The Politics of Authenticity

Protest, Culture, and Society

General editors:
Kathrin Fahlenbrach, Institute for Media and Communication, University of Hamburg
Martin Klimke, New York University, Abu Dhabi
Joachim Scharloth, Waseda University, Japan

Protest movements have been recognized as significant contributors to processes of political participation and transformations of culture and value systems, as well as to the development of both a national and transnational civil society.

This series brings together the various innovative approaches to phenomena of social change, protest, and dissent which have emerged in recent years, from an interdisciplinary perspective. It contextualizes social protest and cultures of dissent in larger political processes and socio-cultural transformations by examining the influence of historical trajectories and the response of various segments of society, political, and legal institutions on a national and international level. In doing so, the series offers a more comprehensive and multi-dimensional view of historical and cultural change in the twentieth and twenty-first century.

For a full volume listing, please see back matter

The Politics of Authenticity

Counterculturs and Radical Movements across the Iron Curtain, 1968–1989

Edited by

Joachim C. Häberlen, Mark Keck-Szajbel, and Kate Mahoney

berghahn
NEW YORK · OXFORD
www.berghahnbooks.com

First published in 2019 by
Berghahn Books
www.berghahnbooks.com

© 2019, 2020 Joachim C. Häberlen, Mark Keck-Szajbel, and Kate Mahoney
First paperback edition published in 2020

All rights reserved. Except for the quotation of short passages
for the purposes of criticism and review, no part of this book
may be reproduced in any form or by any means, electronic or
mechanical, including photocopying, recording, or any information
storage and retrieval system now known or to be invented,
without written permission of the publisher.

Library of Congress Cataloging-in-Publication Data
Names: Häberlen, Joachim C., editor. | Keck-Szajbel, Mark, editor. | Mahoney, Kate, 1989- editor.
Title: The politics of authenticity : counter-cultures and radical movements across the Iron Curtain, 1968-1989 / edited by Joachim C. Häberlen, Mark Keck-Szajbel, and Kate Mahoney.
Description: New York : Berghahn Books, 2019. | Series: Protest, culture and society ; volume 25 | Includes bibliographical references and index.
Identifiers: LCCN 2018018980 (print) | LCCN 2018042198 (ebook) | ISBN 9781789200003 (ebook) | ISBN 9781785339998 | (hardback :alk. paper)
Subjects: LCSH: Counterculture. | Social movements--Europe. | Social movements--Communist countries. | Authenticity (Philosophy)--Social aspects--Europe. | Authenticity (Philosophy)--Social aspects--Communist countries.
Classification: LCC HN373.5 (ebook) | LCC HN373.5 .P63 2018 (print) | DDC 303.48/4094--dc23
LC record available at https://lccn.loc.gov/2018018980

British Library Cataloguing in Publication Data
A catalogue record for this book is available from the British Library

ISBN 978-1-78533-999-8 hardback
ISBN 978-1-78920-824-5 paperback
ISBN 978-1-78920-000-3 ebook

Contents

Acknowledgments — vii

Introduction — 1
  Joachim C. Häberlen and Mark Keck-Szjabel

CHAPTER 1. Revolution as a Quest for an Authentic Life: The 1960s and 1970s in Italy — 25
  Angelo Ventrone

CHAPTER 2. Authenticity through Transgression: Small Acts of Resentment in Post-1968 Czechoslovakia — 45
  Barış Yörümez

CHAPTER 3. The Political, Emotional, and Therapeutic: Narratives of Consciousness-Raising and Authenticity in the English Women's Liberation Movement — 65
  Kate Mahoney

CHAPTER 4. A Genealogy of a Politics of Subjectivity: Guy Hocquenghem, Homosexuality, and the Radical Left in Post-1968 France — 89
  Antoine Idier

CHAPTER 5. New Feminism, Women's Subjectivity, and Feminist Politics: Conceptual Transfers and Activist Inspirations in Yugoslavia in the 1970s and 1980s — 110
  Zsófia Lóránd

CHAPTER 6. Women's Bodies and Feminist Subjectivities in West Germany — 131
  Jane Freeland

CHAPTER 7. The Rise of a New Consciousness: Lesbian Activism in East Germany in the 1980s — 151
  Maria Bühner

CHAPTER 8. The Italian Movement of 1977 and the Cultural Praxis of the Youthful Proletariat — 174
  Danilo Mariscalco

CHAPTER 9. The Struggle for the Minds of the Youth: The Securitate and Musical Countercultures in Communist Romania 191
Manuela Marin

CHAPTER 10. Punk Authenticity: Difference across the Iron Curtain 212
Jeff Hayton

CHAPTER 11. Humanitarianism on Stage: Live Aid and the Origins of Humanitarian Pop Music 233
Benjamin Möckel

CHAPTER 12. Embedded Abstractions: Authenticity, Aura, and Abject Domesticity in Hamburg's Hafenstraße 256
Jake P. Smith

Afterword. Concluding Thoughts: Authenticity's Visual Turn 278
Sara Blaylock

Index 287

Acknowledgments

We would like to thank the institutions and individuals who have supported the project that resulted in this volume, namely the European Union whose generous funding of a Marie Curie Career Integration Grant for the project "Politics of Emotions" helped support this project in its initial stages. We would also like to thank Lewis Smith for careful proofreading of the entire manuscript. Finally, we would like to thank the three anonymous peer reviews for very thorough and thought-provoking reviews that helped improve the book.

Introduction

Joachim C. Häberlen and Mark Keck-Szajbel

"I want to learn how to be myself," wrote five seventeen-year-old girls from West Berlin in a 1977 report about their experiences in a women's group. The group had helped them learn, they claimed, to relate to their feelings and their bodies in a different, more positive, and authentic way.[1] Similar groups existed throughout Europe. Consciousness-raising groups in the women's liberation movement in England and elsewhere offered their members opportunities to express themselves and thus develop a new sense of self-awareness.[2] Meanwhile in France, the radical gay activist Guy Hocquenghem proposed a reconceptualization of politics that would foreground "personal transformation in daily life." Expressing "what we are, what we feel" and thus being able to express an authentic sense of selfhood became essential for the politics Hocquenghem demanded.[3] Radical activists in Italy worried about "inner harmony" that political activism might restore. For the authors of *A/traverso*, one of the leading radical magazines in the 1970s, liberation was a form of "de/lirium," because being in a state of "de/lirium" meant leaving a predestined order behind.[4] All over Western Europe, radical activists believed that they lived in a world that destroyed inner harmony and in which expressing one's true feelings and desires was impossible. Restoring the sense of inner harmony and expressing feelings and desires thus became a central facet of their politics. In the process, activists developed both a new understanding of the political and new political practices for which questions of subjectivity became central.

We find strikingly similar arguments on the other side of the Iron Curtain. Indeed, one could argue that due to both the repressive nature of state socialism and the state's demand for conformity, questions of self-awareness and self-realization became one of the paramount concerns for individuals of every stripe. From punks to feminists, there was increased focus on bodies, feelings, questions of selfhood, and how the state and society sought to regulate and limit them.[5] As early as the 1950s, intellectuals were problematizing how to act independently within a repressive regime. To give but two examples, Nobel-laureate Czesław Miłosz stated in 1953 that the "intellectual elite" had become "actors" in the various people's democracies.[6] The individual had grown so accustomed to his roles—the defamations of Western culture or proclamations of socialist internationalism—that he could "no longer differentiate his true self from the self he simulates, so that even the most intimate of individuals speak to each other in Party slogans."[7] At the time of writing, having escaped the East bloc in the early 1950s, Miłosz suggested that behind the façade of each individual lies the potential of self-realization. Perhaps most famously, Czechoslovak writer and dissident Václav Havel, in his own self-searching exploration of being labelled a "dissident," depicted living under communism as "living in a lie" and thus called for "living in the truth" as a means to resist the communist regime. Similar to Miłosz, for Havel living in truth meant acting according to one's consciousness. Using the parable of the greengrocer, he argued that, by putting up a state-issued sign declaring that "workers of the world, [should] unite," the storekeeper was accepting his life within the system, and even if he did not accept the "lie," he was still giving the communist system legitimacy. Remarkably, however, Havel also referred to Western consumer capitalism as another form of "living in the lie."[8] Miłosz, too, remarked that life in the West was not as perfect as one might expect: "Westerners, and especially Western intellectuals, suffer from a special variety of *taedium vitae*; their emotional and intellectual life is too dispersed. Everything they think and feel evaporates like steam in an open expanse."[9] While Miłosz and Havel are the two most-prominent intellectuals, others individuals—like Lyudmila Zhivkova in Bulgaria or Nina Hagen in East Germany—reveal how self-realization was a problem in both East and West.[10]

That is, of course, not to deny differences between the political contexts of the East and West. One crucial difference was the presence of a superpower in the East bloc that would stop at nothing to ensure the loyalty of a client state. The East bloc had witnessed any number of revolts as early as 1953 in Plzeň or East Berlin. Thereafter, almost each East bloc country tried to either reform the communist state or jettison the camp altogether. Without exception, the reforms suggested both by political leaders or grassroots activists were abandoned and movements violently suppressed.[11] After the largest attempt at reform was forcibly put to an end in Czechoslovakia in 1969 with the occupation of the country by troops from its neighbors, an era of normalization brought citizens of the East in greater contact with consumer goods and higher wages in return for political loyalty (or at least subservience). It was arguably this tacit agreement between the governments of the East bloc with their subjects that fed the dissatisfaction many individuals had toward the communists and their system. Although the experiences of the 1960s were drastically different depending on which side of the Iron Curtain one lived, the resulting quest for authentic subjectivity was, we argue, remarkably similar.

Including case studies from both sides of the Iron Curtain, this book explores how more or less radical activists tried to respond to the sense of living in an inauthentic world in various contexts, ranging from the women's liberation movement to pop and counterculture. On both sides of the Iron Curtain starting in the 1960s, but particularly in the 1970s, individuals from all social strata were looking for an answer to the question of how one might live "authentically" in a world that seemed increasingly commercialized.[12] In West Berlin and Warsaw, Paris and Prague, people were searching for ways to "live in truth." Although there were significant differences from movement to movement and country to country, the following chapters highlight similar desires for authenticity in different places and independent of political and economic systems. With a focus on similarities, the book challenges postwar histories that tend to reproduce Cold War divisions. Engaging in practices such as joining consciousness-raising groups, listening to rock and punk music, or making bodies and sexuality a central aspect of politics, members of countercultural and protest milieus across Europe developed similar styles that can be read as attempts to live more "authentically." Not least, this facilitated communication across the Iron Curtain. As the popularity of the Czechoslovak underground among Western protestors, or (in the case of music) the fascination with the Ramones in the East reveals, the allure of would-be foreign countercultures was prevalent across Europe.[13] Rather than taking states and sociopolitical systems that allegedly shape and confine (counter-)cultural movements as the starting point, this volume inquires how states and societies responded in different ways to similar challenges.

These similarities raise a series of questions. Given the concomitant reassertion of national boundaries after 1945, as well as the attempt to reinforce national identity (particularly in the case of the East bloc, but also in the case of France and Italy), how did people of all walks of life identify with people beyond the state, creating remarkably similar movements and would-be "countercultures"? Should historians argue that such movements were a case of parallelism, or were groups creating transnational networks, global interest groups, or at least consuming goods and reflecting ideals that, in their scope and goals, communicated with others on the opposing side of the Iron Curtain? Our assertion is that the narratives underlying most counterculture groups are too similar to claim parallelism. There were deeper connections, even if they were only tangentially related. Surely, listening to the music of the Ramones in West Berlin was drastically different than listening to the same music group in the East. But the desires were the same: ordinary individuals were seeking to find their authentic selves in movements that spanned traditional nation-state boundaries. Identifying with Western punk groups, youngsters were looking for ways to express themselves outside of typical (national or ideological) molds. Both the narratives as well as the transnational exchanges affirm that counterculture was more deeply interconnected than has been suggested in the past.

In what follows, we first briefly outline what we consider the predominant interpretative frameworks of protest cultures in Europe from the late 1960s to the late 1980s, and how a book focusing on questions of authentic subjectivity engages with these interpretations. Second, we discuss the concept of "politics of authentic subjectivity," before finally presenting some major themes that the chapters in the book address.

Narratives of Democratization and Transnational Exchanges

Scholarship on political and cultural protests from the 1960s to the 1980s abounds. Historians, sociologists, and political scientists have explored themes ranging from terrorism, urban squatting, countercultures like hippies and punks, sexual politics, gay rights and women's movements, tinkering clubs, and all the way to computer geeks.[14] Beyond this plethora of themes, certain general analytical and narrative trends in the historiography can be identified, some of them peculiar to either side of the Iron Curtain, some of them addressing both East and West.

Perhaps the most important narrative framework places protest movements into a context of political democratization, cultural liberalization, and pluralization.[15] Discussing the protests of 1968 in their global dimension, Philipp Gassert notes that activists around the globe shared a "common cause" by "opposing the domestic and international status quo in the name of participatory democracy, political freedom, and personal self-determination." A more radical form of democracy was in the streets in Paris as much as in West Berlin and in Prague.[16] In the West, radical activists and thinkers developed concepts of democracy that went beyond state institutions, demanding what historian Gerd-Rainer Horn has called "participatory democracy" at the workplace or at universities.[17] Thinkers like Johannes Agnoli held state institutions responsible for limiting people's democratic and participatory rights.¹⁸ But demands for radical democracy were not realized, and the revolutions failed, it seemed, since they did not change the government or its structures. Nevertheless, many scholars and other intellectuals regard the revolts around 1968 and in subsequent years as crucial moments for the establishment of liberal and democratic societies in Western Europe. While institutions did not change, cultural and social attitudes did. Democratic values were socially engrained, and especially continental, postfascist Europe became, finally, safe for democracy, the argument goes.¹⁹ Claus Leggewie has, for example, suggested that "1968" constituted a "second foundation" of the Federal Republic of Germany. Only then was democracy truly established in Germany.²⁰

In Eastern Europe, critics opposed Stalinist regimes in all their iterations, yet without embracing Western-style parliamentary democracy. On the contrary: reformers (be they within the state administration or outside of it) consistently called for a different form of socialism. Ironically, the goal of many oppositionists was to make the state more participatory and "genuinely" socialist. An interesting parallel developed in the 1960s and 1970s, when opposition figures on both sides of the Iron Curtain called for more democracy in their respective regimes. Polish dissidents Jacek Kuroń and Karol Modzelewski argued against "parliamentary regimes" and instead called for "workers' democracy," a demand many Western protesters would have found appealing.²¹ In Czechoslovakia, Alexander Dubček also called for a "Third Way," calling for a more open and democratic form of socialism rather than Western democracy.²² In Yugoslavia, students went to the street demanding more autonomy from the state, so as to make the university more communal and socialist in nature.²³ Visions for a radically democratic society that developed in the 1960s informed dissidents and ordinary people of the 1970s and 1980s and thus contributed, in the long run, to the fall of communism in 1989.²⁴ After the fall of state socialism, leaders in almost all East bloc countries initially called for a political system that guaranteed personal freedoms, but which did not slavishly adopt total market capitalism. That is what Václav Havel meant in his speech to the Polish parliament in 1990 when he said that East Central Europe had "spiritual and moral incentives" to offer the West after the various revolutions.²⁵ Thus, while neither protesters in the East or the West accomplished their immediate political goals, their actions ultimately made Europe a more democratic and pluralist continent.

Along similar lines, scholars have proposed that the protesting and countercultural milieus that evolved out of 1968 contributed to changing values and a cultural liberalization.²⁶ Whereas students had lost politically, they seem to have succeeded culturally, as former leading activists from both

France and West Germany frequently claimed.[27] Most famously, attitudes towards sexuality, especially pre- and extramarital intercourse and (eventually) homosexuality, changed dramatically, not least due to the women's and gay rights movements.[28] Yet, it should be noted that processes of cultural liberalization had already begun earlier in the context of the postwar economic boom in Western Europe, and that communist authorities in Eastern Europe did not place particular importance on cultural puritanism to begin with.[29] In particular, the growing youth generation benefited from the economic boom and often joyfully participated in the emerging consumer culture that would become the target of left-wing critics on both sides of the Iron Curtain.[30] Indeed, in the 1970s, postmaterial values, ideals of self-actualization rather than materialistic consumption became increasingly popular. At the same time, an increasingly diversified number of sub- and countercultural scenes emerged with different music and fashion preferences, which indicates a diversification of acceptable lifestyle choices.[31] Whereas men wearing shabby cloths and long hair had caused outrage in the 1960s, by the 1970s, this had become a normal sight not only in large cities, but also in the provinces.[32] All in all, these interpretations suggest a political and cultural success story that ends with the stable liberal democracies that characterize Europe, the rise of populist right-wing parties notwithstanding, at the beginning of the twenty-first century.

These were deeply transnational developments. Protests took place in cities all over Europe and indeed across the globe, and countercultural styles rarely stopped at national boundaries.[33] Activists in different countries learned from each other, making use of protest forms they had encountered, directly or via media, in different places. Young people traveled throughout Europe to sites of protest like the Larzac in France, or full of hope for a better society to Portugal after the Carnation Revolution of 1974.[34] In Eastern Europe, travel restrictions also liberalized in the early 1970s. By 1972, millions of foreigners were visiting Prague, Budapest, or East Berlin in search of the exotic. In this atmosphere, activists met at the Czechoslovak-Polish border to celebrate grassroots contacts, just as Slovak and Hungarian groups formed to protest environmental degradation on the Danube.[35] Numerous studies have thus produced an image of deeply intertwined protest movements and countercultures where a transnational and even European identity developed.[36] Yet, with few notable exceptions, scholars have treated both sides of the Iron Curtain separately.[37] Given the division of the continent into two adversarial economic and political blocs, it seems only natural that opposing these systems and regimes radically differed. Without denying national peculiarities, the studies presented in this volume challenge this perspective.

This scholarship has yielded valuable insights. Yet, it has also faced criticism. Recasting the story of 1968 and the movements that followed as a story of cultural liberalization, Kristin Ross has argued in the French case, obliterates the radical political challenge that 1968 constituted.[38] Ross thus endeavors to restore what she considers the political meaning of the protests, that is, a critique of social categories imposed upon people. In her reading, May 1968 was, above all, an experiment in radical social declassification that is still meaningful in the present. For Ross as well as for other scholars, there is still "unfinished business," issues that were raised in 1968 and not yet solved, such as demands for radical, participatory democracy.[39] Similarly, Jonathan Bolton has reexamined the rise of opposition movements in post-Prague Spring Czechoslovakia, arguing that the role of the dissident in Western historiography has overshadowed most of the country-specific and extensively debated controversies within the opposition.[40] Rather than the typical image of a would-be dissident bloc, his exemplary study reveals the ways that individuals in the underground identified with opposition and how organically groups (and ideas) were formed. These debates indicate how politicized discussions about 1968 still are. A range of scholars have thus expressed skepticism whether looking at these protest movements in terms of democratization and liberalization is ultimately productive. Scholars of West Germany, in particular have drawn our attention to less overt, more, as it were, microscopic forms of power.[41]

The conceptually most innovative and empirically grounded study has been provided by Sven Reichardt, who has studied the West German "Alternative Milieu" during the long 1970s.[42] Reichardt seeks to develop an alternative to the dominant interpretations of the Alternative Left as either "loosening up, liberating and liberalizing," or "totalitarian, restricting and controlling." To this end, he analyzes the Alternative Left as a regime of subjectivity that required its members to be "authentic." Leftists, he argues, wanted to express themselves and their feelings freely; they wanted to be authentic and autonomous subjects, liberated from the impositions of a capitalist economy that only produced false desires and needs. However, rather than taking the rhetoric of authenticity and self-liberation at face value, Reichardt inquires into the relationship between elements of freedom and coercion in creating authentic subjectivities. In the alternative milieu, activists not only had the right to live in a "self-realized" way, but had the "obligation to render account of themselves" and to convey these accounts to others. "Self-therapeutization was intended as a project for the liberation of the alienated individual, but in the practice of the democratic panopticism, it unfolded a normative effect and became a management of the self. The freely chosen culture of self-thematization thus did not only mean 'freedom for', but also an 'obligation to'," Reichardt writes.⁴³ In line with other studies of the contemporary self, Reichardt thus inquires about the practical implications of the alternative search for authenticity.⁴⁴

The approach taken in this book is indebted to Reichardt's work, as the title suggests. At the same time, we draw on the path-breaking work of Padraic Kenney, who has argued that a crucial reason people went to the streets in the late 1980s was thanks to the *konkretny* generation who had been fed by activists in the 1970s and early 1980s. "The *konkretny* activists matched support of the practical with a new attitude toward pluralism. This was not simply a tolerant pluralism of parties or movements ... [but] *internal pluralism*: one mixed and matched identities, and issues, as necessary, depending on what was necessary to defeat the communists."⁴⁵ What was crucial for these new activists was that they were a group of people who coalesced around a collective identity (and, frequently, lifestyle) who sought "to mobilize others around a set of issues."⁴⁶ Addressing case studies from all over Europe, the volume argues that searching for an authentic subjectivity and trying to practice and express this authenticity was a common phenomenon throughout Europe. The contributions inquire how authenticity was practically created in a variety of more or less politically and culturally subversive contexts. Studying authenticity in multiple contexts allows us to see that there was not a single regime of authentic subjectivity, but several and often competing visions of what it meant to be authentic and how one could be authentic. What was at stake with this politics of authenticity?

The Politics of Authenticity

In a famous article published in 1982, Michel Foucault noted that a new kind of struggle was becoming "more and more important." Throughout history, Foucault found "three kinds of social struggles": first, struggles "against forms of domination"; second, "against forms of exploitation which separate individuals from what they produce"; and third, struggles "against that which ties the individual to himself and submits him to others in this way." With the rise of the women's and gay movements of the 1970s, Foucault saw the third kind of struggle on the rise. He tied the rise of this kind of struggle to a peculiar form of political power that he saw emerging with the modern state. Contrary to what most people thought, the state did not ignore individuals, but combined "individualization techniques" and "totalization procedures" in the "same political structures." In a way, the state secularized a Christian form of "pastoral power" that was concerned with individuals' eternal salvation. To ensure this salvation, the Church needed to know about one's inner thoughts and feelings. The modern state, in contrast, concerned itself with individual's worldly well-being, both physically and psychically. Indeed, various state and nonstate institutions seek to shape our sense of self. In this situation, the preeminent philosophical question is no longer "who are we," rather, the political task is, Foucault argues, "to refuse what we are," and to imagine what we could be.[47]

What Foucault is noting here is a fundamental transformation of political struggles that took place in the 1970s across Europe and, arguably, in the United States. Of course, Foucault's writings, which were widely read in leftist circles at the time, contributed themselves to these changes.[48] At the core of these struggles were not merely questions of political participation or the rights of marginalized groups, but questions of subjectivity. The contributions to this volume detail this transformation by discussing a variety of struggles against what Foucault termed "governments of individualization." In different ways, and more or less explicitly, the people that populate the pages of this book, political and countercultural activists as well as ordinary people, questioned and refused who they were supposed to be: heterosexual men or women, productive citizens, or eager consumers.[49] They imagined what they could be: abject subjects who transcended local boundaries while simultaneously remaining grounded in specific and meaningful places, as the squatters of Hamburg's Hafenstraße discussed by Jake Smith suggest; lesbian and gay subjects who embraced their desires and demanded their public recognition, as the case studies on lesbians in the GDR by Maria Bühner and Antoine Idier on gay politics in France show; or "young proletarians" mocking traditional politics by engaging in practices of falsity and nonsense, as the chapter by Danilo Mariscalco on the artistic products of the Italian movement of 1977 shows. By imagining who they could be, activists also inquired who they "really" were. In their understanding, capitalist and socialist societies prevented them from being who they really were, from living a self-realized life "in the truth," as Václav Havel had put it. Creating authentic subjectivities was the central goal of politics.

What does "authentic" mean in our context, and what does a "politics of authenticity" imply? This is not the place to offer a sustained philosophical discussion of what authenticity "really" is.[50] Instead, we would like to offer an albeit brief exploration of the discursive field of authenticity. Above all, the term implies a sense of truthfulness, in contrast to the falsehood that characterized, in the activist perspective, the modern world. More specifically, it refers to being true to one's own personality, to one's own individual "nature," to one's desires and dreams. What mattered for being authentic was, in other words, not only being able to tell the truth, but to tell truth *about oneself*, about one's (sexual) desires, feelings, or dreams, and to act accordingly. Importantly, the desire for authenticity had a deeply emotional and bodily dimension. In a society that seemed to sanction the open expression of feelings, doing so became a way of being authentic. Similarly, activists tried to shape and experience their bodies without social norms or modern technology imposing inauthentic norms. Being authentic, in other words, was also an emotional and bodily way of being.[51] Indeed, it is telling that we can find a rhetoric of desires in many contexts, in part certainly inspired by the work of Gilles Deleuze and Félix Guattari.[52] Pursuing a politics of authenticity was thus about creating the possibilities for living a life that was "true to itself"; it was about enabling people to no longer hide behind "masks," but instead express who they "really" were. This conceptualization of a politics of authenticity means that we do not limit our investigations to actors explicitly using the term "authentic." Even if protagonists did not use the term, we argue that the movements under investigation all pursued a "politics of authenticity," that is, that they tried trying to develop ways of living that would allow people to be true to themselves. Studying the politics of authenticity thus entails examining what people did in order to both create authentic selves, and to create the conditions, not least spatial conditions, that would facilitate authenticity. In different ways, the chapters of the book thus employ praxeological approaches by inquiring in detail how authenticity was practically created in a multiplicity of contexts.

While chapters in this book note that ideals of authenticity came with expectations what one had to do in order to be authentic, and to be recognized as authentic, the book's emphasis lies elsewhere. First, its chapters suggest a fundamental transformation of the political within protest cultures that cannot be grasped in terms of political democratization or cultural liberalization, nor is it sufficient to refer to an "extension of the political." Political struggles, as it were, moved to the self. Hence, forms of activism changed. Expressing one's feelings in consciousness-raising or therapy groups became as important as communal dwelling in abject spaces because both practices would facilitate an authentic self. The book thus seeks to contribute to a "genealogy of the politics of subjectivity," as Antoine Idier writes in his chapter. Indeed, this is neither an exclusively European story, as the influence of US Beat poets and later hippies indicates, nor was it an entirely novel phenomenon in the 1970s, as Angelo Ventrone's remarks about similar desires for harmony around 1900 in Italy indicate.

Second, the chapters highlight how contested questions of authenticity were. Whether in the consciousness-raising groups of the English women's liberation movement, among the squatters of the Hafenstraße in Hamburg, or among lesbians in the GDR: what it meant to be "authentic" was always contested, not least because activists were often quite aware of the impositions and requirements that being recognized as authentic entailed. Recognizing these "external" requirements, the "policing" of authentic subjectivities, as it were, put the very notion of a "genuine" and personal authenticity into question. While some longed for an inner harmony, others in playful and satirical activities mocked any sense of harmony. The chapters in this book thus indicate how creating a sense of authenticity was a process of trying out, often full of conflict. Paying attention to these conflicts, the contributions to this book thus paint a more fluid and unstable picture than merely focusing on regimes of subjectivity would.

Third, the book does not investigate the politics of authentic subjectivity in oppositional or countercultural movements in isolation from mainstream society. As Benjamin Möckel's chapter on the Live Aid concerts and other humanitarian projects indicates, questions of authenticity came to play a role in mainstream pop culture as well, though the role of politics and political criticism in such events was questioned. The desire for authenticity was not limited to oppositional scenes, but it tended to lose its political dimension outside of these scenes. Whereas integrating elements of what constituted an alternative authentic subjectivity an into mainstream society seemed to be possible in Western Europe, the reactions by the state in Eastern Europe were notably different, as Manuela Marin discusses in her contribution about Romania. Here, the state felt threatened by the visions of a different, in its mind Western and destructive, authenticity that questioned its own vision of what it meant to be a good communist citizen. What these examples suggest is that we cannot only observe similarities between East and West, but also a crucial difference with regard to the consequences the new form of struggling had. It would be worthwhile to inquire if they were one factor in the fall of communism.

In the West, in contrast, the desires for authentic self-realization, for creative self-expression and spontaneity contributed to a transformation of capitalism itself, as scholars such as Luc Boltanski, Eve Chiapello, and Ulrich Bröckling have suggested.[53] Creativity, autonomy, and the ability to work in a team, rather than subordination and fulfilling repetitive tasks, are the qualities the "new spirit of capitalism" (Boltanski/Chiapello) requires. And these were also the qualities that alternative activists and cultural critics in countries such as Italy, France, and West Germany celebrated. In this sense, Ulrich Bröckling locates one of the origins of what he calls the "neoliberal self" in the alternative milieus of the 1970s. If this is indeed the case, then observing similar desires in communist Eastern Europe raises the question of how alternative movements contributed to the transformations in Eastern Europe after 1989. Can we observe a "neoliberal" subject in these societies as well, and if so, does it have anything to do with the oppositional and countercultural movements of the 1970s and 1980s? What role did, for example, an emerging Do-It-Yourself culture in these countries play?[54] Answering such questions, though they are outside the scope of this volume, might help us understand European history beyond the East-West divide.

Chapter Overview

Usually, edited volumes such as this one group chapters thematically or geographically. This book, in contrast, proceeds roughly chronologically. The way chapters are arranged might thus seem somewhat incoherent, as the volume jumps from investigations of subcultures to gay and lesbian activists to political movements and back and forth. Yet, by disrupting the common thematic arrangements, for example grouping all chapters dealing with issues of gender and sexuality, we seek to underline the book's central argument, namely that we can find similar themes and problems, that is, the challenging search for authenticity and the development of a new politics of subjectivity, across countries and movements, differences notwithstanding. We need to understand individual movements such as the women's movement or punk in relation to each other.

The book begins with an investigation of revolution as a quest for an authentic life in Italy during the 1960s and 1970s by Angelo Ventrone. Young, radical activists and even terrorists longed for an inner harmony, Ventrone argues, that seemed to have been lost in modern, industrial society. Importantly, Ventrone draws our attention to the fact that this was by no means an invention of the 1960s. Already at the turn of the century, both left- and right-wing critics of capitalist modernity had bemoaned the destruction of human solidarity, excessive individualism, and social isolation, all themes that would recur in the 1960s and 1970s, again on both sides of the political spectrum. Whereas violence as a means to create authenticity plays a fundamental role in Ventrone's chapter, Barış Yörümez, in his study of Czechoslovakia during the 1970s, examines nonviolent small-scale acts of honesty and integrity, not least by telling jokes about the regime, as transgressions that facilitated a sense of authenticity among Czechoslovak citizens who otherwise had to put on "masks" in their public lives. In the third chapter, Kate Mahoney provides an investigation of women's consciousness-raising groups in England during the 1970s. Relying on oral history interviews, her analysis complicates narratives that portray these groups as purely liberating experiences. Instead, she highlights how ambivalent the experience of being in a consciousness-raising group could be: groups could foster feelings of solidarity and liberty, but also create new norms and rules women had to follow. Antoine Idier then turns to the political biography of French gay activist Guy Hocquenghem to examine the "genealogy of a politics of subjectivity" in the French context. Drawing on feminist thought, and indeed early on in collaboration with feminists, Hocquenghem formulated a politics for which expressing (homosexual) desires became central. Zsófia Lóránd discusses similar issues in a Yugoslav context in her investigation of New Yugoslav Feminism. While women in Yugoslavia did not use the term "authenticity" (indeed, not all movements under investigation used the term), they nevertheless asked similar questions as their counterparts in Western Europe. They, too, longed for ways to express their (sexual) desires; they, too, worried about a medicalized health system that alienated them from their bodies, for example when giving birth. They shared these concerns with West German women, as Jane Freeland's chapter on women's bodies in the women's movement shows. She, too, highlights how important it was for women to experience their bodies in a nonalienating and hence authentic way, for example by exploring their bodies in groups, or by learning how to achieve sexual pleasures without men.

Turning from West Germany to the GDR, Maria Bühner examines lesbian activism in East Germany. Similar to what women in Western Europe had longed for, and in some cases making explicit use of Western texts, women in East Germany developed practices, such as consciousness-raising groups, that facilitated "safe spaces" where women could express their (homo-)sexual desires and indeed develop a language for them in the first place. In this sense, lesbians in the GDR, too, tried to create an authentically lesbian subjectivity that questioned hegemonic gender ideals. Danilo Mariscalco's chapter brings us back to the Italian Left. He examines the cultural production of the Autonomist movement of 1977 that made extensive use of techniques of falsity and nonsense as a way to bring "hidden" desires and dreams to the fore. Institutions like Radio Alice sought to develop ways to make "free language" and thus let the body and desires speak directly. Whereas Ventrone emphasizes the longing for inner harmony, Mariscalco's chapter suggests an interpretation of the movement as a struggle for liberating desires. With Manuela Marin's chapter, we move to youth subcultures in Romania. Her chapter suggests that young Romanians turned to Western but also, importantly, Hungarian subcultures to develop an alternative sense of selfhood that challenged the ideals of the "new" socialist man, labor, order, and productivity. Marin also investigates the state's reactions to these youth phenomena, arguing that the alternative subjectivity these youngsters developed was seen as a political threat by the security apparatus, notably the Securitate. Jeff Hayton's chapter turns to another subculture, punk in the late 1970s and early 1980s, in both East and West Germany. Punks in both Germanys rejected, Hayton argues, not only the seemingly boring and monotonous world of Western consumerism and Eastern socialism, but also "alternative" hippies and their search for an authentic inner core. Instead, Hayton explores how punks pursued visions and practices that exposed the instability of authenticity whose genuineness and meaning came not from within but was continuously shifting in response to external conditions.

Whereas punk clearly challenged mainstream aesthetic and cultural norms, the humanitarian pop concerts, namely Live Aid, which Benjamin Möckel discusses, tried to reach as mainstream an audience as possible. His chapter addresses the challenging question of what happened with a sense of authenticity in a consumerist context that was far removed from any radical political activity. Now, what mattered was an "authentic" expression of empathy in the face of suffering, but devoid of (political) rebellion. In the last chapter, Jake Smith turns to the squatters of Hamburg's Hafenstraße in the late 1980s, arguing that we can observe among them two interrelated but also contradictory visions of authenticity that he calls "auratic" and "transcendent" authenticity. He relates both of them to a sense of dwelling, and thus places them in long-term perspectives of a sense of home in West Germany. The often violent struggles of the occupied buildings were, he argues, more than just a struggle for living space: they were a struggle over structures of meaning of urban existence.

Altogether, the chapters suggest that a desire for a more "authentic" life in societies deemed alienating and inauthentic existed throughout Europe, in capitalist countries of the West as much as in socialist countries of the East. Arguably, we could find a similar search for authenticity in cases not addressed in the chapters of this volume, for example in the New Age movement or in alternative medicine.[55] And while political and cultural activists across Europe in many ways agreed on what they criticized—the boredom of urban landscapes, the alienation from feelings and the impossibility of expressing them, the oppression of spontaneity and desires—there was no consensus about what it meant to be authentic and how a more authentic state of being might be achieved. While some engaged in violence, others engaged in self-observation to feel more authentic. Importantly, these were debates within countries or even movements. Opposing "Eastern" and "Western" authenticities would thus miss the point. Not least, this diversity of authenticities should caution us not to buy into the rhetoric of being more authentic. Indeed, authenticity is nothing to be uncovered, but it needs to be practically created, and it is always woven into a network of power.

Joachim C. Häberlen is Associate Professor of Modern Continental European History at the University of Warwick. He is author of *Vertrauen und Politik im Alltag: Die Arbeiterbewegung in Leipzig und Lyon im Moment der Krise, 1929–1933/38* (Vandenhoek & Ruprecht, 2011). He has also authored numerous articles in journals such as *Contemporary European History*, *Central European History*, and the *Journal for the History of Sexuality* and has authored many book chapters. His book *The Emotional Politics of the Alternative Left: West Germany, 1968–1984* is forthcoming with Cambridge University Press.

Mark Keck-Szajbel is an academic research fellow at the Center for Interdisciplinary Polish Studies located at the European University Viadrina in Frankfurt/Oder. He received his Ph.D. from the University of California, Berkeley, with his dissertation on travel and tourism in the East bloc. A recipient of numerous awards and fellowships (including the Fulbright, DAAD, and numerous FLASs), his most recent works focus on the difficult social and cultural changes in late-state socialism and in the 1990s.

Notes

1. Ulla/Birgit/Susan/Sabine/Barbara, "'Ich möchte lernen, ich selbst zu sein.' Siebzehnjährige Oberschülerinnen schreiben über sich," in *Kursbuch* 47, March 1977: 143–158.
2. See Kate Mahoney in this volume.
3. See Antoine Idier in this volume. See also Antoine Idier, *Les vies de Guy Hocquenghem: Politique, sexualité, culture* (Paris, 2017).
4. See Angelo Ventrone and Danilo Mariscalco in this volume. On the Left in Italy, see Angelo Ventrone, *"Vogliamo tutto": Perché due generazioni hanno creduto nella rivoluzione 1960–1988* (Rome, 2012); Phil Edwards, *More Work! Less Pay! Rebellion and Repression in Italy, 1972–7* (Manchester, 2009); Robert Lumley, *States of Emergency: Cultures of Revolt in Italy from 1968–1978* (London, 1990).
5. Cristofer Scarboro, *The Late Socialist Good Life in Bulgaria: Meaning and Living in a Permanent Present Tense* (Lanham, MD, 2012).
6. Czesław Miłosz, *The Captive Mind* (New York, 1990), 54.
7. Ibid., 55.
8. Václav Havel, "The Power of the Powerless," in *From Stalinism to Pluralism: A Documentary History of Eastern Europe Since 1945*, ed. Gale Stokes (Oxford, 1991), 172.
9. Miłosz, *Captive Mind*, 79.
10. Ivanka Nedeva Atanasova, "Lyudmila Zhivkova and the Paradox of Ideology and Identity in Communist Bulgaria," *East European Politics and Society* 18, no. 2 (2004): 278–315; Timothy W. Ryback, *Rock Around the Bloc: A History of Rock Music in Eastern Europe and the Soviet Union* (Oxford, 1990).

11. For an overview of revolts and the communist response to mass protest, see Grzegorz Ekiert, *The State against Society: Political Crises and Their Aftermath in East Central Europe* (Princeton, NJ, 1996).
12. See, for example, the contributions in Pascal Eitler and Jens Elberfeld, eds., *Zeitgeschichte des Selbst: Therapeutisierung—Politisierung—Emotionalisierung* (Bielefeld, 2015); Juliane Fürst and Josie McLellan, eds., *Dropping Out of Socialism: The Creation of Alternative Spheres in the Soviet Bloc* (Lanham, MD, 2017); Uffa Jensen and Maik Tändler, eds., *Das Selbst zwischen Anpassung und Befreiung: Psychowissen und Politik im 20. Jahrhundert* (Göttingen, 2012).
13. Paulina Bren, "1968 East and West: Visions of Political Change and Student Protest from across the Iron Curtain," in *Transnational Moments of Change: Europe 1945, 1968, 1989*, ed. Gerd-Rainer Horn and Padraic Kenney (Lanham, MD, 2004).
14. See, to name only a few studies, Martin Klimke, Jacco Pekelder, and Joachim Scharloth, eds., *Between Prague Spring and French May: Opposition and Revolt in Europe, 1960–1980* (New York, 2011); Belinda Davis et al., eds., *Changing the World, Changing Oneself: Political Protest and Collective Identities in West Germany and the U.S. in the 1960s and 1970s* (New York, 2010); Timothy Brown and Lorena Anton, eds., *Between the Avant-Garde and the Everyday: Subversive Politics in Europe from 1957 to the Present* (New York, 2011); Axel Schildt and Detlef Siegfried, eds., *Between Marx and Coca-Cola: Youth Cultures in Changing European Societies, 1960–1980* (New York, 2006); Alex Vasudevan, *Metropolitan Preoccupations: The Spatial Politics of Squatting in Berlin* (Chichester, 2016); Timothy Brown, *West Germany and the Global Sixties: The Antiauthoritarian Revolt, 1962–1978* (London, 2013); Padraic Kenney, *A Carnival of Revolution: Central Europe 1989* (Princeton, NJ, 2002); Michèlleful Zancarini-Fournel and Philippe Artières, eds., *68, une histoire collective (1962–1981)* (Paris, 2008); Belinda Davis, "What's Left? Popular and Democratic Political Participation in Postwar Europe," *American Historical Review* 113, no. 2 (2008): 363–390.
15. For a critical perspective on these debates in France, see Kristin Ross, *May '68 and Its Afterlives* (Chicago, 2002). For the West German context, see the discussions in Joachim Scharloth, *1968: Eine Kommunikationsgeschichte* (Paderborn, 2011); Quinn Slobodian, *Foreign Front: Third World Politics in Sixties West Germany* (Durham, NC, 2012).
16. Philipp Gassert, "Narratives of Democratization: 1968 in Postwar Europe," in *1968 in Europe: A History of Protest and Activism, 1956–1977*, ed. Martin Klimke and Joachim Scharloth (New York, 2008), 307.
17. Gerd-Rainer Horn, *The Spirit of '68: Rebellion in Western Europe and North America, 1956–1976* (Oxford, 2007).
18. Johannes Agnoli, "Die Transformation der Demokratie," in *Die Transformation der Demokratie*, ed. Johannes Agnoli and Peter Brückner (Frankfurt a. M., 1968), quoted in Gassert, "Narratives," 314.
19. See the discussion in Scharloth, *1968*, 14–20.
20. Claus Leggewie, "1968 ist Geschichte," *Aus Politik und Zeitgeschichte* B 22–23 (2001): 3–6.
21. Jerzy Eisler, "March 1968 in Poland," in *1968: The World Transformed*, ed. Carola Fink, Philipp Gassert, and Detlef Junker (Cambridge, 1998).

22. Kieran Williams, *The Prague Spring and Its Aftermath: Czechoslovak Politics, 1968–1970* (Cambridge, 1997).
23. Madigan Fichter, "Yugoslav Protest: Student Rebellion in Belgrade, Zagreb, and Sarajevo in 1968," *Slavic Review* 75, no. 1 (2016): 99–121.
24. James Krapfl, *Revolution with a Human Face: Politics, Culture, and Community in Czechoslovakia, 1989–1992* (Ithaca, NY, 2013).
25. Václav Havel, "The Future of Central Europe," *New York Review of Books* 29 March 1990: 18
26. See, in addition to the discussion in Ross, *May '68*, Scharloth, *1968*, and Slobodian, *Foreign Front*, for the West German context the contributions in Ulrich Herbert, ed., *Wandlungsprozesse in Westdeutschland: Belastung, Integration, Liberalisierung 1945–1980* (Göttingen, 2002).
27. Silja Behre, *Bewegte Erinnerung: Deutungskämpfe um "1968" in deutsch-französischer Perspektive* (Tübingen, 2016), 363–364.
28. See Peter-Paul Bänziger et al., eds., *Sexuelle Revolution? Zur Geschichte der Sexualität im deutschsprachigen Raum seit den 1960er Jahren* (Bielefeld, 2015); Joachim C. Häberlen, "Feeling like a Child: Visions and Practices of Sexuality in the West German Alternative Left during the Long 1970s," *Journal for the History of Sexuality* 25, no. 2 (2016): 219–245; Gert Hekma and Alain Giami, eds., *Sexual Revolutions* (Basingstoke, 2014); Dagmar Herzog, "Syncopated Sex: Transforming European Sexual Cultures," *American Historical Review* 114, no. 5 (2009): 1287–1308; Dagmar Herzog, *Sex after Fascism: Memory and Morality in Twentieth-Century Germany* (Princeton, NJ, 2005).
29. See Gassert, "Narratives," 315; Andrzej Friszke, *Prl Wobec Kościoła: Akta Urzędu Do Spraw Wyznań 1970–1978* (Warsaw, 2010); Ulrich Herbert, "Liberalisierung als Lernprozess: Die Bundesrepublik in der deutschen Geschichte—eine Skizze," in *Wandlungsprozesse in Westdeutschland: Belastung, Integration, Liberalisierung 1945–1980*, ed. Ulrich Herbert (Göttingen, 2002), 7–49.
30. See Timothy Brown and Andrew Lison, eds., *The Global Sixties in Sound and Vision: Media, Counterculture, Revolt* (Basingstoke, 2014); Ewa Mazierska, ed., *Popular Music in Eastern Europe: Breaking the Post-War Paradigm* (Basingstoke, 2017); Uta G. Poiger, *Jazz, Rock, and Rebels: Cold War Politics and American Culture in a Divided Germany* (Berkeley, CA, 2000); Schildt and Siegfried, eds., *Between Marx and Coca-Cola*; Detlef Siegfried, *Time Is on My Side: Konsum und Politik in der westdeutschen Jugendkultur der 60er Jahre* (Göttingen, 2006).
31. See the contributions in Brown and Anton, eds., *Between the Avant-Garde and the Everyday*; Brown and Lison, eds., *Global Sixties*; Fürst and McLellan, eds., *Dropping Out*.
32. See for West Germany, David Templin, *Freizeit ohne Kontrollen: Die Jugendzentrumsbewegung in der Bundesrepublik der 1970er Jahre* (Göttingen, 2015). For Eastern Europe, see Mark Keck-Szajbel, "A Cultural Shift in the 1970s," *East European Politics and Society* 29, no. 1 (2015): 212–225.
33. See, for example, Slobodian, *Foreign Front*; Daniel A. Gordon, *Immigrants & Intellectuals: May '68 & the Rise of Anti-Racism in France* (London, 2012); Gerd-Rainer Horn and Padraic Kenney, eds., *Transnational Moments of Change: Europe 1945, 1968, 1989* (Lanham, MD, 2004); Richard Ivan Jobs, "Youth Movements:

Travel, Protest, and Europe in 1968," *American Historical Review* 114, no. 2 (2009): 376–404; Martin Klimke, *The Other Alliance: Student Protest in West Germany and the United States in the Global Sixties* (Princeton, NJ, 2010).
34. See, for example, Robert Gildea and Andrew Tompkins, "The Transnational in the Local: The Larzac Plateau as a Site of Transnational Activism since 1970," *Journal of Contemporary History* 50, no. 3 (2015): 581–605.
35. Kenney, *A Carnival of Revolution*; Mark Keck-Szajbel, "Shop Around the Bloc: Trader Tourism and Its Discontents on the East German-Polish Border," in *Communism Unwrapped: Consumption in Cold War Eastern Europe*, ed. Paulina Bren and Mary Neuburger (Oxford, 2012).
36. Jobs, "Youth Movements."
37. For a notable exception, see Robert Gildea, Mark James, and Anette Warring, *Europe's 1968: Voices of Revolt* (Oxford, 2013).
38. Ross, *May '68 and Its Afterlives*.
39. See, for example, Brown, *West Germany*; Horn, *Spirit*.
40. Jonathan Bolton, *Worlds of Dissent: Charter 77, the Plastic People of the Universe, and Czech Culture under Communism* (Cambridge, MA, 2012).
41. See the notable works Scharloth, *1968*; Sven Reichardt, *Authentizität und Gemeinschaft: Linksalternatives Leben in den siebziger und frühen achtziger Jahren* (Berlin, 2014). While the former focuses on communicative styles, the latter explores how a regime of "authentic" subjectification functioned in the Alternative Left.
42. Reichardt, *Authentizität*. See also the contributions in Sven Reichardt and Detlef Siegfried, eds., *Das Alternative Milieu: Antibürgerlicher Lebensstil und linke Politik in der Bundesrepublik Deutschland und Europa 1968–1983* (Göttingen, 2010).
43. Reichardt, *Authentizität*, 71.
44. See, with a focus on West Germany, Eitler and Elberfeld, eds., *Zeitgeschichte*; Jensen and Tändler, eds., *Selbst*; Sabine Maasen et al., eds., *Das beratene Selbst: Zur Genealogie der Therapeutisierung in den "langen" Siebzigern* (Bielefeld, 2011).
45. Kenney, *A Carnival of Revolution*, 13.
46. Ibid., 14.
47. Michel Foucault, "The Subject and Power," *Critical Inquiry* 8, no. 4 (1982): 785.
48. On Foucault's popularity in the Left, see Philipp Felsch, *Der Lange Sommer der Theorie: Geschichte einer Revolte* (Munich, 2015); Julian Bourg, *From Revolution to Ethics: May 1968 and Contemporary French Thought* (Montreal, 2007).
49. See in this context also the reflections in Joachim C. Häberlen, "Conclusion: Dropping Out of Socialism? A Western Perspective," in *Dropping Out of Socialism: The Creation of Alternative Spheres in the Soviet Bloc*, ed. Juliane Fürst and Josie McLellan (Lanham, MD, 2017).
50. For a discussion of the term, see Reichardt, *Authentizität*, 60–64.
51. See, for example, Joachim C. Häberlen and Jake Smith, "Struggling for Feelings: The Politics of Emotions in the Radical New Left in West Germany, c. 1968–84," *Contemporary European History* 23, no. 4 (2014): 615–637. For a theoretical perspective on emotions and bodies, see Pascal Eitler and Monique Scheer, "Emotionengeschichte als Körpergeschichte: Eine heuristische Perspektive auf religiöse Konversionen im 19. und 20. Jahrhundert," *Geschichte und Gesellschaft*

35, no. 2 (2009): 282–313; Monique Scheer, "Are Emotions a Kind of Practice (and Is That What Makes Them Have a History)? A Bourdieuan Approach to Understanding Emotion," *History and Theory* 51, no. 2 (2012): 193–220.
52. See Gilles Deleuze and Félix Guattari, *A Thousand Plateaus*, trans. Brian Massumi (Minneapolis, MN, 1987). For their influence, see Philipp Felsch, "Merves Lachen," *Zeitschrift für Ideengeschichte* 2, no. 4 (2008): 11–30; Felsch, *Lange Sommer*; Bourg, *Revolution to Ethics*. For the rhetoric of "desires" in Italy, see Pablo Echaurren, *La casa del desiderio: '77—Indiani metropolitani e altri strani* (Lecce, 2005).
53. See Luc Boltanski and Eve Chiapello, *The New Spirit of Capitalism* (London, 2005); Paul du Gay and Glenn Morgan, eds., *New Spirits of Capitalism? Crises, Justifications, and Dynamics* (Oxford, 2013); Ulrich Bröckling, *Das unternehmerische Selbst: Soziologie einer Subjektivierungsform* (Frankfurt a. M., 2007); Thomas Lemke, Susanne Krasmann, and Ulrich Bröckling, eds., *Gouvernementalität der Gegenwart: Studien zur Ökonomisierung des Sozialen* (Frankfurt a. M., 2000).
54. On neoliberal Eastern Europe, see Philipp Ther, *Europe since 1989: A History*, trans. Charlotte Hughes-Kreutzmüller (Princeton, NJ, 2016). Questions of subjectivity remain, however, unexplored in his work.
55. On New Ageism and alternative medicine, see for example Pascal Eitler, "'Alternative' Religion: Subjektivierungspraktiken und Politisierungsstrategien im 'New Age' (Westdeutschland 1970–1990)," in *Das alternative Milieu: Antibürgerlicher Lebensstil und linke Politik in der Bundesrepublik Deutschland und Europa, 1968–1983*, ed. Sven Reichardt and Detlef Siegfried (Göttingen, 2010); Pascal Eitler, "'Selbstheilung': Zur Somatisierung und Sakralisierung von Selbstverhältnissen im New Age (Westdeutschland 1970–1990)," in *Das beratene Selbst: Zur Genealogie der Therapeutisierung in den "langen" Siebzigern*, ed. Sabine Maasen, et al. (Bielefeld, 2011); Irina Costache, "The Biography of a Scandal: Experimenting with Yoga during Romanian Late Socialism," in *Dropping Out of Socialism: The Creation of Alternative Spheres in the Soviet Bloc*, ed. Juliane Fürst and Josie McLellan (Lanham, MD, 2017). We should also note that movements such as feminism or punk were not limited to the countries studied here. While both case studies on Italy focus on male actors, the Italian women's movement played a leading role in Europe, see, for example, Maud Bracke, *Women and the Reinvention of the Political: Feminism in Italy, 1968–1983* (New York, 2014). See also the important study by Luisa Passerini, *Autobiography of a Generation: Italy, 1968* (Hanover, NH, 1996).

Bibliography

Atanasova, Ivanka Nedeva. "Lyudmila Zhivkova and the Paradox of Ideology and Identity in Communist Bulgaria." *East European Politics and Society* 18, no. 2 (2004): 278–315.

Bänziger, Peter-Paul, Magdalena Beljan, Franz X. Eder, and Pascal Eitler, eds. *Sexuelle Revolution? Zur Geschichte der Sexualität im deutschsprachigen Raum seit den 1960er Jahren*. Bielefeld: transcript, 2015.

Behre, Silja. *Bewegte Erinnerung: Deutungskämpfe um "1968" in deutsch-französischer Perspektive*. Tübingen: Mohr Siebeck, 2016.

Boltanski, Luc, and Eve Chiapello. *The New Spirit of Capitalism*. London: Verso, 2005.
Bolton, Jonathan. *Worlds of Dissent: Charter 77, the Plastic People of the Universe, and Czech Culture under Communism*. Cambridge, MA: Harvard University Press, 2012.
Bourg, Julian. *From Revolution to Ethics: May 1968 and Contemporary French Thought*. Montreal: McGill University Press, 2007.
Bracke, Maud. *Women and the Reinvention of the Political: Feminism in Italy, 1968–1983*. New York: Routledge, 2014.
Bren, Paulina. "1968 East and West: Visions of Political Change and Student Protest from across the Iron Curtain." In *Transnational Moments of Change: Europe 1945, 1968, 1989*, edited by Gerd-Rainer Horn and Padraic Kenney, 119–135. Lanham, MD: Rowman & Littlefield, 2004.
Bröckling, Ulrich. *Das unternehmerische Selbst: Soziologie einer Subjektivierungsform*. Frankfurt a. M.: Suhrkamp, 2007.
Brown, Timothy. *West Germany and the Global Sixties: The Antiauthoritarian Revolt, 1962–1978*. London: Cambridge University Press, 2013.
Brown, Timothy, and Lorena Anton, eds. *Between the Avant-Garde and the Everyday: Subversive Politics in Europe from 1957 to the Present*. New York: Berghahn Books, 2011.
Brown, Timothy, and Andrew Lison, eds. *The Global Sixties in Sound and Vision: Media, Counterculture, Revolt*. Basingstoke: Palgrave Macmillan, 2014.
Costache, Irina. "The Biography of a Scandal: Experimenting with Yoga during Romanian Late Socialism." In *Dropping Out of Socialism: The Creation of Alternative Spheres in the Soviet Bloc*, edited by Juliane Fürst and Josie McLellan, 23–40. Lanham, MD: Lexington Books, 2017.
Davis, Belinda. "What's Left? Popular and Democratic Political Participation in Postwar Europe." *American Historical Review* 113, no. 2 (2008): 363–390.
Davis, Belinda, Wilfried Mausbach, Martin Klimke, and Carla MacDougall, eds. *Changing the World, Changing Oneself: Political Protest and Collective Identities in West Germany and the U.S. in the 1960s and 1970s*. New York: Berghahn Books, 2010.
Deleuze, Gilles, and Félix Guattari. *A Thousand Plateaus*. Translated by Brian Massumi. Minneapolis: University of Minnesota Press, 1987.
du Gay, Paul, and Glenn Morgan, eds. *New Spirits of Capitalism? Crises, Justifications, and Dynamics*. Oxford: Oxford University Press, 2013.
Echaurren, Pablo. *La casa del desiderio: '77—Indiani metropolitani e altri strani*. Lecce: Manni Editore, 2005.
Ekiert, Grzegorz. *The State against Society: Political Crises and Their Aftermath in East Central Europe*. Princeton, NJ: Princeton University Press, 1996.
Edwards, Phil. *More Work! Less Pay! Rebellion and Repression in Italy, 1972–7*. Manchester: Manchester University Press, 2009.
Eisler, Jerzy. "March 1968 in Poland." In *1968: The World Transformed*, edited by Carola Fink, Philipp Gassert, and Detlef Junker, 237–252. Cambridge: Cambridge University Press, 1998.
Eitler, Pascal. "'Alternative' Religion: Subjektivierungspraktiken und Politisierungsstrategien im 'New Age' (Westdeutschland 1970–1990)." In *Das alternative Milieu: Antibürgerlicher Lebensstil und linke Politik in der Bundesrepublik*

Deutschland und Europa, 1968–1983, edited by Sven Reichardt and Detlef Siegfried, 335–352. Göttingen: Wallstein, 2010.

———. "'Selbstheilung': Zur Somatisierung und Sakralisierung von Selbstverhältnissen im New Age (Westdeutschland 1970–1990)." In *Das beratene Selbst: Zur Genealogie der Therapeutisierung in den "langen" Siebzigern*, edited by Sabine Maasen, Jens Elberfeld, Pascal Eitler, and Maik Tändler, 161–182. Bielefeld: transcript, 2011.

Eitler, Pascal, and Jens Elberfeld, eds. *Zeitgeschichte des Selbst: Therapeutisierung—Politisierung—Emotionalisierung*. Bielefeld: transcript, 2015.

Eitler, Pascal, and Monique Scheer. "Emotionengeschichte als Körpergeschichte: Eine heuristische Perspektive auf religiöse Konversionen im 19. und 20. Jahrhundert." *Geschichte und Gesellschaft* 35, no. 2 (2009): 282–313.

Felsch, Philipp. *Der Lange Sommer der Theorie: Geschichte einer Revolte*. Munich: Beck, 2015.

———. "Merves Lachen." *Zeitschrift für Ideengeschichte* 2, no. 4 (2008): 11–30.

Fichter, Madigan. "Yugoslav Protest: Student Rebellion in Belgrade, Zagreb, and Sarajevo in 1968." *Slavic Review* 75, no. 1 (2016): 99–121.

Foucault, Michel. "The Subject and Power." *Critical Inquiry* 8, no. 4 (1982): 777–795.

Friszke, Andrzej. *Prl Wobec Kościoła: Akta Urzędu Do Spraw Wyznań 1970–1978*. Warsaw: Biblioteka "Więzi," 2010.

Fürst, Juliane, and Josie McLellan, eds. *Dropping Out of Socialism: The Creation of Alternative Spheres in the Soviet Bloc*. Lanham, MD: Lexington Books, 2017.

Gassert, Philipp. "Narratives of Democratization: 1968 in Postwar Europe." In *1968 in Europe: A History of Protest and Activism, 1956–1977*, edited by Martin Klimke and Joachim Scharloth, 307–324. New York: Palgrave Macmillan, 2008.

Gildea, Robert, Mark James, and Anette Warring. *Europe's 1968: Voices of Revolt*. Oxford: Oxford University Press, 2013.

Gildea, Robert, and Andrew Tompkins. "The Transnational in the Local: The Larzac Plateau as a Site of Transnational Activism since 1970." *Journal of Contemporary History* 50, no. 3 (2015): 581–605.

Gordon, Daniel A. *Immigrants & Intellectuals: May '68 & the Rise of Anti-Racism in France*. London: Merlin Press, 2012.

Häberlen, Joachim C. "Conclusion: Dropping Out of Socialism? A Western Perspective." In *Dropping Out of Socialism: The Creation of Alternative Spheres in the Soviet Bloc*, edited by Juliane Fürst and Josie McLellan, 303–318. Lanham, MD: Lexington, 2017.

———. "Feeling like a Child: Visions and Practices of Sexuality in the West German Alternative Left during the Long 1970s." *Journal for the History of Sexuality* 25, no. 2 (2016): 219–245.

Häberlen, Joachim C., and Jake Smith. "Struggling for Feelings: The Politics of Emotions in the Radical New Left in West Germany, c. 1968–84." *Contemporary European History* 23, no. 4 (2014): 615–637.

Havel, Václav. "The Future of Central Europe." *New York Review of Books* 29 March 1990: 18.

———. "The Power of the Powerless." In *From Stalinism to Pluralism: A Documentary History of Eastern Europe Since 1945*, edited by Gale Stokes, 168–174. Oxford: Oxford University Press, 1991.

Hekma, Gert, and Alain Giami, eds. *Sexual Revolutions*. Basingstoke: Palgrave Macmillan, 2014.
Herbert, Ulrich. "Liberalisierung als Lernprozess: Die Bundesrepublik in der deutschen Geschichte—eine Skizze." In *Wandlungsprozesse in Westdeutschland: Belastung, Integration, Liberalisierung 1945–1980*, edited by Ulrich Herbert, 7–49. Göttingen: Wallstein, 2002.
———, ed. *Wandlungsprozesse in Westdeutschland: Belastung, Integration, Liberalisierung 1945–1980*. Göttingen: Wallstein, 2002.
Herzog, Dagmar. *Sex after Fascism: Memory and Morality in Twentieth-Century Germany*. Princeton, NJ: Princeton University Press, 2005.
———. "Snycopated Sex: Transforming European Sexual Cultures." *American Historical Review* 114, no. 5 (2009): 1287–1308.
Horn, Gerd-Rainer. *The Spirit of '68: Rebellion in Western Europe and North America, 1956–1976*. Oxford: Oxford University Press, 2007.
Horn, Gerd-Rainer, and Padraic Kenney, eds. *Transnational Moments of Change: Europe 1945, 1968, 1989*. Lanham, MD: Rowman & Littlefield, 2004.
Idier, Antoine. *Les vies de Guy Hocquenghem: Politique, sexualité, culture*. Paris: Fayard, 2017.
Jensen, Uffa, and Maik Tändler, eds. *Das Selbst zwischen Anpassung und Befreiung: Psychowissen und Politik im 20. Jahrhundert*. Göttingen: Wallstein, 2012.
Jobs, Richard Ivan. "Youth Movements: Travel, Protest, and Europe in 1968." *American Historical Review* 114, no. 2 (2009): 376–404.
Keck-Szajbel, Mark. "A Cultural Shift in the 1970s." *East European Politics and Society* 29, no. 1 (2015): 212–225.
———. "Shop Around the Bloc: Trader Tourism and Its Discontents on the East German-Polish Border." In *Communism Unwrapped: Consumption in Cold War Eastern Europe*, edited by Paulina Bren and Mary Neuburger, 374–392. Oxford: Oxford University Press, 2012.
Kenney, Padraic. *A Carnival of Revolution: Central Europe 1989*. Princeton, NJ: Princeton University Press, 2002.
Klimke, Martin. *The Other Alliance: Student Protest in West Germany and the United States in the Global Sixties*. Princeton, NJ: Princeton University Press, 2010.
Klimke, Martin, Jacco Pekelder, and Joachim Scharloth, eds. *Between Prague Spring and French May: Opposition and Revolt in Europe, 1960–1980*. New York: Berghahn Books, 2011.
Krapfl, James. *Revolution with a Human Face: Politics, Culture, and Community in Czechoslovakia, 1989–1992*. Ithaca, NY: Cornell University Press, 2013.
Leggewie, Claus. "1968 ist Geschichte." *Aus Politik und Zeitgeschichte* B 22–23 (2001): 3–6.
Lemke, Thomas, Susanne Krasmann, and Ulrich Bröckling, eds. *Gouvernementalität der Gegenwart: Studien zur Ökonomisierung des Sozialen*. Frankfurt a. M.: Suhrkamp, 2000.
Lumley, Robert. *States of Emergency: Cultures of Revolt in Italy from 1968–1978*. London: Verso, 1990.
Maasen, Sabine, Jens Elberfeld, Pascal Eitler, and Maik Tändler, eds. *Das beratene Selbst: Zur Genealogie der Therapeutisierung in den "langen" Siebzigern*. Bielefeld: transcript, 2011.

Mazierska, Ewa, ed. *Popular Music in Eastern Europe: Breaking the Post-War Paradigm.* Basingstoke: Palgrave Macmillan, 2017.
Miłosz, Czesław. *The Captive Mind.* New York: Vintage International, 1990.
Passerini, Luisa. *Autobiography of a Generation: Italy, 1968.* Hanover, NH: University Press of New England, 1996.
Poiger, Uta G. *Jazz, Rock, and Rebels: Cold War Politics and American Culture in a Divided Germany.* Berkeley: University of California Press, 2000.
Reichardt, Sven. *Authentizität und Gemeinschaft: Linksalternatives Leben in den siebziger und frühen achtziger Jahren.* Berlin: Suhrkamp Verlag, 2014.
Reichardt, Sven, and Detlef Siegfried, eds. *Das Alternative Milieu: Antibürgerlicher Lebensstil und linke Politik in der Bundesrepublik Deutschland und Europa 1968– 1983.* Göttingen: Wallstein, 2010.
Ross, Kristin. *May '68 and Its Afterlives.* Chicago: University of Chicago Press, 2002.
Ryback, Timothy W. *Rock Around the Bloc: A History of Rock Music in Eastern Europe and the Soviet Union.* Oxford: Oxford University Press, 1990.
Scarboro, Cristofer. *The Late Socialist Good Life in Bulgaria: Meaning and Living in a Permanent Present Tense.* Lanham, MD: Lexington Books, 2012.
Scharloth, Joachim. *1968: Eine Kommunikationsgeschichte.* Paderborn: Wilhelm Fink, 2011.
Scheer, Monique. "Are Emotions a Kind of Practice (and Is That What Makes Them Have a History)? A Bourdieuan Approach to Understanding Emotion." *History and Theory* 51, no. 2 (2012): 193–220.
Schildt, Axel, and Detlef Siegfried, eds. *Between Marx and Coca-Cola: Youth Cultures in Changing European Societies, 1960–1980.* New York: Berghahn Books, 2006.
Siegfried, Detlef. *Time Is on My Side: Konsum und Politik in der westdeutschen Jugendkultur der 60er Jahre.* Göttingen: Wallstein, 2006.
Slobodian, Quinn. *Foreign Front: Third World Politics in Sixties West Germany.* Durham, NC: Duke University Press, 2012.
Templin, David. *Freizeit ohne Kontrollen: Die Jugendzentrumsbewegung in der Bundesrepublik der 1970er Jahre.* Göttingen: Wallstein, 2015.
Ther, Philipp. *Europe since 1989: A History.* Translated by Charlotte Hughes-Kreutzmüller. Princeton, NJ: Princeton University Press, 2016.
Vasudevan, Alex. *Metropolitan Preoccupations: The Spatial Politics of Squatting in Berlin.* Chichester: Wiley and Sons, 2016.
Ventrone, Angelo. *"Vogliamo tutto": Perché due generazioni hanno creduto nella rivoluzione 1960–1988.* Rome: Editori Laterza, 2012.
Williams, Kieran. *The Prague Spring and Its Aftermath: Czechoslovak Politics, 1968–1970.* Cambridge: Cambridge University Press, 1997.
Zancarini-Fournel, Michèlle, and Philippe Artières, eds. *68, une histoire collective (1962– 1981).* Paris: La Découverte, 2008.

Chapter 1

Revolution as a Quest for an Authentic Life

The 1960s and 1970s in Italy

Angelo Ventrone

In the decades around 1900, a cultural critique of bourgeois modernity emerged across the Western world. Critics in different countries and from different political backgrounds worried that society had been devastated by the exaltation of individualism, materialism, hedonism, and utilitarianism. They claimed that all forms of solidarity had been eroded, and that individuals were suffering from feelings of isolation, social displacement, and exhaustion because of ferocious, egocentric competition. In a kingdom of individualism, rivalry, disorder, injustice, desperation, and the despotic dominance of the few over the masses, the peoples of Europe faced not only moral decline, but even physical degeneration, these cultural critics warned.[1] They also railed against a monotonous "mass society" that was perceived to have homogenized tastes, behaviors, ways of living, and minds.[2] Society seemed to have become a giant prison where, as Italian Fascist Sergio Panunzio wrote in the 1930s, "men are machines; the group kills the individual; the cemetery of uniformity makes everything dark and disfigures all."[3]

The society these critics depicted was deeply inhuman and dehumanizing as it deprived life itself of its psychological and emotional dimensions. By distancing man from nature, life seemed to be deprived of sensitivity, in its original meaning of sensory perception: it lacked feeling and was devoid of emotional participation. The tangible, it seemed, was gradually being substituted by the abstract; reality something to be observed with detachment. By distancing individuals from the ability to "sense" themselves, others, and their surroundings, bourgeois modernity, critics argued, was transforming people into abstract, fragile, and isolated beings that lacked social or geographical roots.[4]

A diverse range of cultural and political movements emerged to express—and act on—these critiques of bourgeois modernity. These oppositional movements were driven by shared concerns: how to deal with the impact of massive technological transformations on society; how to save human beings from being crushed by the enormous power of material and anonymous forces such as the economy and finance; and how to save humanity from the corruption, dependency, and fragility caused by the increasing availability of material goods. These were questions asked by critics both on the left and on the right. Indeed, while the answers given to these questions differed, they constituted a common starting point for many if not all movements opposing bourgeois modernity.

In fact, similarities did not end there. Not only did oppositional movements on the extreme left and extreme right share a common enemy—bourgeois society—in some fundamental ways, they also shared a vision of the new society to be built. Throughout much of the twentieth century, groups at both extremes of the political spectrum engaged in an "apocalyptic" struggle to replace a soulless, monotonous modernity with a qualitative, creative, conscious alternative way of living. They fought, or so they claimed, for a politics that would put human beings in their rightful, central place and liberate them from the domination of materiality, economic constraints, and technological machinery. And while it is evidently true that historical experiences differed and should not be flattened, this chapter seeks to underline similarities across political camps: both the left and the right referred, in some ways, to the same imagination, an imagination that expressed the search for a world where human beings were autonomous from material external forces, a place where they could live an authentic life. For both the far left and the far right, sensitivity played a fundamental role in their quest for authenticity; theirs was an aesthetic quest aimed at restoring an emotional intensity to life that had seemingly been corroded by modernization and secularization. Radical activists sought to reverse this process and to restore the importance of living, at the expense of thought. They tried to create the conditions that would enable a return to sensing the self, to rediscovering the body in a way that had been impossible amid the artificiality of contemporary life.[5]

In the 1970s, radical activists at both ends of the political spectrum once again took up these ideas. In Italy, groups comprising the so-called New Left, such as Lotta Continua, Potere Operaio, and Autonomia Operaia; armed leftist groups, such as Brigate Rosse and Prima Linea; and neo-fascist groups such as Ordine Nuovo, Avanguardia nazionale, Costruiamo l'azione, and Terza Posizione, shared, despite their political enmity, a cultural critique of modernity. They all believed that the current system had acquired the ability to penetrate the inner core of individual human beings, to shape and condition them in a fundamental way.

These groups on the extreme left had all emerged from the strong wave of youth protest that had struck Italy in the late 1960s. Between 1967 and 1968 in particular, a student protest movement started in Italy, as it did in many other countries. However, the specificity of the Italian movement was demonstrated by the fact that, from late 1968 to early 1969, the student protest had already begun to meld with that of the workers. At that time, an intense wave of strikes had affected all industrial areas in the north of the country. In 1969, during the "hot autumn," strikes, protests, and demonstrations grew enormously. These actions had a strong impact on public opinion, both pushing broad swathes of public opinion toward the left and, on the opposite side, increasing fears about the left's electoral successes and the eventual arrival of the Communist Party to government.

Ordine Nuovo and Avanguardia nazionale took on new impetus from this polarization of public opinion. The latter had been founded in the second half of the 1950s by former exponents of Movimento sociale italiano, the explicitly neo-fascist party that was now accused of converting to a policy that was too moderate. With the advent of the center-left governments in the early 1960s, these groups had found a greater response in the political, financial, and business environments linked to anti-communism. Eventually, they would be used by the latter as executors of the "strategy of tension": attacks on massacres that would bloody Italy from the end of 1969 (coinciding, in fact, with the "hot autumn") until the massacre in Bologna in 1980.

In this chapter, I argue that these radical movements—although they were, as we know, ideologically opposed—employed the same language, ideologies, and categories of analysis as previous revolutionary generations because they were ultimately fighting for the same cause. They searched for ways to restore the centrality of human beings, to enable them to live an "authentic" life in an increasingly materialistic world. Violence, as the chapter shows, played a vital if contested role in this regard. Whereas some activists engaged in peaceful practices such as growing long hair and wearing shabby clothes, others engaged in violence as a means to liberate themselves, to live a more "authentic" life, and to restore an inner harmony that seemed lost in contemporary society.

The chapter begins with a discussion of the belief that bourgeois modernity was preventing human beings from living a full and meaningful life, showing how critiques formulated in the years around 1900 were taken up by activists on both the left and the right during the 1960s and 1970s. In the second section, I examine how these groups attempted to re-establish an inner harmony that they felt had been lost due to modern society, paying particular attention to the use of violence and the similarities between right-wing and left-wing terrorists.

A Cultural Critique: A "Totalitarian Social System" and the Tailor-Made Man

Throughout the twentieth century, cultural critics of modernity depicted the world in dark terms. In their minds, the very sparks of life seemed to be missing. Critics blamed the exaltation of individualism, hedonism, and utilitarianism not only for destroying all forms of solidarity, but also for transforming human beings into perfect "timepieces." Modern society, they argued, had reduced human beings to nothing but simple cogs in an anonymous and impersonal machine. As slaves to technology, individuals had become deprived of their personality; standardization affected not merely their habits, but their very mentality. Friedrich Pollock, a sociologist and co-founder of the Frankfurt Institute for Social Research, argued in a 1956 study on automation that society was experiencing ever-shrinking freedoms because of the increasing concentration of power in the hands of an elite, while the masses suffered from not only material but also human impoverishment. In his mind, this development paved the way for a "totalitarian social system."[6] International protest movements in the postwar years shared these concerns, worrying that society could decline into a new form of totalitarianism.[7] Another observer from those years felt that there had been a "declaration of open war against joyfulness," because society's primary concern was to demonstrate that "nothing, absolutely nothing" was "special, unique or wonderful," and that everything could be reduced to a mechanical routine. Movies, novels, and theater productions by the likes of Jean-Luc Godard, François Truffaut, Michelangelo Antonioni, and Samuel Beckett expressed similar concerns. Characters in their works often lack feelings, are only capable of automatic reactions, and are utterly indifferent and insensitive to the world and people around them. These are human beings devoid of any humanity. And when their bodies touch each other, they do so without any warmth.[8]

These concerns transcended ideological boundaries. It is not by chance that an Italian neo-fascist terrorist spoke of his desire to use politics to build "places where [it is possible] to live according to our way of feeling, acting, thinking, islands found in the metropolitan desert." Together with his political group, he longed to create "a community … where everyone knew the others truly, profoundly."[9] Another neo-fascist militant said that he fought against the "society of economy, of traffickers" that posed a mortal danger for "human spirituality."[10] This sentiment was echoed by Clemente Graziani, one of the founders of neo-fascist organization Ordine Nuovo. In a pamphlet that proved influential for the emergent "strategy of tension" in

Italy, Graziani called for a struggle against a "materialistic and mechanical" society.[11] The journal of Terza Posizione, one of the leading far right groups in Italy during the late 1970s, similarly wrote:

> We refuse the bourgeois world with its discos and drugs as its symbols; we refuse the suffocating metropolis and this faceless civilization. We want a new people capable of rediscovering the will to stay united and to have not only economic, but also civilized aims. We no longer want parasites or exploiters …, but only better individuals able to lead their people toward freedom.[12]

It is perhaps curious that neo-fascists refer to freedom. However, as Sophie-Anne Leterrier has noted, every "doctrine of regeneration," whether from the right or the left, was also presented as a "doctrine of freedom."[13] Both the left and the right continuously searched for liberty and a fuller life by imagining a society liberated from the constraints of bourgeois modernity. However, the freedom sought by the political Right was markedly different from the freedom called for by the Left. While the Left envisaged freedom of action, thought, and movement, the radical Right emphasized freedom from fear, which would be offered by the protection of one's community.[14]

The Far Right and Far Left also differed with regard to the role violence played in their political thought and practices. Whereas the Far Right discussed the subtle—and horrible—distinction between "selective" and "indiscriminate" terrorism as necessary weapons in the fight against communism,[15] the Far Left found it much more difficult to justify violence, especially against human beings, in the first place. Fighting for people's liberation by using (deadly) violence against them seemed to be—and in fact is—a contradiction. This difficulty becomes evident in the numerous and lengthy texts the Red Brigades produced trying to justify their attacks by blaming the victims for their misdeeds. Indeed, the more the level of violence grew, the longer the justifications by the Red Brigades became.[16] More generally, at least according to Marxist-Leninist theory, violence would be utilized only until the chains of the past were broken and the path toward a new world was open. The Far Right, by contrast, considered it necessary to permanently employ violence in order to ensure the dominance of the elites over the masses.

Many on the Left shared the Right's view that life in modern society was devoid of emotions, and that it was hence necessary to revitalize heart and soul and to shape society around this objective. In a 1969 statement, the Red Brigades, for example, criticized bourgeois notions of freedom: "The freedom of the bourgeoisie is the typical freedom of the isolated individual who lives in the middle of other isolated individuals, where everyone is crushed by a ruthless machine. Whoever defends this kind of freedom, defends an illusionary one and renounces real freedom."[17] The "new man" that the radical Left imagined as an alternative to the isolated individual of bourgeois society would be a collective being; individuality would be completely subordinate to, and fused with, the collective. Indeed, there is an evident tension between competing visions and desires within the New Left: on the one hand, leftists desired a radical autonomy, achieved through resisting social norms, and on the other hand, they held a desire to dedicate themselves to a higher, collective purpose that demanded rigorous loyalty.

In general, the radical Left in Italy during the 1960s and 1970s reflected on society in a more sophisticated way. One argument made by leftists deserves particular attention: that capitalism had gone through a fundamental transformation during the 1950s, resulting in what leftists called "neo-capitalism." According to theorists of *operaismo* (workerism), the most influential neo-Marxist doctrine in the Italian radical Left, neo-capitalism was characterized not only by an ever-increasing production of goods, but also by its capacity to absorb every form of antagonism through the mythology of well-being, the expansion of consumption and the increase of salaries. Alberto Asor Rosa, an intellectual affiliated with *operaismo*, expressed one of the tenets of this political doctrine. In his analysis, contemporary society was organized according to the model of social relationships that characterized the big industries; capital was beginning to exert its control over society as a whole.[18]

Other theorists of *operaismo*, such as Mario Tronti, Raniero Panzieri, and Antonio (Toni) Negri, similarly argued that modern capitalism aimed to shape the entire world to suit its goals, rendering the interests of capitalism and the interest of the general public identical.[19] One influential elaboration of these arguments was Negri's theoretical analysis of the "social worker" (*operaio sociale*) and the "social factory" (*fabbrica sociale*), which suggested that the conditions that characterized life in big industries had become the normal conditions for all kinds of jobs and all spheres of life. According to Negri, nobody was immune to the alienation, oppression, and imposed discipline that had traditionally affected only the working class. The theoretical figure of the "operaio sociale" was thus meant to emphasize that all types of jobs tended to resemble the humiliating and oppressive conditions of the big factories. And the homogenization of life extended beyond work, according to analysis by Negri and other *operaistis*. High costs and strong competition in the West had made it necessary to plan not only production, but also consumption, and hence the consumer. The task for capitalism was thus to eliminate all spontaneous influences and unpredictable elements that escaped calculation and planning, both inside and outside the factory, including the unpredictable behavior of human beings. In that sense, neo-capitalism tried to create a "new man," theorists of *operaismo* argued: a person who would only care about increasing production and consumption. In the society of neo-capitalism, life seemed to have become mere merchandise, deprived of any genuine humanity and subordinated to a productivity that did not care for sensual experiences. Working had turned into punishment, and pleasure merely "inactive and meaningless waste."[20]

To accomplish these goals, capitalism had new and powerful tools at its disposal, theorists claimed. It had the ability to conquer the minds of people, to model them according to its needs, to build the "tailor-made man" that Vance Packard had described in his widely read book *The Hidden Persuaders* (1957).[21] Vittorio Foa, a union leader and one of the most influential leftist intellectuals of the time, formulated this vision drawing on a book by Leo Szilard, a Hungarian scientist who had immigrated to the United States. Szilard's book, *The Voice of Dolphins*, narrates the story of dolphins who had found a way of communicating with humans. Being extremely smart, dolphins had no trouble understanding physics, mathematics, and other sciences, but were incapable of understanding a crucial aspect of the human world: the political and social structure of the United States. When someone tried to explain it to them, one of the dolphins replied: "Is it right [to claim] that Americans are free to say all they think, given that they don't think what they are not free to say?" This, Foa argued, was exactly the logic of modern capitalism: "I don't impede anybody from saying what they think, but I make sure that nobody thinks what I don't want them to think."[22]

One particular focus of criticism was technology. This was true for Far Right activists, too, however leftist thinkers put forward a more substantial critique that focused on the social function of technology. In theory, they argued, modern technology had the capacity to liberate humankind from unnecessarily laborious work and efforts. Yet, this potential remained unrealized because technology was being used solely to extract surplus value from workers for profit. One leftist group argued in 1970 that when capitalist masters bought new machinery capable of doubling production, this did not result in reducing the work time by half, but rather in the dismissal of half the workforce, with the remaining half having to work just as much as before, and with even more intensity.[23]

In sum, the world that leftists in Italy described resembled the world of George Orwell's *1984*, in which the ruling powers exerted total control over minds and languages. Living in the totalitarian system Orwell described meant not only renouncing independent thinking, but, in a much more radical way, to "not have the need of thinking." As one character in the book puts it, "orthodoxy is unconsciousness": it is a literal ignorance of any possible alternative and the acceptance of the present as the eternal and natural environment.[24] In fact, Italian leftists made explicit references to the book. One of the manifestos of terrorist group Prima Linea (Frontline) claimed that a modernized version of the Orwellian nightmare was developing in Italy: "We are on the eve of 1984."[25]

These words point to concerns that ran through the entire twentieth century: the worry that science and scientific thinking would create a society utterly under the control of political and economic powers, a society in which any form of vagueness, ambiguity, and spontaneity was eliminated for the sake of predictability and planning. To contemporary critics, political power seemed to extend infinitely. It was not only capable of ruling the bodies of people, but also able to intervene in their minds, to homogenize, to create a "tailor-made" man, as we have seen, ready for consumer society.

Violence and the Revolution Born from Richness

The assessment that society seemed to have fallen under the total domination of science, technology, and rationality raised important questions regarding the potential and goals of revolutionary politics. Given the level of technological progress, it was possible that knowledge and wealth could, in theory, be accessible to everyone. Social hierarchies that were traditionally based on the possession of superior knowledge had the potential to disappear in this society. If knowledge is indeed power, then a redistribution and democratization of knowledge could lead to an equalization of power and ultimately well-being. For leftists who had traditionally criticized social inequalities, the development of this contemporary utopian vision raised questions about the very nature of politics. Writing about the Beat generation in the United States, Italian novelist Italo Calvino observed:

> The question that the Beat generation posed is: how can we really live our human nature in a world that will be more and more artificial? The beatniks accept this world built entirely by man as if it were a natural scenario. But they do not understand why they should share the principles and rules on which it stands. I believe that a predominant part in the birth of the beat mentality, even more than the atomic danger, is played by the quiet confidence in the prosperity of the affluent society, that is, in the prosperity of abundance.[26]

In Calvino's opinion, the Beat generation, which was in many ways at the root of the protest movement of the 1960s and 1970s, was born out of "the rebellion of young people against the civilization of production and consumption." Yet, at the very same time, the movement also built on what it refused. Only the emergence of consumer society had produced the material wealth that provided those young people with the material means to survive and prosper in the society they contested so much.[27] For the first time, to quote leading US countercultural figure Jerry Rubin, a revolutionary movement appeared from "affluence, not poverty."[28] A few years later, Antonio Negri in Italy reiterated this point by writing about his group, Autonomia Operaia: "we are a reality that derives its reason to hate the masters not from desperation, but from desire, enjoyment, from richness."[29]

How was it possible to engage in revolutionary politics in this situation? How was it possible to escape from the gilded cage of consumer society described above? Young Italians protesting against mainstream society in the 1960s and 1970s gave a variety of answers. Some searched for a mystical fusion with nature or the complete sense of community and sharing in hippie communes. Others turned to collective experiences, such as praying, meditating, chanting Buddhist mantras, or collectively using drugs, to escape from the alienating world. In some respects, we can also include female consciousness-raising groups in this collective effort, which intended to help women to free themselves from the cultural and social conditioning that had, until then, relegated them to a marginal position that was subordinated to the male world. After all, one of their most important objectives was to urge women to discover their own sexuality, and to highlight that in contemporary society. Therefore, in addition to class oppression, there was also that of "gender."

Others still tried to rediscover their bodies as a means of shielding themselves against the mechanization of modern life, following, for example, the teachings of Julian Beck's Living Theater.[30] Growing long hair, which came to signify the generation of dropouts across the continent and the United States, was one example of this. According to Jerry Rubin,

> Long hair gets people uptight—more uptight than ideology, cause long hair is communication. ... Young kids identify short hair with authority, discipline, unhappiness, boredom, rigidity, hatred of life—and long hair with letting go, letting your hair down, being free, being open. ... [Long hair is] instant confrontation. Everyone is forced to become an actor, and that's revolutionary in a society of passive consumers.

He continued: "We're natural men lost in this world of machines and computers. ... Long hair is the beginning of our liberation from the sexual opression that underlies this whole militarized society."[31] Italian hippies shared these sentiments, as their slogans indicate: "Love everts, abstinence perverts"; "Anti-bourgeois of all countries, unite!"; "Beatniks are dirty. Is the atomic bomb clean?"; "The integrated protests. The beatnik challenges."[32]

These were all nonviolent practices. Indeed, for many leftist activists, violence was antithetical to implementing positive change. Retrospectively, some former terrorists attributed the failure of armed struggles to bring about a revolution to the inadequacy of violence as a technique in a much-changed political landscape. Patrizio Peci, once a leader of the Red Brigades and later the first important member of the group to collaborate with the police to destroy it, explained how they had misread the domestic situation in Italy. In contrast to countries in the so-called Third World, in Italy there was neither a seething mass discontent nor a total denial of democratic rights. It was these conditions that had legitimized violent struggles in the Third World:

> What was our mistake? To believe that Italy was a country adapted to a communist revolution. We didn't consider at all that Italy was an advanced capitalist society, that is, a society completely different from the ones where communist revolutions were successful. In Italy, a fundamental element lacked: hunger. Without hunger, or a numerous part of population suffering from it, it is impossible to initiate a revolution. Our mistake has been to believe that, also without hunger, we can somehow start revolution through people who do not want to be economically exploited. People, according to us, had to risk everything they had, starting with their life, to obey a principle. We were completely out of this world.[33]

It was a bitter conclusion. Peci's words also contained an interesting observation: in an advanced capitalistic society, with a high capacity to produce wealth and distribute it to wider parts of the population, revolution was no longer about escaping from misery and hunger, problems of the past that had been resolved in affluent societies. Instead, it pursued a much more abstract and less tangible goal: to end the exploitation and alienation of life itself.

Other members of leftist groups, however, did not share this sentiment. Indeed, the use of violence was a deeply contested and ambivalent issue during this time. Armed organizations such as the Red Brigades portrayed violence in a much more positive manner, claiming it to be redemptive in the world of alienation. Another leader of the Red Brigades, Enrico Fenzi, recalled personal experiences in the armed group:

> We are able to see in more depth than the others; others stop at the surface, at the flesh, and they do not arrive at the skeleton of reality. We

understand that everything is violence, that social relations are a mere fiction, that flesh hides a skeleton of violence. Only violence is real; only by practicing violence can you have real power. So, in order to be strong, we must practice violence. Because we are intelligent and so we have understood that nothing else but violence exists, and only violence lets us exist as strong social and political subjects.[34]

Fenzi conceived of violence as a form of political intelligence in a dual sense: first, as a form of thorough knowledge, because violence enabled those who used it to realize that beyond the surface was a deeper level of reality. And second, violence was a superior category of analysis, because it could help reach that deeper level. In other words, violence was perceived to demonstrate the shortcomings of others, and to itself provide deeper insights. Those who took the step and employed violent means thus constituted, in Fenzi's understanding, an elite of the enlightened, being able to lead those still blind from darkness to light.

Such a statement by a left-wing terrorist might seem surprising. In fact, such ideas are more conventionally associated with the radical Right. And indeed, Far Right and neo-fascist militants would certainly have subscribed to them. Analogies run deeply. Both the radical Left and the radical Right shared the conviction that they were the bearers of a truth that the majority had not (yet) understood, a truth that was waiting to be unveiled. And certain activists within both political extremes considered violence a power that might open the path to a renewed world, to a regeneration of a society that suffered from sickness and mediocrity, from repression and oppression. It is well known that (neo-)fascists regarded violence as a tool to liberate people from the suffocating powers of emasculation, and that they even celebrated violence for fostering feelings of erotic excitement, as indicated by the frequent use of weapons as phallic symbols. But it is worth noting that this rhetoric and symbolism crossed ideological boundaries. For the Far Left, too, violence was a weapon against an impotent society with regenerative potential. Those who opposed violence, in contrast, were deemed incapable of creating something new, incapable of "pro-creating"; they were sterile men, in all senses of the word. The highly sexualized rhetoric that was common on the far right—rhetoric that celebrated virility, violent action, and the desire to dominate—also made appearances in documents and testimonies of the radical Left.[35] For example, one former left-wing terrorist stated that armed struggle was "fascinating, because it was … a break with an emasculated, obsolete, old way of doing politics." Another former terrorist recalled: "Weapons are fascinating in themselves. This fascination is capable of making you feel more virile … stronger. In fact, I often showed them to women, to seduce them."[36] At times, the love for violence and the desire for destruction went hand in hand and reached apocalyptic heights. Declaring that the hate against reformists who were consolidating the system had to be extreme, Antonio Negri wrote in a widely-read text:

> Reformism is miserable ... The misery of reformism is evident in the proletarians' total refusal of repression, of the institutions.... I am part of this rejection that connects me to the world as an agent of destruction.... Nothing reveals the value of the auto-valorization of the workers as sabotage. Nothing more than this perspective of saboteur, deviant, criminal which I am living. Immediately, I feel the warmth of workers and proletarian community, every time I wear a balaclava.... Every action of destruction and sabotage reflects upon me as a sign of connection to the working class. Not even the eventual risk shocks me: on the contrary, it fills me with feverish excitement, as if waiting for my lover.[37]

By engaging in revolutionary politics, activists on both the Far Left and Far Right hoped to overcome the separations that characterized modern society, such as the separation of the public and the private, the separation of mind and body, and the separation of one's inner being and one's outer actions. Overcoming such separations, they hoped, would lead to a fuller, more complete life. For one former leftist terrorist, participating in politics unearthed "a place where I rediscovered myself," where he could develop "relationships in which I was no longer separated from what I did. I no longer had problems with my body, with my gestures; I was no longer shy."[38] Groups such as the Red Brigades sought to re-compose contemporary human beings, whose ego, as the group wrote, was "ultra-weak, neurasthenic, alienated, egocentric, and manipulated."[39] Here, again, violence seemed to be an appropriate and even essential tool, because it was a way to actively construct a new kind of human being. Once more, such sentiments expressed on the left resembled arguments made by far right groups. Giusva Fioravanti, leader of the far right group Nuclei Armati Rivoluzionari (NAR), for example noted that in his search for tools to change mankind, he came to conceive of "armed struggle" as "an act of liberation."[40]

Obviously, not all supporters of revolutionary politics supported violence rhetorically or were, in principle, willing to engage in it, and the number of those who actually did use violence was even smaller.[41] However, to assume that there were no links between those who merely talked about violence and those who engaged in violence would be equally misleading. As juridical investigations have shown, the links between clandestine and legal parts of the movement were strong, and borders between them were extremely thin and permeable, as officially unarmed organizations often supported violent groups by helping them to distribute written statements, falsify identity papers or car plates, or even provide and hide weapons. While legitimizing violence in theory, and actually engaging in violent acts are two quite different things, the distinction is anything but clear-cut. Drawing attention to these complexities is important, not least to refute narratives of former activists who try to distance themselves from violence, that separate a "good season" from the "bad season" of armed struggles. As we have already seen highlighted by Enrico Fenzi, himself a former member of the Red Brigades, such a separation is unfounded, because it would deny the intrinsic links between the revolutionary quest for authenticity of the early 1970s and the violence of the late 1970s, and would put the blame for violence solely on armed groups.[42]

One legitimization of (revolutionary) violence was thus that violence was a tool to build a new and more authentic world. A second legitimization of violence related to the perception that the capitalist system sought to plan and organize everything—human beings included. In this situation, there was a feeling that any oppositional movement had to organize itself as an irrational element in and against the rationality of the system. It had to become the "anarchy," the unpredictable, spontaneous element that the regime could not manage. *A/traverso*, one of the key radical left-wing magazines of the 1970s, linked to Autonomia Operaia, claimed that in order to criticize the present and to even conceive of a revolution, it would be necessary to leave well mapped-out routes; it would be necessary to "rave," in the literal meaning of the term: "Every form of liberation ... comes as de/lirium. De/lirium [which means]: to leave the order ... of forecast," to leave the order that is well known. For liberation to work, it was fundamental to sever and distance oneself from the present, to fully refuse it.[43] This refusal of the rationalized present also entailed a refusal of being useful. As Claudio Gorlier had already written in 1962 about the Beat generation: "When the religion of profit reigns, the most direct way to rebel against it is to be deliberately useless."[44]

Both the Far Left and the Far Right used this reasoning to justify violence, as they considered violence a means to smash the conformist obedience and to disrupt the plans of the corrupt system. The Far Left praised the symbolism of what they called "proletarian expropriations"—thefts and robberies. The Red Brigades, for example, claimed that financing their activities by robbing banks was a first step toward expropriating "finance capital." According to a member of the group, they never took the money of clients, only that of the bank.[45] Former neo-fascist terrorists made the same argument to justify the robberies committed by their group: "We were aware that society was based on economy and so we had to fight it with the same weapons. This is why we began to attack the banks; we were convinced we were taking aim at capital's heart."[46]

The most radical left-wing groups of the mid-1970s, such as Lotta Continua or Potere Operaio, sought to disrupt and disjoint society by taking violent, though not necessarily lethally violent, steps. They deemed it necessary to immediately appropriate and redistribute all the wealth that was now theoretically available, and thus propagated collectively robbing supermarkets as forms of "proletarian expropriation." They also called on people to refuse to pay for movie or theater tickets, phone or electricity bills, or bus tickets on the way to work, which, they argued, should be paid for by the bosses, not by the workers, since the time spent on the bus was time spent for the bosses.[47]

In an economic situation in which material poverty no longer formed the grounds for revolutionary politics, new forms of politics became necessary: politics that aimed at restoring an inner harmony, at making life meaningful again, and at disrupting the rationality of planned capitalist consumer society. In both the Italian far left and the far right during the 1970s, violence became a means, though not the only one, to achieve this. By participating in violent politics, activists felt they could develop a "deeper," more authentic relationship with themselves, with their bodies and with others. It was a way of experiencing life in a more meaningful way. Simultaneously, (non-lethal) acts of violence and robbery, such as "proletarian expropriation," disrupted the capitalist rationality of the system. They introduced an element of unpredictability into a system based on omnipresent calculation. To understand the appeal of violence for a generation of young protesters, it is thus necessary to grasp their critique of life in modern society as oppressively dull, boring, planned, and utterly meaningless.

Conclusion

A piece of graffiti, sprayed on a wall in Bologna in the 1970s, advised: "When you make love don't overdo it, you have to go and fight, but when you fight remember love, [for] what else are you fighting for?"[48] The message points to the centrality of feelings, of desire for radical politics during the 1970s. Indeed, desire was the key concept for young revolutionaries in the 1960s and 1970s, not a desire to possess material wealth, but a desire to give meaning to one's life, to achieve a richness by experiencing deep emotions in oneself and by being able to relate to the emotions of others. This was not a desire for some short "buzz," for a brief moment of excitement, but about re-establishing a sense of emotional intensity, considered an essential element of authentic human life, that had been suppressed in contemporary capitalist society. It was an effort to make life worth living, here, in the present.

A short episode may serve as a conclusion to highlight the quest for giving meaning to life, for sensitivity, which this chapter has discussed and which is fundamental for understanding revolutionary desires throughout the twentieth century. The story concerns Renato Curcio, the founder and leader of the Red Brigades. After many years in prison, he reflected on the time he spent behind bars. He recalled that one day, because of a dream that had impressed him deeply, he made the decision to write down all his dreams, as soon as he woke up in the morning. Soon after, he realized that the more he wrote, the more he dreamed. This was a surprise, not least because he had begun to think that, perhaps, in recent years, he had stopped dreaming. After this revelation, he started to involve his cellmates, and organized meetings in which everybody told their dreams to the others. Unexpectedly, an amazing dynamic was born. Curcio later described what happened in the meetings:

> A disturbing magma came to light.... Our sexual misery, our distance from life, our existential solitude, the confusion of our inmate bodies, suddenly emerged in the light. Our dreams told a story that up until then we had not heard. They showed a scene we had looked at many times, but we had never seen, they threw out images of mutilated bodies, injured in thousands of parts, horribly covered with scars. An extraordinary experience that changed my view.[49]

Searching at first for meaning, the former terrorists became aware of having been living until that moment in the total abstractness of ideology, in the tragic disappearance of any sensitivity. After this discovery, Curcio decided to establish a publishing house, called Sensibili alle foglie (Sensitive to the leaves). The name was inspired by the words of a homeless woman who had once written to him: "Who is sensitive can destroy himself, can die. I am sensitive to the leaves, to the poor, to suffering."[50]

Angelo Ventrone is Full Professor of Contemporary History at the University of Macerata, Italy. He studies political cultures in the twentieth century, parties and political movements, political violence, political communication. His works include *La seduzione totalitaria: Guerra, modernità, violenza politica (1914–1918)* [The totalitarian seduction: War, modernity, political violence, 1914–1918] (Donzelli, 2003); *Il nemico interno: Immagini, parole e simboli della lotta politica nell'Italia nel '900* [The enemy within: Images, words and symbols of the Italian political struggle in the twentieth century] (Donzelli, 2005); *La cittadinanza repubblican: Come cattolici e comunisti hanno costruito la democrazia italiana (1943–1948)* [The republican citizenship: The way in which Catholics and communists have built the Italian democracy, 1943–1948] (Il Mulino, 2008); *"Vogliamo tutto": Perché due generazioni hanno creduto nella rivoluzione 1960–1988* ["We want it all": Why two generations believed in revolution 1960–1988] (Laterza, 2012) and *Il terrorismo di destra e di sinistra in Italia e in Europa: Storici e magistrati a confronto* [The Far Right and Left terrorism in Italy and Europe: Historians and judiciaries in comparison] (Padova University Press, 2018).

Notes

1. Arthur Herman, *The Idea of Decline in Western History* (New York, 1997); George L. Mosse, *The Image of Men: The Creation of Modern Masculinity* (Oxford, 1996); André Reszler, *Mythes politiques modernes* (Paris, 1981), 58–82.
2. Daniel Pick, *Faces of Degeneration: A European Disorder, 1848–1918* (Cambridge, 1989).
3. Cited in Michela Nacci, *L'antiamericanismo in Italia negli anni Trenta* (Turin, 1989), 132–133.
4. Angelo Ventrone, *La seduzione totalitaria: Guerra, modernità, violenza politica (1914–1918)* (Rome, 2004), 143–146.
5. Ventrone, *La seduzione totalitaria*, 147–148; Roger Griffin, *Modernism and Fascism: The Sense of a Beginning under Mussolini and Hitler* (Basingstoke, UK, 2007).
6. Friedrich Pollock, *Automation: A Study of Its Social and Economic Consequences* (New York, 1957). German original, *Automation: Materialien zur Beurteilung der ökonomischen und sozialen Folgen* (Frankfurt a. M., 1956). For similar conclusions, see Jacques Ellul, *Technique ou L'enjeu du Siècle* (Paris, 1954).
7. Jerry Hopkins, ed., *The Hippie Papers* (New York, 1968). See also the immensely influential book by Herbert Marcuse, *One-Dimensional Man: Studies in the Ideology of Advanced Industrial Society* (Boston, MA, 1964).
8. Theodore Roszak, *The Making of a Counter Culture: Reflections on the Technocratic Society and Its Youthful Opposition* (London, 1970).
9. Franco Ferraresi, "Il rosso e il nero: terrorismi a confronto," in *Destra/Sinistra: Storia e fenomenologia di una dicotomia politica*, ed. Alessandro Campi and Ambrogio Santambrogio (Rome, 1997), 202n46.
10. These were the words of a neo-fascist militant, cited in Enrico Pisetta, "Militanza partitica e scelte eversive nei terroristi neofascisti," in *Ideologie, movimenti, terrorismi*, ed. Raimondo Catanzaro (Bologna, 1990), 205.
11. Clemente Graziani, *La guerra rivoluzionaria* (Rome, 1963), 30–33. The author was one of the founders of Ordine Nuovo and his pamphlet was a fundamental landmark for the forthcoming "strategy of tension" in Italy. See also Franco Freda, *La disintegrazione del sistema* (Padova, 1969).

12. "Lotta e vittoria," *Terza Posizione*, November/December 1979, and "Crisi di dimensione," *Lotta studentesca* 1 [n.d., likely Fall 1977]. Both magazines belonged to the same political camp. All translations are my own unless otherwise stated.
13. Sophie-Anne Leterrier, "L'homme nouveau, de l'exégèse à la propagande," in *L'Homme nouveau dans l'Europe fasciste (1922–1945): Entre dictature et totalitarisme*, ed. Marie Anne Matard-Bonucci and Pierre Milza (Paris, 2004), 27.
14. See, for example, Zeev Sternhell, *La droite révolutionnaire* (Paris, 1978); Zeev Sternhell, *Naissance de l'idéologie fasciste* (Paris, 1989).
15. Eggardo Beltrametti, ed., *La guerra rivoluzionaria* (Rome, 1965).
16. Ferraresi, "Il rosso e il nero," 177–178; Ferraresi, "Il sentito e il vissuto: La violenza nel racconto dei protagonisti," in *La politica della violenza*, ed. Raimondo Catanzaro (Bologna, 1990), 204–207. For more examples see the documents of the Red Brigades published in *Controinformazione* 7–8 (June 1976), 158–160, 177–178.
17. Collettivo Politico Metropolitano (CPM), "Lotta sociale e organizzazione nella metropoli (1969)," in *Dossier Brigate rosse: 1969–1975*, ed. Lorenzo Ruggiero (Milan, 2007). The Collettivo Politico Metropolitano was the main group out of which the Red Brigades emerged.
18. Alberto Asor Rosa, "Il punto di vista operaio e la cultura socialista," *Quaderni Rossi* 2 (June 1962), 119. The *Quaderni rossi* (1961–1965) was the most important magazine for the elaboration of the theory of *Operaismo*.
19. Two of the main theoretical writings are Mario Tronti, *Operai e capital* (Turin, 1966), and Antonio Negri, *Crisi dello Stato-piano: Comunismo e organizzazione rivoluzionaria* (Milan, 1979). For a recent interpretation of this political experience, see Angelo Ventrone, *"Vogliamo tutto": Perché due generazioni hanno creduto nella rivoluzione (1960–1988)* (Rome, 2012).
20. "Intervento di Lucio Magri," in *Tendenze del capitalismo italiano: Atti del Convegno di Roma 23–25 marzo 1962*, vol. I (Roma, 1962), 327–333.
21. Vance Packard, *The Hidden Persuaders* (New York, 1957).
22. "Intervento di Vittorio Foa," in *Tendenze del capitalismo italiano: Atti del Convegno di Roma 23–25 marzo 1962*, vol. I (Roma, 1962), 233.
23. See, for example, "Comunicazioni interne dell'Organizzazione consiliare," *Acheronte*, 14 November 1970, *Archivio 68–77: Gruppi e movimenti si raccontano*.
24. George Orwell, *Nineteen Eighty-Four: A Novel* (London, 1950).
25. "Sarà che nella testa avete un maledetto muro (1983)," in *Le parole scritte* (Rome, 1996), 279.
26. Italo Calvino, "I beatniks e il sistema," in *Una pietra sopra: Discorsi di letteratura e società* (Turin, 1980), 78.
27. Italo Calvino, "L'antitesi operaia (1964)," in *Una pietra sopra: Discorsi di letteratura e società* (Turin, 1980), 102–103.
28. Jerry Rubin, *Do It! Scenarios of the Revolution* (New York, 1970), 115.
29. Antonio Negri, "Partito operaio contro il lavoro," in *Crisi e organizzazione operaia*, ed. Sergio Bologna, Paolo Carpignano, and Antonio Negri (Milan, 1974), 126.
30. The main Italian hippie magazine included *Mondo Beat*, *Pianeta Fresco*, and *S* (all of them were published in Milan), but there were also some minor magazines such as *Uomini* and *Off limits* (Turin), *Il Ribelle* (Monza), *Noi la pensiamo così… e via*, and *Esperienza 2* (Lucca), *Stampa Libera* (Cinisello Balsamo), *Pensiero* (Brescia), and *No*

(Rome). For a global perspective on underground magazines, see Richard Neville, *Play Power* (London, 1970).
31. Rubin, *Do it!*, 93–96.
32. In Italian: "L'amore everte, l'astinenza perverte"; "Antiborghesi di tutto il mondo, unitevi!"; "I Beatniks sono sporchi. La bomba atomica è pulita?"; "L'integrato protesta. Il Beatnik contesta," quoted in Mondo Beat, 5 November 1966 and 31 May 1967.
33. Patrizio Peci, *Io l'infame*, ed. by Giordano Bruno Guerri (Milan, 2008 [1983]), 55.
34. Cited in Sergio Zavoli, *La notte della Repubblica* (Rome, 1992), 498.
35. Franco Ferraresi, *Minacce alla democrazia: Minacce alla democrazia e strategia della tensione in Italia nel dopoguerra* (Milan, 1995); Marco Revelli, *La cultura della destra radicale* (Milan, 1985).
36. Ferraresi, "Il sentito e il vissuto," 217.
37. Antonio Negri, *Il dominio e il sabotaggio: Sul metodo marxista della trasformazione sociale* (Milan, 1978), 42–43.
38. Cited in Luisa Passerini, "Ferite della memoria: Immaginario e ideologia in una storia recente," *Rivista di storia contemporanea* 2 (1988): 193.
39. CPM, "Lotta sociale," 49–58.
40. Ferraresi, "Il rosso e il nero," 193–194.
41. Luigi Manconi, *Terroristi italiani: Le Brigate Rosse e la guerra totale 1970–2008* (Milan, 2008), 87–88.
42. Enrico Fenzi, *Armi e bagagli: Un diario dalle Brigate Rosse* (1987; Milan, 2006), 100–101.
43. *A/traverso* 1 (June 1975).
44. Claudio Gorlier, "La Beat generation: Rivolta e innocenza (1962)," in *Beat e Mondo Beat*, ed. Matteo Guarnaccia (Viterbo, 2005), 87.
45. Zavoli, *La notte della repubblica*, 118.
46. Ferraresi, *Il rosso e il nero*, 203n48.
47. "Crisi e insurrezione armata," and "L'appropriazione in fabbrica e nella fabbrica sociale," in *Materiali di discussione, per i militanti in preparazione della III Conferenza d'organizzazione. Roma, 24–25–26 settembre 1971* (Rome, 1971), 26–30; see also "Il sistema è marcio: dobbiamo distruggerlo," *Potere Operaio* 46 (February 1972): 4.
48. Cited in Mino Monicelli, *L'ultrasinistra in Italia 1968–1978* (Bari–Rome, 1978), 98.
49. Renato Curcio, *A viso aperto: Vita e memorie del fondatore delle BR* (Milan, 1993), 199.
50. Ibid., 202–203.

Bibliography

Asor Rosa, Alberto. "Il punto di vista operaio e la cultura socialista." In *Quaderni Rossi* 2 (June 1962): 117–130.
Beltrametti, Eggardo, ed. *La guerra rivoluzionaria*. Rome: Volpe, 1965.
Calvino, Italo. "I beatniks e il sistema (1962)." In *Una pietra sopra: Discorsi di letteratura e società*, 75–81. Turin: Einaudi, 1980.

———. "L'antitesi operaia (1964)." In *Una pietra sopra: Discorsi di letteratura e società*, 100–113. Turin: Einaudi, 1980.

Collettivo Politico Metropolitano (CPM). "Lotta sociale e organizzazione nella metropoli (1969)." In *Dossier Brigate rosse: 1969–1975*, edited by Lorenzo Ruggiero, 21–58. Milan: Kaos Edizioni, 2007.

Curcio, Renato. *A viso aperto: Vita e memorie del fondatore delle BR*. Milan: Mondadori, 1993.

Ellul, Jacques. *Technique ou l'enjeu du Siècle*. Paris: Colin, 1954.

Fenzi, Enrico. *Armi e bagagli: Un diario dalle Brigate Rosse*. Milan: Costlan, [1987] 2006.

Ferraresi, Franco. "Il rosso e il nero: terrorismi a confronti." In *Destra/Sinistra: Storia e fenomenologia di una dicotomia politica*, edited by Alessandro Campi and Ambrogio Santambrogio, 175–223. Rome: Pellicani, 1997.

———. "Il sentito e il vissuto: La violenza nel racconto dei protagonisti." In *La politica della violenza*, edited by Raimondo Catanzaro, 203–244. Bologna: il Mulino, 1990.

———. *Minacce alla democrazia: Minacce alla democrazia e strategia della tensione in Italia nel dopoguerra*. Milan: Feltrinelli, 1995.

Foa, Vittorio. "Intervento". In *Tendenze del capitalismo italiano: Atti del Convegno di Roma 23–25 marzo 1962*, vol. I, 233. Rome: Editori Riuniti, 1962.

Freda, Franco. *La disintegrazione del sistema*. Padova: Edizioni di AR, 1969.

Gorlier, Claudio. "La Beat generation: Rivolta e innocenza (1962)." In *Beat e Mondo Beat*, edited by Matteo Guarnaccia, 51–117. Viterbo: Stampa Alternativa, 2005.

Graziani, Clemente. *La guerra rivoluzionaria*. Rome: La Litograf, 1963.

Griffin, Roger. *Modernism and Fascism: The Sense of a Beginning under Mussolini and Hitler*. Basingstoke, UK: Palgrave Macmillan, 2007.

Herman, Arthur. *The Idea of Decline in Western History*. New York: The Free Press, 1997.

Hopkins, Jerry, ed. *The Hippie Papers*. New York: American Library, 1968.

Leterrier, Sophie-Anne. "L'homme nouveau, de l'exégèse à la propaganda." In *L'Homme nouveau dans l'Europe fasciste (1922–1945): Entre dictature et totalitarisme*, edited by Marie Anne Matard-Bonucci and Pierre Milza, 23–33. Paris: Fayard, 2004.

Magri, Lucio. "Intervento." In *Tendenze del capitalismo italiano: Atti del Convegno di Roma 23–25 marzo 1962*, vol. I, 327–333. Rome: Editori Riuniti, 1962.

Manconi, Luigi. *Terroristi italiani: Le Brigate Rosse e la guerra totale 1970–2008*. Milan: Rizzoli, 2008.

Marcuse, Herbert. *One-Dimensional Man: Studies in the Ideology of Advanced Industrial Society*. Boston, MA: Beacon, 1964.

Monicelli, Mino. *L'ultrasinistra in Italia 1968–1978*. Rome: Laterza, 1978.

Mosse, George L. *The Image of Men: The Creation of Modern Masculinity*. Oxford: Oxford University Press, 1996.

Nacci, Michela. *L'antiamericanismo in Italia negli anni Trenta*. Turin: Bollati Boringhieri, 1989.

Negri, Antonio (Toni). *Crisi dello Stato-piano: Comunismo e organizzazione rivoluzionaria*. Milan: Feltrinelli, 1979.

———. *Il dominio e il sabotaggio: Sul metodo marxista della trasformazione sociale*. Milan: Feltrinelli, 1978.

———. "Partito operaio contro il lavoro." In *Crisi e organizzazione operaia*, edited by Sergio Bologna, Paolo Carpignano, and Antonio Negri, 99–193. Milan: Feltrinelli, 1974.

Neville, Richard. *Play Power*. London: Cape, 1970.

Orwell, George. *Nineteen Eighty-Four: A Novel*. London: Secker & Warburg, 1950.

Packard, Vance. *The Hidden Persuaders*. New York: D. McKay Co., 1957.

Passerini, Luisa. "Ferite della memoria: Immaginario e ideologia in una storia recente." *Rivista di storia contemporanea* 2 (1988): 173–217.

Peci, Patrizio. *Io l'infame*. Edited by Giordano Bruno Guerri. Miland: Mondadori, 2008 [1983].

Pick, Daniel. *Faces of Degeneration: A European Disorder, 1848–1918*. Cambridge: Cambridge University Press, 1989.

Pisetta, Enrico. "Militanza partitica e scelte eversive nei terroristi neofascisti." In *Ideologie, movimenti, terrorismi*, edited by Raimondo Catanzaro, 191–215. Bologna: il Mulino, 1990.

Pollock, Friedrich. *Automation: A Study of Its Social and Economic Consequences*. New York, Praeger, [1956] 1957.

Prima, Linea. "Sarà che nella testa avete un maledetto muro (1983)." In *Le parole scritte*, 275–281. Rome: Sensibili alle Foglie, 1996.

Reszler, André. *Mythes politiques modernes*. Paris: Presses Universitaires de France, 1981.

Revelli, Marco. *La cultura della destra radicale*. Milan: Angeli, 1985.

Roszak, Theodore. *The Making of a Counter Culture: Reflections on the Technocratic Society and Its Youthful Opposition*. London: Faber & Faber, 1970.

Rubin, Jerry. *Do It! Scenarios of the Revolution*. New York: Simon and Schuster, 1970.

Sternhell, Zeev. *La droite révolutionnaire*. Paris: Editions du Seuil, 1978.

———. *Naissance de l'idéologie fasciste*. Paris: Fayard, 1989.

Tronti, Mario. *Operai e capital*. Turin: Einaudi, 1966.

Ventrone, Angelo. *La seduzione totalitaria: Guerra, modernità, violenza politica (1914–1918)*. Rome: Donzelli, 2004.

———. *"Vogliamo tutto": Perché due generazioni hanno creduto nella rivoluzione (1960–1988)*. Rome: Laterza, 2012.

Zavoli, Sergio. *La notte della Repubblica*. Rome: Mondadori, 1992.

Chapter 2

Authenticity through Transgression
Small Acts of Resentment in Post-1968 Czechoslovakia

Barış Yörümez

On New Year's Eve 1979, Slovak National Television broadcast a talk show that featured various celebrity guests, including tenor Peter Dvorský and rock musician Jaroslav Filip. At one point during the program, given that it was being aired on the last day of the decade, the host asked the guests about what they considered to have been the biggest experience of the past ten years. The sarcastic answer that Jaroslav Filip gave to this seemingly mundane question provides a telling anecdote for the mode of transgression and public criticism in the country:

> The biggest experience of the past decade for me was the cutting down of the tree in Primatial Square [*Primaciálne námestie*]. There was this nice big tree and they cut it down. I think this was a big experience and I think they should go on like that ... Now there is this nice, shiny concrete where you can slide in the winter or play golf. It is perfect. I would also recommend getting rid of the square, where the Roland is located. It has to go. These things do not have a place here ... There have already been improvements in Bratislava. Below Bratislava castle, there is a very aesthetically pleasing car wash. That's great. I think there could be three car washes. I have some other possible improvements [in mind]. From Saint Michael's Gate downwards, I would destroy everything.[1] What is it good for? What is this coquetry with history and old buildings good for? These old things should all go ... And we should make everything concrete, beautiful, shiny concrete, concrete, concrete, concrete. This was my experience of the decade.[2]

As Filip was firing off his tirade, the audience in the studio repeatedly burst into laughter and applauded at the end. They all understood what he was talking about. During the 1970s, Bratislava had undergone a massive urban transformation. As a result, many historical buildings and green areas were cut down to give way to new bridges, highways, and housing blocs. Filip's sarcasm took direct aim at the urban policies of the communist government and the audience in the studio gave its approval. All this was filmed in advance, avoided censorship, and aired without issue.

Jaroslav Filip's not-so-covert public criticism was not a rare instance. In fact, the Czechoslovak public sphere, including the media, was filled with tongue-in-cheek mocking and criticisms of the government and political elites. In this chapter, I argue that as the post-Prague Spring Czechoslovak government forcefully suppressed direct political criticism and subjugated citizens through fear and intimidation, people expressed and circulated their discontent through the mass media or behind the back of power in disguised forms. The party, seeking a compromise with a population that had, on the whole, supported the Prague Spring experiment in 1968 and felt humiliated by the Warsaw Pact invasion, did not intervene in public transgressions as long as they did not turn into an open rebellion against the status quo.[3] The transgressive declarations of resentment allowed people to momentarily remove their masks of submission and provided a common jargon for the art and technique of keeping one's own dignity in the face of power. In other words, by performing and participating in small acts of disobedience, individuals insinuated their discontent and, momentarily, distanced themselves from their complicit everyday existence, allowing themselves to express their authentic selves. Moreover, the very acts of participating in transgressive actions produced a sense and culture of authenticity, which provided a common language and emotional unity for the resentful public in the country. In this regard, these modes of transgression functioned as what James C. Scott calls "hidden transcripts" of resistance, allowing a "nonhegemonic, contrapuntal, dissident" discursive realm to be fostered under the post-1968 regime in Czechoslovakia.[4] Building on Scott's conceptualization of hidden transcripts, in this chapter I rethink late-socialist Czechoslovakia beyond the binaries of active resistance and performative complicity.

Until recently, academic interest in East bloc socialism was centered around dissidence and political domination. Inspired by the unexpected revolutions of 1989, many scholars focused on the violation of human rights by East bloc regimes and the resistance of dissident movements.[5] In doing so, most of these studies placed a particular emphasis on the political power play between party elites and dissident intellectuals and largely focused on modes of active resistance such as protests, strikes, or underground publications, which had played an important role in the collapse of communist parties in the region.

In the last decade or so, such an approach has become somewhat unfashionable among historians of late-socialism. Instead of the persecution and resistance narrative of earlier scholarship, a new generation of historians has pointed to the fact that the great majority of citizens did not engage in any dissident activity until the revolutionary days of 1989. Hence, in order to understand the "experience" of living under socialism, they began to focus on everyday life, consumption, compliance, and even the collaboration of individuals in late-socialist societies.[6] Arguably, however, despite their important contributions to understandings of the culture of late-socialism, these studies are largely silent about the communal frustration shared by large segments of society beyond their performative compliance. Paulina Bren's *The Greengrocer and His TV*, for instance, argues that propaganda-free television series, broadcast by party-controlled state television in Czechoslovakia from the mid-1970s onward, helped the party to relocate public criticisms made during the Prague Spring into people's private sphere. In other words, according to Bren, the Party "convinced" people "that the core contexts of politics should be the sphere of private life," and used television as its main ideological apparatus.[7] Unfortunately, however, Bren does not discuss the mechanisms of such "conviction" from the audience's point of view. Although she brilliantly describes the plot, production, and broadcasting of these series, she largely ignores the voices of people who actually watched them. The questions of how and what these "convinced" television-watchers actually thought, felt, and communicated about the authoritarian political predicament in the country remain unanswered. This question is crucial to understanding post-1968 Czechoslovakia, because in 1989 the very same people, who had been complicit for more than two decades, marched on the squares all around the region and made the revolution possible.

Writing about the post-1968 resentment and its insinuation in the public sphere through hidden transcripts compels one to read between the lines of archival documents that largely portray the "actions" and "opinions" of party elites or dissident intellectuals. One challenge is that these opinions and actions rarely reflect on the "emotions" in late-socialist Czechoslovak society. Luckily, there are a wide variety of sources at our disposal such as diaries, feuilletons, memoirs, and popular songs to map out the collective structure of feeling in post-1968 Czechoslovakia. In addition to these written sources, oral history offers a valuable solution to the limitations of archives by democratizing the historical evidence pool. As Paul Thompson once argued, "the use of oral evidence breaks through the barriers between the chroniclers and their audience," and allows the historian to call witness from the people, whose feelings and opinions were absent in written documents.[8] For this reason, I conducted in-depth oral interviews with thirteen people from various class, educational, and age groups (the oldest was born in 1932 and the youngest in 1973) in the city of Bratislava.[9] In addition to my research, Miroslav Vaněk's *Vítězové Poražení* (Winners, losers) and David Leviatin's *Prague Sprung* greatly helped me as they collectively provide oral accounts of people from various social backgrounds.[10] I also made close readings of individual testimonies about life after 1968, as they regularly appear in Czech and Slovak mass media.

This chapter consists of three parts. The first part provides an historical background and discusses what Prague Spring meant for the large majority of Czechs and Slovaks. The second deals with the concept of "authenticity through transgression" by conceptually bringing together dissident writings and oral history. In the third part, I analyze how people voiced and circulated their resentment and criticism through small scale acts of transgressions such as telling political jokes and listening to forbidden iconic songs from 1968.

Spring and Winter in Prague

The Prague Spring, which began in January 1968 with the election of reformist Alexander Dubček as the Party secretary, came to be one of the most significant attempts of twentieth century socialism to reconcile Marxist egalitarian principles with personal freedoms. Almost immediately after Dubček's election, discussions among ruling reform socialists about a democratic future for the country were made public, causing mass euphoria in society, especially among the younger generation. From the very beginning, reformists made it clear that Dubček's appointment was not only a rotation of leaders, but reflected a fundamental shift in the government's orientations. The Party Central Committee Presidium officially declared that it had begun the process of abolishing censorship. Within two weeks, two mass meetings of young people and political and cultural officials were organized in Prague to discuss the matters that had long been forbidden by the Party. It is estimated that around twenty thousand people attended each of these meetings. Never in the history of "actually existing socialisms" had the party enjoyed such a level of enthusiastic support and political participation from its citizens.

The Czechoslovak political experiment to design "socialism with a human face" was closely watched by intellectuals and university students in the East bloc, and this posed a risk to the dictatorial rule of party elites in the region. The leaders of Warsaw Pact countries began to exert heavy diplomatic pressure on the Czechoslovak government to slow down the momentum of the Prague Spring, if not wholly stop it. Arguably, the cardinal sin of the Czechoslovak government's reform government was to form the Action Group for the Restoration of the Social Democratic Party. Soviet leader Leonid Brezhnev simply could not tolerate the idea of multi-party elections as it was in direct conflict with the founding principles of the Soviet Union and other communist regimes in Eastern Europe. After talks between Warsaw Pact leaders and Czechoslovak reform socialists failed to bring any practical solution to the fundamental differences between the two sides, a combined force of Soviet, Hungarian, Polish, and Bulgarian troops entered Czechoslovakia on 20 August 1968 in the name of "friendly aid." In order to avoid bloodshed, the reform government ordered the Czechoslovak army to stay in their barracks and not to confront the foreign armies.[11]

In the absence of military opposition, the only resistance to the "intervention" came from civilians. As the Warsaw Pact troops entered Czechoslovak cities, they were confronted by a large number of protestors who tried to talk to the invading soldiers about the wrongdoing of invasion for the socialist cause, laid barricades on the main streets, changed road signs, and in some cases even tried to fight off the invading force with Molotov cocktails. Yet despite the demonstrations and widespread sense of resistance in society, people soon realized that the only outcome of protests and street clashes with the Warsaw Pact soldiers was civilian deaths. Thus, in the face of Soviet tanks, people's activism gradually lost its momentum. Neither quarrels with Red Army soldiers nor stones and Molotov cocktails managed to have an impact on Brezhnev's interventionist doctrine. Václav Malý, who was one of the protesting students in August 1968, explains this change:

> I remember 1968 very vividly. And I remember those times with mixed feelings. On the one hand, amazing rebellion of people particularly after August 1968. On the other hand, the beginning of hypocrisy, which started to appear at the beginning of 1969. People started to be afraid. They began to change their positions and attitudes in public, and then, this also transferred into the education system where teachers were more careful. In 1968, anyone could—for the first time—talk about the things that one really meant. While after that, cautiousness began to appear.[12]

After the intervention, a newly formed hard-line—or so-called "normalization"—government quickly imposed heavy censorship, mass purges from the party and strict bans on traveling outside the East bloc. In order to increase its legitimacy in society, the new regime increased government spending so as to provide more and better consumer goods for people, and showed an indifference to individuals' personal opinions, as long as any criticism remained within a close circle of friends and family members. In other words, as long as people remained silent about politics in public, they could enjoy relative luxuries such as private cars, cottage houses, or summer holidays in Yugoslavia.[13] Overall, what started out as an effort to combine socialism with democratic values ended up in a welfare dictatorship.

As mentioned above, however, people ultimately accepted defeat in the face of the invasion not because of the relative abundance offered by the new regime but because, perhaps accurately, they reasoned that resistance was futile. One must keep in mind that in 1968 the Czechoslovak public still had a fresh memory of the year 1956, when Hungarians led an armed resistance against the Red Army and suffered great losses. People had every reason to believe that open resistance against the new regime was hopeless as it was backed by thousands of Warsaw Pact troops, who had been permanently stationed in the country.

In addition, one of the most efficient and cruel methods that the State employed to convince citizens to comply was to persecute not only dissenting individuals, but also their close family members. Hence "dissidence" meant preventing one's siblings and children from attending university, or from having any white-collar job in the future. For this reason, many people found themselves at a crossroads between their freedom and integrity on the one hand, and the well-being of their relatives on the other. Intellectuals (academics, journalists, writers) were in a particularly difficult position as "staying out of politics" was not enough for them to keep their jobs. They were expected to publicly support the "normalization" regime. Those who refused to do so were sacked from their positions and forced to work in low-paying, blue-collar jobs. For instance, when reform socialist (and later dissident) Milan Šimečka refused to write a public apology for his earlier reformist beliefs and support the post-invasion government, the regime not only dismissed him from his teaching job at a university, but also barred his son from entering university.[14] After being expelled from his teaching post, Šimečka worked as a truck driver for twenty years until he became an advisor for President Václav Havel after 1989. By that time, his son was already thirty-three years old and married with children. He never went to university.

Milan Šimečka's uncompromising stance against the post-1968 regime was an exception. The regime's blackmailing policy was mostly successful; in some cases, it led people to comply even if they had emigrated to the West. For example, an eighteen-year-old (F. D.) had gone to Switzerland in early 1968, shortly before Warsaw Pact troops occupied Czechoslovakia. When the new government closed the borders, he was sure that he was not coming back to Czechoslovakia. However, it soon became clear that his sister would never be able to go to university if he stayed out of the country. Hence, once the regime declared temporary amnesty for people who had emigrated outside of the East bloc, he came back. But returning home took its emotional toll on him:

> I was young and one of my friends invited me there [to Switzerland], so I said: why not? I really liked it there. At that time, you could easily find a job in Switzerland. So I had a good job, earning good money, having a good life. However, I had to come back because it became very clear that my sister would be in trouble for the rest of her life because of me staying there. So after four years, I came back and everything was so gray and depressing that I could not leave home for three months. It was horrible here.[15]

After this initial period of anger and depression, like the majority of Czechoslovaks, F. D. adapted to the new situation in the country. He found a job, got married, and had children. "Although I somehow got used to situation at home," he says, "I always felt trapped here and wondered how things would be different had I stayed in Switzerland." As in the case of F. D., the great majority of Czechs and Slovaks gradually returned to their everyday lives and adapted to the realities of the new political situation. Yet out of this involuntary collective adaptation, there emerged a social mechanism of transgression, through which people voiced and insinuated their discontent in the public sphere, hence constructing their dignified authentic selves behind their complicit public masks.

Compliance and Its Complications: Authenticity out of Transgression

In his well-known 1978 article on life in post-invasion Czechoslovakia, Václav Havel characterized what he regarded as the average Czechoslovak citizen through a story about a greengrocer who, at the request of the Party, displays a banner saying: "Workers of the world, unite!" amid the fruit and vegetables. For Havel, the greengrocer did not display the banner because of his political ideals, nor did he even give too much thought to it. Yet, although the greengrocer did not share the communist ideals, his very act of compliance signified that he "enters the game, he becomes one of its players, he makes it possible for the game to continue being played, for it basically to continue, simply to exist."[16] According to Havel, the greengrocer can either continue with his or her unquestioning compliance to the regime, or refuse to bend to the regime's *modus operandi,* which was based on falsehood, and finally begin to "live in truth."[17]

For many Czechs and Slovaks however, Havel's moral call for civil disobedience was too idealistic and unpractical. Fellow dissidents like Ludvík Vaculík and Petr Pithart argued that expecting activist courage or, in Pithart's term, "dissi-risk" (*disi-rizika*) from ordinary people in society in their everyday life would simply be asking too much.[18] Vaculík wrote: "Most people are well aware of their own limits and refrain from actions whose consequences they would be unable to bear. Whoever forces people to take more weight than they can carry should not be surprised when they break … A psychologist and politician cannot expect heroism in everyday life … Heroism does not fit into life."[19]

Instead of direct confrontation with the regime, both Vaculík and Pithart saw small-scale acts of honesty, integrity, and goodwill as heroic acts in themselves, and these acts would be capable of improving conditions in the country. Vaculík argued that "while heroism frightens people, by giving them the truthful excuse that they are not made for it, everyone can bravely adhere to the norm of good behavior at the price of acceptable sacrifice, and everyone knows it."[20]

Neither Vaculík nor Pithart explained what they exactly meant by small-scale good acts in society. In fact, whether they realized it or not, a great number of Czechs and Slovaks were actually conducting small-scale acts of transgression in their daily lives. To use Havel's example, the greengrocer may have put the party's signs next to the fruit and vegetables without any protestation, but he or she also privately criticized the system, mocked the party leaders, gossiped about the corruption, or listened to the banned songs of 1968. After all, many citizens were very well aware of their political subordination and, behind their complicit public mask, expressed their discontent in the public sphere through the circulation of popular jokes, urban legends, gossip, songs, and so on. Through such disguised forms, people opened free social space and formed a common language for public dissent. These forms constitute what James Scott calls hidden transcripts of resistance: "a realm of relative discursive freedom outside the earshot of power holders."[21] Milan Šimečka explains this phenomenon in his semi-anthropological work on Czechoslovak society in early 1980s:

> When I listen to adapted citizens talking in private, I have the feeling that they are taking revenge. With ferocity and impotence they avenge their public loss of face, their humiliation, their trepidation, their permanent state of fear, their own hypocrisy, and the lies they must listen

and assent to, not to mention the minor acts of betrayal they have committed against themselves and often against their neighbor.[22]

For many so-called "ordinary" Czechs and Slovaks, who were neither active in dissident circles nor party members, the very act of "avenging public loss of face" through transgression was the mode of constructing an "authentic self" in the face of a regime that demanded performative public compliance from the citizens regardless of their actual opinions and feelings. In other words, as a response to their forced obedience, people performed transgressive actions in their everyday setting to keep their sense of self-dignity. And the more they thought they were pushing to the semi-imagined limits of transgression, the closer they felt to their "authentic being"—as opposed to the collective inauthentic faces of complicity. Z. M. explains how his sarcastic and critical comments about the political situation during his university years possibly led to discrimination later in the army during his military service:

> I am sure the secret police had a report about my comments ... Because I was a university graduate, I could theoretically stay in the Czechoslovak army at the end of my military service and become an officer. But although communists [in the army] made such an offer to almost every university graduate in the unit, they did not have the guts to offer it to me. I was not desirable enough and I felt good about it.[23]

It may seem paradoxical that while Z. M. took pride in what seems to be his exceptional display of transgression, he did not give too much thought about the fact that he could finish his studies (in engineering) and did not face any jail time because of his not-so-private comments. Here it is important to note that the reason why the regime did not persecute transgressors was that, unlike dissidents and counterculture activists, the small-scale acts of transgressions often took place spontaneously and people who engaged in them did not form a politically conscious group. Indeed, one of the most significant dividing lines between "transgression" and "dissidence" was being a member of a resistance (dissident or countercultural) circle, and most citizens did not cross that line. Because the regime successfully implanted a sense of powerlessness in the post-1968 political structure of feeling in Czechoslovakia, the great majority of citizens, while seeking authenticity via their personal, transgressive interactions, regarded their "inauthentic" public face as unfortunate yet unavoidable necessity. Nevertheless, such acceptance did not mean complete surrender. In fact, while the regime was able to corner dissidents and countercultural groups into marginality, popular transgressive acts, as we will see, provided a common language for widespread political resentment in society.[24]

Satire as a Mode of Transgression

Satire was arguably one of the most practiced modes of authenticity in a post-1968 political predicament that was perceived by many to be based on falsehood. Jokes about a lack of personal freedoms, the low quality of goods, and people's own powerlessness to challenge the system that they were forced to live in were widely circulated in the country. One student explained, with a certain sense of nostalgia, the popularity and fast circulation of such political jokes a year after the Velvet Revolution:

> Before the revolution, I remember that we had loads of very, very good jokes. They were about the people and the circumstances we blamed. They weren't only political jokes, they were a special brand of jokes, they were absurd. They were really amazing. You heard a joke in Prague and two days later it was 200 kilometers from Prague. After some time, we heard it in a different form.[25]

Mocking the party elites and their empty rhetoric was a particularly popular "weapon of the weak" as the people at the top ranks of the party were generally perceived as old, careerist, and serious men with a very limited sense of humor.[26] One of the most common themes in these officially-forbidden-yet-popular jokes was the unpopularity of the party and people's inability to challenge it. In one such joke, General Secretary Gustáv Husák and Ronald Reagan "are discussing the number of people who are discontented with their respective governments. Reagan says, 'I am sure the number is not higher than twenty million.' Husák replies: 'To tell you the truth, it is about the same in Czechoslovakia.'"[27] The underlying reality was that the entire population of Czechoslovakia was about fifteen million people, and there were no free multiparty elections in the country. Another joke goes: "Lenin was right in saying that socialism proved to be the era of electrification: you go to work with the sense of resistance, wait for your salary with the pending voltage, but you can never mess with the mainframe [*vedenia*, which also means "leadership" in Czech.]" A more grotesque joke tells the story of a dying man who, on his death bed, wants to be admitted to the Communist Party. "And what would it be good for?" asks his crying wife. The man answers: "I don't want you to cry. You know you always feel good when a communist dies."[28]

Anonymity and being "outside of the earshot of powerholders" let more individuals voice their discontent and intensified the level of sarcasm. One team member of the Czechoslovak Film Studios described how moviegoers reacted differently to party-made newsreels when they turned off the lights in the theaters:

> I remember very well the moment when the lights went out, the curtain opened, and the familiar opening music sequence filled the air. The screen showed an airplane after landing and the well-known face of a political figure descending from stairs. Then came the bouquets of flowers and the usual embraces. Murmurs and giggles were heard from the rows of seats. The laughter was subdued and quiet at first, then it grew louder, words were called out. Parts of the commentary received applause. We were all so brave in the dark.[29]

Here it is important to note that the above testimony was given by a person who herself participated in the production of the newsreels. Even the people working in the media industry harbored critical views. Indeed, from the mid-1970s, the Czechoslovak mass media gained a peculiar autonomy from the party ideology. Transgressive instances, such as Jaroslav Filip's tirade mentioned at the beginning of this chapter, increasingly crept into the public sphere. News programs and newsreels gradually jettisoned the propagandistic tone and occasionally voiced criticism of the inadequacies and inefficiencies in the country.[30] One example of such critical coverage was a newsreel covering the story of construction work in the newly built residential district of Petržalka in Bratislava in 1979. The interviewer spoke with the managers behind the projects and asked about the reasons for the delays in finishing the buildings. The managers provided the usual reasons: delays in the building of the technical equipment; energy connections; the problem of noncontinuous work for various organizational reasons, etc. After the interview finished, the camera began to show various identical blocks with fast-paced cartoon music. The narrator said: "problems and again problems ... Our head starts to spin." Then they showed the shabby exterior and gardens of the supposedly finished buildings. The camera shot children playing next to the debris of construction materials; then the voice said, "this is how the neighborhood looks two years after people moved in." The ironic cartoon music continued; the camera showed the initial plan of the green garden arrangement placed next to the constructed blocks and the current shabbiness, full of dirt and rusty metals from the construction. Then the camera showed a closed grocery store, a small shop, and a cabin with a nonfunctioning telephone inside. The narrator stated: "Let us shine a light on it. So there is light during the day," and the camera showed a street lamp, the only working device in the neighborhood, ridiculously left on in the middle of the day.[31]

Forbidden Box Office of Prerevolutionary Czechoslovakia

Not all acts of resistance were joyful. The painful memory of the Warsaw Pact invasion and the end of the Prague Spring movement had left a lasting legacy in the collective feelings of the country. In this situation, popular songs of resistance to the occupation, which were swiftly banned by the post-invasion regime, reached cult status in the following decades. Listening to and circulating banned music became an important part of the repertoire of transgression, especially among urban classes in Czechoslovakia. The two most memorable of these songs were Karel Kryl's "Bratříčku Zavírej Vrátka" (Little brother, close the gate) and Marta Kubišová's "Modlitba pre Martu" (Prayer for Marta). Unlike the popular jokes, neither of the songs used humor or contained an explicit political message in their lyrics. What made them very popular was their powerful reflection of the emotional frustration shared by many after 1968.

Karel Kryl's debut album *Bratříčku Zavírej Vrátka* (Close the gate, little brother) was released in early 1969 amid the shadow of invasion and self-immolations. Because party hardliners had not yet taken control of the entire cultural sphere, Kryl was able to produce and distribute his album legally. Its opening song, which had the same name as the album, quickly became one of the most iconic symbols of post-invasion Czechoslovakia:

> Little brother, don't sob, it is not a bogeyman
> Don't be frightened, it is only soldiers
> Who arrived in sharp-edged metal caravans ...
> Do not waste your tears
> Hold back the curses and save your strength ...
> The wolf felt a sudden desire for the little ram, little brother, close the gate! Close the gate![32]

Arguably, Kryl's poetic lyrics accompanied by the slow rhythm of his acoustic guitar captured both the resentment ("Hold back your curses") and powerlessness (e.g., wolf and lamb analogy) throughout society. Because of its immense popularity and political connotation, the Party soon banned "Little Brother" and no television or radio stations broadcast any of Kryl's music until 1989. Despite the government ban, "Little Brother Close the Gate" remained one of the most iconic forbidden best-sellers in prerevolutionary Czechoslovakia. Ľudmila Kolesárová, a widely-read blogger from Slovakia, remembers how her mother listened to Kryl in secret: "When I was eight, I heard 'Little Brother, Don't Cry, it's not a Bogeyman' for the first time. When I came into the room, my mother put the disc under the bed and told me not to tell anybody about the song. Then she hid it next to other books and records."[33] Thanks to tape recorders, people could record Kryl's albums, which he recorded in exile, because they were broadcast by Radio Free Europe and circulated illegally throughout the country. P.D. explains Kryl's popularity and the reasons for it: "It was very easy to find his albums. You could buy it on the black market in the street, or somebody would lend it to you. And his songs were very popular and powerful. I would listen to his songs in my room, and look from my window and see what he was singing about, right in front of my eyes."[34]

Kryl composed "Little Brother" shortly after the invasion. It was a figurative reflection of his frustration about the political developments in his country. In this regard, Marta Kubišová's "Prayer for Marta" differed significantly. It was composed before the occupation for the popular television series titled *Songs for Rudolf the Third* (*Píseň pro Rudolfa III*), a comedy about the surreal daydreams of an ordinary butcher from Prague. Kubišová recorded "Prayer" four days after the invasion in the studio of Czechoslovak Radio, which immediately broadcast the song, long before its intended appearance in the television:

> Let peace remain, settle on this country ...
> Now, lost rule over your matters
> shall be returned to you, oh people, shall be returned ...
> This is a prayer, from the whole of my heart:
> let anger burn, time keeps its flowers safe
> beneath a cold balm of winter frost.[35]

Although the song does not have an explicitly political message, its emphasis on peace, self-rule and, perhaps more importantly, the fact that radio stations repeatedly played the song in the first days of Warsaw Pact invasion, made it one of most politically loaded songs of late-socialism in Czechoslovakia.[36] Despite the eventual official ban, "Prayer for Marta" remained a powerful symbol of the discontent the invasion brought to the country and the very act of listening to it became a sign of solidarity among the occupied citizens of Czechoslovakia. As James Krapfl wrote: "when the singer Marta Kubišová—who had been barred from performing since 1970—explained that she had endured the years of silence because 'it was people that helped me' (*pomohli mi lidé*), she was invoking the most fundamental value of the collective effervescence."³⁷

This effervescence reached its peak in November 1989. On 9 November, when Czechoslovaks watched the fall of Berlin Wall on their television screens, it seemed to mark the end of collective powerlessness in the country. Once this happened, long-hidden transcripts of resistance quickly turned into powerful revolutionary slogans expressing their years of resentment in the face of power. Ľudmila Kolesárová, who had been warned by her mother not to tell anybody about listening to Kryl, recalls the moment: "Then suddenly came November 17. I watched it as a child, or rather perhaps as a teenager, who no longer needed to lie and hide. And we turned Kryl on to full volume."³⁸ Both Marta Kubišová and at a later stage Karel Kryl appeared on the podiums of revolution and sang their forbidden songs. Even though their music was banned from official media, people in the square all knew the lyrics and accompanied them as they sang. In particular, Marta Kubišová's appearance on the stage in Prague's Wenceslas Square on 21 November 1989 was one of the epic moments of the Velvet Revolution. Unlike Kryl, Kubišová was not able to go into exile and produce albums. After the government ban on her, she first worked as a manual worker in a toy factory, and then as a low-level clerk in a construction bureau.³⁹ Despite her complete disappearance from public life for more than twenty years, when she stepped on the stage, people in the square began to chant "Long Live Marta." She did not make a speech. Without any instrument or background music, she sang her famous "Prayer for Marta" together with the thousands in the square.⁴⁰ Kubišová recalls the moment: "I didn't cry. I was overcome by the sheer sight of the whole square jammed with people. I said to myself, no singer ever had a comeback like this! Foreign film crews told me people were in tears and when they asked: what are you crying for, they said: it's that woman."⁴¹

These public appearances of Kubišová and Kryl during the Velvet Revolution were what James C. Scott calls "saturnalia of power, the first declaration of the hidden transcript."⁴² Scott argues that in revolutionary times, when the hidden transcripts of resistance (or transgression) were made public in their true meanings, they function as the means for euphoric psychological release of long-held sentiments in the face of hegemonic power. During the Velvet Revolution in Czechoslovakia, the very act of publicly listening to and singing banned music gave people a sense of solidarity comparable only to the immediate aftermath of the Warsaw Pact occupation in 1968. Paradoxically, the symbols of the defeat and suffering after the invasion in 1968 became an empowering rallying cry in 1989.

Conclusion

The rapidity and the swiftness of the so-called Velvet Revolution surprised dissidents and commentators alike. In December 1989, Timothy Garton Ash stated the obvious when he wrote, "in Poland the transition [from communism to democracy] lasted ten years, in Hungary ten months, in Czechoslovakia ten days."[43] Similarly, in the New Year message to the nation in 1990, Václav Havel, who had just transitioned from being a largely obscure dissident to being president, asked: "How is it possible that so many people immediately understood what to do and that none of them needed any advice or instructions?"[44] One of the important reasons for the effective and synchronized mass activism of the civilians in 1989 was the unifying instances of small-scale transgressions that occurred under the post-1968 regime. Because the regime persecuted any organized resistance, a resenting public had developed ways in which it was possible to tear off their masks of complicity and to express their authentic selves without risking being persecuted by the regime.

Unlike dissident activities, these small acts of resentment, such as mocking the party elites or listening to forbidden songs, did not have an explicitly political goal. Nevertheless, they functioned as "hidden transcripts of resistance" providing a free discursive realm through which people could instill their covert criticism into the public sphere. In the fateful year of 1989, when Czechoslovak citizens watched the fall of Berlin Wall on their TVs, the long-hidden and covert transcripts quickly turned into the slogans for the revolution. Finally, they were not small transgressions any more.

Baris Yorumez is a Ph.D. candidate in the Department of History at University of British Columbia. His dissertation is on socioemotional history of the sixties and Prague Spring in Czechoslovakia.

Notes

1. The location Jaroslav Filip describes is basically the entire historical Old Town of Bratislava.
2. Footage of the Filip's tirade can be seen in "Noc v archive: Silvestrovská polnoc v archíve," *RTVS,* 12 January 2014.
3. A survey conducted by Polish sociologists right after the Warsaw Pact intervention shows that only 1.2 percent of Czechoslovak society approved the logic behind the invasion. E. J. Czerwinski and Jaroslaw Piekalkiewicz, *The Soviet Invasion of Czechoslovakia: Its Effects on Eastern Europe* (New York, 1972), 6.

4. James Scott, *Domination and the Arts of Resistance: Hidden Transcript* (New Haven, CT, 1990), 25.
5. For example, see Timothy Gorton Ash, *The Magic Lantern: The Revolution of '89 in Warsaw, Budapest, Berlin, Prague* (New York, 1990); Lawrence Goodwyn, *Breaking the Barrier: Rise of Solidarity in Poland* (New York, 1991); Padraic Kenney, *A Carnival of Revolution: Central Europe 1989* (Princeton, NJ, 2002); Roman Laba, *The Roots of Solidarity: A Political Sociology of Poland's Working Class Democratization* (Princeton, NJ, 1991); Vladimir Tismaneau, ed., *The Revolutions of 1989* (London, 1999).
6. See, for instance, Paulina Bren, *The Greengrocer and His TV: The Culture of Communism after the 1968 Prague Spring* (Ithaca, NY, 2010); Paulina Bren and Mary Neuburger, eds., *Communism Unwrapped: Consumption in Cold War Eastern Europe* (New York, 2012); David Crowley and Susan E. Reid, eds., *Socialist Spaces: Sites of Everyday Life in the Eastern Bloc* (Oxford, 2002); Eli Rubin, *Synthetic Socialism: Plastics and Dictatorship in the German Democratic Republic* (Chapel Hill, NC, 2008); Edith Sheffer, *Burned Bridge: How East and West Germans Made the Iron Curtain* (New York, 2011).
7. Bren, *The Greengrocer and His TV*, 207. Quotation is from Lauren Berlant, *The Queen of America Goes to Washington City: Essays on Sex and Citizenship* (Durham, NC, 1997), 3.
8. Paul Thompson, "The Voice of the Past: Oral History," in *The Oral History Reader*, 3rd ed., ed. Robert Perks and Alistair Thomson (London, 2015), 38.
9. The oral research was part of my master's thesis at Koç University. Barış Yörümez, "In Pursuit of an Errant Act: The Influence of the 'Culture of Late Capitalism' on the Dissolution of Communism in Czechoslovak Socialist Republic," (Istanbul, 2012). The interviewees were both Czechs and Slovaks. The ethnic relationship between Czechs and Slovaks was not within the scope of the research and none of the participants raised the issue.
10. David Leviatin, *Prague Sprung: Notes and Voices from the New World* (London, 1993); Miroslav Vaněk, *Vítězové? Poražení?: I. díl, Disent v období tzv. normalizace : interpretační studie životopisných interview* (Prague, 2006).
11. Harold G. Skilling, *Czechoslovakia's Interrupted Revolution* (Princeton, NJ, 1976); Kieran Williams, *The Prague Spring and its Aftermath: Czechoslovak Politics (1968–1970)* (Cambridge, 1997); Jaromir Navratil, Antonin Bencik, and Vaclav Kural, eds., *The Prague Spring 1968: National Security Archive Documents Reader* (New York, 1998).
12. Vaněk, *Vítězové? Poražení?*, 430–431.
13. Despite the political clash of 1948–1955, Yugoslavia (especially along the Adriatic coast) became one of the most popular travel destinations for Czechoslovak citizens in the late twentieth century. See Igor Tchourakine, "The Yugoslav Road to International Tourism: Opening, Decentralization, and Propaganda in the Early 1950s, " in *Yugoslavia's Sunny Side: A History of Tourism in Socialism (1950s–1980s)*, ed. Hannes Grandits and Karin Taylor (Budapest, 2010), 133.
14. László Rajk and Martin Šimečka, "Dilemma '89: My Father was a Communist," *Eurozine*, 7 May 2010.

15. My personal interview with F. D. on 24 July 2011 in Bratislava. He did not face legal charges when he came back because the government declared a temporary amnesty for people who would return before a certain deadline.
16. Václav Havel, "The Power of the Powerless," in *The Power of the Powerless: Citizens against the State in Central-Eastern Europe*, ed. John Keane (New York, 1985), 31.
17. Havel, "The Power of the Powerless," 31.
18. Ludvík Vaculík, "Poznámky o Statečnosti," in *Z dějin českého myšlení o literatuře 4 (1970–1989) Antologie k Dějinám české literatury 1945–1990*, ed. Kateřina Bláhová and Michal Přibáň (Prague, 2005) 238–241. For an excellent overview and scholarly reflection on the dissident discussion on the topic, see Jonathan Bolton, *Worlds of Dissent: Charter 77, the Plastic People of the Universe, and Czech Culture under Communism* (Cambridge, MA, 2012), 201–239.
19. Vaculík, "Poznámky," 239. Part of the translation is from Bolton, *Worlds of Dissent*, 231. See also Ludvík Vaculík, *A Cup of Coffee with My Interrogator: The Prague Chronicles of Ludvík Vaculík* (London, 1976), 46–51.
20. Vaculík, *A Cup of Coffee with My Interrogator*, 51. Also cited in Bolton, *World of Dissent*, 232.
21. Scott, *Domination and the Arts of Resistance*, 25.
22. Milan Šimečka, *The Restoration of Order: The Normalization of Czechoslovakia, 1969–1976* (London, 1984), 144. The text was smuggled to the West and published in the United Kingdom.
23. My personal interview with Z. M. on 14 July 2011 in Bratislava.
24. Anecdotally, Václav Havel's second wife, actress Dagmar Havlova, remarked that she had not heard about Charter 77 until she met Havel in 1990s. Bren, *The Greengrocer and His TV*, 5.
25. Leviatin, *Prague Sprung*, 23.
26. Phrase is from James Scott, *Weapons of the Weak: Everyday Forms of Peasant Resistance* (New Haven, CT, 1985).
27. Kevin Deegan Krause, "Jokes of the Velvet Revolution and Before," *Wayne State University* Department of Political Science.
28. "Spomienky na November '89: Necenzurované vtipy," *Život*, 13 November 2009.
29. Týždeň vo Filme. [DVD]. Bratislava: Slovenský Filmový Ustav, 2008. The interview appears in the DVD extras.
30. As Paulina Bren's study on Czechoslovak Television convincingly shows, the party elites made a conscious decision to reduce the propagandistic tone in order to increase the ratings and relevance of the state-controlled media. Yet whether it means that non-propagandistic television was "the most effective purveyor" for convincing people for the perks of "quiet life" (as opposed to Havel's dictum of "living in truth") is very debatable. After all, one does not need very much convincing for the quiet life if the alternative is persecution and possible harm to relatives. In addition, by the time Czechoslovak television began to turn into entertainment TV (in the mid-1970s), the Czechoslovak population by and large had already been "convinced." Bren, *The Greengrocer and His TV*, 111.
31. Týždeň vo Filme.
32. This translation is largely based on Adriana Lukas, "Another Remembrance Day," *Samizdata*, 17 November 2007.

33. Ľudmila Kolesárová, "O mojom detstve. (pre premiéra)," *Sme Blog*, 9 January 2014.
34. My personal interview with P. D. on 18 July 2011 in Bratislava.
35. The translation of the song is based on "Marta Kubišová *Modlitba pre Martu* (Supraphon, 1968)," *Eastern Bloc Songs*. I made minor changes to the translation.
36. The line "Now, lost rule over your matters shall be returned to you, oh people, shall be returned" [*Teď když tvá ztracená vláda věcí tvých/ zpět se k tobě navrátí, lide, navrátí*] is borrowed from seventeenth-century Moravian thinker and educator Jan Amos Comenius. For more information about the songs of Velvet Revolution, see Pavla Horaková, "The Soundtrack to the Velvet Revolution," *Radio Prague*, 17 November 2013.
37. James Krapfl, *Revolution with a Human Face* (Ithaca, NY, 2013), 102. Quote is from "M. Kubišová: Pomohli mi lidé," *Svobodne slovo*, 23 November 1989, 5.
38. Kolesárová, "O mojom detstve."
39. Ian Willoughby, "'Prayer for Marta' Singer Kubišová Recalls Dramatic Comeback during 1989's Velvet Revolution," *Radio Prague*. 18 November 2009.
40. Actual footage of the event can be seen at "Marta Kubišová's Modlitba pre Martu (1989)," https://www.youtube.com/watch?v=npMZ7UxwVgU.
41. Willoughby, "Prayer for Marta."
42. Scott, *Hidden Transcripts*, 202–227.
43. Timothy Gorton Ash, "The Revolution of Magic Lantern," *The New York Review of Books*, 18 January 1990.
44. Quoted in Scott, *Domination and Arts of Resistance*, 221. For the full speech, see Václav Havel, "New Year's Address to the Nation," *Czech Republic Presidential Website*, 1 January 1990.

Bibliography

Ash, Timothy Gorton. *The Magic Lantern: The Revolution of '89 in Warsaw, Budapest, Berlin, Prague*. New York: Random House, 1990.

———. "The Revolution of Magic Lantern." *The New York Review of Books*, 18 January 1990. Retrieved 10 January 2017 from http://www.nybooks.com/articles/1990/01/18/the-revolution-of-the-magic-lantern/.

Berlant, Lauren. *The Queen of America Goes to Washington City: Essays on Sex and Citizenship*. Durham, NC: Duke University Press, 1997.

Bláhová, Kateřina, and Michal Přibáň, eds., *Z dějin českého myšlení o literatuře 4 (1970–1989): Antologie k Dějinám české literatury 1945–1990*. Prague: Ústav pro českou literaturu AV ČR, 2005.

Bolton, Jonathan. *Worlds of Dissent: Charter 77, the Plastic People of the Universe, and Czech Culture under Communism*. Cambridge, MA: Harvard University Press, 2012.

Bren, Paulina. *The Greengrocer and His TV: The Culture of Communism after the 1968 Prague Spring*. Ithaca: Cornell University Press, 2010.

Bren, Paulina, and Mary Neuburger, eds. *Communism Unwrapped: Consumption in Cold War Eastern Europe*. New York: Oxford University Press, 2012.

Crowley, David, and Susan E. Reid, eds. *Socialist Spaces: Sites of Everyday Life in the Eastern Bloc*. Oxford: Berg Publishers, 2002.

Czerwinski, E. J., and Jaroslaw Piekalkiewicz. *The Soviet Invasion of Czechoslovakia: Its Effects on Eastern Europe.* New York: Praeger, 1972.
Goodwyn, Lawrence. *Breaking the Barrier: Rise of Solidarity in Poland.* New York: Oxford University Press, 1991.
Grandits, Hannes, and Karin Taylor, eds. *Yugoslavia's Sunny Side: A History of Tourism in Socialism (1950s–1980s).* Budapest: Central European University Press, 2010.
Havel, Václav. "New Year's Address to the Nation." *Czech Republic Presidential Website,* 1 January 1990. Retrieved 23 December 2016 from https://chnm.gmu.edu/1989/archive/files/havel-speech-1-1-90_0c7cd97e58.pdf.
———. "The Power of the Powerless." In *The Power of the Powerless: Citizens against the State in Central-Eastern Europe,* edited by John Keane, 23–97. New York: M. E. Sharp, 1985.
Horaková, Pavla. "The Soundtrack to the Velvet Revolution." *Radio Prague,* 17 November 2013. Retrieved 26 May 2014 from http://www.radio.cz/en/section/sunday-music-show/the-soundtrack-to-the-velvet-revolution
Kenney, Padraic. *A Carnival of Revolution: Central Europe 1989.* Princeton, NJ: Princeton University Press, 2002.
Kolesárová, Ľudmila. "O mojom detstve (pre premiéra)." *Sme Blog,* 9 January 2014. Retrieved 25 May 2014 from http://ludmilakolesarova.blog.sme.sk/c/346131/O-mojom-detstve-pre-premiera.html.
Krapfl, James. *Revolution with a Human Face.* Ithaca, NY: Cornell University Press, 2013.
Krause, Kevin Deegan. "Jokes of the Velvet Revolution and Before." Wayne State University Department of Political Science. Retrieved 24 May 2014 from http://www.la.wayne.edu/polisci/kdk/stuff/jokes.htm.
Laba, Roman. *The Roots of Solidarity: A Political Sociology of Poland's Working Class Democratization.* Princeton, NJ: Princeton University Press, 1991.
Leviatin, David. *Prague Sprung: Notes and Voices from the New World.* London: Praeger, 1993.
Lukas, Adriana. "Another Remembrance Day." *Samizdata,* 17 November 2007. Retrieved 25 May 2014 from http://www.samizdata.net/2007/11/another-remembe/.
"Marta Kubišová *Modlitba pre Martu* (Supraphon, 1968)." *Eastern Bloc Songs.* Retrieved 25 May 2014 from http://easternblocsongs.wordpress.com/2011/11/07/marta-kubisova-modlitba-pro-martu-supraphon-1968/.
Navratíl, Jaromir, Antonin Bencik, and Vaclav Kural, eds. *The Prague Spring 1968: National Security Archive Documents Reader.* New York: Central European University Press, 1998.
"Noc v archive: Silvestrovská polnoc v archíve." *RTVS,* 12 January 2014. Retrieved 15 August 2016 from https://www.rtvs.sk/televizia/archiv/10272/30610.
Perks, Robert, and Alistair Thomson, eds. *The Oral History Reader.* New York: Routledge, 1998.
Rajk, László, and Martin Šimečka. "Dilemma '89: My Father was a Communist." *Eurozine,* 7 May 2010. Retrieved 27 May 2014 from http://www.eurozine.com/articles/2010-05-07-debate-en.html.
Rubin, Eli. *Synthetic Socialism: Plastics and Dictatorship in the German Democratic Republic.* Chapel Hill: University of North Carolina Press, 2008.

Scott, James. *Weapons of the Weak: Everyday Forms of Peasant Resistance.* New Haven, CT: Yale University Press, 1985.

———. *Domination and the Arts of Resistance: Hidden Transcript.* New Haven, CT: Yale University Press, 1990.

Sheffer, Edith. *Burned Bridge: How East and West Germans Made the Iron Curtain.* New York: Oxford University Press, 2011.

Skilling, Harold Gordon. *Czechoslovakia's Interrupted Revolution.* Princeton, NJ: Princeton University Press. 1976. Šimečka, Milan. *The Restoration of Order: The Normalization of Czechoslovakia, 1969–1976.* London: Verso Books, 1984.

"Spomienky na November '89: Necenzurované vtipy." *Život,* 13 November 2009. Retrieved 25 December 2016 from http://zivot.azet.sk/clanok/217/spomienky-na-november-89-necenzurovane-vtipy.html.

Tchourakine, Igor. "The Yugoslav Road to International Tourism: Opening, Decentralization, and Propaganda in the Early 1950s." In *Yugoslavia's Sunny Side: A History of Tourism in Socialism (1950s–1980s),* edited by Hannes Grandits and Karin Taylor, 107–138. Budapest: Central European University Press, 2010.

Tismaneau, Vladimir, ed. *The Revolutions of 1989.* London: Routledge, 1999.

Thompson, Paul. "The Voice of the Past: Oral History." In *The Oral History Reader,* 3rd ed., edited by Robert Perks and Alistair Thomson, 33–39. London: Routledge, 2015.

Týždeň vo Filme [DVD]. Bratislava: Slovenský Filmový Ustav, 2008.

Williams, Kieran. *The Prague Spring and Its Aftermath: Czechoslovak Politics (1968–1970).* Cambridge: Cambridge University Press, 1997.

Willoughby, Ian. "'Prayer for Marta' Singer Kubišová Recalls Dramatic Comeback during 1989's Velvet Revolution." *Radio Prague,* 18 November 2009. Retrieved 26 May 2014 from http://www.radio.cz/en/section/czechstoday/prayer-for-marta-singer-kubisova-recalls-dramatic-comeback-during-1989s-velvet-revolution.

Vaculík, Ludvík. *A Cup of Coffee with My Interrogator: The Prague Chronicles of Ludvík Vaculík.* London: Readers International, 1976.

———. "Poznámky o Statečnosti." In *Z Dějin českého myšlení o literature (1970–1989) Antologie k Dějinám české literatury 1945–1990,* edited by Kateřina Bláhová and Michal Přibáň, 238–241. Prague: Ústav pro českou literaturu AV ČR, 2005.

Vaněk, Miroslav. *Vítězové? Poražení?: I. díl, Disent v období tzv. normalizace : interpretační studie životopisných interview.* Prague: Prostor, 2006.

Yörümez, Barış. "In Pursuit of an Errant Act: The Influence of the 'Culture of Late Capitalism' on the Dissolution of Communism in Czechoslovak Socialist Republic." MA Thesis. Istanbul: Koç University, 2012.

Chapter 3

The Political, Emotional, and Therapeutic

Narratives of Consciousness-Raising and Authenticity in the English Women's Liberation Movement

Kate Mahoney

Consciousness-raising groups have been presented as integral to the development of the Women's Liberation Movement (WLM) in late 1960s England.[1] Consciousness-raising entailed women coming together to talk about their individual experiences of oppression. These communal discussions enabled participants to situate their experiences within the society-wide patriarchal repression of women.[2] WLM members could draw on this understanding to publicly agitate for gender equality and social change.[3] Participants and historians alike suggest that consciousness-raising aided the development of a feminist authenticity within the WLM. Positive accounts of consciousness-raising, referred to as a "practice of the self," document how women used it to explore how they could align their lives with the politics of Women's Liberation, drawing support from one another as they sought to live authentically as WLM members.[4] This chapter critically assesses the association of predominantly positive accounts of consciousness-raising with the construction of a feminist authenticity within the WLM. Documenting WLM members' negative experiences of the practice, it argues that consciousness-raising groups had the capacity to promote a specific form of authenticity that participants felt compelled to adhere to. Women who were unable to comply with these expectations often felt marginalized and were obliged to justify their authenticity as movement members. Recognizing these negative accounts facilitates a more comprehensive assessment of women's experiences of consciousness-raising, as well as the issues that they faced as they attempted to live authentically as WLM members.

This chapter draws on the individual and group narratives of consciousness-raising contained in contemporary periodicals, existing oral history projects, and personal oral history interviews. First, it traces the development of the practice within the English WLM. It highlights how the promotion of specific forms of authenticity within Women's Liberation groups was associated with the perceived rules of consciousness-raising. Second, this chapter critically assesses two areas in which consciousness-raising was seen to foster the development of a feminist authenticity within the WLM: personal transformation through the articulation of individual experiences and the establishment of politicized forms of female friendships. Finally, the chapter traces how WLM members responded to women's negative experiences of consciousness-raising. It explores how the London Women's Liberation Workshop Psychology Group used psychotherapeutic techniques to understand the creation and impact of destructive dynamics in consciousness-raising groups, therefore contributing to the development of a more expansive politics of the self within the WLM.[5]

Authenticity and the Women's Movement

This chapter assesses authenticity as the external set of standards that women felt compelled to adhere to in order to live their lives as politically effective WLM members. These standards were not officiated by the WLM at a national level. Women's Liberation groups and individual activists held different perceptions about the criteria for effective and authentic engagement with the politics of the WLM. Ideas about what it meant to be an authentic WLM activist were influenced by contrasting interpretations of prominent Women's Liberation literature, the divergent collective identities that groups fostered through practices like consciousness-raising, and members' variant personal experiences. In being seen to aid the development of a feminist authenticity among WLM members, consciousness-raising groups played an integral part in establishing what that feminist authenticity could and should be.

Discussions about authenticity within the British and US women's movements have focused on intergenerational debates between second- and third-wave feminists.[6] Writing in 1995, Rebecca Walker, a self-defined third-wave feminist and daughter of prominent author and activist Alice Walker, argued that women had to conform to a specific identity and lifestyle that limited their individuality when engaging with second-wave feminism.[7] Responding to Rebecca Walker's assertions in 2002, feminist theorist Cathryn Bailey employed a Foucauldian framework to argue that the operation of power in women's movements had the capacity to be both liberating and repressive.[8] Bailey theorized how some activists came to militate against the politics and practices of a women's movement that they had initially sought to be part of. She documented how the promotion of specific practices and values within women's movements resulted in the "very kinds of pressures that serve to produce feminist subjects who can then be expected to resist that same feminism."[9] Bailey rejected, however, the presence of an "authentic self" in feminist politics, arguing that an "external standard of authenticity relative to which individuals' desires can be assessed" simply did not exist.[10]

It is important to recognize discussions on intergenerational conflict and authenticity when deciphering developments in women's movement theory and activism since 1990. Authenticity was a key concept in the debates about individuality and choice that dominated facets of the women's movement in the 1990s.[11] Foregrounding these perspectives, however, overlooks WLM members' perceptions of authenticity in the late 1960s and 1970s. Feminist theorists have rejected the existence of an external standard of authenticity in the contemporary women's movement. I argue, however, that it remains a useful historical concept for understanding how WLM activists defined their personal politics, their position within the movement, and their responses to other members, therefore contextualizing subsequent debates between second- and third-wave feminists about the perceived prescriptiveness and exclusivity of Women's Liberation politics. From 1970 onward, Black feminist critics challenged the presumed universal womanhood promoted in Women's Liberation rhetoric as exclusive and unrepresentative.[12] Exploring women's perceptions of what it was to be an authentic movement member helps to decipher the emergence of the WLM in late 1960s and 1970s England, highlighting the complexities inherent in their personal and political transformations. It uncovers activists' emotional responses and experiences as they incorporated the politics of Women's Liberation into their everyday lives by negotiating what an authentic feminist identity could and should be.

The Development of Consciousness-Raising in the English WLM

The WLM emerged in England in the late 1960s, consisting of local women's groups that formed regional networks and convened at annual Women's Liberation conferences.[13] Between 1970 and 1971, the movement's four demands were defined as equal pay, equal access to education, free contraception and abortion, and twenty-four-hour childcare.[14] For many WLM members, community-based consciousness-raising groups constituted the "building blocks" of Women's Liberation and initiated their involvement in the movement.[15] The establishment of these groups in community-based settings appears to contrast with Zsófia Lóránd's portrayal (see her chapter in this volume) of consciousness-raising in Yugoslavia as a political and intellectual endeavor, initially developed by women in academia.[16] The emergence of consciousness-raising in the English WLM was influenced by the Maoist politics promoted within the British New Left, as well as the dissemination of American Women's Liberation literature.[17] Assessing how WLM members responded to these publications highlights their view that there were rules or recommendations that they should adhere to in order to practice consciousness-raising authentically and effectively. Consciousness-raising groups drew on recommendations in existing literature to ensure that their practice was both tailored to the needs of their individual members and suitably aligned with the politics of Women's Liberation. Some groups, however, directly contravened the "rules" of consciousness-raising because they felt more comfortable articulating their emotions in a playful atmosphere.[18] Examining consciousness-raising participants' responses to these recommendations highlights the role that they played in defining how to enact authentic Women's Liberation practices at a community level in the early English WLM.

In the United States and Britain in the 1960s and 1970s, students drew on Maoist literature to develop their own radical political practices.[19] Mao Zedong's 1937 essay "On Practice" was particularly influential in the development of the personal politics of the students' movement. Activists drew on the essay's assertion that "all genuine knowledge originates in direct experience" to promote self-reflection and undermine the explanations of social inequality provided by professional experts.[20] WLM members also emphasized the importance of "On Practice." In 1971, the London-based Tufnell Park Women's Liberation Group published an edition of the London Women's Liberation Workshop periodical *Shrew*, in which they discussed their own approach to consciousness-raising.[21] The group described how they had drawn on the pamphlet "On Strategy," produced by Britain-based Maoist Geoff Richman in direct reference to "On Practice," when conducting their own small group discussions.[22] In an oral history interview, Joanna Ryan, who joined a consciousness-raising group in Cambridge between 1968 and 1969, further argued that the practice was inspired by the combined influence of Maoism and the work of revolutionary and psychiatrist Frantz Fanon on the British New Left in the 1960s.[23]

References to Maoist politics were also present in seminal American Women's Liberation publications, including Robin Morgan's 1970 edited collection *Sisterhood is Powerful*.[24] Consciousness-raising participants such as Sue Bruley, who joined a group in Camden, London, in the mid-1970s, argued that the dissemination of this literature aided the development of the practice across England.[25] Articles including the New York-based Sappho Collective's "Rapping in Small Groups," were widely distributed among English Women's Liberation groups.[26] Originally published in *Women: A Journal of Liberation*, the first national periodical to emerge out of the American WLM, the article recommended that consciousness-raising groups contain between six to ten members.[27] It also detailed potential discussion topics that consciousness-raising participants should choose before each meeting.[28]

Consciousness-raising groups across England responded to these recommendations when organizing the practice. Group members believed that, in following these recommendations, they would practice a form of consciousness-raising that aided participants' development into authentic WLM members. Writing in the *Birmingham Women's Liberation Newsletter* in May 1974, the Monday Consciousness-Raising Group emphasized the importance of tailoring their practice to the needs of individual participants due to the group's varied membership.[29] Participants defined themselves as a "mixed bunch of women, married and single, covering a wide age range and all from very different social backgrounds and occupations."[30] In seeking to encompass the varied experiences of its members, the Monday Group initially rejected a rigid or preplanned approach to their meetings.[31] However, participants became increasingly concerned about this flexible approach, stating in the *Newsletter* that meetings deviated from the "merely boring to the bloody diabolical."[32] The Monday Group drew on the recommendations contained in the Sappho Collective's "Rapping in Small Groups" to remedy these organizational issues. In an advertisement published in the July/August 1974 edition of the *Birmingham Women's Liberation Newsletter*, the group described how they were using the article to structure their meetings and expand their consciousness-raising program.[33] The Monday Group therefore believed that they could use the recommendations contained in American Women's Liberation literature to bolster the effectiveness of their consciousness-raising practice. This demonstrates that suggestions formulated by groups like the Sappho Collective came to represent a series of requirements that consciousness-raising participants should recognize in order to engage in the practice correctly.

Consciousness-raising groups also responded to recommendations contained in existing Women's Liberation publications by capping the size of their membership. In 1970, New York-based WLM members A. Sunshine and J. Gerard published the article "Small Group: Big Job," in which they suggested that consciousness-raising participants establish additional groups for new members to join if they became unmanageable.[34] This advice was also heeded by Birmingham-based consciousness-raising groups. In the summer of 1974, a consciousness-raising group based in the Moseley area of the city advertised for new members. The group had been forced to split into two after it reached its "maximum number" of participants.[35] WLM members documented the impact that capping the size of consciousness-raising groups had on individual participants.[36] In a 1978 interview with national WLM magazine *Spare Rib*, London-based acupuncturist and photographer Sally Fraser described how her group, the Belsize Lane Women's Liberation Group, had to close to new members after its size became problematic. Fraser stated that "sometimes fifty or sixty women would arrive; each week six to ten were new … the group was becoming unmanageable, even disintegrating as women left in frustration at the increasing numbers."[37] On closing the group to new members, Fraser and her fellow members were accused of elitism. Despite this, she maintained that the group would have collapsed if the numbers had not been capped. Maintaining a core membership allowed participants to easily reflect and expand on issues that they had previously discussed.[38] Fraser therefore suggested that capping the number of consciousness-raising participants enhanced existing members' experience of the practice. Her account also indicates, however, that capping group sizes in accordance with the recommendations contained in American Women's Liberation literature had a negative impact on WLM members who were subsequently unable to participate. While adhering to the perceived "rules" for effective consciousness-raising was beneficial to existing participants, it also resulted in the marginalization of new WLM members who wanted to become involved.

The perceived existence of an external set of standards for the effective practice of consciousness-raising is reinforced by the fact that some consciousness-raising participants deliberately rejected these stipulations when formulating their own approach to the practice. In an oral history interview with sociologist Anna E. Rogers, a Yorkshire-based WLM member called Linda described how she and her fellow group members actively rejected the "rule" that consciousness-raising participants should listen to one another's personal concerns before offering advice.[39] Linda referred to the contravention of recommendations as an "ironic mode of defiance" that mocked traditional masculine or patriarchal responses to women's personal issues.[40] Rejecting recommendations with "exaggerated disobedience" also provided participants with some "humorous relief from their emotionally-charged discussions."[41] Many participants regarded the process of developing a feminist authenticity through consciousness-raising as a traumatic or painful experience.[42] Linda's account demonstrates the ways in which some consciousness-raising group members played with the perceived rules of consciousness-raising to support one another through the practice.[43]

Assessing the development of consciousness-raising in the English WLM therefore highlights participants' perception of an external set of standards to which they had to adhere in order to carry out the practice effectively and authentically. Participants either employed or rejected these recommendations, often contained in American Women's Liberation literature, in their pursuit of an emergent feminist authenticity. Other WLM members, however, found themselves marginalized as groups adopted these stipulations. Examining the initial organization of consciousness-raising groups contextualizes the development of assumptions about what it meant to authentically engage in the politics of Women's Liberation.

Consciousness-Raising and Personal Transformation

WLM members have documented the personal transformation they experienced as a result of consciousness-raising. Participants described how the practice encouraged them to overcome patriarchal repression by developing new understandings of themselves and making changes to their everyday lives. Consciousness-raising therefore enabled women to develop ideas and approaches that meant that they could live as increasingly authentic WLM members. Positive accounts of consciousness-raising present the personal transformation the practice encouraged as integral to their engagement with the politics of Women's Liberation.[44] However, some consciousness-raising participants spoke negatively of the practice, detailing how it resulted in their alienation from the movement. Participants attributed their marginalization to the fact that their personal experiences contrasted to those of other consciousness-raising group members.[45] They felt unable to uphold popular expectations of consciousness-raising, notably its emphasis on discursive politics and personal transformation. Highlighting these negative experiences destabilizes the notion that the practice fostered a personal and political transformation among its participants that was central to the development of the WLM. Women who had experiences of consciousness-raising that did not conform to the popular narrative of personal transformation, had to defend and redefine their authenticity as WLM members.

Numerous positive accounts of consciousness-raising draw on language associated with transformation to highlight the initial impact that the practice had on their perceptions of themselves and their everyday lives. Interviewed in the early 2000s for the Bristol-based oral history project *Personal Histories of Second Wave Feminism*, artist Sarah Braun described how she joined a consciousness-raising group in 1971 while married with a small child and running a printing business.[46] Braun initially found the group challenging because women were expected to discuss highly personal issues. She subsequently valued these discussions because they enhanced her understanding of women's lives from different backgrounds. Braun stated that consciousness-raising was "the most important experience of my life for my own personal growth because of the way it just took me by the neck and shook me."[47] In her interview, Braun used violent imagery to emphasize the suddenness with which her new understanding of herself and others influenced her life. Writing in *Spare Rib* in 1978, Mica Nava used similarly dramatic language to describe her realization that she could alter her life to live authentically as a WLM member and agitate for social change.[48] The London-based research student referred to the year following her attendance at a consciousness-raising group as then "probably the most explosive and passionate of my life. We had embarked on the long and difficult task of 'Changing the Way We Lived.'"[49] Braun and Nava's accounts emphasize the immediacy of the personal transformation that they experienced through consciousness-raising. Both participants asserted that this personal transformation provided them with the understandings required to subsequently align their lives with the politics of Women's Liberation. The "discursive politics" of consciousness-raising were deemed transformative because they allowed women to discuss their previously unexplored experiences.[50]

Assessing formerly taboo topics in a comfortable and safe environment also aided participants' emotional expression.[51] As demonstrated in Roger's Yorkshire-based oral history interviews, participants' assessments of Women's Liberation politics while consciousness-raising improved their confidence as intellectual thinkers.[52] Consciousness-raising also allowed women to express emotions that they had previously been discouraged from articulating, such as anger.[53] Sarah Browne argues that participants' expression of anger aided the development of a personalized, experience-led politics of Women's Liberation.[54] The practice further bolstered participants' self-confidence because it enabled them to articulate their emotions more authentically, allowing them to stand up for what they believed in and transforming their feelings into positive, political action.[55] Therefore the personal transformation fostered by the "discursive politics" promoted in consciousness-raising groups allowed participants to develop new understandings about themselves and others, as well as new kinds of emotional and intellectual expression. These forms of expression were also deemed political because they contravened patriarchal assumptions about what constituted normative feminine behavior. Women drew on these understandings when aligning their own lives with the politics of Women's Liberation in order to lead increasingly authentic lives as movement members.

Attributing the historical development of a feminist authenticity to the personal transformations that consciousness-raising encouraged overlooks the accounts of participants who had negative experiences of the practice. Women who felt unable to contribute to the discursive politics of consciousness-raising were compelled to justify the fact that their involvement in the WLM remained authentic and effective. Sally Carter joined a Women's Liberation group in St. Albans in 1970 before becoming involved in the Bristol WLM in 1979.[56] In an oral history interview, Carter stated that she never felt comfortable attending Women's Liberation groups because she grew up as an only child with few friends her own age.[57] Feeling more at ease talking to people one-on-one, Carter remained very quiet and was afraid to speak up at the Women's Liberation group meetings that she attended. She thought that the other women in the group were more informed about oppositional politics because they had attended university and were already involved in both the Communist Party of Great Britain and the Socialist Worker's Party. Carter felt that her lack of a university education meant that she was only accepted "to a point" by the other group members.[58]

Carter's feelings of inclusivity within the group were also influenced by the other members' responses to her quietness. She recalled how one group member challenged her for being too reserved, stating that Carter's perceived lack of participation worried her and made her nervous. Carter described how she thought, "Well, I'm quite nervous of you!" and stated that the exchange had an irreconcilable impact on her relationship with the group member.[59] In calling out Carter's quietness, the group member asserted that she did not adequately contribute to the discursive politics of consciousness-raising and questioned her authenticity as a WLM member. In her oral history interview, Carter felt it necessary to defend her authenticity by distinguishing her engagement with Women's Liberation politics from other movement members. Carter asserted that she took an alternative route into the WLM by "living the opposite of feminism" as a young, married mother throughout the 1960s.[60] She stated that "it was my experience as a woman and actually finding out that being female in 1960s Britain was not acceptable for me anyway and there should be more options basically."[61] In actively living out what she perceived to be the patriarchal confines of femininity and motherhood, Carter deemed herself different from other WLM members who had joined as a result of their educational backgrounds and previous political engagements. Carter's quietness represented a form of authentic self-expression reflective of her personal experiences as an only child and isolated housewife that she felt subsequently facilitated her politicization.

Carter's account destabilizes celebratory narratives that only equate the personal transformation fostered through consciousness-raising with the development of a feminist authenticity in the WLM. Exploring participants' negative experiences of consciousness-raising demonstrates that WLM members expressed what it meant to authentically live out the politics of the movement in variant and conflicting ways. While the discursive politics of consciousness-raising were seen to encourage women's personal transformation into WLM members, they also represented a standard of political practice that participants had to adhere to in order to be perceived as authentic. It is therefore problematic to foreground participants' positive experiences of consciousness-raising when historicizing the development of standards of authenticity within the WLM. This overt focus does not recognize the experiences of women who felt excluded from consciousness-raising groups because they were unable to contribute to the discursive politics that the practice encouraged. Overlooking these negative experiences contributes to the continued promotion of valedictory as opposed to critical narratives of consciousness-raising.

Female Friendships and Emotional Support

Popular narratives of consciousness-raising also emphasize the new and politicized forms of friendship that the practice encouraged. Foregrounding honesty and sisterhood, WLM members argued that these friendships demonstrated women's increasingly authentic interactions with one another.[62] Positive accounts of consciousness-raising document how participants drew on the support fostered through these relationships when attempting to align their lives with the politics of Women's Liberation.[63] Incorporating negative experiences into discussions on female friendship and authenticity highlights the fact that the relationships fostered in consciousness-raising groups were not always beneficial to participants, hindering their engagement with Women's Liberation politics. This assessment highlights how perceived standards of authenticity informed the development of female friendships and collective identities within consciousness-raising groups in the English WLM. Women who expressed attitudes and experiences that did not conform to the collective identities constructed in consciousness-raising groups were marginalized and found their authenticity as WLM members questioned.

Numerous WLM members have attributed their positive experiences of consciousness-raising to the collective ideas, identities, and experiences that the practice fostered. In an interview for the *Personal Histories of Second-Wave Feminism* project, Bristol-based Jilly Rosser described how she became involved in WLM activism at university.[64] She recalled the "terrific strength" she experienced when she joined a consciousness-raising group, stating that the connections that she formed with other participants left her "feeling that you can do anything, anywhere, and you were part of this supportive network."[65] In a personal oral history interview, Rukshana Afia also emphasized the importance of the female friendships that she made through consciousness-raising. She described how "women were so committed to one another, and you never lacked friends, and you never lacked support, and you could pick up on the phone and reach twenty or thirty people who really thought you mattered."[66] In her interview, Afia expressed nostalgia for the connections she made in the WLM, stating that she missed those kinds of relationships now that she was no longer involved in the movement.

Both Rosser and Afia attributed the strength of the friendships they developed through consciousness-raising to the support that they offered. This support was deemed synonymous with the WLM because it represented women's increasingly authentic and politicized interactions with one another. In the minutes of a Birmingham Women's Liberation meeting, held in the summer of 1974, members of the Pershore Road Group described how consciousness-raising provided emotional support because it "taught them to relate to women in ways they had not previously" and enabled members to realize that their "past and present experiences were part of a common pattern for women."[67] Women representing the Moseley Group, also based in Birmingham, reiterated the emotional support that consciousness-raising fostered, stating that the practice allowed them to form increasingly honest relationships with one another.[68] This perspective has been further bolstered in oral history interviews carried out by Rogers. Her interviewees—Lee, a feminist author who became involved in the WLM in Leeds in the late 1960s, and Joanna, a member of a women's group from 1981—described the friendships that they developed in the movement as unlike anything that they had experienced before.[69] Joanna and Lee attributed the newness of these friendships to the fact that they had previously only formed relationships with women that they were connected to through men.[70] In supporting one another without male involvement, WLM members challenged the "heteronormative tendency for social relations to be portrayed as organized around marriage."[71] In an interview with the historian Thomas Dixon, WLM member Barbara Taylor, who cofounded the socialist feminist magazine *Red Rag*, emphasized the politicized nature of these new relationships, stating that they reflected the Women's Liberation tenet "the personal is political."[72] WLM members drew on the support fostered through consciousness-raising both when contending with personal and emotional issues, and while participating in public protests together.[73] The forms of friendships and support fostered through consciousness-raising were therefore regarded as increasingly authentic because they reinforced key political ideas promoted within the WLM.

However, the strong emphasis placed on communal support in the development of these increasingly authentic friendships had negative implications for members who felt that they did not conform to the collective identities that Women's Liberation groups promoted. In a July 1971 edition of the *Women's Liberation Workshop Newssheet*, a contributor named "Disgruntled Hazel" described the alienation she experienced while attending a consciousness-raising group.[74] Defining herself as a "Misfit" and an "out-and-out individualist," Hazel believed that the issues she had experienced deviated from those of the other group members.[75] As a result, she was asked to leave after six months attendance. Hazel called on the London Women's Liberation Workshop, the umbrella organization to which London-based Women's Liberation groups were affiliated, to be more tolerant of the "Misfit in society" and encouraged other women who had similar experiences to contact her.[76] Hazel's letter demonstrates the emphasis that her consciousness-raising group placed on conformity. Hazel's ejection due to her pursuit of individualism and her belief that her experiences contrasted to those of the other women present, suggests that she was seen to contravene the collective identity that the group was trying to foster. Carter also felt that she did not comply with the collective identity of her women's group because she was not university-educated.[77] While the collective identities fostered in consciousness-raising groups were seen to represent new and politicized forms of female friendship, their formation was still reliant on group members initially sharing common interests or experiences.[78] This meant that women who did not share these features found it difficult to engage with the group's collective identity and often felt as if their authenticity as WLM members was questioned.

Other consciousness-raising participants highlighted their encounters with marginalization due to contrasting educational and class backgrounds in Rogers's series of oral history interviews. Interviewee Judith joined a women's group in Bradford in 1977. The group consisted of women from comparable professional and educational backgrounds. The majority of members were social workers; Judith was a teacher. She referred to herself and her fellow members as an "incredibly intellectual middle-class group of people."[79] One new member, a secretary who did not have a university education, was described as displaying a lack of awareness about issues that had clicked with all the other participants. Because it was felt that "her thinking was on a different level," the woman was "implicitly excluded from the group."[80] Judith later reflected that this was "horrible of us."[81] Rogers argues that the woman was rejected from Judith's group because she did not display the "'correct' feminist consciousness."[82] Judith's account therefore reiterates the emphasis placed on conformity, mutual interests, and common experiences as consciousness-raising groups sought to formulate collective identities and authentic interactions among their members.

Assessing positive and negative accounts of the friendships and collective identities fostered within consciousness-raising groups demonstrates the complexities and contradictions inherent in the ways in which these interactions promoted increasingly politicized and authentic forms of female engagement. While these friendships were deemed more authentic because they fostered common experiences and communal support among women, the ejection of some participants suggests that members were expected to conform to the tenets of collective identity that the group encouraged. By promoting identities that were exclusionary, certain consciousness-raising groups undermined the authenticity of the interactions that they sought to foster, endorsing elitist social and relational structures that the WLM opposed.

Recognizing and Responding to Negative Experiences of Consciousness-Raising

In the early 1970s, some WLM members highlighted participants' negative experiences of consciousness-raising and the pressure that they felt to conform to a specific standard of authenticity. The London Women's Liberation Workshop Psychology Group used psychotherapeutic ideas and approaches to understand why some consciousness-raising groups fostered destructive and alienating dynamics.[83] Assessing why women had negative experiences of the practice, the Psychology Group queried the wider organization and effectiveness of the WLM, and explored the position of individual women within the movement. They aimed to expand existing political ideas of authenticity and the self, using psychotherapy to explore how women consciously and subconsciously engaged with the politics of Women's Liberation as they sought to live increasingly authentic lives.

In 1973, WLM members Vivienne, Judy, Trish, Sheila, and Sheila compiled a series of questions for a radical feminist workshop that explored the pressure placed on women to align their lifestyles with the politics of the WLM and their resultant emotional responses.[84] The WLM members questioned whether identifying with radical feminism meant "living your politics twenty-four hours a day" and documented the "apparent imperatives" women felt that they had to comply with in order to remain part of the movement: "Be a lesbian, don't be a lesbian, have kids, don't have kids, get out of exclusive relationships, stay in them, fuck with everybody, don't fuck at all, be sisterly (whatever that means), etc. etc. etc."[85]

The WLM members described how women's inability to adhere to these contradictory expectations left them feeling guilty at "not being there yet" in their fostering of authentic and empowered lifestyles.[86] The questions raised demonstrated that women's anxieties surrounding their authenticity as WLM members were aggravated by wider concerns about the effectiveness of the Movement in instigating social change. Responding to these concerns, the WLM members used the radical feminist workshop to call for the movement to tackle these negative emotional responses. They stated that guilt was manifesting itself in "real and dangerous crises … women are dying—in a sense killed by the Movement."[87]

The London Women's Liberation Workshop Psychology Group responded to WLM members' experiences of emotional distress as a result of consciousness-raising by holding discussion groups and facilitating self-help therapy schemes.[88] Established in 1972 by WLM member and playwright Dinah Brooke, the Psychology Group was initially promoted as an opportunity for women to explore their individual experiences of mental illness in a supportive setting.[89] Some members joined the Psychology Group to specifically explore how women's mental health concerns were aggravated through their participation in Women's Liberation. In an oral history interview, filmmaker Carola Klein stated that she joined the Psychology Group after her friend Jane was forced to leave a Women's Liberation group in Notting Hill.[90] Klein believed that Jane was ejected from the group after being scapegoated for its numerous organizational issues. She asserted that the other members were jealous of Jane because she held a prominent position in the WLM and made a speech at the first Women's Liberation march in London in 1971. Klein described how Jane was unsure how to contend with her own emotions and those of her fellow members when she left the group.[91] Klein therefore joined the Psychology Group to explore the negative emotions fostered in Jane's Women's Liberation group and to develop strategies to overcome them.

In April 1972, the Psychology Group produced an edition of *Shrew*, a periodical published every one to two months by groups affiliated with the London Women's Liberation Workshop in which they detailed their aims.[92] The Psychology Group suggested that consciousness-raising was "semi-therapeutic" because it explored the "emotions aroused by the process of changing."[93] However, Psychology Group members also argued that consciousness-raising could be destructive. They described how some gay women had felt isolated when engaging in the practice because other participants struggled to recognize their own anxieties about homosexuality. Members of the Psychology Group also asserted that consciousness-raising only explored women's emotions at a theoretical level.[94] While consciousness-raising allowed women to express their emotions, its predominantly political framework meant that it did not support women in understanding and overcoming their feelings as they articulated them within the group.

The Psychology Group developed strategies to support WLM members who were experiencing emotional distress. They called for the establishment of a "flexible self-help scheme" within the movement that provided therapeutic support and initiated a "re-evaluation of the dynamics of local, project and actions groups and certain casualties associated with them, which we feel will only increase our strength."[95] The Psychology Group outlined plans for their scheme in *Shrew*, aiming to compile a list of sympathetic London Women's Liberation Workshop members who women could telephone if they felt depressed and isolated and required one-on-one informal support.[96] In petitioning for a scheme that supported women within the movement, the Psychology Group argued the importance of recognizing the negative emotional responses associated with living authentically as a WLM member. Writing in *Spare Rib* in 1973, Psychology Group member Carol Morrell stated that "the way we cope with beginning to be ourselves will affect the rest of our progress."[97] The Psychology Group deemed the movement's recognition of participants' negative experiences integral to the wider development of Women's Liberation politics and practices.

The Psychology Group asserted that incorporating psychotherapeutic ideas into their discussions not only supported individual WLM members but also bolstered the politics of Women's Liberation.[98] Group members argued that psychotherapeutic ideas could be used to understand why women might continue to subconsciously endorse patriarchal norms while participating in oppositional activism. In an article written for *Shrew*, one Psychology Group member compared psychoanalytic ideas with Women's Liberation politics, arguing that both called for a "reorganization of cultural patterns, for a reappraisal of how people need each other and a new form of communication."[99] She argued that women could draw on the understandings of their individual experiences and social positioning that they developed through psychoanalysis to comment on women's repression in society more broadly.

The Psychology Group therefore offered a new understanding of women's negative experiences of consciousness-raising and the pressures individual members felt to conform to perceived standards of authenticity within the WLM. The Psychology Group promoted psychoanalysis as a means to explore women's emotional responses to both patriarchal repression and their engagement with Women's Liberation politics. Critiquing consciousness-raising groups for not providing adequate support to their participants, the Psychology Group called for the WLM to further recognize the significance of emotions in the politics and practices that it promoted. The Group developed perspectives on how individual women perceived themselves within the movement politically and emotionally. In recognizing WLM members as both political and emotional subjects who required increased inclusivity and support, the Psychology Group developed strategies for enhancing the wider effectiveness of the WLM.

Conclusion

Positive accounts of consciousness-raising emphasize the role that the practice played in facilitating participants' development of a feminist authenticity in the English WLM during the late 1960s and 1970s. Through the intimate discussions encouraged in consciousness-raising groups, participants developed new understandings of themselves and other women and forged tight-knit, honest, and politicized relationships. They drew on these intellectual understandings and support networks to lead increasingly authentic lives as WLM members, engaging in public protest and aligning their everyday lifestyles with the politics of Women's Liberation. However, accounts that foreground positive narratives of consciousness-raising and authenticity in the WLM overlook participants' negative experiences of the practice. Some WLM members found that their personal experiences rendered them unable to participate in the discursive politics that consciousness-raising promoted. Other participants felt marginalized for having experiences and backgrounds that deviated from those shared by other group members. Highlighting these negative experiences demonstrates the ways in which consciousness-raising groups defined what constituted authentic engagement with the politics of Women's Liberation, on occasion marginalizing or ejecting women who did not conform to these standards or expectations. The equation of consciousness-raising with specific standards of authenticity was partly due to the perception that WLM members had to follow particular rules or suggestions in order to practice it effectively. Women who did not appear to conform to these standards felt obliged to defend their engagement with the WLM as authentic, highlighting their own experiences of patriarchal repression in order to distinguish themselves from movement members.

In the early 1970s, however, some WLM members sought to understand and respond to women's negative experiences of consciousness-raising. Several women used a radical feminist workshop to explore why women felt extreme levels of guilt in response to the WLM's protracted capacity to facilitate social change. They highlighted both the conflicting standards of authenticity promoted within the WLM, and the emotional impact of the movement's organizational issues on individual members. The London Women's Liberation Workshop Psychology Group drew on psychotherapeutic ideas and practices to explore why destructive dynamics were sometimes fostered in consciousness-raising groups and developed strategies to help individual WLM members overcome their emotional distress. The Psychology Group argued that consciousness-raising encouraged women to express their emotions but did not provide them with the tools to either comprehend or overcome them. By critiquing this absence of support in consciousness-raising discussions, the Psychology Group made a case for the greater alignment of the political and emotional in Women's Liberation practices. In reappraising standards of authenticity present in the WLM, the Psychology Group aimed to develop the politics of Women's Liberation by further recognizing women's individual political and emotional experiences as movement members. In late twentieth-century England, the development of authentic feminist identities was not simply attributable to the personal and political transformation women experienced when practicing consciousness-raising. Women also defined their identification with feminist politics based on how it felt to be excluded from an organized women's movement like the WLM. They fostered what they perceived to be authentic feminist identities through personal negotiation rather than transformation, seeking to align the excitement and expectation of a political movement with their contrasting backgrounds, lived experiences, and emotional responses.

Kate Mahoney is a postdoctoral researcher on the Wellcome Trust-funded project "Body, Self and Family: Women's Psychological, Emotional and Bodily Health in Britain, c. 1960–1990," based in the Department of History at the University of Essex. Her research focuses on women's health activism in late twentieth-century Britain. Her publications include: "'It's Not History; It's My Life': Researcher Emotions and the Production of Critical Histories of the Women's Movement," in Tracey Loughran and Dawn Mannay, eds., *Emotion and the Researcher: Sites, Subjectivities and Relationships*, forthcoming from Emerald Books.

Notes

1. The Women's Liberation Movement (WLM) emerged across Britain in the late 1960s, with women's groups operating in England, Scotland, and Wales. This chapter, however, largely focuses on WLM activism in England. This is due to

the fact that the development of women's movements in Scotland and Wales was readily influenced by the contrasting national contexts in which they were situated, an assessment of which simply cannot be contained within the confines of this chapter. Elisabeth Armstrong, *The Retreat from Organization: U.S. Feminism Conceptualized* (Albany, 2002), 66; Sarah Maddison, "Discursive Politics: Changing the Talk and Raising Expectations," in *The Women's Movement in Protest, Institutions and the Internet: Australia in Transnational Perspective*, ed. Sarah Maddison and Marian Sawer (Oxford, 2013), 41; Geoff Eley, *Forging Democracy: The History of the Left in Europe, 1850–2000* (Oxford, 2002), 371; Anna E. Rogers, "Feminist Consciousness-Raising in the 1970s and 1980s: West Yorkshire Women's Groups and Their Impact on Women's Lives," Ph.D. dissertation (Leeds, 2010), 1.
2. Sarah Browne, *The Women's Movement in Scotland* (Manchester, 2014), 50; Margaret A. McLaren, *Feminism, Foucault, and Embodied Subjectivity* (Albany, 2002), 155.
3. Armstrong, *Retreat*, 66; Eley, *Forging Democracy*, 371; Maddison, "Discursive Politics," 41; Rogers, "Feminist Consciousness-Raising," 1.
4. McLaren, *Feminism*, 156.
5. Feminist Archive [South], London Women's Liberation Workshop Psychology Group, *Shrew* 3, no. 2 (1972), 1–16.
6. Cathryn Bailey, "Unpacking the Mother/Daughter Baggage: Reassessing Second- and Third-Wave Tensions," *Women's Studies Quarterly* 30, no. 3/4 (2002); Shelley Budgeon, *Third Wave Feminism and the Politics of Gender in Late Modernity* (Basingstoke, UK, 2011); McLaren, *Feminism*; Alessandro Ferrara, *Reflective Authenticity: Rethinking the Project of Modernity* (London, 2002); Briony Lipton and Elizabeth Mackinlay, *We Only Talk Feminist Here: Feminist Academics, Voice and Agency in the Neoliberal University* (Basingstoke, UK, 2016).
7. Rebecca Walker, "Being Real: An Introduction," in *To Be Real: Telling the Truth and Changing the Face of Feminism*, ed. Rebecca Walker (New York, 1995), xxxii–xxxiii.
8. Bailey, "Unpacking," 139, 144.
9. Ibid., 139.
10. Ibid.
11. Astrid Henry, *Not My Mother's Sister: Generational Conflict and Third-Wave Feminism* (Bloomington, IN, 2004), 42.
12. Natalie Thomlinson, *Race, Ethnicity and the Women's Movement in England, 1968–1993* (Basingstoke, UK, 2016), 1. "Black" was a political formulation employed across the 1970s and 1980s that, in a British context, recognized "all those who were colonized rather than colonizers" and was "contingent on the supposedly shared experiences of Afro-Caribbean, African, and Asian immigrants to Britain" (Thomlinson, *Race, Ethnicity and the Women's Movement in England*, 14).
13. Jane Pilcher, *Women in Contemporary Britain: An Introduction* (London: 1999), 160.
14. Rogers, "Feminist Consciousness-Raising," 148; Penny Welch, "The Politics of Teaching Women's Studies," *Women's Studies Quarterly* 27, no. 3/4 (1999): 70.
15. Armstrong, *Retreat*, 66; Rogers, "Feminist Consciousness-Raising."
16. Zsófia Lóránd, "New Feminism, Women's Subjectivity, and Feminist Politics: Conceptual Transfers and Activist Inspirations in Yugoslavia in the 1970s and 1980s," this volume.

17. Sue Bruley, *Women Awake: The Experience of Consciousness-Raising* (London, 1976), 2; Sue Bruley, "Consciousness-Raising in Clapham: Women's Liberation as 'Lived Experience' in South London in the 1970s," *Women's History Review* 22, no. 5 (2013): 717–738; Joanna Ryan, personal interview (2012).
18. Rogers, "Feminist Consciousness-Raising," 106; Morwena Griffiths, "Keeping Authenticity in Play, Or Being Naughty to be Good," in *Feminist Politics: Identity, Difference, and Agency*, ed. Deborah Orr et al. (Lanham, 2007), 119.
19. Robin D. G. Kelley and Betsy Esch, "Black like Mao: Red China and Black Revolution," in *Afro Asia: Revolutionary Political and Cultural Connections between African Americans and Asian Americans*, ed. Fred Ho and Bill V. Mullen (Durham, NC, 2008), 147.
20. Ibid.; Mao Zedong, "On Practice: On the Relation between Knowledge and Practice, between Knowing and Doing," July 1937.
21. Feminist Archive [South], Tufnell Park Women's Liberation Group, "Organising Ourselves," *Shrew* 2, no. 3 (1971): 1.
22. Ibid.; Celia Hughes, *Young Lives on the Left: Sixties Activism and the Liberation of the Self* (Manchester, 2015), 147; Celia Hughes, "The Socio-Cultural Milieux of the Left in Post-War Britain," Ph.D. dissertation (Coventry, UK, 2011), 201.
23. Ryan, personal interview.
24. Claudia Mary Cuevas, "Organizational Development and Coalition Building among Domestic Violence Agencies in California: Conflict and Compromise between Grassroots Groups and Established Institutions," Ph.D. dissertation (Columbia, NC, 2006), 114; Robin Morgan, ed., *Sisterhood is Powerful: An Anthology of Writings from the Women's Liberation Movement* (New York, 1970). Morgan's *Sisterhood is Powerful* was one of the first anthologies of women's movement writing to emerge in early 1970s America (Donna Langston, *A to Z of American Women Leaders and Activists* [New York, 2002], 156).
25. Bruley, *Women Awake*, 2; Bruley, "Consciousness-Raising in Clapham."
26. Bruley, *Women Awake*, 2; Sappho Women's Collective, "Rapping in Small Groups: Perspectives on Consciousness-Raising," *Women: A Journal of Liberation* 2, no. 2 (1971): 49.
27. Sappho Women's Collective, "Rapping in Small Groups," 49.
28. Ibid.
29. Feminist Library, The Monday Group, "Our Attempts at Consciousness-Raising: The Monday Group," *Birmingham Women's Liberation Newsletter* (May 1974): 24.
30. Ibid.
31. Ibid.
32. Ibid.
33. Feminist Library, "Monday Consciousness-raising Group," *Birmingham Women's Liberation Newsletter* (July/August 1974), 2.
34. A. Sunshine and J. Gerard, "Small Group: Big Job," *Leviathan* 2, no. 1 (1970): 20–21; Rogers, "Feminist Consciousness-Raising," 12–13.
35. Feminist Library, *Birmingham Women's Liberation Newsletter* (July/August 1973): 2.
36. Rogers, "Feminist Consciousness-Raising," 12–13.
37. Belsize Lane Women's Liberation Group, "Nine Years Together: A History of a Women's Liberation Group," in *Spare Rib Reader: 100 Issues of Women's Liberation*, ed. Marsha Rowe (Harmondsworth, UK: Penguin, 1982), 565, 570–571.

38. Ibid., 571; Rogers, "Feminist Consciousness-Raising," 12.
39. Rogers, "Feminist Consciousness-Raising," 106.
40. Linda, quoted in ibid.
41. Ibid.
42. Griffiths, "Keeping Authenticity in Play," 119; Nancy Hartsock, "Foucault on Power: A Theory for Women?" in *Feminism/Postmodernism*, ed. Linda Nicholson (New York, 1990), 172.
43. Griffiths, "Keeping Authenticity in Play," 119.
44. McLaren, *Feminism*, 156; Rogers, "Feminist Consciousness-Raising," 1; Voichita Nachescu, "Becoming the Feminist Subject: Consciousness-Raising Groups in Second-Wave Feminism," Ph.D. dissertation (Albany, 2006), 242.
45. Sally Carter, personal interview (2012); Feminist Library, Disgruntled Hazel, "A Warning to Misfits," *Women's Liberation Workshop Newssheet* 42 (1971): 2.
46. Sarah Braun, interviewed by Ilona Singer in *Personal Histories of Second Wave Feminism*, ed. Viv Honeybourne and Ilona Singer (Bristol, UK, 2004), 7–8.
47. Ibid., 8.
48. Belsize Lane Women's Liberation Group, "Nine Years Together," 43–44.
49. Ibid.
50. Maddison, "Discursive Politics," 41.
51. Ibid.
52. Rogers, "Feminist Consciousness-Raising," 148.
53. Browne, *The Women's Movement in Scotland*, 50.
54. Ibid.
55. Ibid.
56. Carter, personal interview.
57. Ibid.
58. Ibid.
59. Ibid.
60. Ibid.
61. Ibid.
62. Barbara Taylor, interviewed by Thomas Dixon, "Five Hundred Years of Friendship: Families of Choice," *BBC Radio 4*, 10 April 2014.
63. Ibid.
64. Jilly Rosser, interviewed by Ilona Singer, in *Personal Histories of Second Wave Feminism*, ed. Viv Honeybourne and Ilona Singer (Bristol, UK, 2004), 140.
65. Ibid.
66. Rukshana Afia, personal interview (2012).
67. Feminist Library, *Birmingham Women's Liberation News/Views Letter* (July/August 1973): 4.
68. Ibid.
69. Rogers, "Feminist Consciousness-Raising," 176–178, 270–271.
70. Ibid., 176–178.
71. Michael Warner, "Introduction," in *Fear of a Queer Planet: Queer Politics and Social Theory*, ed. Michael Warner (Minneapolis, MN, 1993), ix–x; Rogers, "Feminist Consciousness-Raising," 179.

72. Taylor, interviewed by Dixon, "Five Hundred Years of Friendship"; Sisterhood and After: An Oral History of Women's Liberation, "Barbara Taylor," *British Library*; Barbara Caine, *English Feminism, 1780–1980* (Oxford, 1997), 256; Redchidgey, "Red Rag: A Magazine of Women's Liberation," *Grassroots Feminism*, 12 November 2009.
73. Taylor, interviewed by Dixon, "Five Hundred Years of Friendship."
74. Disgruntled Hazel, "A Warning to Misfits."
75. Ibid.
76. Ibid.
77. Carter, personal interview.
78. Rogers, "Feminist Consciousness-Raising," 184–185.
79. Ibid.
80. Ibid.
81. Judith, quoted in ibid.
82. Ibid.
83. Feminist Archive [South], London Women's Liberation Workshop Psychology Group, 1–16.
84. Women's Library @ LSE, 7/SEB/A/16, Vivienne, Judy, Trish, Sheila, and Sheila, "Other Questions" (1973).
85. Ibid.
86. Ibid.
87. Ibid.
88. Feminist Archive [South], London Women's Liberation Workshop Psychology Group, 1–2; Feminist Library, London Women's Liberation Workshop, *Women's Liberation Workshop Newsletter* 47 (1971): 1; Feminist Library, London Women's Liberation Workshop, "Meetings and Events," *Women's Liberation Workshop Newsletter* 54 (1971): 1; Femnist Library, Carol Morrell, "Co-Counselling Group," *Women's Liberation Workshop Newsletter* 103 (1972): 2.
89. Feminist Library, Dinah Brooke, "Women and Psychotherapy," *Women's Liberation Workshop Newssheet* 33 (1971): 1.
90. Carola Klein, personal interview (2016).
91. Ibid.
92. Feminist Archive [South], London Women's Liberation Workshop Psychology Group, 1–2; Redchidgey, "Shrew: Women's Liberation Workshop (1969–1978)," *Grassroots Feminism*, 12 November 2009.
93. Feminist Archive [South], London Women's Liberation Workshop Psychology Group, 1.
94. Ibid.
95. Ibid.
96. Ibid.
97. Ibid.
98. Ibid.
99. "Yes No," *Shrew* 4, no. 3 (1972): 9.

Bibliography

Afia, Rukshana. Personal interview. Leeds, 17 July 2012.
Armstrong, Elisabeth. *The Retreat from Organization: U.S. Feminism Reconceptualized.* Albany: State University of New York Press, 2002.
Bailey, Cathryn. "Unpacking the Mother/Daughter Baggage: Reassessing Second- and Third-Wave Tensions." *Women's Studies Quarterly* 30, no. 3/4 (2002): 138–154.
Belsize Lane Women's Liberation Group. "Nine Years Together: A History of a Women's Liberation Group." In *Spare Rib Reader: 100 Issues of Women's Liberation*, edited by Marsha Rowe, 561–575. Harmondsworth, UK: Penguin, 1982.
Braun, Sarah. Interviewed by Ilona Singer. In *Personal Histories of Second Wave Feminism.* edited by Viv Honeybourne and Ilona Singer, 7–9. Bristol, UK: Feminist Archive [South], 2004.
Browne, Sarah. *The Women's Movement in Scotland.* Manchester: Manchester University Press, 2014.
Bruley, Sue. "Consciousness-Raising in Clapham: Women's Liberation as 'Lived Experience' in South London in the 1970s." *Women's History Review* 22, no. 5 (2013): 717–738.
———. *Women Awake: The Experience of Consciousness-Raising.* London: the author, 1976.
Budgeon, Shelley. *Third Wave Feminism and the Politics of Gender in Late Modernity.* Basingstoke, UK: Palgrave Macmillan, 2011.
Caine, Barbara. *English Feminism, 1780–1980.* Oxford: Oxford University Press, 1997.
Carter, Sally. Personal interview. Bristol, 4 July 2012.
Cuevas, Claudia Mary. "Organizational Development and Coalition Building among Domestic Violence Agencies in California: Conflict and Compromise between Grassroots Groups and Established Institutions." Ph.D. dissertation. Columbia: University of South Carolina, 2006.
Eley, Geoff. *Forging Democracy: The History of the Left in Europe, 1850–2000.* Oxford: Oxford University Press, 2002.
Ferrara, Alessandro. *Reflective Authenticity: Rethinking the Project of Modernity.* London: Routledge, 2002.
Griffiths, Morwena. "Keeping Authenticity in Play, Or Being Naughty to Be Good." In *Feminist Politics: Identity, Difference, and Agency*, edited by Deborah Orr, Dianna Taylor, Eileen Kahl, Kathleen Earle, Christa Rainwater, and Linda López McAlister, 119–140. Lanham, MD: Rowman & Littlefield Publishers, Inc., 2007.
Hartsock, Nancy, "Foucault on Power: A Theory for Women?" In *Feminism/Postmodernism*, edited by Linda Nicholson, 157–175. New York: Routledge, 1990.
Henry, Astrid. *Not My Mother's Sister: Generational Conflict and Third-Wave Feminism.* Bloomington: Indiana University Press, 2004.
Hughes, Celia. "The Socio-Cultural Milieux of the Left in Post-War Britain." Ph.D. dissertation. Coventry, UK: University of Warwick, 2011.
———. *Young Lives on the Left: Sixties Activism and the Liberation of the Self.* Manchester: Manchester University Press, 2015.
Kelley, Robin D. G., and Betsy Esch. "Black like Mao: Red China and Black Revolution." In *Afro Asia: Revolutionary Political and Cultural Connections between African*

Americans and Asian Americans, edited by Fred Ho and Bill V. Mullen, 97–154. Durham, NC: Duke University Press, 2008.

Klein, Carola. Personal interview. Birmingham, 28 October 2016.

Langston, Donna. *A to Z of American Women Leaders and Activists*. New York: Facts on File, 2002.

Lipton, Briony, and Elizabeth Mackinlay. *We Only Talk Feminist Here: Feminist Academics, Voice and Agency in the Neoliberal University*. Basingstoke, UK: Palgrave Macmillan, 2016.

Maddison, Sarah. "Discursive Politics: Changing the Talk and Raising Expectations." In *The Women's Movement in Protest, Institutions and the Internet: Australia in Transnational Perspective*, edited by Sarah Maddison and Marian Sawer, 37–53. Oxford: Routledge, 2013.

McLaren, Margaret A. *Feminism, Foucault, and Embodied Subjectivity*. Albany: State University of New York Press, 2002.

Morgan, Robin, ed. *Sisterhood is Powerful: An Anthology of Writings from the Women's Liberation Movement*. New York: Random House, 1970.

Nachescu, Voichita. "Becoming the Feminist Subject: Consciousness-Raising Groups in Second-Wave Feminism." Ph.D. dissertation. Albany: State University of New York, 2006.

Pilcher, Jane. *Women in Contemporary Britain: An Introduction*. London: Routledge, 1999.

Redchidgey. "Red Rag: A Magazine of Women's Liberation." *Grassroots Feminism*, 12 November 2009. Retrieved 27 November 2016 from http://www.grassrootsfeminism.net/cms/node/521.

Redchidgey, "Shrew: Women's Liberation Workshop (1969–1978)." *Grassroots Feminism*, 12 November 2009). Retrieved 9 March 217 from http://www.grassrootsfeminism.net/cms/node/520.

Rogers, Anna E. "Feminist Consciousness-Raising in the 1970s and 1980s: West Yorkshire Women's Groups and Their Impact on Women's Lives." Ph.D. dissertation. Leeds: University of Leeds, 2010.

Rosser, Jilly. Interviewed by Ilona Singer. In *Personal Histories of Second Wave Feminism*, edited by Viv Honeybourne and Ilona Singer, 139–146. Bristol, UK: Feminist Archive South, 2004.

Ryan, Joanna. Personal interview. London, 12 July 2012.

Sisterhood and After: An Oral History of Women's Liberation. "Barbara Taylor." *British Library*. Retrieved 26 April 2015 from http://www.bl.uk/learning/histcitizen/sisterhood/biographies/144001.html.

Sunshine, A., and J. Gerard. "Small Group: Big Job," *Leviathan* 2, no. 1 (1970): 20–21.

Taylor, Barbara. Interviewed by Thomas Dixon. "Five Hundred Years of Friendship: Families of Choice." *BBC Radio 4*, 10 April 2014. Retrieved 24 April 2015 from http://www.bbc.co.uk/programmes/b04009c6.

Thomlinson, Natalie. *Race, Ethnicity and the Women's Movement in England, 1968–1993*. Basingstoke, UK: Palgrave Macmillan, 2016.

Tse-tung, Mao. "On Practice: On the Relation between Knowledge and Practice, between Knowing and Doing." July 1937. Retrieved 29 May 2015 from https://www.marxists.org/reference/archive/mao/selected-works/volume-1/mswv1_16.htm.

Walker, Rebecca. "Being Real: An Introduction." In *To Be Real: Telling the Truth and Changing the Face of Feminism*, edited by Rebecca Walker, xxix–xl. New York: Anchor, 1995.

Warner, Michael. "Introduction." In *Fear of a Queer Planet: Queer Politics and Social Theory*, edited by Michael Warner, vii–xxxi. Minneapolis: University of Minnesota Press, 1993.

Welch, Penny. "The Politics of Teaching Women's Studies." *Women's Studies Quarterly* 27, no. 3/4 (1999): 70–76.

Chapter 4

A Genealogy of a Politics of Subjectivity

Guy Hocquenghem, Homosexuality, and the Radical Left in Post-1968 France

Antoine Idier

One of the most significant figures of the French gay liberation movement was Guy Hocquenghem. Having been a Marxist activist in the mid-1960s, Hocquenghem went on to become the figurehead of the Front homosexuel d'action révolutionnaire (FHAR), which was founded in Paris in February 1971. He became the public face of the organization following the publication of a self-portrait entitled "La Révolution des Homosexuels" in the moderate left-wing magazine *Le Nouvel Observateur* in January 1972. That year, he also published *Le Désir Homosexuel*, an essay that theorizes gay liberation (and that is today considered one of the founding texts of queer theory).[1]

This chapter examines Hocquenghem's evolution as an activist to demonstrate how the politicization of homosexuality in post-1968 France entailed the invention of a new political subjectivity that opposed dominant subjectivities within the Left. Tracing Hocquenghem's progression allows us, to use a terminology proposed by Pierre Bourdieu, to describe a "symbolic revolution": an upheaval "of cognitive structures and sometimes … social structures," a transformation of the "categories of perception and of appreciation, those that we ordinarily use to understand the representations of the world and the world itself" and a "*mise en question* of the forms of thought in force."[2]

In 1971, aged twenty-four and inspired by gay liberation movements in the United States and the slogan "say it loud, we're gay and proud," Hocquenghem publicly proclaimed his homosexuality and its political character. In doing so, Hocquenghem, formerly a political activist who happened to be a homosexual man, became a "homosexual activist for revolutionary action." How did this "symbolic revolution" happen? Answering this question requires a retracing of how he became able to think about and affirm his own sexuality as political and revolutionary, and thus to retrace the appearance and the appropriation of categories of perception for speaking of the self, and for affirming oneself as a certain political subject. The task is, in other words, to understand how a new political activist came into being: the "gay activist," who, in the same vein as Bourdieu's painter of the Impressionist revolution, "completely changed the vision of the world, the hierarchy of importance, the function of the painter."[3]

The chapter provides an analysis of subjectivity—political subjectivity as well as individual subjectivity—as a historical and social phenomenon. While protagonists did not refer directly to the concept of "authenticity," it was nevertheless used implicitly and, as we will see, constituted the substance of a "symbolic struggle" (in the sense of Pierre Bourdieu's terminology) over the definition of a true radical self. As highlighted in this chapter, in the political debates that took place between members of the radical left, activists discussed the veracity of political movements such as the gay movement or the feminist movement, and argued the legitimacy of the new subjectivities that these movements created.

Therefore, retracing the genesis of the FHAR requires resituating "homosexual liberation" within the landscape of the revolutionary Left in the period after 1968. It is both within the radical Left and against it that the gay movement appeared. The FHAR was inspired by the vitality of post-1968 protests, of their references and political categories, but at the same time called some of these categories into question. More specifically, the initiative for homosexual politics and a revolutionary homosexuality developed *because* homosexuality was not allowed its own space within "gauchism" (an invented term, originally negative, to designate movements to the left of the Communist Party). This chapter thus examines the homophobia that characterized the revolutionary Left, before exploring the political struggles that ran through post-1968 gauchism, the influence of the counterculture, and the birth of the feminist movement—all of which provide the context for the birth of the FHAR.

Kissing and Partying as Activism

Emotions played a fundamental role in the discourses of gay liberation. For example, in a 1988 autobiographical piece, Hocquenghem gave a gripping summary of what the years following 1968 represented for him and his friends. About the "post-May '68" period, he wrote: "We fumble like children in the dark trying to catch hold of each other, we fumble to grasp the evanescent idea of an absolute happiness, of a life reconciled with itself. And what we believed to grasp, this phantom of liberty, always escaped us."

The terminological register Hocquenghem uses is striking: childhood, absolute happiness. A few lines earlier, he also speaks of the "erotic" experience of the May-June 1968 riots and shares an anecdote about his lover: "When I came home in the early morning, salted with the smell of tear gas, he licked my skin steeped in the perfumes of riot."[4] Of course, this association between May 1968 and the vocabulary of emotion is not Hocquenghem's alone. In *May '68 and its Afterlives*, Kristin Ross points to numerous accounts that share this vocabulary of pleasure and emotion and attributes a particular temporality to the spring of 1968. Ross evokes "the temporal acceleration of those days ... unforeseen, spiraling developments that catch up with and ultimately surpass the protagonists," the "exaltation" and the "exhaustion," the "transformation of relations with others," and even "the workings of a different social order." Along similar lines, novelist Leslie Kaplan described her experience of the strikes of 1968 as "something difficult to grasp" and of having the power "to surprise you, to take you away, to raise you up, to undo you." Kaplan adds: "Love can create this feeling, or art; it is rare to feel it in society, where one is almost always confronted with a kind of obligatory inertia, where the activity one pursues, the activity that one can pursue, goes almost always hand in hand with the painful feeling of its limitations."[5]

Emotions also occupied a large place in the vocabulary of the FHAR. In a text published in the *Rapport Contre la Normalité*, a book-length manifesto of the FHAR, homosexual activists insisted on their "joyous conduct" during the May Day march of 1971. May Day marches were—and still are—the traditional place of assembly for left-wing organizations. The participation of the FHAR, alongside the Mouvement de la libération des femmes (MLF), in 1971 was thus a gesture that powerfully demonstrated the existence of homosexual struggles. The manifesto explains that this 1 May demonstration "was the start of the party for us." This reference to a festivity deserves our attention. The authors added that, having broken with "solemn" and "boring" conduct and with "the order and dignity" that usually characterize a march, they "danced ... kissed ... fondled one another ... sang." In another passage from the *Rapport Contre la Normalité*, a homosexual activist describes his feelings, especially his anger: "Not a single heterosexual will know what our hell was for so many years: this contained rage, this desire to bite, this powerless want, that remains there, in the deepest part of us, to destroy this world. That none of it remain!" Speaking about the FHAR, Hocquenghem himself noted a "nebula of feelings and action," something "at once political and vital," a space where "affective relations" could multiply.[6]

This emphasis on emotions indicates that the birth of the FHAR and the appearance of the gay radical movement transformed the ways of doing politics, the ways of considering oneself both a political activist and a subject. Henceforth, feelings had a central place in these matters. Returning to the march of May Day 1971, the FHAR explained: "Our joyous conduct greatly displeased, of course, respectable leftists. … Our presence alone in this march and the fact that we spoke openly seemed to challenge the scenario of different 'gauchisms.'" While the emphasis on joyous feelings suggests a radical break, it is worth noting that the FHAR also inscribed itself into certain post-1968 protest dynamics. In particular, it shared the Marxist terminology common in the post-1968 Left, though with a notable twist: "For us, the class struggle also occurs in the body. … It is thus not a question of separating our sexual struggle from our daily one in order to realize our desires, our anti-capitalist struggle, our struggle for a classless society, with neither master nor slave."[7] While on the one hand participating in the mainstream discourse of the anti-establishment Left that emphasized class struggle, the FHAR also developed its own discourse that contested conventional radical politics and proclaimed a politics that took the body, desires, and sexuality as fundamentally political objects.

"Proletarian Terrorism"

The roots of the sexual politics of the FHAR that gave emotions a fundamental role are located in a very strong and aggressive homophobia within French protest movements of the 1960s and early 1970s. Proclaiming that homosexuality had a political character was far from self-evident, and expressing emotions, especially (homo)sexual desires, was taboo. This homophobia explains why FHAR activists expressed great hostility towards *gauchistes*. Hocquenghem himself was confronted with such homophobia during his time with the UEC (Union des étudiants communistes), then the JCR (Jeunesses communistes révolutionnaires), and finally the UNEF (Union nationale des etudiants de France), all major youth organizations of the *gauchiste* Left.

One episode exemplifies the point. Hocquenghem recounts it in *L'Amphithéâtre des Morts,* an autobiographical essay published in 1994, six years after the death of its author. He describes a general assembly of the UNEF that took place in late 1967 or early 1968: "We adopt motions, we count the 'Shall Not Votes,' within the frame of an obscure quarrel between two opposing wings of Trotskyism. Suddenly, Chisseray gets up, and starts shouting. Chisseray leads the other wing, the one to which I do not belong. ... 'And, what's more, H. is homosexual. Your group lets in perverted and degenerate petty bourgeois.'"

Hocquenghem continues his story: "I had not thought that this could be known. I had constructed a wall between my private life—my weekends in the country, my first nights out clubbing, my love for Romain—and the embryo of my public life, that I believed to be impassable."

Hocquenghem then described how he left the room and took refuge in a café where his friends joined him. There was Henri Weber, one of the leaders of the JCR, his companion Pascale Werner, and another activist of the JCR, Jean-Michel Gerassi, who is referred to as Jean-René in the story. Hocquenghem stresses that these were not only fellow activists, but friends, to whom he was intimately tied. The scene goes on: "Suddenly, Jean-René ..., out of the blue, asks: 'But is it true that you are homosexual?'"

According to his autobiographical account, Hocquenghem was "unsettled, frozen," because he had not "expected this from him, from them, my comrades." He finally answered "in a quiet voice": "You're crazy! What an idea!" It was a response that left him "still ashamed, half a century later."[8]

The episode is revealing for how Hocquenghem navigated his homosexuality before the emergence of the FHAR. It was not an isolated incident: over and over again, Hocquenghem was forced to endure sarcasm and attacks, which he referred to in a 1986 statement as "proletarian terrorism," of which he was a victim.[9] In the 1960s, homosexuality did not have a place in the revolutionary Left, whether it was among uncompromising Trotskyists like the "Lambertist" movement,[10] or among the Jeunesse communiste révolutionaire.[11] The attitude of left-wing leaders such as Werner, Weber, and Gerassi is representative of the period: even for one's friends, homosexuality was taboo. The JCR was, however, a rather liberal organization when it came to sexuality in general; citing Wilhelm Reich, a leaflet of the University of Nanterre chapter of the JCR, for example, criticized the "sexual regulations within university residences" and called for the "forming of committees against sexual repression."[12]

Oppression on account of one's homosexuality did not end after 1968. Nor did it limit itself to Trotskyism: it touched all spheres of gauchism, including the then dominant Maoism. Anecdotes from FHAR activist Michel Cressole, a close friend of Hocquenghem, Claude Arnaud, and Jean Rolin all demonstrate this violence.[13] When Hocquenghem himself, after having split with the JCR and aligning himself with Maoism (within a group deemed "Mao-Spontex," Vive la Révolution), wished to join the Base ouvrière de Flins, a group active in Renault's factories, he was rejected. Later, he described the incident to the feminist film-maker, Carole Roussopoulos: "The Flint comrades ... said: 'a queer, it's out of the question.' Half of them saying, 'look, it's not that we're against it, but it would shock the workers.' … The other half saying quite simply that it was a vice due to bourgeois degeneration and that it was not a matter of accepting me."[14]

If we are to believe the representation of homosexuality in *Tigre en Papier*, Olivier Rolin's novel on the Gauche prolétarienne (one of the major Maoist organizations post-1968, of which he was a leader) such incidents were commonplace. In the novel, the narrator discovers that "the leader of worker base number one is a queer!" He comments on this "really astounding revelation": "A worker, and what's more a revolutionary worker, cannot be a queer."[15]

These episodes document the widespread homophobia within the French Left. For Hocquenghem, this meant that, prior to becoming a public figure in the struggle for gay rights, he had led a "double life." Indeed, in 1972, he described "a life split in two, a schizophrenic life": "On the one hand, activist life, revolution. On the other hand, affective life, homosexuality. And a permanent obsession: the idea that these two irreconcilable worlds would meet." He added: "I was condemned to lies and concealment."[16] In his autobiographical account, Hocquenghem describes the atmosphere in revolutionary political circles before the foundation of the FHAR as being full of fear, "censorship" of emotions, and "affectivity," "shame," and guilt.[17] Compared with the emotional vocabulary Hocquenghem used to depict the experience within the FHAR in 1971, the contrast could not be greater. The emphasis on joy within the FHAR was also a deliberate response to the impossibility of expressing such emotions elsewhere. In that sense, the foundation of the FHAR was also a reversal of the emotional cultural within the *gauchiste* political sphere.

Politics in the First Person

The appearance of the homosexual movement in 1971 was, as the discussion above has shown, an emotional upheaval and reversal: whereas feelings of embarrassment and shame had predominated in the Left around 1968, the expression of joy and pride had marked the presence of the FHAR at the May Day demonstration of 1971. This was not only an emotional transformation, it was also a shift in terms of political subjectivity—that is, of how people thought of themselves as political subjects. The rupture thus not only concerned the emotions that were expressed; it constituted a wider redefinition of politics. According to the FHAR, politics were intimately connected to one's subjectivity as a political activist. One of the key points of Hocquenghem's trajectory was a reconceptualization of the political: he implored for revolution to be conceived of as a personal transformation in daily life. His writings thus raised questions about the nature of the political and political subjectivity.

To understand this reconfiguration of the political, it is necessary to examine the political unrest that shook the entirety of the radical Left after 1968. There was a widespread sense that "something" happened in 1968 that made this symbolic revolution occur. From its very inception, the May 1968 movement was loaded with meaning and perceived, to use Félix Guattari's term, as a "shock" (*ébranlement*).[18] In the years following 1968, a variety of movements emerged that were engaged in intense symbolic struggles over the (re)definition of politics and how to move on in the wake of May 1968.

Individual trajectories characterized by important ruptures are telling in this regard, and Hocquenghem provides a good example for such an investigation. At the start of 1969, he was excluded from the Ligue communiste, which followed the JCR that had dissolved in the summer of 1968. He was reproached for having been, during the debates that preceded the forming of the Ligue communiste, a proponent of "spontaneity"—an anti-organizational political tendency that refused to rely on Leninist and Trotskyist organizational principles and opposed adhering to the Fourth International.[19] Hocquenghem's trajectory—breaking away from traditional leftist understandings of politics and organizational practices—is far from unique. As the 1974 publication of *La Leçon d'Althusser* attests, Jacques Rancière, whose formative experience had been in the entourage of Louis Althusser and the Marxism of Rue d'Ulm, broke with his academic mentor in the wake of 1968. To justify this rupture, Rancière refered to a "misunderstanding," a "surprise," an "enigma of '68," and to the "perception of an important gap between the concrete reasons for these revolts and what theory said about them."[20] The work of André Glucksmann, a friend of Hocquenghem, provides an example for the numerous uncertainties and interrogations as well as political and intellectual reconfigurations. In 1974, Glucksmann declared on television: "Since May 1968, one no longer knows what pure literature is. Nor does one know what pure politics is."[21] Glucksmann's statement sums up the challenges to the definition of the political that the post-1968 period saw in France. Even if Glucksmann did not mention these challenges explicitly, one can assume that he referred to the inclusion of discourses, claims, forms of protest, and also feelings that were previously excluded from the political sphere.

Hocquenghem's book *L'Après-Mai des Faunes*, published in 1974, is a collection of texts written in the preceding years that explores the upheaval of political categories instigated by 1968. In a 1969 essay, he wrote: "One must systematize the new ideas that appeared in May." And in 1970: "The term proletariat itself must be seen again in the light of May."²² The texts, though they sometimes give contradicting answers, all address a burning question: what is politics now? The founding of the FHAR took place within this context of debates about the boundaries of the political, the place of personal subjectivity in politics, and the relevance of certain political categories inherited from Marxism.

Maoism occupied a dominant position in the political landscape of the Left during these years. Both Jean-Paul Sartre and Michel Foucault, to give just two famous examples, moved closer to the Gauche Prolétarienne, a Maoist organization, during this time.²³ Hocquenghem himself wrote in May 1971 that "the first political analysis that really served me in my life was that of the Chinese in the Cultural Revolution."²⁴ Already in June 1969, he had argued that "the only revolutionary way today is the way of the Cultural Revolution, a form finally found of proletarian power such as it was inaugurated in China."²⁵ Within Maoism, he defended a minority position, and the "cultural revolution" he celebrated not only had little to do with what was happening in China, but also had very little in common with the way it was typically represented by French Maoist groups. In particular, Hocquenghem continued to oppose the Gauche prolétarienne. If, in a 1970 tract entitled "Changer La Vie," he referenced Mao five times, it was only to contest French Maoism, qualified as "ossified Marxism-Leninism" and as "French Chinese-Khrushchev." He later wrote: "The sad forgery of Maoism that the majority of pro-Chinese groups in France offered to us systematically erased all the vital energy from the figure of Mao himself."²⁶

In Hocquenghem's reading, the "cultural revolution" had a particular meaning, that of "not letting any of the bourgeois institutions nor any of their mores escape the critiques of the masses." The "culture" Hocquenghem referred to encompassed an ensemble of values, the "bourgeois ideas and mores," modeled on the image of the family, of the "parental function, pillar of oppression," of medicine and psychiatry, of the university, and of "daily life."²⁷ Hocquenghem especially contested "the falsified image given of the *cultural revolution*" that results from reducing "it to an *individual moral progression* of the activist."²⁸ He particularly opposed an essential component of leftist and notably Maoist movements, namely the idea of workerism according to which a good activist, often a student, must adopt the "qualities ascribed ... to the working class: discipline, the spirit of sacrifice, etc." Hocquenghem castigated such a "submission to a pseudo-model of proletarian life." He lamented: "The activist becomes the object of the organization, the principal problem becomes his individual transformation; the central instruction is to 'Serve the people' and, to serve them, to identify with the image that has been assigned to them: conjugal fidelity, regularity at work, etc."²⁹

The text posed a range of questions: What is a revolutionary? What is a political activist? And even: how does one do politics? Hocquenghem contested what he described as "politicism" (*politisme*), which is to say, "the fact of considering that there is an absolute break between politics (meetings, mimeographing, postering etc.) and daily life."[30] This rejection of "politicism" seems in a large part tied to his homosexuality, even though it was not explicit at this point.

For Hocquenghem, the "establishment" (*établissement*; not to be confused with the "establishment" that students elsewhere attacked) tendency was the clearest example of how Marxism-Leninism had gone wrong. For activists following this tendency, "to establish oneself" meant to become a factory worker. A dynamic of "establishment" was, for example, promoted in the fall of 1967 within the Maoist group UJC(ml) (Union des jeunesses communistes marxistes-léninistes).[31] Robert Linhart, whose book *L'Etabli* is a remarkable description of the factory, provides an account of this dynamic. He got hired at Citröen in September 1968 and organized a strike there.[32] After 1968, the Gauche Prolétarienne, founded by a minority of the UJC(ml), argued that "the solution to youth revolt is not in the high schools, but in the factories." According to Virginie Linhart, after 1969, "anti-authoritarian high schoolers and students [would] be sent systematically to establish themselves in factories, to install themselves in shanty towns and working class suburbs, from where they will organize the resistance."[33]

Hocquenghem was deeply critical of this movement. In his 1970 article "Changer La Vie," he contested the notion that "the revolutionary student who refuses ... to 'establish' himself ... is no more than a progressive petty bourgeois." He wrote: "Certain French comrades went all the way to exalting the formative value of factory discipline and assembly line work." Then he specified: "For us, the formula 'share the life of the masses' has to be abandoned in favor of the slogan: 'Share the revolt of the masses.'" Hocquenghem thus problematized the point of view of politics. In his mind, anti-establishment students did not need to renounce their point of view in order to assume the identity of workers and of the "masses." To the contrary, politics had to start from their own position; they had to critically question their position, interrogate themselves as to how their position could be revolutionary, and ask what they would contribute to the revolution. Denying the specificity of their situation would be useless, because only their own position could form the basis from which they might find the proverbial seeds of the revolution. Thus, he wrote, "the first duty of revolutionaries is to revolutionize themselves in their union with the revolt of the masses," adding that "the activist who accepts following the family model in his personal life accepts in this way to present it to the masses as the only possible and imaginable model of life."[34] Such political positions, which were also shared by other activists, anticipated the problems posed by the birth of the radical homosexual movement and offered a rich and fertile ground on which to pose these problems. In effect, they simultaneously contested positions of traditional Marxism and brought up the question of activists' subjectivity and of the possibility of a political struggle based on one's individual circumstances.

Despite its name, this "cultural revolution" had, in the end, very little to do with the Chinese revolution. Rather it drew on ideas developed in US counterculture, from which Hocquenghem took the idea of a cultural transformation of the way of life. Indeed, Hocquenghem's work is full of references to William Burroughs, Jimi Hendrix, Janis Joplin, Aretha Franklin, and Otis Redding. Jerry Rubin and Abbie Hoffman, who had, in 1967, founded the Yippies in New York, were also two important figures for Hocquenghem.[35] Drawing on ideas of communal living popularized by North American movements, Hocquenghem and his friends spent several months living in a commune in 1970—first in Ivry-sur-Seine, then in a newly founded commune in Asnière, both municipalities in the suburbs of Paris. While other activists strongly criticized this decision to live in a commune with activists and workers, Hocquenghem emphasized the political dimension of commune life and described it as a "new attitude to rediscover life" and an "instrument of struggle."[36]

The launch of the newspaper *Tout!*, in which Hocquenghem played a large part, illustrates the tensions within the French radical Left. Created by activists from *Vive la Révolution*, a Maoist-spontaneist group ("mao-spontex"), *Tout!* was considered a "journal of the masses" or, to follow the expression of Roland Castro, head of the VLR, a "red *France-Soir*" (a major daily tabloid in France). As Manus McGrogan writes, the paper was an encounter of "three major currents in the post-'68 leftist milieu." First, it straddled Marxist and libertarian movements that broke with traditional activist models by contesting hierarchies and oppressions in the most informal and provocative ways. Second, it facilitated the spread of "underground" themes coming from the United States such as music, communal living, and drugs.[37] Third, by printing an increased number of sometimes colored caricatures, illustrations, and, under the influence of the underground press, by breaking with the red and black against white background used by Maoist papers, the *Tout!* tried "to broaden the class struggle into a struggle for civilization." It offered a platform for budding political movements such as the MLF, the FHAR, the FLJ (Front de libération des jeunes), and even immigrant struggles.[38]

The article that Hocquenghem wrote for the first issue of *Tout!* in September 1970 was revelatory for the path taken since 1968 and the speed of change that had occurred. It showed how much he had distanced himself from previous positions and underlined his argument for a politics of the personal. "Revolution is a rupture," he writes: "they will no longer do it to us, there will not be a socialist justice for us, a socialist university, socialist factories, a socialist family, that would be themselves repainted in red." For Hocquenghem, revolutionaries "are no longer rebels": "Leftists are noteworthy in that they never speak of their background, of their family, but always of that of others. ... That is what we no longer want to be. We want to speak from our guts. We want to say what we are, what we feel."[39] The quote—particularly the last two sentences—points to a fundamental rupture by linking the expression of emotions with a political project that distanced itself from traditional ideas of socialist revolution. The expression of feelings is portrayed as an essential aspect of the politics of the first person, a politics that does not deny the relevance of the activist's subjectivity, but, on the contrary, assumes its centrality for politics.

Even though Hocquenghem does not mention his homosexuality in the texts written a few months before the birth of the FHAR in 1971, his political positions seem deeply influenced by his homosexuality. His words in the first issue of *Tout!* in September 1970, seem to express the founding inspiration of FHAR—calling for the expression of one's true feelings.[40] The text speaks of the family and the misogyny of activists, but not of homosexuality. Arguing against medical advice regarding drugs in February 1971, he allowed himself only the slightest allusion to sexuality: "The scandal is that doctors legislate our sexuality or what they call the 'drug.' ... Their only criteria, the sole basis of their reasoning, is the classification of 'normal' or 'abnormal,' of the unusual and the usual, of that which is done and that which is not."[41] Immediately after the birth of the homosexual movement, he made the connection between his politics and homosexuality more explicit. Drawing a parallel between the support offered by *gauchiste* activists to the Chinese repression of Bengal, which outraged him, and leftist attitudes toward homosexuality, he wrote in May 1971: "I feel that those who condemn this [Bengali] uprising as nonconformist are also those who condemn mine [i.e., my uprising], as a living being and not as a bunch of principles." In *Le Désir Homosexual*, published in 1972, he was more specific: "it is ... the struggle against normality that characterized the Bengali movement as nonconforming to the Maoist blueprint for popular war, and ... certain homosexuals supported the first forms of this revolt."[42]

We can thus consider Hocquenghem's positions in relation to the radical French Left in the immediate aftermath of 1968 as constitutive of a silent subversion: his ideas and actions were evidently linked to his sexuality, but this influence remained implicit. Hocquenghem could not yet speak of his homosexuality—in part because of the hostilities he faced within the Left, but also, as will be discussed, because he had not yet acquired the categories of perception to realize its subversive potential. The (counter)cultural revolution advanced a number of themes that were to shape what was to come, but it was anything but immune to adversity.

The Feminist Breach

Any genealogy of the FHAR, of its invention of homosexual politics and a new political subjectivity, must considerer the FHAR as the result of a process that included several reconfigurations of radical politics in post-1968 France. Hocquenghem's desire "to say what we feel, what we are" was part of a broader political project. The question of emotions in the gay liberation movement was indeed part and parcel of a more general reconfiguration of relationships between politics and subjectivity. In particular, the feminist movement played a key role in this development that led to the birth of the FHAR. Even though feminists did not directly address the question of emotions and emotional politics, their political project raised the question of a "politics of the first person," the situation of women in political struggles and the relation between the private and the political.

The French Mouvement pour la libération des femmes (MLF) that emerged a few months before the FHAR in 1970 brought the decisive impetus. A single photograph documents what the homosexual movement owed to feminism. Taken by Catherine Deudon on 10 March 1971 in front of the Salle Pleyel (one of the most popular concert halls in Paris), it immortalizes a group of women dancing the French cancan. Leading figures of the French feminist movement are in the forefront of the photo: Christine Delphy, Monique Wittig, Elisabeth Salvaresi, Antoinette Fouque, and Anne de Bascher. They have just interrupted a program by Ménie Grégoire on RTL about homosexuality that was broadcast live and in front of an audience. The action quickly became legendary, and the interruption is considered to be the founding act of the homosexual movement. That same evening, the name Front homosexuel d'action révolutionnaire was chosen. The episode shows how the feminist movement and its protagonists, who participated in the founding of the FHAR, were of crucial importance for homosexual politics.

In a public discussion recorded by Carole Roussopoulos in 1971, Hocquenghem explained that FHAR's existence was "essentially due to the breach that was opened by the MLF," because the foundation of the MLF was "the moment where they said to people: 'we are going to depart from what we are, and not simply from our political ideas.'"[43] In 1972, Hocquenghem elaborated, stating that the feminist movement "creates the conditions of a new understanding of what we call struggles. ... One is a woman before being a Trotskyist or Maoist, why not a queer? It was private life, thus private in the political sense, and that becomes a struggle."[44] He elaborated on these points in *Désir Homosexuel*, a book inspired by Gilles Deleuze and Félix Guattari's *Anti-Œdipus*: "It is no longer sufficient to analyze society in terms of a conflict between conscious groups united by their interests (the classes). We must also recognize the existence, besides conscious (political) investments, of unconscious libidinal investments which sometimes conflict with the former."[45] Hocquenghem's claims echoed an assertion by feminist and lesbian theorist Monique Wittig that Marxism "prevented [women] from being aware that they are a class and therefore from constituting themselves as a class for a very long time." In her mind, "Lenin, the party, all the communist parties up to now, including all the most radical political groups, have always reacted to any attempt on the part of women to reflect and form groups based on their own class problem with an accusation of divisiveness."[46] Feminists like Wittig had thus started questioning the political categories of Marxism, and this had a profound impact on the nascent gay movement.

Feminist activists and ideas crucially influenced the foundation of the FHAR. Already in the "homophile" movement *Arcadie* (a homosexual movement founded in 1954 that the FHAR denounced as archaic and reactionary), a young woman, Anne-Marie Fauret (pseudonym of Anne-Marie Grélois), together with her partner Maryse, formed a lesbian group. She frequented Maoist circles from which she distanced herself as a result of their machismo, before discovering the MLF in the fall of 1970 in an issue of the review *Partisans* entitled "Libération des femmes, année zero."[47] She joined Namaskar Shaktini, an American student traveling in Europe who, on 26 August 1970, participated in the demonstration at the foot of the Arc de Triomphe that is considered to be the founding act of the MLF, where feminists declared that there one who is more "unknown than the unknown soldier: his wife."[48] This group also included Françoise d'Eaubonne, a heterosexual writer born in 1920, who published a book in support of Simone de Beauvoir and her *Deuxième Sexe*, as well as Marie-Jo Bonnet, born in 1949, who met Anne-Marie Fauret and her partner Maryse through the feminist reading group founded by Shaktini, called the "Polymorphes perverses."[49]

The women's liberation movement was so important to the gay liberation movement because it had already enacted a "symbolic takeover" (*coup de force symbolique*)—to use Pierre Bourdieu's expression—against gauchism. FHAR activists drew on both feminist rhetoric and practice. The FHAR's manifesto

Rapport Contre la Normalité, published anonymously in the fall of 1971, echoed ideas that can be found in the foundational texts of the MLF. To give but one example: Gille Wittig, Monique Wittig, Marcia Rothenburg, and Namaskar Shaktini proclaimed in an article entitled "Combat pour la libération de la femme" (Struggle for the liberation of the woman), published in the *Idiot International* in May 1970:

> To the revolutionaries who presume that we are putting the cart before the horse, that it is only *after* the proletariat has taken power that women's "problems" (so petty in truth) will solve themselves, we reply: all the power to the people. We are the people and we want to participate in the taking of power in order to stand for our own interests.[50]

The feminists maintained that "already existing revolutionary organizations are led by men," and that the importance of women's liberation is always minimized: "We always hear men saying that our struggle is a 'secondary problem.'" The signatories turned to their comrades: "Men—revolutionary activists for example—all participated in our oppression on any given day, they were all complicit in male chauvinism at one time or another, they are all guilty." They continued: "We are tired of fighting against our revolutionary comrades in order to highlight our oppression. ... The time is over where we ask men—were they revolutionary activists—the permission to rise up."

Feminists criticized "revolutionaries who presume that we are putting the cart before the horse," "those who accuse us of provoking division among workers," "those who tell us that we cannot constitute the primary front due to our relation with production," "those who tell us that in society there exists two contradictions: the principal contradiction between workers and the capitalist class, and secondary contradictions, those between men and women being a secondary contradiction."[51]

Members of the FHAR, notably Hocquenghem, were directly inspired by this text: he used the same formulas to address leftists and to question their political discourses. He authored an "address to those who consider themselves 'normal,'" writing: "You who want revolution, you who wanted to impose on us your repression. You fought for Blacks and you treated the cops like buggers (*enculés*), as if there were no worse insult. You, lovers of the proletariat, have encouraged with all of your strength the upholding of the virile image of the worker."[52] The same parallels can be seen in both groups' subversion of the *Communist Party Manifesto*: where the feminist writer Christiane Rochefort asked "Proletarians of all countries ... who washes your socks?" the FHAR proclaimed: "Proletarians of all countries, fondle one another!"[53] Feminists made themselves known by "agit-prop," laying a wreath at the Arc de Triomphe and disturbing an "Estates-General" of *Elle* magazine; the gay liberation movement similarly took up these modes of action by interrupting a conference of Professor Lejeune, a doctor opposed to abortion, on 10 February 1971, an anti-abortion meeting held by the association "Laissez-les vivre" on 5 March 1971, or again, 10 March 1971, on Ménie Grégoire's show.

Not only did the two movements share political slogans, but also forms of political mobilization. In reaction to gauchism, both movements embraced a libertarian influence and refused rigid organization. "The term 'organization' is a trap," feminists stated in their paper *Le Torchon brûle*. The organization, they added, is akin to "dads and honest morals, order, security, with their kind (in fact, paternalistic) air."[54] Hocquenghem expressed a similar thought in June 1971 by emphasizing how delighted he was at the absence of a "minimal political base": "I think that we will not make any manifesto, that the chaos of the general meetings is constitutive. ... We are a nebula of feelings and action. And I do not agree with hasty clarifications; with the race for identification: knowing who one is, find one's way amid the gauchistes."[55] Here, Hocquenghem opposed "a nebula of feelings" to political behaviors he considered traditional and classical. He later states, in *Le Désir homosexuel*, "we must give up the dream of reconciling the official spokesmen of revolution to the expression of desire. We cannot force desire to identify with a revolution which is already so heavy with the past history of the 'workers' movement.'" And further: "Not only is a new revolutionary model needed, but also a new questioning of the content traditionally associated with the term 'revolution,' particularly the notion of the seizure of power."[56]

While these quotes suggest fundamental agreements between the feminist and homosexual movements, disagreements quickly emerged. By the spring of 1971, a group of lesbian activists condemned the mechanisms of masculine domination that endured within the FHAR and decided to form a splinter group called "Gouines rouges" (Red Dykes).

Conclusion: "Political" Gauchism and "Cultural" Gauchism

This chapter has argued that the foundation of the FHAR needs to be placed in a larger context and chronology. Not only were matters of sexuality at stake, but also the very meaning of politics. The rise of a radical homosexual movement in the post-1968 period was inseparably linked to a range of reconfigurations of, and struggles about, the political. While this chapter has drawn attention to the importance of the feminist movement, one could also examine relations with other movements, such as the GIP (Groupe d'information sur les prisons) or the CERFI (Centre d'études, de recherches et de formations institutionnelles) that, under the leadership of Félix Guattari, conducted research on "institutional psychotherapy."[57]

In his 1974 book *L'Après-Midi des Faunes*, Guy Hocquenghem reflects on the preceding years and considers the consequences of the turmoil in which he took part. In the six years since 1968, politics had been radically transformed. "In this way an old story dies, that of engagement," he writes. He opposes a past and a present, an old and a new way of being an activist: "We no longer engage in just struggles; we act by stances. ... We do not directly take on the big questions that preoccupy humanity. We slip askew between two layers of guilty conscience, sneaking up from behind into a multitude of the social body's quaking, into an infinity of imperious localizations, the boxes where one tries to enclose us."[58] Referring to the writings of Jean-François Lyotard, he also opposes the "volutionary" attitude to the "revolutionary" attitude, in order to claim an end to this revolutionary horizon. This is not a renunciation of political contestation: Hocquenghem calls for "moving in all directions," for "dispersing throughout the civilizing powers," for "burrowing, everywhere possible, mining underneath the edifice." His text refers to Marxism, to the "transcendence for the gauchistes," "the incessant judging of revolutionary normality," the "despotic subject of history," the "dialectical temporality," and even "the order of a great transcending power."[59] Hocquenghem was not the only one to affirm the advent of a new politics. In 1977, in his preface to the English edition of *Anti-Œdipus*, Michel Foucault also evoked "five brief, impassioned, jubilant, enigmatic years" that paved the way for a new "style of political discourse" and "a movement toward political struggles that no longer conformed to the model that Marxist tradition had prescribed."[60]

Such comments call for a reinterpretation of the extant historiography on May 1968 and an interrogation of the use of categories such as "cultural," that are frequently employed in an uncritical manner. Much of the historiography therefore draws an unquestioned distinction between "political" and "cultural" *gauchism*, with the FHAR belonging to the second category. It is commonly seen as part of a "larger cultural contestation" that reached "from medical school to the judiciary, prison, the army, the Church, ecology, the regional question, sexuality, male-female relations or children's education."[61] Kristin Ross expresses a similar idea in her book, *May '68 and Its Afterlives*, a noteworthy study because it reattributes a historical significance to May 1968. Criticizing interpretations, prominent in the 1980s, which depict May 1968 as merely a cultural event, Ross seeks to repoliticize our understanding of events. Yet, despite Ross's admirable critique of various falsifications of

May 1968, her own interpretation is equally problematic. Writing about those who are, in her mind, the true inheritors of May 1968, she examines the Marxist-inspired journals *Forum-Histoire* or *Révoltes Logiques*: "It is here that we should look, rather than to the sociologists, or to the philosophers of Desire like Lyotard or Deleuze frequently summoned up to embody the legacy of May within intellectual production, to find some of the most interesting and radical political experiments around the question of equality.[62]

Ross's interpretation can be read as an example of how May 1968 and its later lives inaugurate a hierarchy between the diverse political and intellectual experiences that flourished in the 1970s. Yet, by affirming such hierarchies, Ross herself does little more than strengthen the schisms that occurred at the time. This chapter has suggested a different approach. Rather than establishing a hierarchy between different experiences, it is essential to consider the relations between different movements and contestations, and to see how the post-May 1968 period was characterized by an ensemble of "symbolic struggles." Indeed, the major political battle of the time was, as the development of the FHAR exemplifies, a battle about the nature of the political, about what was inside and what was outside the boundaries of the political. In the course of these debates, a new political subjectivity was invented.

Antoine Idier holds a master's degree in Political Science from Sciences-Po Lyon and a doctorate in Social Science from the University of Amiens. He is the author of several publications on sexuality, politics, and the history of ideas as well as contributions about contemporary art. His last book *Les Vies de Guy Hocquenghem: Politique, sexualité, culture* was published in 2017 by Fayard Editions. He also edited a collection of press articles written by Guy Hocquenghem, *Un journal de rêve: Articles de presse (1971–1987)* published in 2017 by Éditions Verticales. He is currently study and research coordinator at the École nationale supérieure d'arts de Paris-Cergy (ENSAPC), where he is jointly responsible for the postgraduate research program *Moving Frontiers—Do and undo/Faire et défaire,* in partnership with Triennale SUD2017 in Cameroon. He also coordinates the implementation of a practice-led doctorate in arts.

Notes

The original draft of the chapter was translated from French by Allison L. Faris.

1. Guy Hocquenghem, *Homosexual Desire*, trans. Daniella Dangoor (Durham, NC, 1993). *Le Désir Homosexuel* (Paris, 2000, for the French edition; Paris, 1972, for the first edition). This chapter stems from research conducted for a doctoral thesis in

sociology that resulted in the book: *Les vies de Guy Hocquenghem: Politique, sexualité, culture* (Paris, 2017).
2. Pierre Bourdieu, *Manet: Une Révolution Symbolique* (Paris, 2013), 13–14; Pierre Bourdieu, *Les Règles de L'Art* (Paris, 1998), 165. All translations are mine unless otherwise stated.
3. Pierre Bourdieu, "La Révolution Impressionniste," *Noroit*, 303 (1987).
4. Guy Hocquenghem, *L'Amphithéâtre des Morts* (Paris, 1994), 94 (this and the previous quotation).
5. Kristin Ross, *May '68 and Its Afterlives* (Chicago, 2002), 102–103 and 141–142, citing Leslie Kaplan, *Depuis maintenant: Miss Nobody Knows* (Paris, 1996), 61–63.
6. FHAR, *Rapport Contre la Normalité* (Montpellier, France, 2013), 68, 41 and 71–72.
7. FHAR, *Rapport Contre la Normalité*, 68–69.
8. Hocquenghem, *L'Amphithéâtre des Morts*, 89–92.
9. Hocquenghem, *La Dérive Homosexuelle*, 24.
10. The Trotskyist movement included several different organizations referring to the 4th International founded by Leon Trotsky. The members of the OCI (Organisation communiste internationaliste) were considered "Lambertists" because of the name of its leading figure, Pierre Lambert.
11. Representing another branch of Trotskyism, the JCR (Jeunesse communiste révolutionnaire) was founded in 1966 by students and young Marxist activists excluded from the Union des étudiants communistes (UEC), the student organization of the French Communist Party. The JCR especially denounced the "Stalinism" of the Communist Party. Forbidden in 1968, the JCR became the Ligue communiste and then the Ligue communiste révolutionnaire.
12. "Pour une Nouvelle Politique Sexuelle," leaflet reproduced in the appendix of Véronique Faburel, "La Jeunesse communiste révolutionnaire: 1966–1968," MA Thesis (Paris, 1988).
13. Alain Prique, "Rencontre avec Michel Cressole," *Résister—Vivre la Mémoire. Acte I*, 1994; Claude Arnaud, *Qu'As-Tu Fait de Tes Frères?* (Paris, 2010), 122–124, 154, and 187–188; Jean Rolin, *L'Organisation* (Paris, 1996), 33.
14. *Le FHAR*, directed by Carole Roussopoulos (France, 1971).
15. Olivier Rolin, *Tigre en Papier* (Paris, 2003), 183–184.
16. Guy Hocquenghem, *La Dérive Homosexuelle* (Paris, 1977), 29–30.
17. Hocquenghem, *La Dérive Homosexuelle*, 29–30; Hocquenghem, *L'Amphithéâtre des Morts*, 90; "Trois milliards de pervers," *Recherches* no. 12 (1973): 214.
18. Gilles Deleuze, "Entretien sur *L'Anti-Œdipe*," in *Pourparlers 1972–1990* (Paris, 2003), 26.
19. *Construire le Parti, Construire L'Internationale. 2. de L'Internationalisme à L'Internationale* (Paris, no. 8/9, 1969).
20. "Entretien avec Jacques Rancière," in *La Parole Errante: De Mai 68 à ...*, retrieved 10 July 2018 from http://www.la-parole-errante.org/fichiers/Expo68/chantierranciere.pdf.
21. "Ouvrez les Guillemets," Première Chaîne de l'ORTF, 24 June 1974.
22. Guy Hocquenghem, *L'Après-Mai des Faunes* (Paris, 1974), 48 and 58.
23. Annie Cohen-Solal, *Sartre 1905–1980* (Paris, 1999); Didier Eribon, *Michel Foucault* (Paris, 2011).

24. Hocquenghem, *L'Après-Mai des Faunes*, 90.
25. Ibid., 49.
26. Ibid., 55, 59, and 62.
27. Ibid., 52–53.
28. Ibid., 54. Emphasis in original.
29. Ibid., 54–55.
30. Ibid., 56.
31. Virginie Linhart, *Volontaires pour L'Usine: Vies D'établis, 1967–1977* (Paris, 2010), 32–34. See also Marnix Dressen, *De L'Amphi à L'Etabli: Les Etudiants maoïstes à l'usine (1967–1989)* (Paris, 1999); Nicolas Hatzfeld, "Les établis: du projet politique à l'expérience sociale," in *68, une histoire collective*, ed. Philippe Artières and Michelle Zancarini-Fournel (Paris, 2008).
32. Robert Linhart, *L'Établi* (Paris, 1978). Translated as *The Assembly Line* by Margaret Crosland (Amherst, 1981).
33. Linhart, *Volontaires pour L'Usine*, 114 and 46–47.
34. Hocquenghem, *L'Après-Mai des Faunes*, 61–62.
35. Ibid., 114–119, 84–85; Andrew J. Diamond, Romain Huret, and Caroline Rolland-Diamond, *Révoltes et Utopies: La Contre-Culture Américaine des Années 60* (Paris, 2012), 88–89.
36. Hocquenghem, *L'Après-Mai des Faunes*, 55, 80–81.
37. Manus McGrogan, *Tout! in Context 1968–1973: French Radical Press at the Crossroads of Far Left, New Movements and Counterculture*. Ph.D. Dissertation (Portsmouth, 2010), 82–83 and 2–3.
38. McGrogan, *Tout! in Context 1968–1973*, 87 and 100.
39. Hocquenghem, *L'Après-Mai des Faunes*, 77–80.
40. Ibid., 79.
41. Ibid., 125–126.
42. Ibid., 91. See also Hocquenghem, *Le Désir homosexuel*, 167–168 (surprisingly, this sentence is absent from the English translation of the book).
43. *Le FHAR*, Roussopoulos.
44. Hocquenghem, *L'Après-Mai des Faunes*, 188.
45. Hocquenghem, *Homosexual Desire*, 72.
46. Monique Wittig, *The Straight Mind and Other Essays* (Boston, MA, 1992), 17–18.
47. *La Révolution du Désir*, directed by Alessandro Avellis (France, 2006); "Le Témoignage d'Anne-Marie Fauret," *Gai Pied* no. 25 (April 1981): 36; Anne-Marie Fauret, "Libération des Femmes, Année Zéro," *Arcadie* no. 297 (March 1971): 142–146.
48. Gildas Le Dem, "Cette Américaine qui a Allumé le FHAR," *Têtu* no. 165 (April 2011); Françoise Flamant, *À Tire d'Elles: Itinéraires de Féministes Radicales des Années 1970* (Rennes, 2007), 149–159.
49. Françoise d'Eaubonne, "Le FHAR, Origines et Illustrations," *La Revue H* no. 2 (1996). Interview of the author with Marie-Jo Bonnet, 5 November 2012.
50. Emphasis in original.
51. Mouvement de libération des femmes (MLF), *Textes Premiers* (Paris, 2009), 33–35 (this and the previous quotations).
52. FHAR, *Rapport Contre la Normalité*, 8.

53. FHAR, *Rapport Contre la Normalité*, 49; *Gulliver* no. 1 (November 1972).
54. MLF, *Textes Premiers*, 139–141.
55. Hocquenghem, *L'Après-Mai des Faunes*, 158–159.
56. Hocquenghem, *Homosexual Desire*, 135.
57. In 1973, around Hocquenghem, a group born of the FHAR is behind the publication of an issue dedicated to homosexuality in the review *Recherches*, review of the CERFI edited by Guattari ("Trois Milliards de Pervers," *Recherches* no. 12 [1973]: 214).
58. Guy Hocquenghem, *L'Après-Mai des Faunes*, 203–204.
59. Guy Hocquenghem, "Volutions," trans. Ron Haas, *Radical Philosophy Review* 11, no. 1 (2008): 27–33.
60. Michel Foucault, Preface to *Anti-Œdipus: Capitalism and Schizophrenia* by Gilles Deleuze and Félix Guattari (Minneapolis, MN, 1983), xi–xii.
61. Bernard Brillant, "Le Gauchisme et Ses Cultures Politiques," in *68, une histoire collective*, ed. Philippe Artières and Michelle Zancarini-Fournel (Paris, 2008), 553.
62. Ross, *May '68 and Its Afterlives*, 116.

Bibliography

Arnaud, Claude. *Qu'As-Tu Fait de Tes Frères?* Paris: Grasset, 2010.
Bourdieu, Pierre. *Manet: Une Révolution Symbolique*. Paris: Seuil/Raisons d'agir, 2013.
——— "La Révolution Impressionniste." *Noroit*, 303 (1987).
———. *Les Règles de L'Art*. Paris: Seuil, 1998.
Brillant, Bernard. "Le Gauchisme et Ses Cultures Politiques." In *68, une histoire collective*, edited by Philippe Artières and Michelle Zancarini-Fournel, 556–562. Paris: La Découverte, 2008.
Cohen-Solal, Annie. *Sartre 1905–1980*. Paris: Gallimard, 1999.
Deleuze, Gilles. "Entretien sur *L'Anti-Œdipe*." In *Pourparlers 1972–1990*, 24–38. Paris: Éditions de Minuit, 2003.
Deleuze, Gilles, and Félix Guattari. *Anti-Œdipus: Capitalism and Schizophrenia*. Minneapolis: University of Minnesota Press, 1983.
Dressen, Marnix. *De L'Amphi à L'Etabli: Les Etudiants maoïstes à l'usine (1967–1989)*. Paris: Belin, 1999.
d'Eaubonne, Françoise. "Le FHAR, Origines et Illustrations." *La Revue H* no. 2 (1996): 18–30.
Elias, Norbert. *Mozart: Portrait of a Genius*. Cambridge: Polity Press, 1993.
"Entretien avec Jacques Rancière," In *La Parole Errante: De Mai 68 à....* Retrieved 10 July 2018 from http://www.la-parole-errante.org/fichiers/Expo68/chantierranciere.pdf.
Eribon, Didier. *Michel Foucault*. Paris: Flammarion, 2011.
———. *Returning to Reims*. Boston, MA: The MIT Press, 2013.
Faburel, Véronique. "La Jeunesse communiste révolutionnaire: 1966–1968." MA Thesis. Paris: University of Paris I, 1988.
FHAR. *Rapport Contre la Normalité*. Montpellier, France: GayKitschCamp, 2013.
Flamant, Françoise. *À Tire d'Elles: Itinéraires de Féministes Radicales des Années 1970*. Rennes: Presses universitaires de Rennes, 2007.

Foucault, Michel. Preface to *Anti-Œdipus: Capitalism and Schizophrenia* by Gilles Deleuze and Félix Guattari. Minneapolis: University of Minnesota Press, 1983.
Hatzfeld, Nicolas. "Les établis: du projet politique à l'expérience sociale." In *68, une histoire collective*, edited by Philippe Artières and Michelle Zancarini-Fournel, 546–549. Paris: La Découverte, 2008.
Hocquenghem, Guy. *L'Amphithéâtre des Morts*. Paris: Gallimard, 1994.
———. *L'Après-Mai des Faunes*. Paris: Grasset, 1974.
———. *La Dérive Homosexuelle*. Paris: Éditions Jean-Pierre Delarge, 1977.
———. *Homosexual Desire*. Translated by Daniella Dangoor. Durham, NC: Duke University Press, 1993.
———. *Un journal de rêve: Articles de presse (1970–1987)*. Paris: Verticales, 2017.
———. "Volutions." Translated by Ron Haas. *Radical Philosophy Review* 11, no. 1 (2008): 27–33.
Idier, Antoine. *Les Vies de Guy Hocquenghem: Politique, sexualité, culture*. Paris: Fayard, 2017.
Kaplan, Leslie. *Depuis maintenant: Miss Nobody Knows*. Paris: P.O.L., 1996.
La Révolution du Désir, directed by Alessandro Avellis (France: Hysterie Prod, 2006), 80 min.
Le FHAR, directed by Roussopoulos (France: Vidéo Out, 1971), 26 min.
Le Dem, Gildas. "Cette Américaine qui a Allumé le FHAR," *Têtu* no. 165 (April 2011).
Linhart, Robert. *L'Établi*. Paris: Éditions de Minuit, 1978.
Linhart, Virginie. *Volontaires pour L'Usine: Vies D'établis, 1967–1977*. Paris: Le Seuil, 2010.
McGrogan, Manus. *Tout! in Context 1968–1973: French Radical Press at the Crossroads of Far Left, New Movements and Counterculture*. Ph.D. Dissertation, Portsmouth: University of Portsmouth, 2010.
Mouvement de libération des femmes (MLF). *Textes Premiers*. Paris: Stock, 2009.
Prique, Alain. "Rencontre avec Michel Cressole." In *Résister—Vivre la Mémoire. Acte I*, 1994.
Rolin, Jean. *L'Organisation*. Paris: Gallimard, 1996.
Rolin, Olivier. *Tigre en Papier*. Paris: Seuil, 2003.
Ross, Kristin. *May '68 and Its Afterlives*. Chicago: University of Chicago Press, 2002.
Wittig, Monique. *The Straight Mind and Other Essays*. Boston, MA: Beacon Press, 1992.

Chapter 5

New Feminism, Women's Subjectivity, and Feminist Politics

Conceptual Transfers and Activist Inspirations in Yugoslavia in the 1970s and 1980s

Zsófia Lóránd

Emotions, subjectivity, and personal experience have been at the heart of feminist activism since the 1960s, not only in Europe and North America but across the globe. When researching, analyzing, and presenting movements that have explored female agency and sought to make what women feel a political matter, it is essential to focus on what women thought and what women had to say about the way they saw the world, how they expressed their subjectivity. This is especially true with regard to the era of state socialism in Central and Eastern Europe in the 1970s and 1980s. In these years, as recent historiography has highlighted, new approaches to subjectivities, emotions, and politics were developed in intellectual dissident and (pop) cultural underground scenes.[1] A fascinating example of this is the emergence of *Žena i društvo* (Woman and society), a well-organized and highly active radical feminist group in Yugoslavia during the time of state socialism. New Yugoslav feminism, as the protagonists in this story often referred to it, should be interpreted as both an intellectual enterprise and as a discursive and physical space where alternative subjectivities and lifestyles could be fashioned.

In this chapter, I examine the personal and the subjective in the interactions between intellectual and political texts (including artwork and literary writing), and the social practices that these texts both drew on and criticized. The material varies from the academic writings of social scientists and humanities scholars, such as Gordana Cerjan-Letica, Rada Iveković, Nada Ler Sofronić, Nada Popović Perišić, Ingrid Šafranek, and Jelena Zuppa, to psychologists such as Lepa Mlađenović and Vera Smiljanić, and writers such as Slavenka Drakulić. I also draw on interviews with other activists and members of feminist groups. My aim in this chapter is to show how women's subjectivity and feminist politics were shaped by the Yugoslav feminist discourse and feminist practice, and how this can be put in dialogue with other subcultures west of the Iron Curtain. My analysis pays particular attention to how political contexts changed meanings and stakes: in a socialist context, critiques of capitalism and critiques of state socialist practices carried different messages, and new Yugoslav feminism found a way to formulate both.

Feminist intellectuals in Yugoslavia at the time were looking for ways to reframe the "women's question" and the approach toward gender equality under state socialism in accordance with feminist ideas about a woman's place in society. Their achievement is particularly important considering how often female thinkers have been neglected within histories of political thought and philosophy. Looking at the history of feminism in Yugoslavia in the 1970s and 1980s, ideas about subjectivity and the self were embedded into a discourse that is intellectually fascinating for various reasons. Several texts reflect on the questions that this volume raises regarding people's search for the "truth about oneself," and the way in which activists (or in this case, critical intellectuals who later became activists) searched for an "authentic" form of subjectivity. And even though new Yugoslav feminists did not explicitly engage in discussions about authenticity, they searched for meanings of womanhood and female subjectivity. The new feminist discourse in Yugoslavia was thus not only connected with North American and Western Europe through transfers and translations, but also through similar questions and answers.

For the most part, this chapter provides an intellectual history of new feminism in Yugoslavia, but it is also infused with cultural and social history and a study of the interaction between individual biographies and the broader history of the feminist movement and its members. This approach allows me to look at subjectivity and emotions, and examine the way these can be related to discourses and practices of authenticity elsewhere, as a matter of intellectual history.

In his study of the changing field of the history of political thought, Michael Freeden emphasizes how movements shape ideologies.[2] This is certainly true in the case of Yugoslav feminism: practices were often translated into theory. A broad pool of actions contributed to changes in ideas, including the practices through which the feminist groups operated: the circumstances under which they met, the ways the participants behaved toward each other, who could participate in what and how. After establishing that the sociopolitical mattered, we also need to understand that the personal mattered; in my analysis, I will turn the "personal is political" argument "upside down" by arguing that feminists in Yugoslavia wrote political texts to prove the importance of the personal. I examine these texts to show that these, in turn, offer new approaches to the self.

When studying countercultures under state socialism in Eastern and Central Europe, and the role of leftist, anticapitalist ideas and movements within this region, it is crucial to bear in mind that the ideas so important for the Western New Left, such as alienation within the capitalist system of labor, were part of the official discourse that countercultural and dissenting groups were challenging. However different from context to context, the post-1945 state discourse sought to create a new and real identity for socialist society: the new man and the new woman who were hardworking, progressive, revolutionary, sincere, and true in these attitudes. They were, according to the state prescribed ideal, authentic socialist subjects.[3] Any reference or claim to new identities meant having to engage with this discourse. At the same time, as the ideologies of these regimes were discredited, dissidents returned to the idea of truth, as opposed to the lies of the corrupted regime. The position of dissidents who called for "living in truth,"[4] was on one end of the spectrum of being critical. On the other end were new Yugoslav feminists, who took a different position. These activists engaged with the state from the outset and were therefore closer to "political civil society," rather than to the antipolitics (that is, the turning away from state-controlled politics) of the dissidents of the 1980s.[5] The New Yugoslav feminist position, therefore, can be seen as a middle ground between the dissident practice of total secession from the state and acceptance of the regime as entirely legitimate. By focusing their critique on patriarchy, however, Yugoslav feminists were in debate with both the socialist state and other dissenting, dissident, and countercultural groups. As we shall see, their anticapitalism and the acknowledgement of at least some of the achievements of the regime with regard to women's emancipation (an issue mostly ignored by liberal dissidents and seen as one of the crimes of the regimes by the conservative-nationalist critics) went hand-in-hand with a strong critique of what others had failed to do or even to problematize.

The New Yugoslav Feminists: Ideas, Practices, Institutions

It was a group of mostly young women based at the universities in Zagreb and Ljubljana and in students' cultural centers in Belgrade and Ljubljana who began reading and writing about feminism in the early 1970s. Starting with publications in the field of the humanities and social sciences and subsequently by investigating feminist issues through literature and art, the *Žena i društvo* collective introduced feminist matters to the public through the mass media. Eventually, they turned to activism. Inspirations came from the feminist movements of the 1960s and 1970s in North America and Western Europe. Activists were especially interested in radical and socialist feminist ideas as well as French post-structuralism; revisionist Marxist texts and new approaches to psychoanalysis were also extensively read and discussed. There is a strong overlap between the language they developed through their intellectual endeavors and their activism: language created practice and practice created discourse. One way of theory becoming "practice" was the establishment of SOS helplines and shelters in Zagreb, Belgrade, and Ljubljana in the 1980s for women and children who had been victims of domestic and gender-based violence. These shelters served as semi-institutions, replacing the missing infrastructure the state failed to provide.

Between the 1970s and the early 1990s, the Yugoslav socialist system first opened up and then fell apart. But before the system collapsed, there were a few years of hope. These years of openness and relative stability gave women the opportunity to engage in feminist activism. In their endeavor, they were inspired by the partisan myth of the emancipated woman: according to official historiographies, hundreds of thousands of women had participated in the National Liberation Struggle during World War II. The new feminists' generation (with a small number of exceptions, such as the philosopher Blaženka Despot and Gordana Bosanac) was born after the war, from mothers who had firsthand experience of the war and who had very often been active participants in the partisan movement. Unlike their mothers, who saw movements toward gender equality in the post-World War II years as a drastic improvement, this new generation of women was puzzled by the contradiction between the promises of equality from the regime and their own perceived lack of emancipation.[6] The new feminists realized that despite the implementation of legislation ensuring suffrage, equal pay, childcare services and, with the exception of one year, access to abortion, and despite the changes in social status brought about by attempts of socialist modernization (alphabetization, urbanization, industrialization), ultimately, patriarchy had not disappeared. Women were still struggling with an unequal share of domestic labor, with what we today would call the "glass ceiling," as well as violence in their homes; even their reproductive rights were not safe beyond doubt.

By engaging in a dialogue with the state, premised on its supposed commitment to gender equality, the new Yugoslav feminists did not directly oppose the Yugoslav state, but instead saw women's roles as constantly keeping the state in check. As Nada Ler-Sofronić put it:

> throughout the thousand-year long oppression of women, women could maintain a relatively autonomous position ... [while they] had

to obey the rule of those in power, fit into the system and the existing order. While doing so, they remained in opposition and they managed to preserve an inner, a different sociability in themselves [*društvenost*], with the help of psychological resistance and by constantly reminding themselves of their dissatisfactory position.[7]

The approach that suggested that women's oppression created an inner resistance characterized the ways in which feminists in Yugoslavia related to institutions. To offer one example: many of the new feminists worked at the students' centers and at the universities, and actively used the space offered by these state institutions to resist and criticize the state.

Reconsidering the Private-Public Divide in Theory and Practice

The new Yugoslav feminists joined feminists in North America and Western Europe in arguing that the personal was political.[8] Placing "the personal" and women's everyday life experiences at the center of intellectual debates resulted in discussions about female subjectivity and the very meaning of the concept of "womanhood." It is impossible to provide a single definition of this concept, which might be best described as "real womanhood," not least because of the highly theoretical, postmodern, debates that characterized feminist thinking during this time. This was as much the case in Yugoslavia as it was in Italy or France (consider, for example, the writings of Julia Kristeva, Hélène Cixous, Luce Irigaray).[9] In the hands of theorists such as Rada Iveković, Nada Popović-Perišić, Ingrid Šafranek, and Jelena Zuppa, the concept of "womanhood" gained a new meaning.[10] The resistance against a single definition created a certain tension in the discussions. These thinkers addressed the silenced, hidden, and suppressed as opposed to addressing a fixed category, such as the category of authenticity, which would only replace previous fixed categories.

The main terrain where many of these arguments took place was in the discussion of the concept of the *écriture féminine*, a concept that had been developed by French post-poststructuralist feminist theorists and that entered Yugoslav discourse through reinterpretation and re-appropriation. New Yugoslav feminists used it to replace the concept of "women's literature," (*ženska književnost*), which reduced the idea to texts written by women, with their version of the *écriture féminine*, the *žensko pismo*. The precise wording matters here. As opposed to the most common English translation of the *écriture feminine* ("women's writing"), *žensko* means "feminine," rather than "women's," closer to the French original *feminine*; *žensko* thus points towards the constructed, the façade, the attributed. The concept was already being employed in the discussions of the time and became even more common with the spread of the sex-gender differentiation from the mid-1980s onward. Yugoslav authors used the idea of the *žensko pismo* in their explorations of the results of women's oppression. Rada Iveković, for example, relied on Irigaray and her argument from *Speculum de l'autre femme* that in a man's world, a woman is left to the role of an image in the mirror: "a woman is what is not, her history is empty history, non-history, the history of the other, a history of power from which she is excluded."[11]

This predefined, subjugated woman is not what Iveković, relying on Irigaray, wanted to recreate. Iveković, a philosopher by training, together with literary scholars Nada Popović-Perišić, Ingrid Šafranek, and Jelena Zuppa, argued against fixed meanings of the concept of womanhood and tried to relate feminism as activism and as theory.[12] A debate in 1983 that resulted from an essay written by Ingrid Šafranek reveals the main concerns about the celebration of even a reinterpreted concept of *écriture féminine*.[13] Šafranek expressed fears of the reductionist potential of the concept and criticized Cixous's refusal to give a concrete and fixed definition of *écriture féminine*. Cixous's refusal was also mocked by sociologist Vjeran Katunarić, who suggested that if a definition was impossible, it would make no sense to stay at the public forum, and that everyone might as well just go home. Literary scholar Jelena Zuppa in turn argued that "the drama" Katunarić proposed was unnecessary, and supported Šafranek's explanation that, while it would be hard to articulate a definition due to the "natural openness" of the concept, it was not impossible.[14] A series of articles explored the further implications of the concept, providing both arguments for a search for women's experience and a language in which experiences could be conveyed, an endeavor for which knowing women's sexuality and imagination was essential.[15]

Besides the explorations of *žensko pismo*, several other texts that address key concepts such as *consciousness* and *subjugation* (of women) offered feminist reinterpretations and critical assessments of the previous conceptualizations of what being a woman meant. Feminist authors argued that solving the problems of women's subjugation would be impossible within the overarching framework of the class question, and that explaining this subjugation with biological reasoning would be equally impossible. They also frequently emphasized that the personal plays a crucial role in society, and that we can understand the human psyche only in its social context. Psychologist Vera Smiljanić was one of the first to publish on the relation between the psyche and society, arguing that social factors explain psychological differences between men and women.[16] This was one of the many ways in which Yugoslav feminists reassessed differences between men and women and spoke about women's subjectivity. The role of psychologists became even more crucial during the 1980s when Yugoslav feminists moved toward grassroots activism and fought violence against women.

Women first problematized the private-public division and the role of consciousness in feminist thought and practice by reading and critically reassessing Marx and Marxism.[17] Reading Marxist texts through a psychological lens demonstrated the possibilities of reconsidering the role of consciousness in new feminist discourse and politics. In fact, consciousness as a topic entered Yugoslav feminist discussions via a detour: contemporaries in the United States had taken the Marxian concept of consciousness and adopted it within their grassroots, radical feminist groups to suit their cause.[18] Yugoslav feminists became fascinated by the concept of women's consciousness as it was used by the American feminists. In 1981, Nada Ler-Sofronić located "the radicalization of women's consciousness in their awareness of their own subordination and exploitation in private life and in their interpersonal relations."[19] She emphasized the possibilities of reaching and developing women's consciousness, based on the acknowledgement that there were different types of oppression, each of which required different qualities and depths of "revolutionary praxis." While feminists used consciousness for their own agenda, they also argued that the feminist reassessment of the private could enrich Marxist thought. As sociologist Gordana Cerjan-Letica argued, "the feminist theoretical penetration into the sphere of the 'private' reveals to Marxism a multitude of new and not insignificant elements of social relations in the family and in smaller communities of contemporary capitalism."[20] These critical interventions into questions of womanhood, femininity, women's consciousness, and subjectivity meant an evolution of discussions about how women participated in society and the possibilities of, and strategies for, women's emancipation in a socialist society.

Claiming Space: The Body between the Public and the Private

In order to put the idea that the "personal is political" into practice within Yugoslav new feminism, the first necessary step was to turn to the experience of individual women, as the ultimate proof that, even if emancipation was guaranteed on paper, it had many flaws in reality. These experiences provided a basis for political action. Activist work thus became a new kind of research and a source for gaining a different kind of knowledge. Both chronologically and intellectually, the new Yugoslav feminists' trajectory can be described as a transition from theory to activism. In the meantime, feminist scholarship developed new approaches to the most burning issues of feminist activism that created a discourse that shaped the tools and agenda of the women who would later become activists. The shift toward activism around 1985–1986 was seen as a "second wave" of new Yugoslav feminism. Feminists now began to turn to higher-level politics. This development fits into the more general emergence of a new civil society in the region, as the political landscape in Yugoslavia and the entire region of Eastern Europe was changing. Finally, lesbian group members were gaining more and more of a voice, which led to a significant restructuring of the *Žena i društvo* groups and re-energized them. The most important step, also signaling a "second wave" of new Yugoslav feminism, was the creation of women-only groups in the mid-1980s.

This was also a time for other types of organizing: the earlier work that had taken place in private or semi-private spaces prepared participants for activism in the public sphere. The highly informal meetings of earlier times, which had taken place in kitchens, cafés, or pubs, and the talks about psychoanalysis at the psychologist Vera Smiljanić's apartment (which the Belgrade activist and psychologist Sofija Trivunac remembers as "consciousness-raising meetings"), grew into university seminars, conferences, parties, and activist projects. By entering the public sphere, private issues could be discussed in that space too. It should be mentioned that even in the 1970s, groups of young women got together in pubs without male company (for example, the *Marjež kafana*, which journalist Lina Vušković attended and recalled that they "never left in a bad mood"), and kitchen tables were used for far more than social reproduction (cooking), as sites for discussing political issues and organizing a movement. But by the 1980s, feminists in Yugoslavia were entering the streets too, within the available possibilities. For example, they conducted street polls (*anketiranje*) on topics such as "what do you think of equality" or "solidarity among women." If academic work created a feminist language, the *tribine*, seminars and informal talks were also scenes of activist socialization, while women-only groups became a nest for explicit political participation. The turn happened around 1985–1986. The "mastermind" behind it was Lepa Mlađenović. A psychologist by training, she started traveling to workshops about women's health and thereby learned about new methods of organizing. If Zagreb was the most prominent site for developing academic strands of "new Yugoslav feminism," primarily because most journals and intellectuals were based there, the Belgrade Students' Cultural Centre (the SKC) and the Ljubljana group contributed significantly to the movement's shift toward activism.

As the focus shifted increasingly toward the body, sexuality (including sexual identity and orientation, contraception, and sexual life), health and violence, and after years of experience with male members as regular participants at different events and meetings, the question of whether it was appropriate for men to be allowed to participate eventually arose. Lepa Mlađenović argued that in women's health workshops, it was easier for women to share their experiences and work for change in an exclusively female environment. Her experiences convinced her that the *Žena i društvo* group needed reorganization too. Mlađenović believed that "safe spaces"— that is, spaces free of men—not only helped the consciousness-raising activities of women, but also had the potential to facilitate a learning environment that was significantly better than mixed groups.

The question of men's participation proved to be a divisive one, and it resulted in changes for the new Yugoslav feminist groups in the three big cities. Some women left, others joined; certain incumbent members became stronger and more vocal. Whether someone was for or against women-only groups depended on how they perceived the participation of men before, as well as one's sexual identity. Participating men were often partners of feminists, mostly from left-wing or liberal circles. Intellectual men, who would later become important members of the antinationalist opposition against Milošević, often attended the meetings of the *Žena i društvo* group at SKC. However, women had mixed feelings about the presence of men, and the decision to exclude men divided the group members.[21]

For some women, the exclusion of male participants was a reason to leave the group. Sofija Trivunac, for example, gave the following explanation: "When the group decided that we would exclude men, I left. After my training in England, I believed that women should feel equal and strong in mixed company, and this women-only group felt like a step back in history." However, Trivunac admitted that there were other reasons to leave: "I was also tired already and wanted to focus more on my research, my private practice and my clinical work." Other members stayed, even though they disagreed with the exclusion of men. Lina Vušković emphasizes that some men who were genuinely interested in feminism attended the meetings, like Ivan Vejvoda and Nebojša Popov. In Ljubljana, members also debated whether men should be allowed to participate. The group's first big public event was a women-only party, a huge success with hundreds of guests. Recalling their experiences of having male participants in meetings in Zagreb, Vesna Kesić and Nadežda Čačinović note that much depended on the individuals.

She refines the picture by adding that there were also men who were supportive and contributed to the discussion in a meaningful way, for example Vjeran Katunarić, who she claimed really did understand what feminism was about. Lepa Mlađenović remembers the situation in a simple and balanced way: there were always one or two men who came to the meetings, asked the same questions and made the same comments, constantly forcing the group to return to the beginnings of the discussion.

Sexual Politics: Redefining the Female Body

Women's sexuality and women's bodies were common topics of discussion within the new Yugoslav feminist groups. Finding a language about their bodies helped women to express and experience their sexuality. The feminist discourse in Yugoslavia, as much as anywhere else, sought to re-appropriate the female body. The unique political context in Yugoslavia altered the stakes of the feminist endeavor: women in Yugoslavia lived in a state that provided access to abortion (no matter the quality of the service) and free health care (paid for in taxes), but still did not imagine the "new socialist woman" as being sexually liberated. In general, the health advice books and leaflets accessible to women after 1945 depicted women as mothers and workers.[22] Artists and writers, influenced by the new feminist discourse around them, wanted to offer a different type of idea of women's lives and women experiencing their bodies, challenging the proclaimed truth about the subject.

Feminist ideas about sexuality were first explored in the arts, literature, and essays. The discourse of the sexual revolution, which was still patriarchal but nevertheless stretched boundaries, was a first step toward liberating the language. It was very much present in the Yugoslav countercultural and even popular cultural scenes.[23] Writers and artists such as Slavenka Drakulić, Katalin Ladik, Vlasta Delimar, Sanja Iveković, even Marina Abramović, made contributions. These artists participated in exhibitions at major contemporary art galleries, and published novels that were accessible in any bookstore. As literary scholar Jasmina Lukić writes, Slavenka Drakulić was the first author in Yugoslav literature who introduced female sexuality from a woman's point of view into the discourse.[24] In her essays as well as in her two early novels, *Holograms of Fear* and *Marble Skin*, Drakulić draws attention to the troubled relationship between women and their bodies that were shaped by expectations, discipline, and violence, but were also a surface of desire and appreciation. The women in her novels do not easily accept the objectification of their bodies, posing a "long war of the naked Venus." The trope characterizes her work as well as the contemporary women's art scene: the naked Venus is demanding its moment and its space in art history. These bodies often bear resemblance to the Venuses and caryatides of the male artists in their appearance, but not in their behavior. They scream (Katalin

Ladik), they speak of their orgasms (Vlasta Delimar), they speak of their lack of orgasm, they pretend to masturbate (Sanja Iveković: *Trokut*), or they lie down in the middle of a fire circle and almost die (Abramović: *Rhythm 5*). In some cases, their bodies have ceased to be beautiful and become ill. These representations and recreations of the female body contrasted the patriarchal construction of womanhood.

Similar to many other feminists of the time, Drakulić refuted and refused the ideology of the "sexual revolution" as liberating for women.[25] Presenting sociological arguments in her essays, she addresses the alienation and objectification of the female body which the so-called sexual revolution did not question at all. Sanja Iveković, a visual artist starting her career in Yugoslavia in the 1970s, produced a sarcastic series of drawings of the unfulfilled promises of this revolution, with the title *Čekajući revoluciju (Alice)* (Waiting for a revolution [Alice], 1982). In the four identical drawings, a girl or young woman stares at a frog, the only difference between the drawings being the color of the frog. Expecting a revolution, in a context that is supposedly post-revolutionary and where women have more than a princess could ever have dreamt of, is already sarcastic. The colors of the frog are the wrapping of the promises of a revolution, and although the colors may change, neither these promises nor the prince will ever arrive. The drawing is a gesture to both the partisan and the sexual revolutions: they changed the colors, but the same little frog still remained. Iveković and Marina Abramović, also a visual artist, most explicitly reflect on the political regime: putting the symbols of the Titoist regime and their own bodies in interaction facilitates multilayered interpretations of the place and possibilities of the female body within the system.

In her piece *Trokut* (Triangle), Sanja Iveković uses the act of masturbation to disrupt a political charade. She reclaims the discourse surrounding orgasms in women's magazines, finally bringing the topic into the public discourse after it had been silenced in the popular educational publications about women's health. In these publications, a woman's right to sexual pleasure and fulfillment was either not discussed at all, or, if it was discussed, was simply taken for granted: in *Higenija žene*, the author quotes statistics of women's orgasms during sexual intercourse with a man they are married to. More progressive statements in the book argued that the frigidity that caused the lack of orgasm was not the woman's fault, but caused by her partner's inability to please her. According to the author, "women with normal sexual sensitivity experience orgasm during all, or almost all sexual intercourse."[26] The claim implied that women's ability to reach orgasm would be a proof of their "normal" sexuality, which excluded non-heterosexual women from the sphere of normality. It also posited that reaching orgasm did not depend on both partners, but was simply an objective quality of women's normality.

The Role of the Body in the New Activism against Violence against Women

The possibility for women to talk about the gender-based violence they endured gave way to changes in the ways women organized, spoke, and lived. This was the case in Yugoslavia too. Several small group discussions took place in the Belgrade SKC, where women shared experiences and gathered knowledge about gendered violence. These discussions related to the way feminists reconceptualized womanhood. Challenging the official image of the emancipated, new woman, liberated by the socialist regime, feminists made violence against women a central issue, pointing out several layers of women's oppression that questioned the official success story. Discussions about the body shifted from theory and art toward women's health, reproductive rights and violence, emphasizing the deep interconnectedness of these issues.

Women discussed a broad range of topics that went beyond the topics addressed by magazines and journals, because the discussion format allowed for more flexibility. Belgrade group *Feministička grupa žena i društvo* (FGŽD, Feminist Group Women and Society) enjoyed great freedom in this regard. The group organized an entire series of events about women's health in March-April 1986, mostly women-only events due to the sensitive topics. It began with an event about the "feminist approach to women's health" in general, at which Lepa Mlađenović talked.[27] At another event, Gordana Cerjan-Letica, a sociologist working on health and medicine, gave a talk with the provocative title, "Medicine or Poison: Medicine as the Tool of Social Control," while Sofija Trivunac facilitated a discussion about abortion entitled: "What Does Abortion Mean to Us?" Mlađenović recalls that twenty-five women came together and shared their experiences; it was surprising for them to learn how many of them had already had an abortion.

Women also discussed health, body images, and nutrition and the contradictions and difficulties this entailed, both in terms of how it affected their health and looks, and in terms of their roles as mothers and housewives feeding others. The discussion was facilitated by Vesna Dražilović, who later continued to work on women's issues and the healthcare system. Sladjana Marković led a further *tribina* about women and AIDS, and Sonja Lončar organized a meeting on the myth of women's heterosexuality. To make women more aware of their bodies, a medical doctor, Svetlana Mitraković was asked to give a talk about hormonal change and menopause.[28]

Feminists elaborated on their critique of health care institutions in a discussion about violence-free childbirth and alternative modes of giving birth, which featured Snežana Simić, Danica Radović-Solomun, and Snežana Adašević-Petrović. At another event, the Belgrade feminists invited former patients of psychiatric hospitals to share and discuss their experiences. Again, Western movements inspired Yugoslav feminists, as the example of Lepa Mlađenović shows. Mlađenović's views on the violence produced by institutions of psychiatry and more generally on the ways in which women's health and violence against women were treated by the institutions, were heavily influenced by the Democratic Psychiatry movement in Italy and the antipsychiatry movement in Britain. Her understanding was that the institution of psychiatry is totalitarian, violent, and does not accommodate difference. Mental hospitals, she argued, should be demolished and replaced by new mental health centers. Within the wide and complex set of approaches of antipsychiatry activists, Mlađenović's was primarily focused on ensuring a more humane treatment of psychiatric patients.[29]

In 1981, an entire series of reports were published in magazines, on the various facets of violence that women had to endure in patriarchal society. In one piece, Jasenka Kodrnja wrote about her experience of giving birth, and suggested that giving birth in a hospital environment was a form of violence against women: "I imagined giving birth to one's own baby to be a joyful event, in which staff help us, because it's their job. After giving birth, I felt as if I had been raped: by some unknown people, institutions, circumstances."[30]

In an interview, Sofija Trivunac said that her experiences of giving birth resembled the experience that Kodrnja had described in her account. Trivuanc also explained how this unpleasant experience inspired her to begin focusing on the topic.

> After I gave birth to my second daughter, I started working more intensely on trauma prevention during child birth. This was based on my very bad experience in a socialist hospital. At the time, I wasn't participating in the feminist group any more, but I think that this was serious feminist work: we focused a lot on power relations and stereotypes.[31]

Other articles, some written by local authors and some translated from Western authors, further challenged the notion that the health care system was unbiased and operating with the single objective of healing its patients in the best possible way. These writings pointed out how gendered and class-based power relations defined the ways the health care system works. As highlighted above—in Kodrnja's story about her personal experience and in Trivunac's comments during the interview—activists reflected on the social and gender imbalances within the health care system, and questioned the prescribed ways in which women were expected to do things with their bodies.

These authors and articles also problematized the ways in which existing institutions exerted violence on women in order to make them obey. The discourse on violence against women was closely related to the foundation of the first SOS-helplines aiming to support women and children victims of domestic violence. The creation of the helplines provides a final example of how the feminist slogan "the personal is political" came to life. Publications, such as the work of the criminologist Vesna Nikolić-Ristanović on violence against women, the writings of the helpline volunteers in academic journals, and political newspapers, made the personal political, and the private public.[32] The inspiration and the source of courage for women to make their personal issues political came from intellectual debates and publications. Transforming texts into action and practice, turning ideological dissent into political disagreement, is one of the most valid ways to describe what happened within new Yugoslav feminism.

Feminists set an agenda and developed a practice through discourse. Understanding their own position through theoretical concepts such as subjugation, oppression, women's identity, subjectivity, and consciousness made intellectual women in Yugoslavia realize that change was necessary. The theoretical texts gave them courage to question existing paradigms and discuss problems that were treated as nonexistent. Writing about the *écriture féminine* made them aware of the importance of the body. Reading gender-conscious literature in the field of psychology made them question institutionalized knowledge. The ideas of the "new man" and "new woman" were challenged by finding a new language to delineate existing problems and through activist practices, such as the discussion groups, the street polling, or the SOS helplines, to suggest solutions to them.

Conclusion

The Yugoslav feminist discussions, be they theoretical texts, magazine articles, activist pamphlets or small group meetings where women shared their experiences with each other, all reacted to the ways womanhood and femininity were prescribed to women. Whereas these critical reflections on the existing definitions can easily be read through the concept of "authenticity," it was not part of the new Yugoslav feminist vocabulary. Nevertheless, the way discussions about female subjectivity in the new Yugoslav feminist movement were framed does take us very close to explorations of authenticity that were prominent in other contexts, for example in the alternative milieu of West Germany or in feminism of the United States.[33] Ruth Colker, in one of her early writings on the radical feminist movement in the United States, argued: "Feminism ... recognizes that both women and men are far from exploring their authentic selves. Men's inauthenticity provides them with the tools of domination and power; women's inauthenticity provides them with the disabilities of subordination and weakness."[34] This concept of authenticity is very similar to West German and other New Leftist interpretations. As Sven Reichardt has shown, activists blamed oppressive systems, such as capitalism, for not allowing people to live an authentic life.

In Yugoslavia, however, as was the case in most state socialist regimes, the concept of authenticity had already been taken by the state. Therefore, other concepts needed to be utilized to frame criticism. Reclaiming women's subjectivity, reconceptualizing the idea of consciousness in a way that differed from existing Marxist interpretations, and talking about the personal and intimate opened up the idea of womanhood and femininity. By creating spaces where women could share their experiences and by building on these experiences in political activism, activists placed the personal back into the public space and offered alternative interpretations of what it meant to be a woman in Yugoslavia during this time.

Zsófia Lóránd is an intellectual historian of feminism in post-World War II socialist Eastern Europe. She got her Ph.D. at the Central European University in Budapest and has held positions at the European University Institute in Florence and the Lichtenberg-Kolleg in Göttingen. Her book *The Feminist Challenge to the Socialist State in Yugoslavia* is published in the Palgrave Macmillan series "Genders and Sexualities in History" in 2018. For eight years, she worked as an SOS-helpline volunteer and trainer in the field of domestic violence.

Notes

Short excerpts of this chapter have been published as part of the book: Zsófia Lóránd, *The Feminist Challenge to the Socialist State in Yugoslavia* (London: Palgrave Macmillan, 2018).

1. E.g., Daniel J. Goulding, ed., *Post New Wave Cinema in the Soviet Union and Eastern Europe* (Bloomington,, IN, 1989); Michal Kopeček and Piotr Wciślik, eds., *Thinking through Transition: Liberal Democracy, Authoritarian Pasts, and Intellectual History in East Central Europe after 1989* (New York, 2015); Piotr Piotrowski, *In the Shadow of Yalta: Art and the Avant-Garde in Eastern Europe, 1945–1989* (London, 2009);

Sabrina P. Ramet, ed., *Rocking the State: Rock Music and Politics in Eastern Europe and Russia* (Boulder, CO, 1994).
2. Michael Freeden, *Liberal Languages: Ideological Imaginations and Twentieth-Century Progressive Thought* (Princeton, NJ, 2005), 14.
3. For the Yugoslav context, see Igor Duda, *Danas kada postajem pionir: Djetinjstvo i ideologija jugoslavenskoga socijalizma* (Zagreb, 2015). For a variety of socialist contexts, see Yinghong Cheng, *Creating the New Man: From Enlightenment Ideals to Socialist Realities* (Honolulu, 2009); Lynne Attwood, *Creating the New Soviet Woman: Women's Magazines as Engineers of Female Identity, 1922–53* (New York, 1999); Libora Oates-Indruchová, "The Beauty and the Loser: Cultural Representations of Gender in Late State Socialism," *Signs* 37, no. 2 (2012): 357–383.
4. "They may be teachers who privately teach young people things that are kept from them in the state schools; clergymen who … try to carry on a free religious life; painters, musicians, and singers who practice their work regardless of how it is looked upon by official institutions; everyone who shares this independent culture and helps to spread it," Václav Havel, "The Power of the Powerless," trans. Paul Wilson.
5. Juan J. Linz and Alfred Stepan, *Problems of Democratic Transition and Consolidation: Southern Europe, South America, and Post-Communist Europe* (Baltimore, MD, 1996); Alan Renwick, "Anti-Political or Just Anti-Communist? Varieties of Dissidence in East-Central Europe and their Implications for the Development of Political Society." *East European Politics and Societies* 20, no. 2 (2006): 288.
6. See Sharon Zukin about Praxis: "For several older members of this group, the collective odyssey in dissent began in an unlikely way, in teenage heroism with the Partisans during World War II. … They were still party members and, unlike Đilas, remained in the party until the late 1960s." Sharon Zukin, "Sources of Dissent and Nondissent in Yugoslavia," in *Dissent in Eastern Europe*, ed. Jane Leftwich Curry (New York, 1983), 131.
7. Nada Ler-Sofronić, "Odiseja ljudskog identiteta žene", *Pitanja* no. 7–8 (1978): 21. All translations are mine unless otherwise stated. This text is very enigmatic in the Serbo-Croatian original.
8. Starting with the essay "What is Happening to American Women?" (Silva Mežnarić, "Što se događa s američkom ženom?" *Žena* 30, no. 6. [1972]: 57–62), followed by a variety of interpretative texts and translations in the coming two decades, in special issues of the journals such as *Student* no. 9 (1976), *Pitanja* no. 7–8 (1978), and *Argumenti* no. 1 (1979).
9. See e.g., Toril Moi, *Sexual/Textual Politics: Feminist Literary Theory* (London, [1985] 2002). *Sexual/Textual Politics* "starts with 'literary theory,' and ends with the concept of 'theory' that is starting to mean what is means today, namely someone like Marxist, poststructuralist, postcolonial, psychoanalytical, queer, feminist or variously postmodern thoughts about subjectivity, meaning, ideology and culture in their widest generality." Moi, *Sexual/Textual Politics*, 176.
10. Rada Iveković, "Ženska kreativnost i kreiranje žene" [Women's creativity and the creation of women], *Argumenti* no. 1 (1979): 139–147; Nada Popović-Perišić, *Literatura kao zavođenje* [Literature as seduction] (Beograd, 1986); Ingrid Šafranek, "'Ženska književnost' i 'žensko pismo'" ["Women's literature" and "women's

writing"], *Republika* no. 11–12 (1983): 7–28; Jelena Zuppa, "Novo žensko pismo: da bi se kazalo život" [New women's writing: So that life can show itself], *Delo* no. 4 (1981): 16; Jelena Zuppa, "Žena pisac i součenje s vlastatim položajem žene" [The woman as author and the confrontation with her position as a woman], *Žena* 38, no. 6 (1980): 50–62.

11. Iveković, "Ženska kreativnost i kreiranje žene," 143. Without quotation marks, from Irigaray's *Speculum de l'autre femme* (Paris, 1974 edition).
12. Popović-Perišić, *Literatura kao zavođenje*; Zuppa, "Žena pisac i součenje s vlastatim položajem žene"; Zuppa, "Novo žensko pismo: da bi se kazalo život."
13. Šafranek, "'Ženska književnost' i 'žensko pismo.'"
14. "Diskusija" following the essay in Šafranek, "'Ženska književnost' i 'žensko pismo,'" 23.
15. Zuppa, "Žena pisac i součenje s vlastatim položajem žene", 52.
16. Vera Smiljanić, "Socijalno poreklo psiholoških spolnih razlika" [The social origin of psychological sexual difference], *Psihološka istraživanja*, no. 3 (1984): 109–129.
17. I write about this in greater detail in "New Yugoslav Feminism during Socialism between 'Mainstreaming' and 'Disengagement': The Possibilities of Resistance, Critical Opposition and Dissent," *The Hungarian Historical Review* 5, no. 4 (2016): 854–881.
18. In Christine Stansell's opinion, the radical feminist vocabulary in the United States is more Marxist than feminist as such. See Christine Stansell, *The Feminist Promise: 1792 to Present* (New York, 2010), 230, 245.
19. Nada Ler-Sofronić, "Dijalektika odnosa polova i klasna svijest" [The dialectics of the relation of the sexes and class consciousness], *Dometi* 13, no. 2 (1980): 5–14.
20. Gordana Cerjan-Letica, "Feministička pitanja i marksistički odgovori" [Feminist questions and Marxist answers], *Naše teme* 24, no. 11 (1980): 1974. The two texts introduced: Sheila Rowbotham, "Dijalektičke smetnje" [Dialectical disturbances], *Naše teme* 24, no. 11 (1980): 1975–1993. [From Sheila Rowbotham, *Women, Resistance and Revolution* (London, 1975)]; Juliet Mitchell, "Položaj žene" [Women's estate], *Naše teme* 24, no. 11 (1980): 1994–2012. [From Juliet Mitchell, *Woman's Estate* (London, 1971)].
21. My interviewees' recollections. Oral history interviews with Nadežda Čačinovič, Zagreb, 5 March 2014; Mojca Dobnikar, Ljubljana, 8 April 2012; Slavenka Drakulić, Zagreb, 12 November 2012; Vesna Kesić, Zagreb, 6 March 2014; Lepa Mlađenović, Belgrade, 16 April 2014; Sofija Trivunac, Belgrade, 3 June 2011; Lina Vušković, Belgrade, 24 January 2011.
22. See e.g., Mary Senechal, *Sačuvajte zdravlje svoje obitelji* [Guarding your family's health] (Zagreb, 1974); Blagoje Stambolović, *Higijena žene: kako žena da sačuva svoje zdravlje* [The hygiene of women: How to take care of your health] (Beograd, 1959); Živka Vidojković, *Žena i dom: lečenje lekovitim biljem, ishrana i zdravlje, kozmetika* [Woman and home: Healing with herbs, nutrition and health, cosmetics] (Beograd, 1973).
23. See Zsófia Lóránd, "'A Politically Non-Dangerous Revolution is Not a Revolution'— Critical Readings of the Concept of Sexual Revolution by Yugoslav Feminists in the 1970s," *European Review of History / revue européenne d histoire*, 22, no. 1 (2015): 120–137.

24. Jasmina Lukić, "Women-Centered Narratives in Contemporary Serbian and Croatian Literatures", in *Engendering Slavic Literatures*, ed. Pamela Chester and Sibelan Forrester (Bloomington, 1996), 236.
25. See Lóránd, "'A Politically Non-Dangerous Revolution is Not a Revolution.'"
26. Stambolović, *Higijena žene*, 112–115.
27. The documentation of the FGŽD in the ŽINDOK Centar and the list of events of the SKC do not always agree on the exact dates. The reason is probably that events sometimes had to be rescheduled. It is certain, however, that the "Women and Health" series took place in March and April 1986. About the first event, the date in the ŽINDOK file is 8 April 1987. See ŽINDOK D-76/1987. The SKC events are listed in Marina Blagojević, ed., *Ka vidljivoj ženskoj istoriji: ženski pokret u Beogradu 90-ih* (Beograd, 1998), 49–60.
28. ŽINDOK Centar Archive (Belgrad), D-28/1988.
29. Her selected publications in the field include Lepa Mlađenović et al., eds., *Alternative psihijatriji: Materjali sa medjunarodnog skupa "Psihijatrija i društvo"* [Alternatives of psychiatry: Materials from the international conference "Psychiatry and society"] (Belgrade, 1985); "Implikacije feminističke terapije" / "The Implications of Feminist Therapy," *Knjiga rezimea sa 31 sabora psihologa* (Belgrade, 1983), 132; "Proizvodnja majke: nacrt za odnos majke i ćerke" [The production of mothers: A sketch to the mother-daughter relationships], *Vidici* 1–2 (1984): 23–35; with Biljana Branković, "Mreža—Alternative Psihijatriji" [Alternatives to Psychiatry], *Kultura* no. 68–69, (1985): 170–178; with Aleksandar Petrović, eds., *Mreža alternativa* [Network of alternatives] (Kragujevac, 1987).
30. Jasenka Kodrnja, "Dnevnik jedne rodilje" [Diary of a woman giving birth], *Start* 335 (1981): 56–57.
31. Interview with Sofija Trivunac, Belgrade, 3 June 2011.
32. Nevenka Gruzinov-Milovanović, "Sociološki i kulturni aspekti silovanja" [Sociological and cultural aspects of rape], *Gledišta* 1–2 (1990): 170–184; Vesna Nikolić-Ristanović, *Žene kao žrtve kriminaliteta* [Women as crime victims] (Beograd, 1989); "Okrugli stol Žene: Nasilje u obitelji" [Roundtable *Žena*: Violence in the family], *Žena* 47, no. 1–2 (1989): 54–83; Feministička grupa "Žena i društvo" SKC Beograd, "Još jednom o SOS-telefonu: Nasilje je politički problem" [Once more about the SOS telephone: Violence is a political problem], *Student* 29 March 1989; Dražena Peranić and Merima Hamulić, "Ko to lomi adamovo rebro" [The one who is cracking Adam's ribs], *Oslobođenje* 6 November 1988. (Both sources are the courtesy of the press archive, "Presarijum SKC," of the Students' Cultural Centre in Belgrade.)
33. See Sven Reichardt, *Authentizität und Gemeinschaft: Linksalternatives Leben in den siebziger und frühen achtziger Jahren* (Berlin, 2014).
34. Ruth Colker, "Feminism, Sexuality, and Self: A Preliminary Inquiry into the Politics of Authenticity," *Boston University Law Review* 8, no. 1 (1988): 218.

Bibliography

Attwood, Lynne. *Creating the New Soviet Woman: Women's Magazines as Engineers of Female Identity, 1922–53*. New York: St. Martin's Press, 1999.

Blagojević, Marina, ed. *Ka vidljivoj ženskoj istoriji: ženski pokret u Beogradu 90-ih*. Beograd: Centar za ženske studije, istraživanja i komunikaciju, 1998.

Čačinovič, Nadežda. Personal interview. Zagreb, 5 March 2014.

Cerjan-Letica, Gordana. "Feministička pitanja i marksistički odgovori." *Naše teme* 24, no. 11 (1980): 1970–1974.

Cheng, Yinghong. *Creating the New Man: From Enlightenment Ideals to Socialist Realities*. Honolulu: University of Hawai`i Press, 2009.

Colker, Ruth. "Feminism, Sexuality, and Self: A Preliminary Inquiry into the Politics of Authenticity." *Boston University Law Review* 68, no. 1 (1988): 217–264.

Dobnikar, Mojca. Personal interview. Ljubljana, 8 April 2012.

Drakulić, Slavenka. Personal interview. Zagreb, 12 November 2012.

Duda, Igor. *Danas kada postajem pionir: Djetinjstvo i ideologija jugoslavenskoga socijalizma*. Zagreb: Srednja Europa and Pula: Sveučilište Jurja Dobrile u Puli, 2015.

Feministička grupa "Žena i društvo" SKC Beograd. "Još jednom o SOS-telefonu: Nasilje je politički problem." *Student* 29 March 1989.

Freeden, Michael. *Liberal Languages: Ideological Imaginations and Twentieth-Century Progressive Thought*. Princeton, NJ: Princeton University Press, 2005.

Goulding, Daniel J., ed. *Post New Wave Cinema in the Soviet Union and Eastern Europe*. Bloomington: Indiana University Press, 1989.

Gruzinov-Milovanović, Nevenka. "Sociološki i kulturni aspekti silovanja." *Gledišta* 1–2 (1990): 170–184.

Havel, Václav "The Power of the Powerless." Translated by Paul Wilson. Retreived 15 August 2014 from http://vaclavhavel.cz/showtrans.php?cat=eseje&val=2_aj_eseje.html&typ=HTML.

Iveković, Rada. "Ženska kreativnost i kreiranje žene." *Argumenti* 1 (1979): 139–147.

Kesić, Vesna. Personal interview. Zagreb, 6 March 2014.

Kodrnja, Jasenka. "Dnevnik jedne rodilje." *Start* 335 (1981): 56–57.

Kopeček, Michal, and Piotr Wciślik, eds. *Thinking through Transition: Liberal Democracy, Authoritarian Pasts, and Intellectual History in East Central Europe after 1989*. New York: Central European University Press, 2015.

Ler-Sofronić, Nada. "Dijalektika odnosa polova i klasna svijest." *Dometi* 13, no. 2 (1980): 5–14.

Linz, Juan J., and Alfred Stepan. *Problems of Democratic Transition and Consolidation: Southern Europe, South America, and Post-Communist Europe*. Baltimore, MD: Johns Hopkins University Press, 1996.

Lóránd, Zsófia. "New Yugoslav Feminism during Socialism between 'Mainstreaming' and 'Disengagement': The Possibilities of Resistance, Critical Opposition and Dissent." *The Hungarian Historical Review* 5, no. 4 (2016): 854–881.

———. "'A Politically Non-Dangerous Revolution is Not a Revolution'—Critical Readings of the Concept of Sexual Revolution by Yugoslav Feminists in the 1970s." *European Review of History / revue européenne d histoire* 22, no. 1 (2015): 120–137.

Lukić, Jasmina. "Women-Centered Narratives in Contemporary Serbian and Croatian Literatures." In *Engendering Slavic Literatures*, ed. Pamela Chester and Sibelan Forrester, 223–243. Bloomington: Indiana University Press, 1996.

Mežnarić, Silva. "Što se događa s američkom ženom?" *Žena* 30, no. 6 (1972): 57–62.

Mitchell, Juliet. "Položaj žene." *Naše teme* 24, no. 11 (1980): 1994–2012.
Mlađenović, Lepa. "Implikacije feminističke terapije" / "The Implications of Feminist Therapy." *Knjiga rezimea sa 31 sabora psihologa*, Belgrade, 1983.
———. 1984. "Proizvodnja majke: nacrt za odnos majke i ćerke." *Vidici* no. 1–2 (1984): 23–35.
——— with Biljana Branković. "Mreža—Alternative Psihijatriji." *Kultura* no. 68–69 (1985): 170–178.
Mlađenović, Lepa. Personal interview. Belgrade, 16 April 2014.
Mlađenović, Lepa, and Aleksandar Petrović, eds. *Mreža alternativa*. Kragujevac: Svetlost, 1987.
Mlađenović, Lepa, with the editorial group Međunarodni skup "Psihijatrija i društvo", eds. *Alternative psihijatriji: Materjali sa medjunarodnog skupa "Psihijatrija i društvo."* Belgrade: Lila Ulica, 1985.
Moi, Toril. *Sexual/Textual Politics: Feminist Literary Theory*. London: Routledge, [1985] 2002.
Nikolić-Ristanović, Vesna. *Žene kao žrtve kriminaliteta*. Beograd: Naučna knjiga, 1989.
Oates-Indruchová, Libora. "The Beauty and the Loser: Cultural Representations of Gender in Late State Socialism." *Signs* 37, no. 2 (2012): 357–383.
"Okrugli stol *Žene*: Nasilje u obitelji." *Žena* 47, no. 1–2 (1989): 54–83.
Peranić, Dražena, and Merima Hamulić. "Ko to lomi adamovo rebro." *Oslobođenje*, 6 November 1988.
Piotrowski, Piotr. *In the Shadow of Yalta: Art and the Avant-Garde in Eastern Europe, 1945–1989*. London: Reaktion, 2009.
Popović-Perišić, Nada. *Literatura kao zavođenje*. Beograd: Prosveta, 1986.
Ramet, Sabrina P., ed. *Rocking the State: Rock Music and Politics in Eastern Europe and Russia*. Boulder, CO: Westview Press, 1994.
Reichardt, Sven. *Authentizität und Gemeinschaft: Linksalternatives Leben in den siebziger und frühen achtziger Jahren*. Berlin: Suhrkamp Verlag, 2014.
Renwick, Alan. "Anti-Political or Just Anti-Communist? Varieties of Dissidence in East-Central Europe and their Implications for the Development of Political Society." *East European Politics and Societies* 20, no. 2 (2006): 286–318.
Rowbotham, Sheila. "Dijalektičke smetnje." *Naše teme* 24, no. 11 (1980): 1975–1993.
Šafranek, Ingrid. "'Ženska književnost' i 'žensko pismo.'" *Republika* no. 11–12 (1980): 7–28.
Senechal, Mary. *Sačuvajte zdravlje svoje obitelji*. Zagreb: Naprijed, 1974.
Smiljanić, Vera. "Socijalno poreklo psiholoških spolnih razlika." *Psihološka istraživanja* no. 3 (1984): 109–129.
Stambolović, Blagoje. *Higijena žene: kako žena da sačuva svoje zdravlje*. Beograd: Medicinska knjiga, 1959.
Stansell, Christine. *The Feminist Promise: 1792 to Present*. New York: The Modern Library, 2010.
Trivunac, Sofija. Personal interview. Belgrade, 3 June 2011.
Vidojković, Živka. *Žena i dom: lečenje lekovitim biljem, ishrana i zdravlje, kozmetika*. Beograd: Dom i porodica—Preševo: Progres, 1973.
Vušković, Lina. Personal interview. Belgrade, 24 January 2011.

Zukin, Sharon. "Sources of Dissent and Nondissent in Yugoslavia." In *Dissent in Eastern Europe*, edited by Jane Leftwich Curry, 117–137. New York: Praeger, 1983.

Zuppa, Jelena. "Novo žensko pismo: da bi se kazalo život." *Delo* no. 4 (1981): 15–28.

———. "Žena pisac i součenje s vlastatim položajem žene." *Žena* 38, no. 6 (1980): 50–62.

Chapter 6

Women's Bodies and Feminist Subjectivities in West Germany

Jane Freeland

The formation of the female subject has figured centrally in West German feminist organizing and in the project of liberating women. Writing in 1969, Münster lecturer Karin Schrader-Klebert argued that the emancipation of women would only be realized through the "self-realization and politicization of women."[1] For Schrader-Klebert, "women are the negroes of all people and their collective history."[2] They needed to transform themselves into subjects, rather than continue to be the objects and victims that society made them. Exactly how to do this was a question that preoccupied the women's movement of the 1960s and 1970s.

Indeed, Schrader-Klebert's call for liberation and self-realization found clear resonance among women in West Germany. Shared feelings of frustration and disillusionment at the way men and male-dominated society limited their life choices created solidarity among women. Women felt they did not know who they were, their personal development stalled through motherhood and marriage. "I married, because I was pregnant, and for economic reasons could not afford to remain unmarried," West German filmmaker Helke Sander revealed in her 1968 leaflet "first attempt. to find the right question." Giving up her studies to take care of the baby, she argued that "it was obvious, that the man must study, just as it is natural that the man must support his family, that the man must have an education and that the woman must take care of the children." Living this way, having "suddenly renounced any further personal development," however, had left her unfulfilled and "aggressive."

Sander believed she was not alone; instead, "women wander homeless in this system, living alone with their experiences and not collectively. … but every thinking woman is emotionally fed up with this system, even if she can't articulate it. she's fed up because she senses that this system will never be ready to even slightly fulfill her desires".[3] Indeed, such feelings of being unfulfilled, of unhappiness and dissatisfaction were commonplace within the early women's movement.[4] Sander's revelations of her frustration closely echo those made by American feminist Betty Friedan five years earlier in *The Feminine Mystique*, when she asked "is this all?"[5] These feelings were key to bringing the women's movement together, as women coalesced around a shared sense of anger and disillusionment and a desire for fulfillment and subjecthood.

For women like Sander, who were associated with the New Left, the creation of a female subject was a socialist project. Gathering in groups, mostly without the presence of men, women forged a space for the discussion of women's issues in Leftist politics: in 1968, Sander helped create an Action Council for the Liberation of Women in West Berlin, while in Frankfurt socialist women organized a Women's Revolutionary Council. These groups "did not want to wait for the socialist revolution" to address women's issues.[6] They wanted to do so now. Together they opened communal childcare services in empty West Berlin shopfronts and attempted to liberate women from motherhood and the "tyranny of the private sphere."[7]

For others, women's solidarity came in the form of protest against West Germany's restrictive abortion law, which only permitted abortion in cases where the mother's health was seriously at risk. With an estimated 300,000 illegal abortions in the Federal Republic in 1965, by the early 1970s, women began to call for the decriminalization of abortion provided for in §218 of the West German criminal code.[8] Using the tactic of "self-incrimination," feminist journalist Alice Schwarzer organized women to admit they had had an abortion, even though it was illegal. This culminated in the 6 June 1971 issue of the magazine *Stern* where the article "We Had Abortions," presented 374 women's experiences of unwanted and unexpected pregnancy.[9] Women's activism against §218 was widespread and very public, with Schwarzer even attempting to televise an abortion. This period of women's activism has broadly been understood by scholars as a period of consensus and unity among the growing women's movement in West Germany.[10] This is thought to change, however, by the mid-1970s. Although the governing Social Democratic Party was able to pass a reform law that allowed abortion in the first trimester in 1974, only a year later it was overturned by the Federal Constitutional Court. In its place came a revised §218, which allowed abortion in the first trimester only if a doctor certified that the woman met strict criteria, including risk to maternal health, eugenic reasons, if the pregnancy had resulted from rape, or if there was a "social need" for an abortion.[11] This decision was a major defeat for feminist activists, who at the same time were becoming frustrated with the New Left and socialist politics. Indeed, the women's movement of the mid to late 1970s and early 1980s is understood as marked by growing tensions, as feminists struggled with the realization that their activism had not created the change they had envisioned.

Instead, the years between 1975 and 1985 have been labeled the "women's project movement."[12] During this time, activists opened innumerable spaces for the emancipation of womanhood. Two major feminist magazines began during this period—*Courage* (1976–1984) and *EMMA* (1977–present). At the same time, women's centers, bookstores, cafes, and shelters multiplied throughout West Germany, as activists attempted to put the politics of West German feminism into practice. However, focusing on mainstream and popular women's activism this chapter shows that what has been characterized as a period of plurality and division among the women's movement can also be understood as united by a shared concern with the body.

Indeed, the creation of women's spaces was central to the cultivation of the body as a site for the construction of an authentic feminist subjectivity. Taking inspiration from radical feminist organizing in the United States, women's spaces in West Germany, both discursive and physical, opened the possibility of ending women's isolation and creating a "positive female role model that did not yet exist."[13] In the face of patriarchal society, feminists wanted spaces where they could explore what being a woman meant. As one feminist book warned women: "the idea of entering into and mixing as equals in male institutions will not break the thousand year old power of men, will not bring into question their values that hide within every fiber of these institutions."[14] Women's publications, groups, and centers enabled women to come together and realize their shared oppression, and in doing so build their subjectivity collectively.

Engaging with the body in women's spaces was a key part of this process. Throughout the mid to late 1970s and the 1980s, feminist students, artists, journalists, and writers promoted the body as a site for the development and construction of a feminist subjectivity. By engaging with the body, they argued that women could both discover who they were and perform feminist ideals of womanhood. Learning how to conduct physical self-examinations, how to give themselves sexual pleasure, and critiquing the way their bodies were used by men and society, these feminists attempted to uncover who they were without the pressure of patriarchal norms and values. By taking back control over their bodies and sexuality, they believed they could both liberate themselves from male oppression and find personal fulfillment.

This chapter examines how the body was a site for feminist self-exploration and self-definition. Focusing on three examples—women's health, sexuality, and violence against women—it shows how mainstream

West German feminists used their activism in service of the construction of an "authentic" subjectivity. Drawing from US radical feminism, women activists attempted to wrest control of their bodies and their selves from men by discussing women's sexuality, founding self-help clinics, and politicizing violence against women. This was a collective project involving bringing women together to reclaim control of their bodies. Discussing and exploring the body together, these predominantly well-educated women attempted to find wholeness and fulfillment, showing that they were both sexual subjects and people with rights. However, as this chapter concludes, by using the body as a key marker of feminist subjectivity, West German feminist activists also concretized middle class patriarchal gender differences and affirmed biological determinism.

Women's Health and Self-Help

In 1973, around three hundred women arrived at the West Berlin Women's Center to hear two American feminists, Debbie Law and Carol Downer, talk about the self-help clinic they had founded in California. After speaking to them about performing illicit abortions and showing slides on how to detect early pregnancy, Law suddenly took off her jeans and underwear, climbed up on a table and opened her legs. Inserting a speculum, she encouraged the audience to come and look at her vagina. What the women saw looked different "from what we feared … Not ugly and unappetizing, but beautiful and aesthetic."[15] "Like an orchid," gushed one woman in attendance.

The now-prominent feminist and founder of *EMMA* magazine, Alice Schwarzer, was in attendance that evening. Her report on the event reveals not only the political importance of such consciousness-raising events, but also the transformative effect of such encounters with the body. Law's act shook the gathered crowd. "It was incredible," Schwarzer enthused, "that a woman dared to reveal what we've been trained to believe is shameful." Empowered by Law's act and surprising even themselves, the women "dared to look" and, at least for Schwarzer, "from that moment on, I understood so much more about my own body and my sexuality."[16]

Learning about and overcoming the shame that was associated with female sexuality and sex organs was a way for feminists to wrest control over women's bodies away from men. Men, as medical professionals and husbands and fathers, not only had physical, but also discursive power over women's bodies. "What we saw was banal for any male gynecologist, but a secret to us women: we saw our own body," Schwarzer argued.[17] In doing so, feminist women's health activists saw the body as a conduit to an authentic womanhood, an expression of femininity unrestricted by the power of male authority.

Of course, the body had been a site of feminist concern prior to the late 1970s. The sexual revolution brought nudity, pornography, birth control, and promiscuity into the West German conscience like never before. However, as young women activists discovered, this was a masculinist project, even within the New Left. As historian Dagmar Herzog argues, "misogyny was woven into the very fabric of the sexual revolution."[18] Women's bodies were not only used as marketing tools, but were sexual conquests for male activists, with one antiauthoritarian slogan even declaiming "whoever sleeps twice with the same woman, already belongs to the establishment."[19]

This chauvinism did not pass women by. In a 1968 leaflet, the Frankfurt Women's Revolutionary Council complained about the "socialist pressure to fuck" and the "potent socialist lechery," calling for the male socialist elites to be liberated "from their bourgeois cocks."[20] Accompanying the text was a drawing of a naked witch reclining on a chaise-longue. In her hand, she holds a battle-ax, while above her head are erect penises mounted on the wall, each labeled with the name of a prominent German male socialist.

At the same time, the §218 campaign drew attention to the question of women's physical autonomy and self-determination, as feminists argued that women had the right to make decisions about their own bodies. Schwarzer directly linked §218 activism to the rise of women's self-help, arguing that the abortion rights campaign was "a dark hour in the history of women's struggle. But not a total defeat. The §218 campaign shook women awake. The fight against compulsory motherhood must be thanked for making women realize what §218 has to do with their stunted sexuality and being underpaid in their jobs."[21]

Indeed, at the West Berlin Women's Center that evening in 1973 were three women—Christiane Ewert, Dagmar Schultz, and Gaby Karsten—who were frustrated with the failure of the §218 campaign. After hearing Downer and Law speak about self-help, they were determined to use what they learned to do something concrete to help women with their reproductive choices. In the words of Schultz, they wanted to "not be so hopeless."[22] Instead, they believed that self-help "could mean that abortion and sexual misery could one day be superfluous, because we know our own bodies and our own needs so well that unwanted pregnancies hardly ever occur."[23]

Women's "self-help" encompassed values of anti-authoritarianism, equality, and women helping women. It was a key concept for feminism in West Germany, as activists attempted to empower women to determine the course of their own lives. As Schwarzer argues, self-help took on new prominence in response to the §218 campaign, as feminists learned to distrust the ability of petitions to create change.²⁴ It was central to the quest for women's authentic subjectivity as it enabled the creation of a community of women, who, together, could discover who they were, learning and drawing strength from one another. More broadly, it was used as a tool for addressing systemic power imbalances, whether between rich and poor, social worker and client, or between abusive spouse and battered wife. In West Germany, if not also Western Europe, the late 1960s and 1970s saw a proliferation of protest groups who used grassroots methods and politics "from below" as a way of giving voice to marginalized people and opinions. In Berlin, the language of self-help was particularly prevalent in the squatting movement of the early 1980s, as those most vulnerable to processes of urban renewal in traditionally working class areas like Kreuzberg took back and occupied apartments as a way of protesting the lack of affordable housing.²⁵

Drawing from these politics, Ewert, Schultz, and Karsten began organizing courses in self-help at West Berlin community colleges. Small groups of women would gather every Monday night at the West Berlin Women's Center to learn about their bodies. Groups were kept purposefully small so that the women could get to know one another. On the night Schwarzer joined them, there were six women in attendance, ranging from 18 to 34 years old and all well-educated. That evening they were due to practice breast exams, but before doing so, the women discussed their experiences conducting vaginal self-exams. Provided with a speculum and a "self-help map," they quickly learned that "there is no such thing as normal."²⁶ Examining themselves and one another, they discovered that they each had their own bodily rhythm and their own physical structure. Before getting to the topic at hand, one woman even showed the class a slight reddening on her cervix that she was concerned about.

By getting women to explore their bodies, these courses sought to enable the discovery of an authentic womanhood. This was a collective process that involved women exploring each other and themselves. Alongside technical, medical explanations, conversations between women were an important element of the self-help course. Talking with one another, examining one another, the organizers sought to end women's isolation and the shame surrounding women's bodies. In doing so, they wanted women to question norms and in the process discover how much they had in common with one another. Free from feelings of shame and sexual objectification, women would then be able to enjoy their bodies and themselves. For Schwarzer, the transformative effect of these women's encounters was visible in their relationship with one another. Rather than seeming uncomfortable or awkward at the sight of a cervix, Schwarzer noted that "it was significant to see how the women liked each other, how gentle, attentive and loving they are with one another."²⁷ Emphasizing this point, three photos accompany the article. In one, two women smile as they examine a third. A second shows a blonde woman smiling as she was physically examined, presumably by another woman. The final shows a woman gazing lovingly at the mirror as she examines herself.

This was not only about enabling women to discover who they were, but was also a way of challenging the male-dominated medical establishment's control over women's bodies. Indeed, according to the organizers of the courses, regular observation of the body was thought to give women a better sense and judgment than medical practitioners, even when it came to determining pregnancy. Further, as a group they discovered home remedies for simple gynecological issues (e.g., yeast infections) that, compared with chemical medicines, were gentler on the body. In doing so, they underscored a prioritization of female knowledge and experience of the body over male.

Out of these courses, the group developed a Feminist Women's Health Center (FFGZ), housed within the Berlin Women's Center. Opened in 1977, the FFGZ continued to run self-help courses for women, alongside sexual and women's health counseling, gynecological exams, pregnancy tests, and offering women information on various health issues.[28] The FFGZ concretized many of the principles and ideals established in the initial self-help courses. For example, through group counseling they attempted to connect women with one another and their bodies, and they wanted to improve women's knowledge and relationship with their bodies, so that one day abortion might not be needed.[29] They also continued to challenge the male-dominated medical system, informing women of the side effects of birth control, offering natural alternatives to drug treatments, and keeping records of women's experiences with various doctors.[30] They continued this task in their 1975 self-help manual *Witches Whispering*.

More than this, the FFGZ and their self-help courses were about helping women to uncover their true selves. By removing the shame associated with the body, and opposing male medical authority, feminists sought to enable women to perform a more authentic femininity. They wanted women to "find new ways of expressing their feelings, ways that question the 'technical', misogynistic, male sexuality and lead to a more enjoyable and relaxing sexuality."[31] This was a task that could only take place among other women.

However, in doing so, these women's health activists perpetuated the very gender norms they professed to challenge. Women's knowledge of the body was contrasted to the male medical elite. While women were thus connected with nature and simplicity, men, meanwhile, inhabited the realm of culture and science. They also tied the feminist struggle to biological sex. Despite highlighting that there was no "normal" female body, being a woman in these groups still meant having a vagina and cervix. Gender was therefore not presented as a construction or a performance, but was tied to biological sex, subtly underscoring biological determinism. This meant that true womanhood could be uncovered through self-exploration and women's solidarity. By getting to know their bodies and to reject the shame that shrouded them, feminists wanted women to discover how their health and their bodies had been limited and controlled by men. Only then would women be able to live authentically and reach their full potential.

Women's Sexual Pleasure

> Whenever female orgasm and frigidity are discussed, a false distinction is made between the vaginal and the clitoral orgasm. Frigidity has generally been defined by men as the failure of women to have vaginal orgasms. Actually the vagina is not a highly sensitive area and is not constructed to achieve orgasm. It is the clitoris which is the center of sexual sensitivity and which is the female equivalent of the penis.
> —Anna Koedt, "The Myth of the Vaginal Orgasm"

So began the 1970 article "The Myth of the Vaginal Orgasm," from American feminist Anna Koedt. Taking aim at psychoanalytical definitions of women's heterosexuality and critiquing it from a feminist standpoint, Koedt showed how Freud's concept of the vaginal orgasm had been used to medicalize women's sexual pleasure, and to shroud female reproductive organs in feelings of shame and fear. In doing so, Koedt outlined the "political significance of sexual pleasure."[32]

In his work on sexuality, Sigmund Freud counterposed the vagina and clitoris as sites of mature versus immature sexuality.[33] Whereas the clitoris was central to girlhood sexual excitement, during puberty this transferred to the vagina. As Koedt summed up: "The vagina, it was assumed, was able to produce a parallel, but more mature, orgasm than the clitoris."[34] Women who were unable to have such an orgasm, or who were believed to enjoy clitoral stimulation excessively were labeled by psychoanalysts and medical specialists as frigid and abnormal. Indeed, the very existence of such women threatened familial and societal cohesion, as "frigid women, like feminists and lesbians, could not tolerate men being the leader in sexual matters and so instead they harbored neurotic fantasies about their own powers."[35]

Drawing from the scientific work of sexologists Alfred Kinsey, and William Masters and Virginia Johnson, Koedt argued that the "myth of the vaginal orgasm" had not only left women feeling sexually inadequate, but had seriously damaged their mental health. "Frigid" women either "suffered silently with self-blame, or flocked to psychiatrists looking desperately for the hidden and terrible repression that had kept from them their vaginal destiny." Even more frustrating for Koedt:

> women who were perfectly healthy sexually were taught that they were not. So in addition to being sexually deprived, these women were told to blame themselves when they deserved no blame. Looking for a cure to a problem that has none can lead a woman on an endless path of self-hatred and insecurity. For she is told by her analyst that not even in her one role allowed in a male society—the role of a woman—is she successful.[36]

Although she was not alone in making these critiques, Koedt's work found clear resonances in the West German women's movement, who were frustrated by the way that ideas about sex and pleasure inhibited women's self-development. As Dagmar Herzog has shown in the 1950s and even in to the 1960s, penetrative heterosexual sex was the prescribed norm in West Germany, with oral sex only mentioned in one sex advice magazine from the 1950s.[37] More than this, Herzog argues that sex advice literature from this period disdained sexual "petting"—the very act feminists encouraged as a path to women's sexual fulfillment—as a cause of women's frigidity in later life. While Elizabeth Heineman has shown that people's intimate lives often differed from the pronouncements of sex advice literature, the overwhelming emphasis on penetrative sex as "normal" and the best source of women's pleasure was criticized by West German feminists for perpetuating dangerous gender norms.[38] Indeed, sexuality was a political concern for the Alternative Left more generally in the 1970s in West Germany.[39]

Initially circulated in English in the early 1970s in West Germany, the German translation of "The Myth of the Vaginal Orgasm" appeared in the 1974 collection *First Women's Publication from the Berlin Women's Center*. Many West German feminists were attracted to Koedt's critique of the abuse of women's sexuality by medical professionals and men, and helped to bring "The Myth of the Vaginal Orgasm" to a broader German audience. One such woman was Alice Schwarzer. In her book *The "Small Difference" and Its Big Consequences* (1975), Schwarzer showed that women in West Germany were unsatisfied in their sexual relationships with men. She argued that for most young women having sex for the first time was a "compulsory exercise," not done out of desire, but out of fear—either because they had to do it or because their male partner wanted to.[40] She further stated that while many women experienced sex with their husbands/boyfriends as prostitution, all women felt used during sex and reacted with frigidity. Schwarzer attributed this to women's ignorance of their emotional and physical needs and their dependence on men.[41]

Like Koedt, Schwarzer highlighted the dangerous impact of patriarchal societal norms on women. "When she doesn't want to sleep with her husband every day, when she doesn't have any orgasms, when she is not fulfilled by housework and raising children—it always means: you are not normal," Schwarzer critiqued. Indeed, women were most endangered through sexual norms. Hardly able to verify them, women had to accept what "men and the media" told them about sex.[42] She also took aim at the "vaginal orgasm," stating that none of the women she interviewed had experienced one. Instead, she highlighted the importance of alternative sexual practices (not just penetrative sex) to women's sexual pleasure.

For Schwarzer then, the path to women's emancipation lay in sexuality. Indeed, she emphatically proclaimed that "only the destabilization of the male sex-monopoly can completely shake gender roles."[43] To do this, women needed to talk about and question gender and sexuality together: "all women should have the opportunity to question what is thought as natural ... women should finally be able to speak the truth. They should not be allowed to remain in fear of apparent norms, they must see that their problems are shared by other women."[44] In support of this argument, she stated that only women active in the women's movement could come close to meeting their male partners halfway in sexual matters.[45] This was because "their increasing sense of self-identity was no longer so dependent on their relationship to men."[46] However, despite arguing that gender is constructed, Schwarzer's call to reclaim female sexuality still fed into patriarchal ideals. According to Schwarzer, gendered power imbalances also impacted women's ability to experience sexual pleasure: "the more manly and potent a man behaves the less likely he can fulfill a woman sexually."[47] Of course, such an argument only underscores a logic that associates femininity with care and compassion for other people and masculinity with arrogance and selfishness.

This points to the political importance of women's sexuality to the formation of a feminist subjectivity. Like the FFGZ, throughout the 1970s, feminists worked to provide women with a greater knowledge of their sexuality. Alongside reclaiming the body from feelings of shame and anxiety and from male medical expertise, feminists encouraged women to discover the body as a source of sexual pleasure. This was not only a way to liberate women from male expectations, but was also a way for women to "discover" who they authentically were and what they wanted—in the bedroom and out of life.

This was certainly true for one author in the feminist magazine *Courage*, who found that learning about her body and what gave her pleasure opened her eyes to who she really was. In the 1977 article, "Desire for My Own Body," author Gudula L., wanted "to ask every woman who reads this article: do you masturbate? Can you talk about it? Can you describe it to me?"[48] Describing how she gives herself sexual pleasure—by squeezing her legs together in the fetal position—Gudula acknowledges that some readers might find such information uncomfortable, but explains that:

> It's important for me to explain this because it has a lot to do with why I am so focused on the topic of masturbation. When I, as a young girl, without instruction, without knowledge, developed this kind of sexuality, then that means that is my very own sexuality. Something exclusively from me and for me.[49]

In comparison, sex with men felt like "an imposition from outside, an alienating behavior, conformity and subordination. Not MY sexuality."[50]

In spite of this, when Gudula read Koedt's "The Myth of the Vaginal Orgasm," she was baffled. "Where was my clitoris?" she asked herself.[51] Despite having masturbated since she was a child, she did not know what her clitoris was. This cut to the heart of Gudula's sense of self. She could find no peace, worrying that she was abnormal and all alone with her problems. With these fears spinning in her mind, she gathered all her might and looked at herself in the mirror.

From that moment on Gudula was overrun with "questions, thoughts, feelings." "Why did I wait till I was 30; why am I so unfamiliar with 'down there.'" It was as if a whole new world had opened, and Gudula was determined to "get to know her vagina, to like her and to develop a passionate love for her." For Gudula, this was about more than just giving herself pleasure, this was about discovering who she was at her core. "I'm tracking down MY sexuality, MY desire, MY self," she wrote.[52] This sexual awakening impacted the rest of her life. The more she got to know herself, the freer she felt. She was increasingly clear about what she wanted, what she liked and what she got a kick out of, even going so far as to say that it was as if she could finally "breath freely, move freely." Her vagina was no longer just "down there," but was instead a part of her.[53]

Gudula's reflection highlights just how important engaging with the body was for feminists. This was an act of reclamation. Women were taking back physical and discursive control of the female body from husbands and doctors. Looking at themselves in the mirror, touching themselves and getting to know their sex organs was a political act, as women sought to reconnect with parts of themselves shrouded in feelings of shame. More than this though, as Gudula shows, it was about women discovering their authentic selves—who they were before society and men placed expectations on them.

It is likely that Gudula L. is Gudula Lorez, a West German feminist journalist, who wrote various articles on women's sexuality in *Courage*. In 1977 alone, she published three other articles in the magazine: one on older women's sexuality, an article on lesbian love, and an interview with American feminist and author of the Hite-Report, Shere Hite. Similarly to Koedt, the Hite-Report presented findings from a survey on women's sexual experiences. It also critiqued the research of Kinsey, and Masters and Johnson, arguing that, while important, their work continued to uphold the primacy of penetrative sex and in doing so concretized gender norms. Lorez's interview with Hite ends with Hite affirming the importance of sexuality and sexual pleasure to women's identity. "The 'problem' of women and female sexuality is always being talked and written about. But it's not a problem, it is something we can be proud of, it is a real reason to celebrate," Hite concluded.[54] Lorez's dedication to women's sexuality even led her to open a publishing house in the late 1970s. The Gudula-Lorez Verlag was dedicated to publishing erotic literature, written by women for women.

Alongside encouraging women to use masturbation and pleasure as a pathway to self-discovery, it was also a feminist performance of authentic womanhood. Giving one's self sexual pleasure was a way to protest the orthodoxy of penetrative sex. As historian Joachim Häberlen argues "reaching orgasm without men remained a key goal for many women active in the women's movement."[55] As he has shown, this involved more than just masturbation, but also required the creation of new sexual practices that reflected leftist principles.[56] In doing so, however, new sexual norms were created among the alternative and feminist milieu, as "in and out" was replaced by "rub, rub."[57] Indeed, Gudula's fear that she had been masturbating "wrong" and not through clitoral stimulation, reflects the anxieties the feminist emphasis on the clitoris could produce. Consequently, despite challenging norms that limited women's sexual experiences and alienated them from their sexuality, feminist discourse on sexuality often only left women feeling isolated.[58]

Violence against Women

Alongside critiquing how medical professionals misused women's bodies, feminists in West Germany were drawn to the issue of violence against women and throughout the mid to late 1970s, violence became a key component of feminist women's emancipation. Defining violence in particular, became a central part of delimiting women's oppression. Indeed, as one of the earliest pieces on violence made clear, all forms of women's subjugation were perpetuated and enabled by male violence. Specifically, a 1974 flyer from a Frankfurt women's group highlighted the connection between women's objectification in film and pornography, patriarchal gender roles, abortion, and even women's frigidity to sexual violence against women.[59] Dealing with violence then, was a way for feminists to get to the core of women's oppression, and in the process enable the creation of an authentic subjectivity.

For feminists, violence against women was an everyday occurrence – "not only in legal provisions, not only committed by men against women, not only in psychiatric institutions or in prisons" proclaimed feminist journalist Sibylle Plogstedt on the pages of *Courage*.[60] Instead, it was the silencing of women's sexuality and male fantasies of passive women.[61] For a women's group in Marburg, violence was "being chatted up on the street, a hand suddenly touching your ass … wolf-whistles, suggestive glances and leers … ignoring our thought processes in seminars."[62]

With such a broad definition, feminists saw the potential for violence within all men. "Rape is no more and no less than a conscious attempt at intimidation, through which all men hold all women in a position of fear," anti-violence activist and Berlin artist Sarah Haffner quoted from American feminist Susan Brownmiller.[63] One of the most influential texts to make this argument was *Everyday Violence in Marriage: Texts for a Sociology of Power and Love* authored by two feminist sociologists, Cheryl Benard and Edit Schlaffer. While the majority of the book focuses on women's experiences of physical and emotional violence in marriage and relationships, one chapter examines "normal marriages." In this section, Benard and Schlaffer highlight how even in these marriages gendered power imbalances create conflict and unhappiness, rhetorically linking all marriage to the potential for violence, a message powerfully presented in the book's cover description: "Unhappiness in marriage is a part of everyday life, and the number of abused women is too high to be dismissed as individual unfortunate cases. We must realize that violence does not just play out in public, but frequently in kitchens and bedrooms."[64]

Defining violence in this way enabled feminists to cast womanhood in opposition to manhood: women were universal victims and men were the oppressors and perpetrators. Sharing their experiences with one another in women's groups across the Federal Republic, feminists began to see how their identities and subjectivities were controlled and shaped by the fear and experience of male violence. Consequently, like the politicization of women's sexuality and health, much of the activism against violence toward women took the form of reclamation of the body.

One of the most prominent examples of this is the Walpurgis Night March in Berlin. Starting in 1977, women have taken to the streets on the evening of April 30 to reclaim the night, rejecting their typical vulnerability and using the occasion to point to the failure to protect their rights as citizens. The flyer for the first march specifically dealt with violence against women, highlighting the damaging role it played in women's lives and underscoring the importance of taking action against it: "From earliest childhood it is drummed into our head that we should be careful around men. This fear hinders us from moving freely, enfeebles us when we need to defend ourselves—it is our invisible prison," the authors from the Berlin Women's Center argued. Instead, they called on women "to yell back, to hit back and to defend each other together."[65]

An even more radical reclamation of the self was publicized in the 1976 *Women's Year Book*, which not only stated that "every woman has the right to kill the man who raped her," but it also recounted a story—its veracity is unclear—of a group of women who flew to Paris to attack the man who raped two of them. For one of these women, attacking her rapist was her "one chance to hold on to myself and my self-worth … finally to be myself with my anger."[66] Only by taking back the violence that had been enacted upon her body could she discover and reclaim who she was.

Other women's groups worked to open shelters and services for women living with violence. The first battered women's shelter opened in Germany in 1976, as a group of women based out of the West Berlin Women's Center came together to create a service for women living with violence.[67] Drawing from the principle of self-help, they wanted to open a house outside of the typical bureaucracy of the state and formal welfare system, which they believed not only treated people and families like case files, but had failed to provide safety or protection for women living with a violent partner.[68] Instead, they wanted to empower women to leave a violent spouse.

Like the FFGZ, this shelter and the others opened in its wake, practiced self-help and were spaces intended to enable women's empowerment, using the discussion of violence as a way for women to come to terms with their oppression by men and in the process understand more about themselves. In reality, however, soon after opening many shelters were quick to professionalize as the initial activists involved left, frustrated that the battered women who arrived sought assistance—legal and medical—not emancipation.[69]

Conclusion

Part of the process of constructing a feminist subjectivity then, was giving women the space to engage with their bodies, sexuality, and identity without the pressure, expectations, or even fear of men. Only among other women could an authentic expression of womanhood be uncovered, as together they could realize how the male-dominated world shaped and controlled their lives. Within these spaces, the body was both a conduit for the "discovery" and a site for the practice of this subjectivity. Reclaiming their bodies, women could find out who they were without the pressure of societal norms and, in doing so, protest patriarchy.

In contrast to a vision of the West German women's movement as divided throughout the later 1970s, this chapter has instead shown how—despite addressing diverse issues—feminists were united in an attempt to politicize the female body, using it as a site for the formation of authentic subjectivities. Although this chapter has only focused on women's health, sexuality, and violence against women, it could equally have examined the feminist politicization of women's work, ongoing reproductive rights activism, or the backlash against the objectification of women in Alice Schwarzer's PorNo! campaign.

In reality though, expressions of authentic womanhood in women's spaces were far more limiting than at first glance. By linking female subjectivity with the body, West German activists fused gender identity with biological sex and in the process unwittingly reified a biologically-based vision of gender difference and patriarchal norms. Women were varyingly presented by feminists as strong and powerful, as connected with nature, as victims. Indeed, despite critiquing gender norms, being a woman still meant having female sex organs. It also called for a particular performance of femininity, revealing the class-based values underpinning much of the mainstream women's activism in West Germany. The women activists studied here were mostly well-educated. They were journalists, teachers and lecturers, university students, they even ran publishing houses and magazines. The truly authentic feminist was like them: she read and wrote for women's magazines, engaged in political discussions, she had the confidence to discuss her sexuality and sexual life openly, she had free time in which to attend rallies and women's groups, and had the money to shop at the right stores. These were fused with bodily practices of masturbation, self-cervical examination, having orgasms, and owning her body. These visions of authentic feminist womanhood and its connection to the female body point are perhaps prescient of contemporary tensions surrounding the intersections of class, gender identity, sexuality within the feminist movement.

Jane Freeland is a Teaching Associate in Modern European History at the University of Sheffield. Her research interests focus on the histories of feminism in divided Germany, and historical and contemporary issues of gender violence, citizenship, and legal reform. She is currently working on her monograph *Feminist Transformations: Domestic Violence in Divided Berlin, 1969–2002*, which examines women's activism against domestic abuse on both sides of the Berlin Wall.

Notes

1. Karin Schrader-Klebert, "Die kulturelle Revolution der Frau," *Kursbuch* 17 (June 1969): 41. All translations are mine unless otherwise stated.
2. Ibid., 1.
3. Helke Sander, "1. versuch" in Ilse Lenz, ed., *Die Neue Frauenbewegung in Deutschland: Abschied vom kleinen Unterschied. Eine Quellensammlung*, 2nd ed. (Wiesbaden, 2010), 53. Lack of capitalization in the original.
4. Sara Ahmed, "Happiness and Queer Politics," *World Picture* 3 (2009): 1–20.
5. Betty Friedan, *The Feminine Mystique* (New York, 2001), 57.
6. "Selbstverständnis des Aktionsrat zur Befreiung der Frauen," A Rep 400 17.20 0-4, Frauenforschungs-, -bildungs- und Informationszentrum (FFBIZ).
7. Ibid.
8. Susanne von Paczensky, *Gemischte Gefühle: Von Frauen, die ungewollt schwanger sind* (Munich, 1987).
9. "Wir haben abgetrieben," *Stern* (6 June 1971).
10. Lenz, *Die Neue Frauenbewegung*.
11. Myra Marx Ferree, *Varieties of Feminism: German Gender Politics in Global Perspective* (Stanford, CA, 2012). See also Atina Grossmann, *Reforming Sex: The German Movement for Birth Control and Abortion, 1920–1950* (Oxford, 1995).
12. Ferree, *Varieties of Feminism*; Lenz, *Neue Frauenbewegung*.
13. Ute Kätzel, *Die 68erinnen: Porträt einer rebellischen Frauengeneration* (Berlin, 2002), 16.
14. *Frauenjahrbuch '76* (Munich, 1976), 79. See also Anne Enke, "Smuggling Sex through the Gate: Race, Sexuality, and the Politics of Space in Second Wave Feminism," *American Quarterly* 55, no. 4 (2003): 635–667.
15. Alice Schwarzer, "Die neuen Hexen," *EMMA* (May 1977), 6.
16. Ibid.
17. Ibid.
18. Dagmar Herzog, *Sex after Fascism: Memory and Morality in Twentieth Century Germany* (Princeton, NJ, 2005), 231.

19. Ibid. See also Timothy Brown, *West Germany and the Global Sixties: The Anti-Authoritarian Revolt, 1962–1978* (London, 2013).
20. "Rechenschaftsbericht," A Rep 400 17.20 0-4, FFBIZ.
21. Alice Schwarzer, "Nach 100 Jahren wieder Frauenklinik," *EMMA* (May 1977): 9.
22. Schwarzer, "Die neuen Hexen," 7.
23. Ibid.
24. Schwarzer, "Nach 100 Jahren wieder Frauenklinik," 9.
25. Carla MacDougall, "Cold War Capital: Contested Urbanity in West Berlin," Ph.D. dissertation (New Brunswick, NJ, 2011); Steven Katz and Margit Mayer, "Gimme Shelter: Self-Help Struggles Within and Against the State in New York City and West Berlin," *International Journal of Urban and Regional Research* 9, no. 1 (1985): 15–46; Anna Ross, "Photographing Reurbanization in West Berlin, 1977–84," in *The Ethics of Seeing: German Documentary Photography Reconsidered*, ed. Jennifer Evans, Paul Betts, and Stefan-Ludwig Hoffmann (New York, 2018).
26. Schwarzer, "Die neuen Hexen," 7.
27. Ibid, 8.
28. Jutta Lauterbach, Doris Scharf, and Dagmar Schultz, "Es geht um unseren Körper als Ganzen," *Courage* 11 (1977): 13–18.
29. Ibid.
30. Ibid.; Frankfurter Frauen, *Frauenjahrbuch 75* (Frankfurt, 1975), 56–67. This was also practiced by feminist activists in California in the mid/late 1960s, when the Association to Repeal Abortion Laws published lists of verified Mexican abortionists. See Leslie J. Reagan, "Crossing the Border for Abortions: California Activists, Mexican Clinics, and the Creation of a Feminist Health Agency in the 1960s," *Feminist Studies* 26, no. 2 (2000): 323–348.
31. Ibid., 14.
32. Jane Gerhard, "Revisiting 'The Myth of the Vaginal Orgasm': The Female Orgasm in American Sexual Thought and Second Wave Feminism," *Feminist Studies* 26, no. 2 (2000): 449.
33. Sigmund Freud, *Three Essays on the Theory of Sexuality*, trans. James Strachey (London, 1949).
34. Anna Koedt, "The Myth of the Vaginal Orgasm" (1970) from *The Feminist eZine*.
35. Gerhard, "Revisiting 'The Myth of the Vaginal Orgasm,'" 458.
36. Koedt, "The Myth of the Vaginal Orgasm."
37. Herzog, *Sex after Fascism*, 124.
38. Elizabeth Heineman, "The Economic Miracle in the Bedroom: Big Business and Sexual Consumption in Reconstruction West Germany," *The Journal of Modern History* 78, no. 4 (2006): 846–877; Elizabeth Heineman, *Before Porn was Legal: The Erotic Empire of Beate Uhse* (Chicago, IL, 2011).
39. Brown, *West Germany and the Global Sixties*; Sven Reichardt, *Authentizität und Gemeinschaft: Linksalternatives Leben in den siebziger und frühen achtziger Jahren* (Berlin, 2014); Joachim C. Häberlen, "Feeling like a Child: Dreams and Practices of Sexuality in the West German Alternative Left during the Long 1970s," *Journal of the History of Sexuality* 25, no. 2 (2016): 219–245.
40. Alice Schwarzer, *Der "kleine Unterschied" und seine großen Folgen: Frauen über sich. Beginn einer Befreiung* (Frankfurt, 1975), 184.

41. Ibid.
42. Ibid., 185.
43. Ibid., 207.
44. Ibid., 210–211.
45. Ibid., 186.
46. Ibid.
47. Ibid., 185.
48. Gudula L., "Lust am eigenen Leib," *Courage* 6/7 (1977), 31–32.
49. Ibid., 31.
50. Ibid., emphasis in original.
51. Ibid.
52. Ibid., 32.
53. Ibid.
54. Gudula Lorez, "Wir Frauen haben Grund zum Feiern: Interview mit Shere Hite," *Courage* 9 (1977): 43.
55. Häberlen, "Feeling like a Child," 238.
56. Ibid.
57. Sylvia, "Die Last meiner Lust," *Erotik und Umbruch: Zeitung zu Sexualität*, Midsummer (1978), 32–33 as quoted in Häberlen, "Feeling like a Child," 230. On the topic of the creation of norms within the left see Reichardt, *Authentizität und Gemeinschaft*; Andrea Bührmann, *Das authentische Geschlecht: Die Sexualitätsdebatte der neuen Frauenbewegung und die Foucaultsche Machtanalyse* (Münster, 1995); Andrea Trumann, *Feministische Theorie: Frauenbewegung und weibliche Subjektbildung im Spätkapitalismus* (Stuttgart, 2002).
58. Häberlen, "Feeling like a Child," 242.
59. "Daß Du untergehst, wenn Du nicht wehrst, wirst Du doch einsehn!," in Lenz, *Die Neue Frauenbewegung*, 290–291.
60. Sibylle Plogstedt, "Die Gewalt in unseren Köpfen: Kölner Kongreß," *Courage* 6 (1978): 7–8.
61. Ibid.
62. "Dokumentation der Marburger Gruppe: Gewalt gegen Frauen," A Rep 400 BRD 22 Broschüren gegen Gewalt (1976–2001), FFBIZ. For a parallel example of the way other women's experiences of violence were experienced, if not embodied by activists, see Pascal Eitler, "Das 'Reich der Sinne'? Pornographie, Philosophie und die Brutalisierung der Sexualität (Westdeutschland, 1968–1988)," *Body Politics* 1 (2013): 259–296.
63. Sarah Haffner, "Die Angst ist unser schlimmster Feind: Sarah Haffner auf der Kundgebung nach dem Tod von Susanne Schmidtke am 1.3.1977," *Courage* 4 (1977): 5.
64. Cheryl Benard and Edit Schlaffer, *Die ganz gewöhnliche Gewalt in der Ehe: Texte zu einer Soziologie von Macht und Liebe* (Hamburg, 1978), jacket cover.
65. "Frauen, wir erobern uns die Nacht zurück!" A Rep 400 Berlin 21.22.6-21.22a (DFB), FFBIZ.
66. "Antwort auf eine Vergewaltigung," *Frauenjahrbuch '76* (Munich, 1976), 202.
67. Alice Schwarzer, "Ein Tag im Haus für geschlagene Frauen," *EMMA*, March 1977.

68. Projektantrag zur Einrichtung eines Frauenhauses in Berlin (West) (1976), B Rep 002/12504, Landesarchiv Berlin (LAB); Ferree, *Varieties of Feminism*; Myra Marx Ferree, "Equality and Autonomy: Feminist Politics in the United States and West Germany," in *The Women's Movements of the United States and Western Europe: Consciousness, Political Opportunity, and Public Policy*, ed. Mary Fainsod Katzenstein and Carol McClurg Mueller (Philadelphia, PA, 1987), 172–195.
69. Jane Freeland, "Behind Closed Doors: Domestic Violence, Citizenship and State-Making in Divided Berlin, 1969–1990," Ph.D. dissertation (Ottawa, 2016).

Bibliography

Ahmed, Sara. "Happiness and Queer Politics." *World Picture* 3 (2009): 1–20.
Benard, Cheryl, and Edit Schlaffer. *Die ganz gewöhnliche Gewalt in der Ehe: Texte zu einer Soziologie von Macht und Liebe*. Hamburg: Rowohlt Taschenbuch Verlag, 1978.
Brown, Timothy. *West Germany and the Global Sixties: The Anti-Authoritarian Revolt, 1962–1978*. London: Cambridge University Press, 2013.
Bührmann, Andrea. *Das authentische Geschlecht: Die Sexualitätsdebatte der neuen Frauenbewegung und die Foucaultsche Machtanalyse*. Münster: Westfälisches Dampfboot, 1995.
Eitler, Pascal. "Das 'Reich der Sinne'? Pornographie, Philosophie und die Brutalisierung der Sexualität (Westdeutschland, 1968–1988)." *Body Politics* 1 (2013): 259–296.
Enke, Anne. "Smuggling Sex through the Gate: Race, Sexuality, and the Politics of Space in Second Wave Feminism." *American Quarterly* 55, no. 4 (2003): 635–667.
Ferree, Myra Marx. "Equality and Autonomy: Feminist Politics in the United States and West Germany." In *The Women's Movements of the United States and Western Europe: Consciousness, Political Opportunity, and Public Policy*, edited by Mary Fainsod Katzenstein and Carol McClurg Mueller, 172–195. Philadelphia, PA: Temple University Press, 1987.
———. *Varieties of Feminism: German Gender Politics in Global Perspective*. Stanford, CA: Stanford University Press, 2012.
Frankfurter Frauen, *Frauenjahrbuch 75*. Frankfurt: Verlag Roter Stern, 1975.
Frauenjahrbuch '76. Munich: Verlag Frauenoffensive, 1976.
Freeland, Jane. "Behind Closed Doors: Domestic Violence, Citizenship and State-Making in Divided Berlin, 1969–1990." Ph.D. dissertation. Ottawa: Carleton University, 2016.
Freud, Sigmund. *Three Essays on the Theory of Sexuality*. Translated by James Strachey. London: Imago, 1949.
Friedan, Betty. *The Feminine Mystique*. New York: W.W. Norton, 2001.
Gerhard, Jane. "Revisiting 'The Myth of the Vaginal Orgasm': The Female Orgasm in American Sexual Thought and Second Wave Feminism." *Feminist Studies* 26, no. 2 (2000): 440–476.
Grossmann, Atina. *Reforming Sex: The German Movement for Birth Control and Abortion, 1920–1950*. Oxford: Oxford University Press, 1995.

Häberlen, Joachim C. "Feeling like a Child: Dreams and Practices of Sexuality in the West German Alternative Left during the Long 1970s." *Journal of the History of Sexuality* 25, no. 2 (2016): 219–245.

Haffner, Sarah. "Die Angst ist unser schlimmster Feind: Sarah Haffner auf der Kundgebung nach dem Tod von Susanne Schmidtke am 1.3.1977." *Courage* 4 (1977): 5.

Heineman, Elizabeth. *Before Porn was Legal: The Erotic Empire of Beate Uhse.* Chicago: University of Chicago Press, 2011.

———. "The Economic Miracle in the Bedroom: Big Business and Sexual Consumption in Reconstruction West Germany." *The Journal of Modern History* 78, no. 4 (2006): 846–877.

Herzog, Dagmar. *Sex after Fascism: Memory and Morality in Twentieth Century Germany.* Princeton, NJ: Princeton University Press, 2005.

Katz, Steven, and Margit Mayer. "Gimme Shelter: Self-Help Struggles Within and Against the State in New York City and West Berlin." *International Journal of Urban and Regional Research* 9, no. 1 (1985): 15–46.

Kätzel, Ute. *Die 68erinnen.* Berlin: Rowohlt, 2002.

Koedt, Anna. "The Myth of the Vaginal Orgasm" (1970), *The Feminist eZine*, retrieved May 10 2017 from http://www.feministezine.com/feminist/modern/The-Myth-ofthe-Vaginal-Orgasm.html.

Lenz, Ilse, ed. *Die Neue Frauenbewegung in Deutschland: Abschied vom kleinen Unterschied. Eine Quellensammlung,* 2nd ed. Wiesbaden: VS Verlag, 2010.

MacDougall, Carla. "Cold War Capital: Contested Urbanity in West Berlin." Ph.D. dissertation. New Brunswick, NJ: Rutgers, The State University of New Jersey, 2011.

von Paczensky, Susanne. *Gemischte Gefühle: Von Frauen, die ungewollt schwanger sind.* Munich: Beck, 1987.

Reagan, Leslie J. "Crossing the Border for Abortions: California Activists, Mexican Clinics, and the Creation of a Feminist Health Agency in the 1960s." *Feminist Studies* 26, no. 2 (2000): 323–348.

Reichardt, Sven. *Authentizität und Gemeinschaft: Linksalternatives Leben in den siebziger und frühen achtziger Jahren.* Berlin: Suhrkamp Verlag, 2014.

Ross, Anna. "Photographing Reurbanization in West Berlin, 1977–84," in *The Ethics of Seeing: German Documentary Photography Reconsidered,* edited by Jennifer Evans, Paul Betts, and Stefan-Ludwig Hoffmann, 205–226. New York: Berghahn Books, 2018.

Schwarzer, Alice. *Der "kleine Unterschied" und seine großen Folgen: Frauen über sich. Beginn einer Befreiung.* Frankfurt a. M.: Fischer Taschenbuch Verlag, 1975.

Trumann, Andrea. *Feministische Theorie: Frauenbewegung und weibliche Subjektbildung im Spätkapitalismus.* Stuttgart: Schmetterlingsverlag, 2002.

Chapter 7

The Rise of a New Consciousness

Lesbian Activism in East Germany in the 1980s

Maria Bühner

For most of the German Democratic Republic (GDR)'s existence, lesbians and lesbian desires in East Germany remained invisible, unnamed, and hidden in the private sphere. This changed in the 1980s, when lesbians not only increasingly became seen and heard, but also developed new ideas about what it meant to be a lesbian. New networks of lesbian rights activists emerged during this period, and campaigned for visibility, recognition, and respect. Positioning this activism within the broader narrative of dissidence in the former GDR helps us gain a greater understanding of the nature of the political crisis in the 1980s, and the rise of a political consciousness under the umbrella of the Protestant Church at this time. Lesbian rights activists actively participated in the processes of political transformation before, during, and after the reunification.[1] They not only criticized the omnipresence of heteronormativity and their limited opportunities to live an emancipated life, but, in doing so, also ultimately questioned the legitimacy of the Socialist Unity Party (SED).[2] In the GDR, living an authentic life as a lesbian seemed impossible.

A variety of developments made homosexuality a political issue in the second half of the 1980s: new academic understandings of homosexuality; the politicization of homosexuality by activist groups that had close relationships to groups from Western Europe (a security risk in the eyes of the Stasi); and the emergence of AIDS. Sensing a loss of control, the regime developed official policies on homosexuality in an attempt to reassert its authority. Different public agencies collaborated so that the "welfare-dictatorship" (Konrad Jarausch) could "solve the problems of the homosexuals."[3] Using mass media and culture to "educate" the public, these agencies worked for the "integration of homosexuals into socialism." Academic research was commissioned to gain a better understanding of homosexuality, although it reproduced an estranged gaze by mostly male academics. By permitting the publication of same-sex dating adverts in 1985, and abolishing the discriminatory StGB-DDR §151 law—which had criminalized homosexual "sexual acts" between an underage person and an adult with an age of consent that differed from that of heterosexuals—in 1989, the regime attempted to improve the situation for homosexuals. These changes must be understood in the context of lesbian rights' activism, because it was here that the politicization of female homosexuality began.

Emotions played a crucial role in the politicization of female homosexuality.[4] As Deborah Gould has argued, the regulation of emotions is a fundamental aspect of governance.[5] At the same time, however, emotions are an important tool for social and political movements that challenge hegemonic powers. Emotions motivate, shape, and alter activism. As illustrated by lesbian rights activism in the GDR, identities are not only policed by power-knowledge complexes, but also by emotional regimes that can be challenged and changed.[6] In this chapter, I discuss the emotional politics and practices of lesbian activists, focusing particularly on the lesbian activist group Lesben in der Kirche (LiK), the first and perhaps most influential lesbian rights group in the GDR. The group acted in the milieu of political activism that formed under the umbrella of the Protestant Church from the late 1970s. A study of this group highlights the importance of lesbian subjectivity and agency, offering insights into how activists tried to situate themselves in socialist society and develop their own ideas of what it meant to be a lesbian. In the context of this lesbian rights activism, a specific lesbian subjectivity developed that was inherently political.

In this chapter, I examine this subjectification process and explore how new politics and new subjectivities were developed through lesbian rights activism. I argue that the repressive emotional regime of the GDR, which had constricted the expression of homosexuality, ultimately motivated the political activism that pushed for social and political change. As a result of their isolation, activists faced an affective state defined by invisibility and marginalization, and dominated by shame, guilt, fear, and self-hatred. Activists created a language for, and an understanding of, these very affects. They conceived of homosexuality as a political rather than a private issue and hence insisted on the necessity of political change. Transforming personal negative feelings into self-awareness and belonging was an important practice of self-empowerment, and essential for the creation of a new emotional habitus. Lesbians gained a sense of how and what to feel, and how to understand, name, and express their feelings in a political horizon. In short, the lesbian rights movement provided a language to make sense of, and respond to, their emotions.⁷ Emotion work was therefore important because it helped activists to name and reframe their feelings.⁸ At the core of the movement was a belief in the centrality of sexuality to the formation of one's personality, and hence, coming out became a necessary step on the quest to authenticity. Coming out can be considered emotion work as it helped lesbians to clarify and thus transform their feelings.⁹ Often, this emotion work took place in consciousness-raising groups comparable to those that were formed in Western countries like the United States, the United Kingdom, and West Germany. These female-only groups were supposed to create a safe space for sharing one's feelings and experiences.

I first explore the (emotional) effects of marginalization and invisibility. Second, I offer an introduction to the lesbian movement in the GDR. Third, I discuss what it meant to be a lesbian according to LiK. Finally, I examine the transnational and radical practices of lesbian consciousness-raising groups as a form of emotion work.

From Invisibility and Marginalization to Emancipation and Normalization

After suffering brutal persecution during National Socialism, homosexuals and their desires continued to remain socially marginalized in the GDR until the 1980s. There was hardly any representation, either positive or negative, of (female) homosexuality in the public sphere. In the 1980s, an emerging network of homosexual and lesbian rights activists was formed in response to this lack of visibility. Limited access to knowledge about lesbians created an affective state that was characterized by isolation, fear, shame, and confusion. Some lesbians did not even have a word to name their desire, as an excerpt from a monologue by a woman named Christiane, shows: "But when I remembered this first woman and started to think about what my feelings towards women were like, I began to consider this alternative: to live with a woman. But I believed that I was the only lesbian in this town—lesbian, that wasn't clear to me back then—the only woman that felt this way."¹⁰ This passage also highlights how feelings of social isolation went hand in hand with the absence of concepts to define one's desires. A ban on publishing same-sex dating adverts until 1985 made it hard for women, especially those living in the countryside, to find like-minded women. This further added to the social marginalization of lesbian desires.¹¹

Marginalization in the media worked in conjunction with social marginalization. One woman, who was born in 1961 and had been living in a small town, explained to me in an interview that she had hardly any access to information about homosexuality. She had no contact with homosexual groups and lacked a positive understanding of her homosexual desires, which resulted in inner conflicts, alcohol abuse, strong feelings of guilt and shame, and the fear that others might find out that, as she had put it for decades, "I'm not interested in men." This situation prevented her from identifying with her homosexuality and from being honest with herself and others. She did have intimate relationships with women, but these relationships never felt real to her for various reasons, not least because they remained a secret and took place only behind closed doors.[12] Not only did she describe a sense of social isolation, but also what retrospectively appeared to be an inability to live authentically, in accordance with her own desires. The marginalization of homosexual desires had made it impossible for her to live an authentic life.

The reflections of Bärbel Klässner, who was active in a lesbian group in Jena, show how important finding a label was for forming a self-identity and subsequently a political movement. While reading feminist publications from West Germany in the early 1980s, Klässner had come across the word "lesbian" for the first time: "Certainly, without the term 'lesbian' there wouldn't have been a lesbian political movement. ... Lesbian, lesbian, lesbian. A word with the potential for fight, with spike, with courage. It had not been mentioned in GDR-publications beforehand, even if they were speaking of female homosexuals."[13] The word "lesbian" named previously unnamed desires. In doing so, it created an opportunity to rethink one's sexuality in a different and, importantly, political way.

Following a church assembly on homosexuality in 1982, an increasing number of Arbeitskreise Homosexualität (working groups on homosexuality) emerged in larger cities. However, at least until the second half of the 1980s, only one group had a significant impact on the development of a political lesbian subjectivity: Lesben in der Kirche (LiK). The group grew out of a circle of friends in East Berlin who shared a desire to make lesbianism visible to the wider public. Different factors then encouraged the foundation of a specific political organization to achieve this aim, including the National Service Act of 1982, which stipulated the potential mobilization of women into the army, a desire to meet other women and, to put it plainly, the numerous questions that its members sought answers to: "We wanted to learn more about ourselves: How did other lesbians in the GDR live? Were there even others or were we the only ones? We wanted to talk about women in general. What do women do, how are they living in this society, are there differently minded women?"[14]

Curiosity and an interest in politics, informed by feminism and the peace movement, motivated these friends to find ways to meet like-minded people. At the first LiK meeting, about fifteen women gathered in an apartment but, when the police intervened, it became apparent that it was not safe to meet in private places. As a result, the women looked for shelter in the Protestant Church. LiK was not the only group in Berlin that engaged with questions of homosexuality. At first, LiK collaborated with gay men in the Arbeitskreis Homosexuelle Selbsthilfe, but it did not take long for the group to split into two distinct gay and lesbian groups.[15]

Given the challenges that unofficial political movements faced in the GDR (such as being unable to freely assemble, publish literature, and form associations), the protection offered by the Protestant Church was crucial for LiK's activism. As early as 1978, the Protestant Church started to provide space to oppositional groups such as environmental, feminist, and peace groups.[16] These were the only semipublic and nongovernmental places where political activists in the GDR could gather. Only under the Protestant Church's umbrella was LiK able to engage in the kind of activism it envisioned. As members of the group stated in a 1992 interview: "We conceived of lesbian work from the very beginning as political work, because we criticized the existing conditions. If you did this in the GDR, you had to do it in the Church."[17] Alongside this willingness to engage in social criticism, members of LiK also considered their activism to be political because they sought to challenge taboos around lesbian sexuality.[18]

It took the group some time to find a parish that would accept them. Not all parishes and pastors were tolerant enough to host a lesbian group but, in the summer of 1983, the group secured an arrangement to hold meetings on a biweekly basis at the Philippus-Kapelle (Hohenschönhausen) and, in 1984, they found shelter in the more central Gethsemane parish (Prenzlauer Berg).[19] A small group of activists, numbering around ten, prepared meetings that were attended by up to sixty people. Over the years, the core group changed significantly because several original members emigrated to West Germany. These changes made it difficult for the group to engage in constant activism. The core group included not only lesbians but also at least two bisexual women. All of them were in their mid-twenties. Most of them did not have "proper" or steady jobs, only insecure employment, which meant that most group members had a rather small income.[20] Some group members thus combined their critique of the system and heteronormativity with a critique of the omnipresent demand to find personal fulfillment in regular wage labor and in a heterosexual nuclear family. Marina Krug makes this point when reflecting on her activism: "Under the conditions of a political dictatorship, engaging in critiques of the state and feminist activism meant, as a lesbian, at the same time to critically question the careers we aspired to, or to give them up because of pressure from the state."[21] The core group provided an important support system; it was, as long-term member Bettina

Dziggel remembered, "a big queer family."²² People who felt that they were "different" from the rest of society found a safe space to try out other ways of living and new forms of political activism. Not only were issues of sexuality at stake, but also broader critical perspectives that manifested themselves through personal decisions and practices.

Regular meetings were central to LiK. These events created a place where people could meet each other and learn more about lesbianism in the past and present. Participants discussed topics like lesbian history and lesbian literature; art; female sexuality; women in other countries; and state authority. They also organized regular coming-out evenings as well as parties and trips.²³ To deal with their experiences of discrimination, activists engaged in personal and collective emotion work. They also believed that they had to take action to make lesbians more visible in the public sphere, in governmental institutions, and among "experts." To this end, the group contacted psychologists, doctors, and social institutions, and actively participated in a series of workshops called "Psychosoziale Aspekte der Homosexualität" that started in 1985 and brought activists and scientists together.²⁴ In the mid-1980s, LiK also attempted to make lesbians and their history more visible by publicly commemorating lesbian victims of Nazi persecution at the memorial site of the Ravensbrück concentration camp.²⁵

In the second half of the 1980s, other lesbian groups formed and started to create a lesbian network that was based on personal connections and pushed for a new kind of politics inspired by feminist and lesbian ideas. In Dresden, some women split away from Arbeitskreis Homosexualität Dresden to form their own group in 1985. From 1985 to 1987, they organized three women's festivals, each of which involved around three hundred guests.²⁶ In 1987, a lesbian group in Erfurt called Erfurter Lesben formed as part of the Erfurter Lesben- und Schwulen Arbeitskreis bei der Evangelischen Stadtmission.²⁷ In Leipzig, efforts to form a lesbian group that was distinct from the Arbeitskreis Homosexualität Leipzig was not immediately successfully; only in January 1989 was the lesbian group Lila Pause formed.²⁸ In Jena, lesbian meetings started in 1985 and, in 1987, they organized a lesbian festival that hosted around a hundred guests.²⁹ In 1988, a lesbian group was formed in Halle as well as the Unabhängige Frauengruppe Brandenburg and the Unabhängige Frauengruppe Magdeburg.³⁰

The reasons why lesbians split away from mixed homosexual rights groups differed from place to place. In Jena, lesbians felt that their issues did not have a lot in common with the problems that men faced. In Berlin, activists wanted to create a space free from male dominance.³¹ Nevertheless, lesbian groups and individual lesbians still continued to participate in homosexual activist networks, events, and groups. In 1989/90, around twenty mixed Arbeitskreise Homosexualität existed.[32] The visibility of lesbians and their concerns varied from group to group.

Lesbian networks were closely connected to the independent women's rights movement. Therefore, it comes as no surprise that female homosexuality was also a topic that was explored in some women's groups.[33] Activists formed connections on the basis of personal contacts, GDR-wide women's meetings and festivals, as well as lesbian workshops and meetings. In 1988, some members of the lesbian group based in Jena founded the Samizdat publication *frau anders* (Miss Different), which promoted the creation of further networks and the development of a collective lesbian identity by shining a spotlight on different lesbian groups and their events.[34] A lesbian workshop in Dresden followed in 1988. A second workshop then took place in Hanstorf (near Rostock) in 1989.[35] Festivals, workshops, and meetings not only facilitated networking, but also created self-organized safe spaces where participants could exchange experiences, discuss future projects, and socialize. Not least, these events were important because they showed women that there were many other feminists and lesbians who shared similar experiences and visions. They also mattered emotionally. The experience of taking part in such events created a feeling of great joy and empowerment among participants that contrasted with their widespread sense of loneliness.[36]

A variety of political positions and understandings of homosexuality existed within the diverse lesbian and homosexual groups that emerged in the 1980s. Not all groups met under the umbrella of the Protestant Church. In contrast to the groups that worked within the church, so-called secular groups focused on the assimilation and integration of homosexuals into socialist society. They campaigned for official recognition and used, for example, clubhouses provided by the official youth organization Freie Deutsche Jugend (FDJ). These groups included Sonntags-Club in Berlin (formed in 1986), RosaLinde in Leipzig (formed 1987), and the Sonntags-Club in Cottbus (formed in 1986).[37] By 1989/90, approximately eleven of these clubs had been established.[38] Their attempts to make homosexuality part of the official political discourse caused tensions between "secular" and "clerical" groups. However, the existence of these diverse groups ultimately contributed to the increasing visibility of homosexual desires in the GDR. They questioned the heteronormative order and the traditional gender roles that had been at the heart of the regime's biopolitical agenda. It is difficult to tell how many people in total were organized in the lesbian and homosexual rights groups. The size of the groups varied from between ten and sixty members, and some of their events, like the women's festivals in Dresden, attracted up to three hundred people. Despite the fact that only several hundred individuals participated in these groups and events, their activism and ideas influenced people more broadly.

LiK maintained an openly political approach, and therefore differed from most other homosexual groups that focused more readily on the integration and normalization of homosexuality. Marinka Körzendörfer, a member of LiK, recalled: "Our self-understanding was radical and we understood our homosexuality to be a political decision."[39] The fact that LiK developed such a political understanding of homosexuality reveals how sexuality and gender were considered to be inextricably linked to regimes of power. Beyond questions of sexuality and gender, LiK could draw on a network of different political groups that were active within the Protestant Church, including feminist groups like Frauen für den Frieden and other peace and homosexual rights groups.[40]

Activist networks also extended beyond the GDR. Members of LiK, for example, had personal contacts with lesbians and activists in West Berlin, West Germany, and the Netherlands. Personal meetings offered new perspectives. A visit by the black lesbian feminist writer and civil rights activist Audre Lorde in 1985 gave LiK activists insights into the rise of the Afro-German feminist movement in West Germany and drew their attention to racism.[41] From 1987, members of the Homosexuelle Initiative Wien organized East European Information Pool meetings, which provided LiK members with the opportunity to meet activists from other European countries, especially those in Eastern Europe.[42] The accounts subsequently provided by activists indicate that politics and political activism meant something different in the GDR than in the "West." Activists in the East faced extensive spying and repression by the Stasi and lacked freedom of assembly, publication, and association. Indeed, any form of political activism outside of the governmental or official party organizations was outlawed. Stasi surveillance, however, had paradoxical effects. Everything could become suspicious and therefore political, as this comment by Bärbel Klässner shows:

> The sphere of influence of the state did not even stop at the corner of the bed, if it was in its [i.e., the state's] (alleged) interests. The Stasi made use of the fact that lesbians and gays who were not living openly (and who would back then?) could be blackmailed. In that sense, it was already a political issue for female citizens of the GDR not to follow the predestined ways of life and not to hide this fact. And it was political to take a stand in private, against the interventions of the state.[43]

Stasi surveillance of lesbians is an issue that has yet to be studied in depth.[44] The archives are extensive. What is clear, however, is that the surveillance of lesbians was widespread, took place in every single one of the lesbian and homosexual activist groups, and that the Stasi specifically targeted lesbians who were actively participating in homosexual or lesbian rights groups. Confidential informants infiltrated groups and, in some cases, the beds of activists, or at least they tried to do so.[45] For the Stasi, lesbian groups were perceived to pose a security risk due to their contact with activists from other countries and their questioning of the existing political regime. The Stasi feared, as one report from February 1986 stated, a "political abuse of homosexuals" by the "usurpation by hostile forces" and understood them as part of the opposition movement. To deal with the growing homosexual movement, the Stasi sought to "destroy organizational structures and make certain involved persons insecure." The Stasi employed these methods against LiK, as it was considered to be disloyal to the political system.[46]

Such measures made political activism, including that which took place in groups such as LiK, a risky endeavor that could, at worst, result in imprisonment. In light of this, it is perhaps unsurprising that LiK member Marinka Körzendörfer stated in June 1989 that: "From the moment a lesbian meets another and they start to do something together for themselves and other lesbians, the lesbian work has already started."[47] Körzendörfer speaks of "lesbian work," thus avoiding potentially risky terms like "political" or "activism." The second part of Körzendörfer's statement is also revealing. For Körzendörfer, as well as other activists, "lesbian" or "homosexual work" started at the very basic level of two or more lesbians meeting and doing something to improve their situations. However, even these very basic forms of activism were regarded as political and potentially dangerous acts by the state.

The Lesbian Subject between Regulation and Politicization

Lesben in der Kirche developed a distinct understanding of what it meant to be a lesbian, and why this was a political issue. Two documents by LiK, a working paper from 1983 and an information paper published between 1985 and 1986, provide insights into their political understanding of homosexuality.[48] They show how the group's activism was informed by their analysis of the difficult living conditions that lesbians in the GDR faced. Though both texts are written in a reflexive and analytic rather than emotional style, emotions were nevertheless important, especially to their understanding of what being a lesbian meant: being a woman who desires women and who wants to share intimacy, romance, and sexuality with women. In line with feminists in other countries, Lesben in der Kirche argued that lesbians experienced a double oppression, both as women and as lesbians. According to their analysis, women internalized heterosexuality and motherhood as a norm when they lived in an oppressive, patriarchal system. "How shall a woman who was brought up in an anti-sexual way, who had to learn to suffer passively, understand and communicate her sexual needs? How does a woman make out, if her own body is 'a closed book'?"[49] In their understanding, the oppression of women in the patriarchal system had a bodily dimension, since not knowing their own bodies made it difficult to explore sexual desires and thus have an authentic sexuality. Women remained estranged from their bodies, their sexuality, and ultimately, their entire lives. As LiK highlighted, women were still socialized into a passive role and were supposed to become married, heterosexual mothers. These unspoken but powerful social expectations made it difficult for women to accept their identity as lesbians.[50] In their analysis, LiK therefore linked a collective subjectification of political lesbianism with individual women's personal acceptance of their sexuality.

LiK's understanding of women as oppressed subjects diverged from the official political position of the GDR, which stipulated that men and women were equal. In contrast to many Western European countries, gender equality was, to a certain extent, an essential aspect of official politics in the GDR. Even though complete gender equality was never accomplished, it was common for women to be employed. They enjoyed equal rights, had autonomy over their bodies with regard to abortion, and access to childcare and affordable housing that was provided by the state. During the 1970s, the figure of the single mother became increasingly common. These developments also offered opportunities for lesbians to live their lives differently. Women, and lesbians, had greater independence from men in comparison to countries such as West Germany. However, just as in Western countries, family and social politics in the GDR were mainly focused on heterosexual married couples with children. Despite legal equality, women were not equal to men in practice, and this inequality was not addressed in public discourse.[51] During the 1980s, Lesben in der Kirche and other lesbian and feminist groups sought to challenge such inequalities.

LiK did not simply promote the understanding that lesbians were oppressed and constrained by sexism. They also criticized the tabooing of homosexuality and the widespread idea was homosexuality was an "illness" and "perversion." They challenged discriminatory laws, inaccurate media reports, and homophobia in general. LiK argued that the tensions between the institutionalized and omnipresent heterosexuality and a marginal homosexual identity affected individuals on a personal level, as they believed that social oppression caused physical and mental illnesses.[52] In this sense, they construed the lesbian subject as vulnerable. Indeed, the notion that homosexuals were deficient, ill, and in need of professional help was widespread, especially within psychology.[53] LiK asserted that a legal discourse that portrayed homosexuals as potentially criminal and dangerous further contributed to widespread "feelings of guilt," "fear," "bias," a "self-definition as deviant," and therefore to the "inner rejection of the 'homosexual' ego" and the suppression of lesbian desires.[54] The understanding of lesbian subjectivity that LiK developed was a response to the impositions and constraints that they faced in East German society. LiK defined their own subjectivities in response to these forms of regulation. Echoing West German homosexual activist Rosa von Praunheim's famous film "It is not the homosexual who is perverse, but the society in which he lives" (1971), LiK called for society to change rather than for homosexuals to change: "our homosexuality needs to be addressed and we need to realize that it is not our sexuality that is problematic, but the situation in which we live."[55]

Such a statement indicates that the politicization of gender and sexuality was a transnational process. Typically, ideas and concepts traveled east from the United States to West Germany and, from there, through personal meetings and books to the GDR. With help from the Netherlands, West Germany, and donations from the International Lesbian and Gay Association, Lesben in der Kirche built a small, illegal library with feminist and lesbian fiction and non-fiction from the United States and West Germany.[56] The books that they received from the West provided East German activists with both feminist theories of female homosexuality and practical advice that they sometimes adopted for their own activism. The phrase "coming out," for example, was first coined by US-American homosexual rights activists in the 1970s, before spreading to other countries. LiK activists were clearly aware of the origins of "coming out" as a concept, as the reference to a US source in their "information paper" indicates.[57]

Coming out was central to the creation of a lesbian political subject. Indeed, the very concept of "coming out" suggested a clear distinction between hetero- and homosexuality and hence a gender binary. The assumption of clearly distinguished categories made it possible to form an identity based on differentiation. For Lesben in der Kirche, coming out could "redefine" a "deviant" identity into a "minority identity." They understood coming out as a "conflict with one's own homosexuality." By accepting one's homosexuality, a lesbian woman would discover her "true sexuality."[58] Being a lesbian, however, was not simply about sexuality, but also authentic subjectivity.

In the understanding of the LiK, the self-definition as "deviant" included an internalized conflict with behavioral patterns, expectations and the way of life that society had declared to be the norm. For these reasons the lesbian woman often reacts with feelings of guilt without wanting to accept this "normality" for herself. If the lesbian woman realizes and accepts her life choice, different behavioral patterns become visible that reflect the problem of homosexuality as part of a social reality.[59]

One aspect of the transformative process that LiK described concerned the transformation of negative feelings. Developing a genuine "self-awareness" meant overcoming feelings of shame, fear, and self-hatred.[60] They understood "coming out" to be an essential step toward developing a true, authentic lesbian subjectivity. However, becoming a self-conscious and authentic lesbian was not an individualized process. "We need to develop a lesbian solidarity," Lesben in der Kirche proclaimed.[61] Self-awareness was something that should be accomplished with the help of consciousness-raising groups. These groups were supposed to function as a "communication center" and aimed to offer "support" in the coming-out process.[62] In these groups, lesbians developed a new emotional habitus that offered them a different understanding of their situation, as well as a transformation of their feelings.

Consciousness-Raising and Writing as Emotion Work

In practice, activist groups engaged in emotion work during their regular meetings. While some meetings were devoted to discussions, lectures, or cultural activities, others provided a space to get to know each other, to socialize and to talk about one's life, feelings, and experiences. Opportunities to advertise meetings to a broader audience were limited. As a result, LiK promoted their events at regular church assemblies, and relied on word of mouth.[63] In many cases, meetings were attended by friends and personal acquaintances.[64] Participants had rather diverse expectations and interests: finding a partner; getting support for coming-out; socializing; political activism to improve the living conditions of lesbians; and activism to change society more fundamentally.[65]

Half of LiK's events were open to everyone. These events were usually devoted to discussions or lectures about a specific topic. The group's other events, which were exclusively for women to get to know each other, socialize, and talk about their lives, feelings, and experiences, were deemed more important. These meetings aimed to offer a safe space to deal with emotions and coming-out, providing shelter from patriarchal and antihomosexual oppression and an arena "for communication, dealing with problems and consciousness-raising as homosexuals."[66] Talking about sexuality played a central role in lesbians' emotion work at these meetings. The introductory comments at an event by the AK Homosexuality Dresden, dedicated to exchanging personal experiences of homosexuality, create an impression of how lesbians talked about sexuality. Karin Dauenheimer, the founder of the AK, explained how the group worked and encouraged people to share their feelings about their homosexuality. She also discussed her own feelings: "In a long and difficult process, I realized that my homosexuality is not something bad, inferior. That it is not something that needs to be fought, derided, oppressed. I realized that I have the opportunity, also as a homosexual, as a lesbian woman, to become an equal human."[67]

Accepting her sexual orientation was not only central to her self-understanding as a lesbian, but also carried a political dimension. Dauenheimer asserted that accepting oneself and thus gaining a sense of authenticity was a long-term process. The safe space that consciousness-raising groups provided also offered an opportunity to break taboos. Ramona Dreßler, former member of LiK, remembered how: "We also spoke about our sexuality. This was an even bigger taboo than lesbianism. It was very difficult to speak about it, but it was a very positive experience."[68] LiK explicitly addressed such themes. A discussion evening that took place on 1 November 1984, for example, was dedicated to the question: "Happy Childhood—Happy Sexuality?"[69] Questions had been prepared to encourage discussion, the first of which read: "What is your earliest sexual experience, feeling, or thought that you can remember? How did you feel about it?" The event then went on to collectively examine the sexual feelings of the participants. Other questions addressed menstruation, further sexual experiences, and (the lack of) sexual education. Sharing these personal experiences was a central aspect of the groups' emotion work, because it highlighted that these were not isolated or individual experiences, but rather the result of the social conditions that lesbians and women had to face.

Lesbian activists also wrote about their feelings and sexuality, producing anonymized tracts that chronicled individual life stories. Through the act of writing, the authors sought to understand their personal trajectories, how they became lesbians, and why they had suppressed their lesbian desires for so long. One of the authors explained that it took her a long time to accept the reality of her homosexual desires in the face of private and public rejections:

> For a long time, I had this idea of myself, how I want to be, that had nothing to do with who I really am and certainly did not question my sexuality ... a lesbian relationship as a pursuit of happiness was never an option. My mother had spoken to me about homosexuality because

she was working with a homosexual man; she also showed understanding for him, but without saying it, it was clear that it is something abnormal, that could only ever be something that happens to others, not oneself. ... This prevented me for a long time from confessing to myself my longing for a sexual relationship with a woman.[70]

From 1985 onwards, a lesbian group in Jena held weekly meetings to talk about personal experiences, discrimination due to their homosexuality, drug addiction, their relationship with their bodies, sexuality, sexual violence, experiences of psychiatry and abortions. Every woman who joined the group had a chance to tell her story at a dedicated meeting. Other participants then asked her questions and documented her answers. These documents were used as material for a performance.[71] In 1988, some members of the group started to compile the samizdat publication *frau anders* that served as a semi-public forum for lesbians to share their experiences and, more broadly, as a platform for the lesbian movement that was not subject to the censorship and concessions of the authorities. The magazine accepted submissions from groups as well as individuals. In its fifth issue, published in 1989, co-editor Bärbel Klässner promoted the foundation of a lesbian writing group:

> I think that writing ... always moves between understanding ourselves and the need to talk. Doing both is really important to us—to live in accordance with oneself as well as to talk to a public that has ignored us for too long—shows that these are the concerns of our lesbian groups, yes, a necessity for every lesbian woman who wants to escape from shame, fear and isolation.[72]

Klässner's words draw our attention once again to the fact that talking about one's situation, whether in consciousness-raising groups or through writing, was considered an essential tool for creating an authentic lesbian subjectivity. Much like the places where women met, *frau anders* offered a safe space that encouraged lesbians to write about themselves and their experiences, a place that had been absent in the public discourse of homosexuality in the GDR.

When drawing up rules and guidelines for consciousness-raising groups, women in the GDR relied on Western models from the United States and West Germany. The private archives of Marinka Körzendörfer, for example, include a list of rules for group discussions, which originated in West German and US contexts.[73] The rules instructed participants on how to behave in group discussions, especially regarding how to communicate in this "unusual" setting. They were meant to facilitate a reflective, communicative, and emancipated subject. The first rule called for being "your own chairman," which meant everyone should decide for herself what she wanted to share and act according to her own needs. Central to all the rules was a focus on the individual and on strategies for becoming aware of oneself, one's needs, and one's feelings. The rules also urged participants to communicate as directly and as clearly as possible with one other. They instructed participants to take themselves and their needs seriously, regarding their feelings and bodily signals as important clues on how to do so. Following these rules would help create a self-aware, individual subject.

Many of the instructions were taken word for word from the book *Anleitung zum sozialen Lernen für Paare, Gruppen und Erzieher* (*Instructions for Social Learning for Couples, Groups, and Educators*) by Lutz Schwäbisch and Martin Siems, a bestseller that was first published in West Germany in 1974, where it had informed the practices of numerous consciousness-raising groups.[74] Drawing on theme-centered interaction theory, which was itself based on humanist psychology, the book provided its readers with guidelines on how to better understand themselves and change their behavior. The book proposed that consciousness-raising groups were a crucial tool in this regard.[75]

Besides Schwäbisch and Siems's book, lesbians in the GDR also adopted rules proposed by a West German group from Freiburg.[76] The rules stated, for example, that a consciousness raising group should consist only of women: "This is very important, because this group is supposed to be a free space to become aware of our experiences as women."[77] They addressed organizational questions, dictating for example that the group should be small, should not have leader, should meet every week for two or three hours, that no new members should join the group after the first meeting, and that all members should attend on a regular basis. Other rules addressed communication. Members were advised to pick a specific topic for each session and to encourage everyone to share their experiences regarding this issue. It would be up to every woman to decide what she wanted to share and when she shared her experiences, other group members should not interrupt her. Rather, participants were advised to listen carefully, ask questions to gain a better understanding, and express their concerns. They were not allowed to criticize or give advice, except when it was asked for. Once every woman had shared her experiences on the topic, the group was supposed to reflect on the session based on their feelings throughout the evening. Ideally, the meetings created a space to develop a shared language that expressed individual experiences of oppressions and the (negative) feelings these experiences caused, before transforming these feelings within the group.

When comparing the two texts, the book by Schwäbisch and Siems and the rules proposed by the women's group in Freiburg, an interesting difference emerges: whereas the rules for group discussions developed by Schwäbisch and Siems focused on individual self-awareness, the rules developed by the Freiburg women's group not only concentrated on self-awareness, but also emphasized awareness of shared experiences. This indicates the political dimension of the work done in women's groups.

Concluding Thoughts

Lesbian rights activism in the late GDR can be understood, to a large extent, as emotional politics. During the 1980s, both the homosexual rights movement and the separate lesbian rights movement, which emerged slightly later, facilitated the creation of new homosexual subjectivities, emotions, networks, and modes of politics. Lesben in der Kirche, with its ideas of a regulated lesbian subject and its demand for societal change, played a leading role in the lesbian rights movement. Lesbians in the GDR faced an affective state that was characterized by isolation, shame, and fear. The formation of lesbian and homosexual rights groups can be understood as a reaction to this affective state. Supported by exchanges with activists from other countries, these groups sought to make sense of the negative emotions that many lesbians described. The ideas behind consciousness-raising were inspired by homosexual and feminist activism in "Western" countries. Compared to the situation in the other East bloc countries, GDR activists were in a relatively "privileged" position. They had quite easy access to groups and literature from the West. The situation for lesbians and gays within the East bloc was diverse. In Czechoslovakia, Hungary, Poland, and Slovenia, relatively strong groups were formed within a subculture that was able to access Western films and books with homosexual themes. In the Soviet Union, however, lesbian groups were not created before 1990 due to the massive repression and tabooing of homosexuality. Due to the work of the Eastern European Information Pool, some elements of Western activism and identities were adopted within specific national contexts.[78]

For each of the groups discussed in this chapter, lesbian identity was deeply political. The concept of consciousness-raising was central to the emotion work that occurred in these groups, as was the idea that coming-out was a process through which women could learn to accept their homosexuality despite the constant discrimination that they experienced. The concept of consciousness-raising and coming-out first emerged in the US feminist and homosexual rights movements, and were later adapted in other countries. Female-only consciousness-raising meetings were important spaces in which women could engage in deep conversations about their lives, sexuality, and coming-out. Talking and writing about their experiences and feelings helped participants to see their lives in a broader perspective and to transform their emotional habitus, not least because groups offered support and ideas of a positive self-understanding. The practice also challenged the prevailing emotional regime that offered hardly any positive emotions regarding female homosexuality. In this context, consciousness-raising groups offered spaces for communication and support. The groups helped participants raise awareness of their suppressed emotions and desires, and to develop authentic feelings and an authentic self. Consciousness-raising encouraged an entirely new set of practices. Lesbian groups offered a space for trying out different ways of being a lesbian, articulating oneself in different ways, and learning how to do politics in a manner that was directly democratic. All these practices had the potential to challenge the legitimacy of the GDR.

The case study presented here highlights the central role of emotions to political activism. Emotions motivated and informed lesbian activists. Their emotion work facilitated the formation of new subjectivities and a political understanding of homosexuality. It also shows the important and transformative work that took place within the lesbian movement in East Germany during the 1980s. These transformations challenged the prevailing regime. They offered alternative, authentic subjectivities and new political practices, therefore contributing to the transformations that ultimately resulted in the fall of the Berlin Wall. Much of the research on the opposition movement in the GDR excludes the lesbian movement. However, as Michel Foucault has argued, sexuality and gender, and their regulation, are central regimes of power. The case of Lesben in der Kirche demonstrates how the questioning of heteronormativity and gender went hand in hand with social criticism to such an extent that it made lesbians a target for the Stasi. In addition, lesbians participated in transregional activist networks that went beyond the homosexual rights and feminist movements. In the GDR, the concept of the "socialist personality" and the "socialist manner of life" came to play a central role in socialist ideology during the 1960s and 1970s. The prevailing doctrine of Marxism-Leninism did not recognize specific individuals, but only "socialist personalities" who had to strongly identify with the socialist system.[79] Therefore, consciousness-raising in the GDR can be understood as a genuinely revolutionary act on a micro level, one that questioned the paradigm of the socialist personality and socialist politics in general.

Maria Bühner is a doctoral candidate and Lecturer at the Institute for Cultural Studies at Leipzig University in the section for Comparative Cultural and Social History of Modern Europe. Her major research interests are history of emotions, gender history, and history of the body. She is currently completing her dissertation on lesbian subjectification in the German Democratic Republic from the 1960s to 1980s. She is a member of the interdisciplinary Graduate School "Global and Area Studies" at Leipzig University and scholar of the German Academic Scholarship Foundation.

Notes

I would like to thank Joachim Häberlen, Kate Mahoney, Alexandra Ghit, and Arbeitsgruppe Kultur- und Sozialgeschichte der DDR in transnationaler Perspektive at Leipzig University for their helpful comments and ideas.

1. Anne Hampele Ulrich, *Der Unabhängige Frauenverband: Ein frauenpolitisches Experiment im deutschen Vereinigungsprozess* (Berlin, 2000), 69–80.
2. Eva Sänger, *Begrenzte Teilhabe: Ostdeutsche Frauenbewegung und Zentraler Runder Tisch in der DDR* (Frankfurt a. M., 2005), 121.
3. Konrad Jarausch, "Realer Sozialismus als Fürsorgediktatur," *Aus Politik und Zeitgeschichte* no. 48 (1998): 33–46; Juliane Scholz, "Die andere Liebe (The Other Love): 'Fürsorgediktatur' and LGBTIQ in the GDR in the 1980s," paper presented at the Fortieth Annual German Studies Association Conference, 29 September–2 October 2016. San Diego, CA.
4. Deborah Gould, *Moving Politics: Emotion and ACT UP's Fight against AIDS*. (Chicago, 2009), 3.
5. Ibid., 40.
6. William Reddy, *The Navigation of Feeling* (Cambridge, 2001), 124.
7. Gould, *Moving Politics,* 1–48, 439–444.
8. Ibid., 1–48.
9. Magdalena Beljan, *Rosa Zeiten? Eine Geschichte der Subjektivierung männlicher Homosexualität in den 1970er und 1980er Jahren der BRD* (Bielefeld, 2014), 106–122.
10. Kerstin Gutsche, *Ich ahnungsloser Engel: Lesbenprotokolle* (Berlin, 1991), 19. All translations are mine unless otherwise stated.
11. Eva Sänger, "'Lieber öffentlich lesbisch als heimlich im DFD': Die Samisdat-Publikation frau anders in der DDR 1988/89," in *Öffentlichkeiten und Geschlechterverhältnisse: Erfahrungen—Politiken—Subjekte,* ed. Susanne Lettow (Königstein [Taunus], 2005), 161.
12. Unpublished anonymized interview by the author, 26 and 27 January 2016.
13. Bärbel Klässner, "Als frau anders war," in *Das Übersehenwerden hat Geschichte— Lesben in der DDR und der Friedlichen Revolution: Tagungsdokumentation,* ed. Daniela Zocholl and Susanne Diehr (Berlin, 2015), 59.
14. Christina Karstädt and Anette von Zitzewitz, *...viel zuviel verschwiegen: Eine Dokumentation von Lebensgeschichten lesbischer Frauen aus der Deutschen Demokratischen Republik* (Berlin, 1996), 160.
15. "Zur Geschichte des Berliner Lesbenkreises," in Robert-Havemann-Gesellschaft Berlin (RHG)/GrauZone (GZ)/1470.
16. See Hampele Ulrich, *Der Unabhängige Frauenverband,* 302.

17. Karstädt and Zitzewitz, *…viel zuviel verschwiegen*, 155.
18. Ibid., 160.
19. Stefanie Krautz, *Lesbisches Engagement in Ost-Berlin 1978–1989* (Marburg, 2009), 56–57.
20. Personal interview with Bettina Dziggel by the author, Leipzig, 13 July 2016.
21. Marina Krug, "Die Gruppe Arbeitskreis Homosexuelle Selbsthilfe: Lesben in der Kirche in Berlin/DDR—November 1982 bis Sommer 1986," in *In Bewegung bleiben: 100 Jahre Politik, Kultur und Geschichte von Lesben*, ed. Gabriele Dennert, Christiane Leidinger, and Franziska Rauchut (Berlin, 2007), 112.
22. Unpublished interview with Bettina Dziggel.
23. Samirah Kenawi, *Frauengruppen in der DDR der 1980er Jahre: Eine Dokumentation* (Berlin, 1995), 84; unpublished interview with Bettina Dziggel.
24. Sektion Ehe und Familie der Gesellschaft für Sozialhygiene der DDR and Sektion Andrologie der Gesellschaft für Dermatologie, ed., *Psychosoziale Aspekte der Homosexualität* (Jena, 1986); idem, ed. *Psychosoziale Aspekte der Homosexualität. II. Workshop* (Jena, 1989).
25. Samirah Kenawi, "Die Ersten werden die Letzten sein: Thesen zur Lesbenbewegung in der DDR," in *Lesben und Schwule in der DDR: Tagungsdokumentation*, ed. Lesben- und Schwulenverband in Deutschland (LSVD)—Landesverband Sachsen-Anhalt e.V. and Heinrich-Böll-Stiftung Sachsen-Anhalt (Magdeburg, 2008), 57–65.
26. Hampele Ulrich, *Der Unabhängige Frauenverband*, 46.
27. Sänger, *Begrenzte Teilhabe*, 104–108.
28. Jessica Bock, "Die Lesbengruppe in Leipzig: Eine Geschichte der Spurlosen?—Ein Werkstattbericht," in *Das Übersehenwerden hat Geschichte—Lesben in der DDR und der Friedlichen Revolution. Tagungsdokumentation*, ed. by Daniela Zocholl and Susanne Diehr (Berlin, 2015), 99–109.
29. Kenawi, *Frauengruppen*, 191–195; Klässner, *Als frau anders war*, 58–69.
30. Kenawi, *Frauengruppen*, 99, 173.
31. Klässner, *Als frau anders war*, 62; "Zur Geschichte des Berliner Lesbenskreises," in RHG/GZ/1470.
32. "Arbeitskreise Homosexualität in der DDR, Stand August 1989 und Stand Januar 1990," in Schwules Museum, Berlin, DDR, AK Homosexualität, no. 7.
33. Kenawi, *Frauengruppen*, 245–246.
34. Sänger, *Begrenzte Teilhabe*, 106–111.
35. "Die Zwischenwerkstatt in Hanstorf—Pfingsten 1989—ein Bericht," in RHG/GZ/A1/1173.
36. E.g., Klässner, *Als frau anders war*, 63.
37. Sänger, *Begrenzte Teilhabe*, 102–103.
38. "Arbeitskreise Homosexualität in der DDR, Stand August 1989 und Stand Januar 1990," in Schwules Museum, Berlin, DDR, AK Homosexualität, no. 7.
39. "Zur Geschichte des Berliner Lesbenkreises," RHG/GZ/A1/1470.
40. Kenawi, *Frauengruppen*, 84.
41. Krug, "Die Gruppe," 110.
42. "Protokoll (Verlaufsprotokoll) des 3. EEIP, 21–23 April 1989," in RHG/GZ/A1/2589.

43. Klässner, *Als frau anders war,* 66.
44. Maria Bühner, "'Beiträge für eine Chronik, die vielleicht einmal geschrieben wird': Perspektiven auf den Forschungsstand zu Lesben in der DDR," in *Das Übersehenwerden hat Geschichte—Lesben in der DDR und der Friedlichen Revolution: Tagungsdokumentation,* ed. Daniela Zocholl and Susanne Diehr (Berlin, 2015), 110–120.
45. Barbara Wallbraun, "Lesben im Visier der Staatssicherheit," in *Das Übersehenwerden hat Geschichte—Lesben in der DDR und der Friedlichen Revolution: Tagungsdokumentation,* ed. Daniela Zocholl and Susanne Diehr (Berlin, 2015), 26–50.
46. Behörde des Bundesbeauftragten für die Unterlagen des Staatssicherheitsdiensts der ehemaligen Deutschen Demokratischen Republik (BStU), BVfS Potsdam, AKG, no. 260, 27–29.
47. Marinka Körzendörfer (1989), "Resümee und Ausblick der Lesbenarbeit in der DDR" in RHG/GZ/A1/2572.
48. Lesben in der Kirche (1983), "Arbeitspapier des Arbeitskreises homosexuelle Selbshilfe Berlin," in RHG/GZ/A1/1453; Lesben in der Kirche (1985/86), "Informationspapier vom Arbeitskreis Homosexuelle Selbsthilfe—Lesben in der Kirche: Homosexualität in der Gesellschaft," in RHG/GZ/A1/29. For a more detailed discussion of this document, see Maria Bühner, "'[W]ir haben einen Zustand zu analysieren, der uns zu Außenseitern macht': Lesbischer Aktivismus in Ost-Berlin in den 1980er-Jahren," in *Clio Online: Themenportal Europäische Geschichte,* 2017.
49. "Informationspapier," in RHG/GZ/A1/29.
50. "Arbeitspapier," in RHG/GZ/A1/1453.
51. Josie McLellan, *Love in the Time of Communism: Intimacy and Sexuality in the GDR* (Cambridge, 2011), 66–68.
52. "Informationspapier," in RHG/GZ/A1/29.
53. Birgit Waberski, *Die großen Veränderungen beginnen leise: Lesbenliteratur in der DDR und den neuen Bundesländern* (Dortmund, 1997), 40–41; Ulrike Klöppel, "Die 'Verfügung zur Geschlechtsumwandlung von Transsexualisten' im Spiegel der Sexualpolitik der DDR," in *Lernen aus der Geschichte,* 2014.
54. "Informationspapier," in RHG/GZ/A1/29.
55. Ibid.
56. Krug, "Die Gruppe," 110; unpublished interview with Bettina Dziggel.
57. Sharon Maxine Raphael, *Coming Out: The Emergence of the Movement Lesbian* (Cleveland, OH, 1974).
58. "Arbeitspapier," in RHG/GZ/A1/1453.
59. "Informationspapier," in RHG/GZ/A1/29.
60. Ibid.
61. Ibid.
62. "Arbeitspapier," in RHG/GZ/A1/1453.
63. Krug, "Die Gruppe," 110–111.
64. Unpublished interview with Bettina Dziggel.
65. Klässner, *Als frau anders war,* 62.
66. "Positionspapier," in RHG/GZ/A1/1453.

67. Karin Dauenheimer (1984), "Stichworte, die ein Gespräch eröffnen können," in RHG/GZ/A1/2774.
68. Karstädt and Zitzewitz, ... *viel zuviel verschwiegen*, 162.
69. Lesben in der Kirche (1984), "Glückliche Kindheit—glückliche Sexualität?," in RHG/GZ/A1/1456.
70. Ibid.
71. Klässner, *Als frau anders war*, 66–67.
72. Bärbel Klässner, in *frau anders* (V/1989), cited in Sänger, "'Lieber öffentlich lesbisch als heimlich im DFD,'" 167.
73. "Regeln für die Gruppendiskussion," in RHG/GZ/2577.
74. Lutz Schwäbisch and Martin Siems, *Anleitung zum sozialen Lernen für Paare, Gruppen und Erzieher: Kommunikations- und Verhaltenstraining* (Reinbek bei Hamburg, 1974), 243–245.
75. Jochen Spielmann, "Was ist TZI?" in *Handbuch Themenzentrierte Interaktion (TZI)*, ed. Jochen Spielmann, Mina Schneider-Landolf, and Walter Zitterbarth (Göttingen, 2014), 15–17.
76. First published in *Frauenjahrbuch* (Münster, 1975) and reprinted in Freiburger Frauengruppe, "Kleingruppen—Erfahrungen und Regeln," in *Autonome Frauen: Schlüsseltexte der Neuen Frauenbewegung seit 1968*, ed. Ann Anders (Frankfurt a. M., 1988), 102–108.
77. "Regeln für eine Frauengruppe," in RHG/GZ/2577.
78. Roman Kuhar, "Ljubljana: The Tales from the Queer Margins of the City," in *Queer Cities, Queer Cultures: Europe since 1945*, ed. Matt Cook and Jennifer Evans (London, 2014), 135–150; Francesca Stella, *Lesbian Lives in Soviet and Post-Soviet Russia: Post/Socialism and Gendered Sexualities* (Basingstoke, UK, 2015); Lukasz Szulc, *Transnational Homosexuals in Communist Poland: Cross-Border Flows in Gay and Lesbian Magazines* (Basingstoke, UK, 2018), 61–90; Judit Takács, "Queering Budapest," in Cook and Evans, *Queer Cities*, 191–210.
79. Ulrike Froböse, "Drei Geschlechter, eine sozialistische Identität? Sex, gender und Begehren zwischen offizieller Politik und lesbischem (Er-)Leben in der DDR," in *"Nie wieder Sex": Geschlechterforschung am Ende des Geschlechts*, ed. Esther Donat, Ulrike Froböse, and Rebecca Pates (Wiesbaden, 2009), 91–133.

Bibliography

Beljan, Magdalena. *Rosa Zeiten? Eine Geschichte der Subjektivierung männlicher Homosexualität in den 1970er und 1980er Jahren der BRD*. Bielefeld: Transcript, 2014.

Bock, Jessica. "Die Lesbengruppe in Leipzig: Eine Geschichte der Spurlosen?—Ein Werkstattbericht." In *Das Übersehenwerden hat Geschichte—Lesben in der DDR und der Friedlichen Revolution: Tagungsdokumentation*, edited by Daniela Zocholl and Susanne Diehr, 99–109. Berlin: Heinrich-Böll-Stiftung Sachsen-Anhalt and Gunda Werner Institut 2015.

Bühner, Maria. "'Beiträge für eine Chronik, die vielleicht einmal geschrieben wird': Perspektiven auf den Forschungsstand zu Lesben in der DDR." In *Das*

Übersehenwerden hat Geschichte—Lesben in der DDR und der Friedlichen Revolution: Tagungsdokumentation, edited by Daniela Zocholl and Susanne Diehr, 110–120. Berlin: Heinrich-Böll-Stiftung Sachsen-Anhalt and Gunda Werner Institut, 2015.

———. "'[W]ir haben einen Zustand zu analysieren, der uns zu Außenseitern macht': Lesbischer Aktivismus in Ost-Berlin in den 1980er-Jahren." In *Clio Online: Themenportal Europäische Geschichte,* 2017. Retrieved 10 December 2017 from www.europa.clio-online.de/essay/id/artikel-4126.

Dziggel, Bettina. Personal interview by the author. Leipzig, 13 July 2016.

Frauenjahrbuch. Münster: Tende-Verlag, 1975.

Freiburger Frauengruppe. "Kleingruppen—Erfahrungen und Regeln." In *Autonome Frauen: Schlüsseltexte der Neuen Frauenbewegung seit 1968,* edited by Ann Anders, 94–110. Frankfurt a. M.: Athenäum, 1988.

Froböse, Ulrike. "Drei Geschlechter, eine sozialistische Identität? Sex, gender und Begehren zwischen offizieller Politik und lesbischem (Er-)Leben in der DDR." In *"Nie wieder Sex": Geschlechterforschung am Ende des Geschlechts,* edited by Esther Donat, Ulrike Froböse, and Rebecca Pates, 91–133, Wiesbaden: Verlag für Sozialwissenschaften, 2009.

Gould, Deborah. *Moving Politics: Emotion and ACT UP's Fight against AIDS.* Chicago: The University of Chicago Press, 2009.

Gutsche, Kerstin. *Ich ahnungsloser Engel: Lesbenprotokolle.* Berlin: Reiher, 1991.

Hampele Ulrich, Anne. *Der Unabhängige Frauenverband: Ein frauenpolitisches Experiment im deutschen Vereinigungsprozess,* Berlin: Berliner Debatte, 2000.

Jarausch, Konrad. "Realer Sozialismus als Fürsorgediktatur." *Aus Politik und Zeitgeschichte* no. 48 (1998): 33–46.

Karstädt, Christina, and Anette von Zitzewitz. *...viel zuviel verschwiegen: Eine Dokumentation von Lebensgeschichten lesbischer Frauen aus der Deutschen Demokratischen Republik.* Berlin: Hoho, 1996.

Kenawi, Samirah. "Die Ersten werden die Letzten sein: Thesen zur Lesbenbewegung in der DDR." In *Lesben und Schwule in der DDR: Tagungsdokumentation,* edited by Lesben- und Schwulenverband in Deutschland (LSVD)—Landesverband Sachsen-Anhalt e.V. and Heinrich-Böll-Stiftung Sachsen-Anhalt, 57–65. Magdeburg: LSVD Sachsen-Anhalt and Heinrich-Böll-Stiftung Sachsen-Anhalt, 2008.

———. *Frauengruppen in der DDR der 1980er Jahre: Eine Dokumentation.* Berlin: GrauZone, 1995.

Klässner, Bärbel. "Als frau anders war." In *Das Übersehenwerden hat Geschichte—Lesben in der DDR und der Friedlichen Revolution: Tagungsdokumentation,* edited by Daniela Zocholl und Susanne Diehr, 58–69. Berlin: Heinrich-Böll-Stiftung Sachsen-Anhalt and Gunda Werner Institut, 2015.

Klöppel, Ulrike. "Die 'Verfügung zur Geschlechtsumwandlung von Transsexualisten' im Spiegel der Sexualpolitik der DDR." In *Lernen aus der Geschichte,* 2014. Retrieved 26 November 2017 from http://lernen-aus-der-geschichte.de/Lernen-und-Lehren/content/11667.

Krautz, Stefanie, *Lesbisches Engagement in Ost-Berlin 1978–1989.* Marburg: Tectum, 2009.

Krug, Marina. "Die Gruppe Arbeitskreis Homosexuelle Selbsthilfe: Lesben in der Kirche in Berlin/DDR—November 1982 bis Sommer 1986." In *In Bewegung bleiben:*

100 Jahre Politik, Kultur und Geschichte von Lesben, edited by Gabriele Dennert, Christiane Leidinger, and Franziska Rauchut, 109–112, Berlin: Querverlag, 2007.
Kuhar, Roman. "Ljubljana: The Tales from the Queer Margins of the City." In *Queer Cities, Queer Cultures: Europe since 1945,* edited by Matt Cook and Jennifer Evans, 135–150. London: Bloomsbury, 2014.
McLellan, Josie. *Love in the Time of Communism: Intimacy and Sexuality in the GDR.* Cambridge: Cambridge University Press, 2011.
Raphael, Sharon Maxine. *Coming Out: The Emergence of the Movement Lesbian.* Cleveland, OH: Case Western Reserve University, Department of Sociology, 1974.
Reddy, William. *The Navigation of Feeling.* Cambridge: Cambridge University Press, 2001.
Sänger, Eva. *Begrenzte Teilhabe: Ostdeutsche Frauenbewegung und Zentraler Runder Tisch in der DDR.* Frankfurt a. M.: Campus, 2005.
———. "'Lieber öffentlich lesbisch als heimlich im DFD': Die Samisdat-Publikation frau anders in der DDR 1988/89." In *Öffentlichkeiten und Geschlechterverhältnisse: Erfahrungen—Politiken—Subjekte,* edited by Susanne Lettow, 159–183, Königstein (Taunus): Helmer, 2005.
Scholz, Juliane. "Die andere Liebe (The Other Love): 'Fürsorgediktatur' and LGBTIQ in the GDR in the 1980s." Paper presented at the Fortieth Annual German Studies Association Conference, 29 September–2 October 2016. San Diego, CA.
Schwäbisch, Lutz, and Martin Siems. *Anleitung zum sozialen Lernen für Paare, Gruppen und Erzieher: Kommunikations- und Verhaltenstraining.* Reinbek bei Hamburg: Rowohlt, 1974.
Sektion Ehe und Familie der Gesellschaft für Sozialhygiene der DDR and Sektion Andrologie der Gesellschaft für Dermatologie, ed. *Psychosoziale Aspekte der Homosexualität.* Jena: Manuskriptdruck, 1986.
———, ed. *Psychosoziale Aspekte der Homosexualität. II. Workshop.* Jena: Manuskriptdruck, 1989.
Spielmann, Jochen. "Was ist TZI?" In *Handbuch Themenzentrierte Interaktion (TZI),* edited by Jochen Spielmann, Mina Schneider-Landolf, and Walter Zitterbarth, 15–17. Göttingen: Vandenhoeck & Ruprecht, 2014.
Stella, Francesca. *Lesbian Lives in Soviet and Post-Soviet Russia: Post/Socialism and Gendered Sexualities,* Basingstoke, UK: Palgrave Macmillan, 2015.
Szulc, Lukasz. *Transnational Homosexuals in Communist Poland: Cross-Border Flows in Gay and Lesbian Magazines.* Basingstoke, UK: Palgrave Macmillan, 2018.
Takács, Judit. "Queering Budapest." In *Queer Cities, Queer Cultures: Europe since 1945,* edited by Matt Cook and Jennifer Evans, 191–210. London: Bloomsbury, 2014.
Waberski, Birgit. *Die großen Veränderungen beginnen leise: Lesbenliteratur in der DDR und den neuen Bundesländern.* Dortmund: Ebersbach, 1997.
Wallbraun, Barbara. "Lesben im Visier der Staatssicherheit." In *Das Übersehenwerden hat Geschichte—Lesben in der DDR und der Friedlichen Revolution. Tagungsdokumentation,* edited by Daniela Zocholl and Susanne Diehr, 26–50. Berlin: Heinrich-Böll-Stiftung Sachsen-Anhalt and Gunda Werner Institut, 2015.

Chapter 8

The Italian Movement of 1977 and the Cultural Praxis of the Youthful Proletariat

Danilo Mariscalco

In 1977, a radical political movement known as Autonomist emerged in Italy and revolutionized traditional forms of political communication and cultural representation. The movement produced magazines, leaflets, comics, graphic novels, photos, posters, graffiti, radio broadcasts and live performances, and drew on avant-garde approaches (Dadaism, Surrealism, Russian and Italian Futurism, Situationism) and the fundamental concepts of Marxism and poststructuralism (particularly notions of *general intellect* and *desire*). In this chapter, I analyze these cultural practices as a means of understanding a new form of antagonistic subjectivity that emerged in the context of the crisis of industrial capitalism in the 1970s: the "youthful proletariat," composed of "students, unemployed youth, precarious workers, and other 'marginals' excluded from the twilight of the Keynesian-Fordist pact."[1] This youthful proletariat was politically aligned with Autonomia Operaia, a radical organization that emerged in 1973 from Italian workerism. Autonomia Operaia promoted the refusal of labor and the sabotage of capitalistic devices, and rejected the "policy of sacrifices" and the "historic compromise" proposed by the Italian Communist Party and the Christian Democrats.[2]

Theorists of Italian workerism such as Antonio Negri, who had investigated how the production process and hence class conflict moved from the factory to society (which Negri thus described as the social factory), argued that the crisis of Fordism made the "social worker"—the new subjective figure of social production—a central cultural and political figure. This figure corresponds, they argued, to the transformation of capitalism and new ways of extracting surplus value; yet, the social worker also exceeds capitalist control and the forms of representation offered by political and cultural institutions. In the analysis of Autonomist Marxism, the emergence of the cultured and educated social worker signaled the proletarianization of intellectual labor, a process that deactivated traditional forms of social mediation.

In this chapter, I interpret the creative praxis of the Autonomist movement of 1977 as a radical form of the new "working-class use" of technology and culture. Drawing on Autonomist and Mao-Dadaist magazines like *A/traverso*, the transmissions of Radio Alice, and the disguise of the Metropolitan Indians, I examine the cultural self-representation of the youthful proletariat and its use of falsity, absurdity, and détournement. The chapter presents some long quotes extrapolated from the texts of the Italian movement: fundamental documents that are difficult to find and that have never been translated before.[3] Such self-representations, I argue, problematize the tendency toward disguise of the revolutionary masses examined by Marx in *The Eighteenth Brumaire of Louis Bonaparte* (1851–1852). While this turn to nonsense and falsehood might be superficially interpreted as a disregard for "authenticity," I argue that in the Italian movement of 1977, the conformity between practice and ideological self-definition was actually viewed as a more spontaneous and concrete representation of subjectivity.

The Youthful Proletariat and its Self-Representation

In the 1970s, hundreds of "young proletarian" circles and collectives appeared in cities such as Milan, Bologna, and Rome. These groups organized workshops on precarious work and parties that were perceived as political situations, and campaigned for expropriations as forms of re-appropriation of goods, subjective satisfaction of desires and the redistribution of wealth. Thanks to the expansion of mass education, the development of mass media and the social diffusion of technical know-how, these groups of young proletarians were cultured and educated. This cultural knowledge provided young proletarians with the means to represent themselves using the languages of the avant-garde art movements, Marxist concepts, as well as the categories of French poststructuralism such as *discourse* and *desire*.[4] It was a movement that was, in the words of Austrian scholar Klemens Gruber, born out of "the desire for a poetics of the social transformation." The "infiltration" of everyday life by avant-garde artistic productions enabled the movement to develop a cultural practice that mixed Dadaism and Futurism: "We find avant-garde fragments everywhere, in pop music, in the advertising and in the Campbell's Tomato Soup cans."[5]

Italian Workerist theory provided the youthful proletariat with a political focus. In particular, activists drew on research about the transition of the production process from the factory to the social factory, which suggested the emergence of a new social reality had revolutionized the class composition of the proletariat and its political and cultural praxis.[6] According to an anonymous author writing in the Autonomist and Mao-Dadaist[7] magazine *A/traverso* (September 1975), knowledge, culture, and everyday life had become essential elements in the radical strategy. The "formation of an educated proletariat" that constituted a "new reality" had allowed the movement to "put onto the agenda theoretical and political issues related to the formation of existence, the need for the liberation of everyday life, the collectivization of writing …, as elements of the general redefinition of the class tactic."[8] Building on the aesthetics of Russian poet Vladimir Majakovskij (1893–1930), the Italian Autonomist movement wanted to transform the production of texts by creating a direct relationship between writing and everyday life, thus establishing a connection with the widespread creativity of the masses.[9]

The cultural praxis of the youthful proletariat was also related to the concept of *refusal of labor*, and Marx's *Grundrisse* became a fundamental theoretical text for the Italian movement of 1977 in this regard. According to Marx, the reduction of the necessary labor, determined by technological development, "corresponds to the artistic, scientific etc. development of the individuals in the time set free, and with the means created, for all of them." In Marx's reading, industrial society had led to a new historical stage that was full of revolutionary opportunities, because capitalism used scientific progress to render the production of wealth independent of the labor time. However, capitalism concurrently used labor time to measure these giant social forces. Capital, Marx asserted, is a "moving contradiction."[10] In Marx's *Grundrisse*, activists of the Autonomist movement acquired the "foundations of the critique of political economy"; they found a convincing theory of radical subjectivities that appeared conducive to both the analysis and the exacerbation of the crisis of Fordism. The young proletarians thus examined the relationship between works of art, culture, communication, and mechanical reproduction, redefining the role of technology and intellectual praxis in the production process. According to the movement, the proletarianization of intellectual labor had produced a tendential deactivation of political and cultural mediations and thus enabled an expression of a radical self-representation, as the editorial staff of *A/traverso* wrote (October 1975):

> The proletarianization of intellectual labor enables the working class to use technology…. According to the power, culture has got to be a mediation between the interests of capitalism and the interests of the intellectual class…. But now, with the massification of this social class, the mystification of the independence of culture from the production process disappears.[11]

In the context of an expanded mass education and the rise of mass media, intellectual labor had become a productive force. Responding to these developments, the movement of 1977 developed a creative praxis that was new and radical in its approach to using technology and culture for political struggles.

Literary Texts, Graffiti, Comics, Performances, and Radio Broadcasts

The Italian Autonomist movement of 1977 is famous for its production of magazines, leaflets, books, comics, graphic novels, photos, posters, graffiti, and radio broadcasts that used the languages of avant-garde art movements and technologically advanced media. The establishment of the alternative press during the 1970s, for example, was correlated with the diffusion of a new medium of mechanical reproduction: the off-set printer, a cheap instrument that made collage and détournement techniques possible and allowed for printing both typewritten and handwritten texts.[12] Between 1975 and 1977 seventy magazines were published, most notably *A/traverso*, *Wow*, *Zut*, *Oask?!*, *Désir*, *Finalmente il cielo è caduto sulla terra*, and *Il complotto (di Zurigo)*. According to the editorial staff at *A/traverso*, it was not merely an underground magazine, rather "it was a new way of understanding the political organization. ... An organization that arises from ... everyday life, from love and friendship, from the rejection of wage labor and the pleasure of being together."[13] Coming out of Bologna, *A/traverso* was published between 1975 and 1981. Other magazines appeared less often. There was, for example, only a single issue of *11 marzo*, which came out in 1977. Other titles included *Finalmente il cielo è caduto sulla terra*, a collective magazine distributed in 1977 by the editorial staff of *A/traverso*, *Zut*, and Radio "Joe Hill." In Milan, *Viola*, *Identikit del sovversivo*, *Macondolore*, *Bi/lot*, and *Wow* were all published between 1976 and 1977 by young proletarian circles. Rome was the nerve center of the magazines produced by the Metropolitan Indians, a radical group famous for dressing up like Native Americans and celebrating spontaneity and desires: *Zut*, *Oask?!*, *Abat/jour*, *La sensazione del soffice blu in una...*, *Strippo teorico*, *Il complotto (di Zurigo)*, *Rifiut/are*, *L'occulto*, *Margine ambiguo*, *Foeminik*, *Zizzania*, and *Altrove/materiali* were all published between 1976 and 1977. Some magazines came out of southern Italy, for example *Fire, fire, fire* and *Pasquale* in Naples, *Désir* in Castrovillari, in the province of Cosenza in Calabria. The cooperative "Punti Rossi," a network of hundreds of libraries and resource centers founded by the Milanese bookseller Primo Moroni, was responsible for organizing the distribution of these magazines throughout the country.

All of these publications used falsity, nonsense, and détournement as artistic techniques to create a political alternative to traditional forms of counterinformation. The *A/traverso* collective, for example, formulated a critique of counterinformation. According to the collective, "counterinformation" had merely "denounced the falsehoods that power produces." Counter-information, they argued, acted "like a mirror" by re-establishing "what is true, but in a purely reflexive manner." Radio Alice, by contrast, was "language beyond the mirror. It has built a space in which the subject does not recognize itself as in a mirror, as restored truth, as fixed reproduction, but as the practice of an existence in becoming." It was not enough to "denounce the lies of power," *A/traverso* wrote; what was necessary was "denouncing and breaking the truth of power." "When power speaks the truth and pretends it is natural, we must denounce what is inhuman and absurd in this order of reality that the order of the discourse reproduces, reflects, and consolidates." Hence, the collective called for "emitting signs with the voice and tone of power. False signs. We produce false information which exposes what power hides, and which produces a revolt against the force of the discourse of order."[14]

Indeed, the cultural output of the Italian movement of 1977 offers many examples of false information with the voice and the tone of power: false reports by the Minister of Interior Francesco Cossiga and other politicians about the "treasonable dens" of the activists, guilty of possession of texts about German Dadaism;[15] false reports of meetings between the mayor of Rome, Giulio Carlo Argan, elected from the list of the Italian Communist Party, and Pope Paul VI to denounce the "historic compromise" proposed by the Italian Communist Party and the Christian Democrats.[16] Activists produced newspapers and magazines that were aesthetically identical to real and well-known periodicals such as *il Resto del Carlino*, *l'Unità*, and *L'Espresso*, but that contained fictional, ironic, and apparently nonsense news stories. For example, headlines proclaimed the capture of the "billionaire" Franco Berardi "Bifo" (an editor of *A/traverso*) or "The price of meat is increasing / Agnelli with cornmeal mush" (a play on words: the surname of Gianni Agnelli, president of the car company Fiat, means "lamb" in Italian).

Activists in the movement also practiced collective writing, for example in the book *Alice è il diavolo*; in novels such as *Boccalone* by Enrico Palandri and *Chi ha ucciso Majakovskij? Romanzo rivoluzionario* by Franco Berardi "Bifo"; and in poetry such as the poem *Cloacale* by Paolo Ricci, the director of Radio Alice. There was also graffiti: the walls of Italian cities where the movement was active were covered with naive pictures next to political slogans that communicated desires ("I want to make a slogan") or contained puns: "After Marx, April!"; "After Mao, June!"; "Lama is in Tibet," an allusion to the general secretary of the Italian General Confederation of Labor, Luciano Lama, who had supported the "policy of sacrifices."

Comics and graphic novels were an important element of the visual production of the movement. The magazine *Cannibale*, founded in 1977 by artists Stefano Tamburini, Massimo Mattioli, Andrea Pazienza, Filippo Scozzari, and Gaetano Liberatore, introduced the underground art form in Italy.[17] Autobiographical fragments by Andrea Pazienza show the intentional and radical exercise of a subjectivity exceeding traditional forms of artistic representation. In fact, before drawing comics Pazienza used to paint pictures espousing political and social condemnation. Yet, as Pazienza noted, these pictures "were bought by pharmacists who put them in their bedrooms." He considered this fact not only a contradiction but also an enormous limitation that ultimately stirred his "desire to write comics."[18]

The choice to produce comics—to produce cultural objects characterized by a highly communicative potential, determined by the rather inexpensive mechanical reproduction and the combination of images and texts—guaranteed a partial solution to the contradiction that existed, according to Pazienza, between the traditional artistic activity and political endeavor. In 1977, he started to draw *Le straordinarie avventure di Pentothal* (1977–1981), published by *Alter*, an appendix of the magazine *Linus*. The comic provided a realistic and dreamlike narrative, addressing the material conditions, experiences, needs, and desires of the social conflicts present at the time. Pazienza shows us the "personal and political" everyday life of Bologna—parties and assemblies, Radio Alice and concerts, conflicts and repression, love affairs and imaginary travels. The final page of the first episode of the graphic novel serves as an interesting example.[19] This page was added belatedly, replacing a page that had been produced prior to the murder of militant Francesco Lorusso and the conflicts between police and demonstrators in March 1977. The page shows the protagonist (Pazienza's alter ego), a radio that reproduces the tactical information diffused by Radio Alice ("Comrades! Tonight, at the end of the various assemblies, don't scatter!"), an alarm clock, and a flag that claims the political and ideal survival of Lorusso ("Francesco is still alive and he fights with us!"). The protagonist's thoughts are also expressed: "Expelled … I'm totally expelled."

This sense of being expelled originated from the admission of the "limits" of the traditional artistic practices. Pazienza explains in lengthy endnote how he started working on the comic in February 1977, believing that he was "drawing a sketch," but he was "totally in error because instead it was a beginning." Had he known what was about to happen, he would have waited, he wrote, "for this beautiful March to happen, and I would have drawn it then." Under the impression of the events of March 1977, he had the final page of the comic replaced. "The original final page had the sentence 'so this is the end' in place of the typical 'end' placed in the lower right corner, which now has the wrong overtones. Good Heavens! I swear to you, I believed it was a sketch, instead it was a beginning. Yeah!" (Andrea Pazienza, 16 March 1977).[20]

In this comic, Pazienza outlined the importance of Radio Alice, the radio station of the movement, because of its ability to constantly update. Other activists made similar arguments, declaring the supremacy of the radio over other "clean" and "paralyzing" practices traditionally used by political activists. These differed from the "dirtiness" of new media, a claim advanced by Hans Magnus Enzensberger in *Baukasten zu einer Theorie der Medien* (1970), which became an influential text in the Italian movement.[21] This point is reaffirmed in the book *Alice è il diavolo* (Alice is the devil), which highlighted that the collective had, even before broadcasting its shows, analyzed "the obsolescence of the written language, of the codified media—within the political code, too—rather than the transformation of the needs of the movement." Using a "'clean,' slow, and ritual medium" such as flyers would not facilitate "an analysis of the 'metropolization' of the figure of the social class." In the 1960s, when "an avant-garde had to extend and develop a revolutionary idea in the masses," the flyer had indeed played a major role. "But when the levels of knowledge rise, and especially when the circulation of the experiences uses communication channels more persuasive than the flyer …, it is necessary to transform the language of the movement," the book concluded.[22]

Alternative radio stations offer instructive examples of how important the relationship between technological development and radical self-representation was. In 1974, the Italian Constitutional Court certified the illegitimacy of the state monopoly of radio stations. In the aftermath of the decision, approximately two hundred stations were founded, among them Radio Alice. Not least, Radio Alice is notable for being the first Italian station to use live phone calls.[23] According to the radio activists, the development of a diffuse intellectuality, even among the lower classes, revolutionized the relationship between emission and reception. Broadcasting live phone calls offered listeners, the young proletarians, an opportunity to represent themselves and thus to become the authors of the transmission. They could disrupt the language of productivity and the cycle of the valorization of capital, in the process of circulation of the sign-value:

> Silence. The subject has changed. [*Pant, hiss*] don't think you're right.…
> The silence, the uncanny, the "unstated," that which "remains to be

said," frightens.... Alice *hisses, yells, contemplates, interrupts herself, pulls*.... We have received a telephone call from the Technological Institute: "We have occupied the office and we are calling from his phone, hear how he yells." Radio for the participants or radio for the uncanny? In the first case the language is univocal: [it is] the announcer's [voice], who announces that the event has happened. They talk about something which means something else and can therefore never be captured because it is over.... In the second case, something continues to flee from language. This is manifest in outbursts of laughter, words in suspension, the word that cannot be found and that refuses to change into another one, stammering, silence. ... Another direct phone call: "We are workers on strike, we want you to play some music and we want to talk to you about the thirty-five-hour week, it's time they talked about that in contracts".... Break the cycle of the valorization of capital in the process of circulation of the sign-value (no more appropriation of merchandise to interrupt the Money – Commodity – Money cycle, but a savage strike in the circulation of the single sign-value Money – Money). Interrupt the language of machines, of work-ethics, of productivity. An invitation to not get up this morning, to stay in bed with someone, to make musical instruments and war devices for yourself.[24]

Young proletarians used the techniques of avant-garde artistic movements—such as détournement,[25] nonsense, and performance—to expose their subjectivity and desires through Radio Alice; to reveal the voice of the excluded, the voice of the body, of sexuality, desires, and obscenity. Indeed, when Radio Alice was accused of "obscenity," they were "a little disconcerted." They had anticipated accusations of being a pirate station, of undermining the state or of being communists, but not the accusation of obscenity. But then they understood that such an accusation was only "natural":

Language, when it is freed from the sublimations which reduce it to the code and makes desire and the body speak, is obscene.... The body, sexuality, the desire to sleep in the morning, the liberation from labor, the possibility to be overwhelmed, to make oneself unproductive and open to tactile, uncodified communication: all this has for centuries been hidden, submerged, denied, unstated. Vade Retro, Satanas. The blackmail of poverty, the discipline of labor, hierarchical order, sacrifice, fatherland, family, general interests, socialist blackmail, participation: all that stifled the voice of the body. All our time, forever and always, devoted to labor. Eight hours of work, two hours of travel, and, afterward, rest, television, and dinner with the family. Everything that is not confined within the limits of that order is obscene. Outside it smells like shit. All the "unstated" is emerging: from the Chants de Maldoror to the struggles for reducing the workday. It speaks in the Paris Commune and in Artaud's poetry, it speaks in Surrealism and in the French May, in the Italian Autumn and in immediate liberation; it speaks across the separate orders of the language of rebellion. Desire is given a voice, and for them, it is obscene.[26]

The "Festival of the Young Proletariat," organized by the magazine *Re Nudo* (Naked king), that took place in June 1976 at Parco Lambro in Milan, offers an example of the political potential of exhibiting the body and sexuality. There were "concerts, shouted readings, mass nudity, Orphic dances and witches' Sabbath."[27] Both the conservative right and the "progressive" Communist Party turned the event into a scandal. For them, it was obscene; it was, in other words, "out of the scene" of political and cultural institutions. Photos taken by Tano D'Amico and Enrico Scuro and other anonymous photographers that show bodies and actions of the so-called Metropolitan Indians similarly exhibit political bodies. The Metropolitan Indians symbolized what characterized the Italian movement of 1977: the creative use of irony, falsity, jokes, and costumes.[28] Until then, such practices had been completely unknown in the context of the class struggle. With the movement of 1977, demonstrations, and political militancy turned into happenings and subversive communication.

The Metropolitan Indians and the Question of Disguise

The Autonomist movement's cultural and communicative practices, in particular those of the Metropolitan Indians, have attracted considerable scholarly attention.[29] According to Umberto Eco, their specific quality was the "amazing" diffusion among social classes that were excluded from the "high" culture. In "La comunicazione sovversiva nove anni dopo il sessantotto" (The subversive communication nine years after 1968) (25 February 1977), Eco wrote: "In contrast to the avant-gardes of the beginning of the twentieth century, these groups are really related to the 'lower' echelons of society, and ... what they say ... seems instinctively understandable also to uneducated people."[30] "There's another language," he asserted, the language of the "Italian-Indian." "New generations speak and live, in their daily practice, the language (that is the multiplicity of languages) of avant-garde. ... This proliferation of messages, apparently without any code, is perfectly understood and practiced by groups ... that are excluded from high culture."[31]

Elsewhere, the art historian Maurizio Calvesi wrote in *Avanguardia di massa* (Mass avant-garde) (1978) that the transgressive language of the movement resembled "the fantastic and automatic writing of Dada and Surrealism, well as the Futurist words-in-freedom."[32] Finally, the scholar Claudia Salaris has compared the characteristic irony of the Italian movement of 1977 with the communicative strategy of German Dadaism, especially with regard to its political undertones: "Dada in Berlin supported the revolt using the [same] techniques of de-contextualization of language and images ... that reappear in the performances of the Metropolitan Indians."[33]

The Italian young proletarians, the Metropolitan Indians, Radio Alice, and the other activists of the movement were not the first to use falsity, nonsense, détournement, irony, and disguise as political weapons. As Patrick Cuninghame has written, such techniques were employed by "the Provos in Amsterdam, Kommune 1 in Germany, Black Mask in New York, and in Britain King Mob, who, dressed as Santa Claus, went into a department store on Christmas [in] 1968 and began handing items from the shelves to children as 'presents.' These were later confiscated by the police while Santa was arrested."[34] However, in his article "'A laughter that will bury you all...,'" Cuninghame highlights a crucial difference between Metropolitan Indians and other international groups, namely the fact that the main characteristic of the Italian movement was "its desire to both express itself through and play with words in a politically subversive fashion."[35]

During the 1970s, radical activists in Italy used Indian imagery at key events. In March 1973, for example, factory workers at Fiat in Turin demonstrated with red bandages and drums. Three years later, Radio Alice called, with "howls of war," for a "party against repression."[36] The vocabulary of the Indians is also present in a 1976 poster (Figure 8.1) for a happening at the University of Milan, organized by "circles of the youthful proletariat."

The text reads: "we have unearthed the ax. It is time for the human tribes to get their act together, to chase away the false friends of man." Alternative magazines spoke the "Italian-Indian" language: "We'll be like lethal snakes in front of you; we'll burn the metropolis in the nights of full moon. We are not Power. You will not capture us. We will flee thanks to spells, Indian circles, carnivorous plants."[37] Arguably the most noteworthy appearance of the Metropolitan Indians happened on 17 February 1977. The Italian Communist Party had organized a rally at the University of Rome, which by then had been occupied by the Autonomist movement. The secretary of the Italian General Confederation of Labor (CGIL), Luciano Lama, was due to speak at the event; however, there was a conflict between the Italian Communist Party and Autonomist militants. Fighting against the organization of the (old, Fordist) working class, a number of the young proletarians

Figure 8.1. Poster of the National Happening of the Youthful Proletariat (27 November 1976). From author's collection.

disguised themselves with masks and carried axes.[38] In the large open area of the campus where he was to speak, Lama found another platform already rigged up, with a dummy of himself on it. There was a big red cut-out of a Valentine's heart, with a slogan punning his name: *Nessuno L'Ama* (Nobody loves him). Around this platform there was a band of Metropolitan Indians. As Lama started to speak, they began to chant "Sacrifices, sacrifices, we want sacrifices!" (a parody of the State's economic policy upheld by the Communist Party). "Build us more churches and fewer houses!" (Italy has more churches than any other European country, and a chronic housing shortage). "We demand to work harder and earn less!" The irony aggravated the humorless heavies.[39]

According to Pablo Echaurren, the Metropolitan Indian expressed the refusal of individual identity, because it was

> the symbolic figure of a movement that was born from disintegration of the monolithic entity of the political groups; he easily tends to resume his life for a long time imprisoned into the rigor of a militancy ... that began to be too tight; the Indian ... unhinged all the certainties about "Who are we? Where are we going? What do we want?"; he challenged the roles, he wrong-footed any attempt to define a course of action.[40]

The social diffusion of knowledge, the self-representation of the Italian movement and the performances of Metropolitan Indians, which broke the "monolithic entity" (and appearance) of political groups, mark a turn away from previous forms of disguise in revolutionary masses that Karl Marx examined in *The Eighteenth Brumaire of Louis Bonaparte*. According to Marx, it is precisely in times of revolutionary crisis that the masses "anxiously conjure up the spirits of the past to their service and borrow from them names, battle cries, and costumes in order to present the new scene of world history in this time-honored disguise and this borrowed language." Marx asserted that the proletarian revolution, by contrast, "cannot draw its poetry from the past, but only from the future." [41] However, as Augusto Illuminati notes, traditional communist movements often turned to the past for symbolic inspiration. For example, "the Communards simulated the Convention, the Bolsheviks imitated the Jacobins, the Trotskyist Left immediately evoked the Stalinist Thermidor." More recently, in the early 1960s, "the working class struggles took on the name New Resistance, the movement of 1968 quoted the Third International and the Chinese Cultural Revolution."[42] In contrast, according to Illuminati, the Italian movement of 1977 was characterized by original forms of representation that corresponded to its political praxis: "There was a greater conformity between practices and ideological self-definition. Autonomism of 1977 renewed the watchwords.... Social movements adopt a collection of clothes to put on a show, but they do not suppress the inner difference."[43] The subject in the Italian movement recognized itself as an "existence in becoming"; it was not like a "mirror" that reflects the language of power or the revolutionary tradition, as *A/traverso* collective emphasized. The different disguises of Metropolitan Indians thus did not celebrate the past, did not evoke a revolutionary uniform. Rather, they showed the inner differences of a new and molecular form of antagonistic subjectivity, imbued with mass culture but able to use the languages of the avant-garde and the fundamental concepts of workerism and poststructuralism; an antagonistic subjectivity that revolutionized the traditional forms of political communication and representation.

Death and Dissemination of the Movement: The Practice of Desire and Happiness, Today

By spring 1977, the autonomous direction of the new radical tendency was broken. In March, the Italian movement was subject to repression. As mentioned above, the militant Francesco Lorusso was killed during a demonstration in Bologna. Other activists were arrested, and Radio Alice was closed. In March 1977, a public notice from the San Giovanni in Monte Prison reported the arrest of Franco Berardi "Bifo." The police had stormed the house where he had been sleeping with comrades with "submachine guns in hand." At first, they had accused him of being a member of the Red Brigades, but within two days, he claimed, the accusation had become "so ridiculous that they had to invent another one." Hence they accused him of "being the ideological organizer of an incredible series of criminal plots committed in Bologna in the last few months." Yet, the true reason from him being put into prison was something else, he argued:

> But then let them say it clearly: the practice of happiness is subversive when it becomes collective. Our will for happiness and liberation is their terror, and they react by terrorizing us with prison, when the repression of work, of the patriarchal family, and of sexism is not enough. But then let them say it clearly. To conspire means to breathe together. And that is what we are accused of. They want to prevent us from breathing because we have refused to breathe in isolation, in their asphyxiating places of work, in their individuating familial relationships, in their atomizing houses. There is a crime I confess I have committed: It is the attack against the separation of life and desire, against sexism in interindividual relationships, against the reduction of life to the payment of a salary. But then let them say it clearly: it is Dada that terrorizes the gray, the obtuse, the dangerous. Guardians of order and of the exploitation of poverty—for them, the transversal writing that runs through the

separate orders and reunites isolated behaviors is not just obscene, any more, it is a crime.[44]

This "attack against the separation of life and desire," the refusal of labor, the political use of mass media, the "transversal writing," the theatricality of Metropolitan Indians, in short: the practice of desire and happiness has changed the language of contemporary oppositional movements. And not only in Italy: it "speaks" in the "apparition" of San Precario (St. Precarious) during May Day and in occupied theaters; it "speaks" through the Guy Fawkes mask (*V for Vendetta*) and the cyber attacks of Anonymous; it "speaks" in the use of social networks in the global anticapitalist mobilizations and in the "creative commons" movement. "Language," Cuninghame stresses, "is the site of political struggle and the derisory laughter born of irony is one of the most potent weapons a social movement has, humiliating the 'powerful' and inspiring the 'powerless.'"[45] Today, as in 1977. In the last reprint of *Alice è il diavolo*, which contains a CD with several radio transmissions, the editors ascribe the preservation of the tapes to the law enforcement agency, with an intentional paradox that resembles the language of Metropolitan Indians and Mao-Dada: "We thank the police officers and magistrates for having conserved, for two decades, the tapes of the radio …, that we have used to make the CD. We would have lost them for sure!"[46]

Danilo Mariscalco is Doctor Europaeus in Cultural Studies. He is member of the scientific committee of Forma, *Revista d'Estudis Comparatius*, Art, Literatura, Pensament (Universitat Pompeu Fabra, Barcelona) and of the book series MaterialiIT (Quodlibet). Among his publications are: *Dai laboratori alle masse: Pratiche artistiche e comunicazione nel movimento del '77* (Ombre Corte, 2014); *Rappresentanza/rappresentazione: Una questione degli studi culturali* (Quodlibet, 2014), with Michele Cometa; *Vita, politica, rappresentazione: A partire dall'Italian Theory* (Ombre Corte, 2016), with Pietro Maltese.

Notes

1. Patrick Cuninghame, "A Laughter That Will Bury You All: Irony as Protest and Language as Struggle in the Italian 1977 Movement," *International Review of Social History* 52, no. 15 (2007): 154. On the gender issue, see Lea Melandri, *L'infamia originaria* (Milan, 1977).
2. See Nanni Balestrini and Primo Moroni, eds., *L'Orda d'oro 1968–1977: La grande ondata rivoluzionaria e creativa, politica ed esistenziale* (Milan, 1997), 469–471.
3. All translations are mine unless otherwise stated.

4. See Danilo Mariscalco, "Sul divenire culturale del general intellect," in *Vita, politica, rappresentazione: A partire dall'Italian Theory*, ed. Pietro Maltese and Danilo Mariscalco (Verona, 2016), 179–190; Danilo Mariscalco, *Dai laboratori alle masse: Pratiche artistiche e comunicazione nel movimento del '77* (Verona, 2014).
5. See Klemens Gruber, *L'avanguardia inaudita: Comunicazione e strategia nei movimenti degli anni Settanta* (Milan, 1997), 15–16.
6. See Antonio Negri, *Dall'operaio massa all'operaio sociale: Intervista sull'operaismo* (Milano, 1979).
7. See Danilo Mariscalco, "Autonomia e abolizione dell'arte: Emergenze maodadaiste nel movimento del '77," *Palinsesti* 1, no. 4 (2014): 21–34.
8. *A/traverso* (September 1975).
9. See Klemens Gruber, *L'avanguardia inaudita: Comunicazione e strategia nei movimenti degli anni Settanta*, 25–27, 29–31.
10. Karl Marx, *Grundrisse* (Harmondsworth, UK, 1973), 706.
11. *A/traverso* (October 1975).
12. Collettivo A/traverso, *Alice è il diavolo: Storia di una radio sovversiva* (Milan, 2002), 10. See Danilo Mariscalco, "Il movimento del '77 nella società dello spettacolo," in *Critica/Crisi: Una questione degli studi culturali*, ed. Michele Cometa and Valentina Mignano (Macerata, 2014), 93–106.
13. Collettivo A/traverso, *Alice è il diavolo*, 10.
14. *A/traverso* (February 1977).
15. Collettivo A/traverso, *Alice è il diavolo*, 103–104.
16. See Collettivo A/traverso, *Alice è il diavolo*, 15.
17. Vincenzo Sparagna, "L'avventura del Male," in *L'Orda d'oro. 1968–1977: La grande ondata rivoluzionaria e creativa, politica ed esistenziale*, ed. Nanni Balestrini and Primo Moroni (Milan, 1997), 596–597.
18. Andrea Pazienza, "Il plesso solare e la tecnica del fumetto," *Il Grifo* 3, no. 23 (1993): 44.
19. See Danilo Mariscalco, "Transizione e risveglio nell'immobilità: Un'immagine di Andrea Pazienza," *roots§routes* 9 (2013).
20. Andrea Pazienza, *Le straordinarie avventure di Pentothal* (Milan, 1982).
21. See Hans Magnus Enzensberger, "Baukasten zu einer Theorie der Medien," *Kursbuch* 20, no. 5 (1970): 159–186; partially reprinted in Paolo Hutter, ed., *Piccole antenne crescono: Documenti, interventi e proposte sulla vita delle radio di movimento* (Rome, 1978), 129.
22. Collettivo A/traverso, *Alice è il diavolo*, 112–113.
23. Hutter, *Piccole antenne crescono*, 12.
24. Collettivo A/traverso, *Alice è il diavolo*, 40–41. Emphasis in original.
25. See *Zut* (1977): "The game of reversal is impassioning the Rome movement; once the trick is discovered the game is easy…. The trick is old, in France it has a precise linguistic expression—"détournement"—and it has long been used by the exponents of the historical vanguard."
26. *A/traverso* (1976).
27. Collettivo A/traverso, *Alice è il diavolo*, 13.
28. Pablo Echaurren, *Parole ribelli: I fogli del movimento del '77* (Rome, 1997), 4–5.

29. See Danilo Mariscalco, "A/traverso la transizione: Le pratiche culturali del movimento del '77 e il paradigma artistico," *Enthymema* 7 (2012): 387–400. The quoted scholars are Eco, Calvesi, Di Nallo, Salaris, and Gruber.
30. Umberto Eco, "La comunicazione sovversiva nove anni dopo il sessantotto," *Corriere della sera*, 25 February 1977, 3.
31. See Umberto Eco, "Il laboratorio in piazza," in *Sette anni di desiderio: Cronache 1977–1983*, ed. Umberto Eco (Milan, 1983), 64–67.
32. Maurizio Calvesi, *Avanguardia di massa* (Milan, 1978), 65.
33. Claudia Salaris, *Il movimento del Settantasette: Linguaggi e scritture dell'ala creativa* (Udine, 1997), 54.
34. Patrick Cuninghame, "A Laughter That Will Bury You All," 168.
35. Ibid.
36. Collettivo A/traverso, *Alice è il diavolo*, 12–13.
37. *Wow* (March 1977).
38. Balestrini and Moroni, *L'Orda d'oro*, 536–541.
39. Sylvère Lotringer and Christian Marazzi, eds., *Autonomia: Post-Political Politics* (New York, 1980): 101.
40. Echaurren, *Parole ribelli*, 4–5.
41. Karl Marx, *The Eighteenth Brumaire of Louis Bonaparte* (Moscow, 1972), 10–13.
42. Augusto Illuminati, *Del comune: Cronache del general intellect* (Rome, 2003), 184–185.
43. Ibid., 185.
44. Collettivo A/traverso, *Alice è il diavolo*, 53.
45. Cuninghame, "A Laughter That Will Bury You All," 168.
46. Collettivo A/traverso, *Alice è il diavolo*, 4.

Bibliography

Balestrini, Nanni, and Primo Moroni, eds. *L'Orda d'oro. 1968–1977: La grande ondata rivoluzionaria e creativa, politica ed esistenziale*. Milan: Feltrinelli, 1977.
Calvesi, Maurizio. *Avanguardia di massa*. Milan: Feltrinelli, 1978.
Collettivo A/traverso. *Alice è il diavolo: Storia di una radio sovversiva*. Milan: ShaKe. 2002.
Cuninghame, Patrick. "A Laughter That Will Bury You All: Irony as Protest and Language as Struggle in the Italian 1977 Movement." *International Review of Social History* 52, no. 15 (2007): 153–168.
Echaurren, Pablo. *Parole ribelli: I fogli del movimento del '77*. Rome: Stampa Alternativa, 1997.
Eco, Umberto, "Il laboratorio in piazza." In *Sette anni di desiderio: Cronache 1977–1983*, edited by Umberto Eco, 64–67. Milan: Bompiani, 1983.
Enzensberger, Hans Magnus. "Baukasten zu einer Theorie der Medien." *Kursbuch* 20, no. 5 (1970): 159–186.
Gruber, Klemens. *L'avanguardia inaudita: Comunicazione e strategia nei movimenti degli anni Settanta*. Milan: Costa & Nolan, 1997.
Hutter, Paolo, ed. *Piccole antenne crescono: Documenti, interventi e proposte sulla vita delle radio di movimento*. Rome: Savelli, 1978.

Illuminati, Augusto. *Del comune: Cronache del general intellect.* Rome: Manifestolibri, 2003.

Lotringer, Sylvère and Christian Marazzi, eds. *Autonomia: Post-Political Politics.* New York: Semiotext(e), 1980.

Mariscalco, Danilo. "A/traverso la transizione: Le pratiche culturali del movimento del '77 e il paradigma artistico." *Enthymema* 7 (2012): 387–400.

———. "Autonomia e abolizione dell'arte: Emergenze maodadaiste nel movimento del '77." *Palinsesti* 1, no. 4 (2014): 21–34.

———. *Dai laboratori alle masse: Pratiche artistiche e comunicazione nel movimento del '77.* Verona: Ombre Corte. 2014.

———. "Il movimento del '77 nella società dello spettacolo." In *Critica/Crisi: Una questione degli studi culturali,* edited by Michele Cometa and Valentina Mignano, 93–106. Macerata: Quodlibet, 2014.

———. "Sul divenire culturale del general intellect." In *Vita, politica, rappresentazione: A partire dall'Italian Theory,* edited by Pietro Maltese and Danilo Mariscalco, 179–190. Verona: Ombre Corte, 2016.

———. "Transizione e risveglio nell'immobilità: Un'immagine di Andrea Pazienza," *roots§routes* 3, no. 9 (2016). Retrieved 21 August 2016 from http://www.roots-routes.org/politics-and-poetics-of-displayingtransizione-e-risveglio-nellimmobilita-unimmagine-di-andrea-pazienza.

Marx, Karl. *Grundrisse.* Harmondsworth, UK: Penguin, 1973.

———. *The Eighteenth Brumaire of Louis Bonaparte.* Moscow: Progress Publishers, 1972.

Melandri, Lea. *L'infamia originaria.* Milan: L'Erba Voglio, 1977.

Negri, Antonio. 1979. *Dall'operaio massa all'operaio sociale: Intervista sull'operaismo.* Milano: Multhipla, 1979.

Pazienza, Andrea. "Il plesso solare e la tecnica del fumetto." *Il Grifo* 3, no. 23 (1993): 44–47.

———. *Le straordinarie avventure di Pentothal.* Milan: Milano Libri, 1982.

Salaris, Claudia, *Il movimento del Settantasette: Linguaggi e scritture dell'ala creativa.* Udine: AAA Edizioni, 1997.

Sparagna, Vincenzo. "L'avventura del Male." in *L'Orda d'oro 1968–1977: La grande ondata rivoluzionaria e creativa, politica ed esistenziale,* edited by Nanni Balestrini and Primo Moroni, 596–598. Milan: Feltrinelli, 1997.

Chapter 9

The Struggle for the Minds of the Youth

The Securitate and Musical Countercultures in Communist Romania

Manuela Marin

In a letter addressed to Radio Free Europe (RFE) on 15 October 1971, a young Romanian provided a summary of the effects of the country's latest cultural reforms: "After the famous date of 7 July 1971, a date that will remain forever inscribed in the calendar as a day of mourning, the lives of the youth in Romania worsened even more: gone were the beards and the long hair, gone was pop, beat or progressive music. Everything was gone!"[1] The event referenced in the letter was a meeting of the bodies of party and state leadership in Bucharest. The decisions adopted on this occasion imposed an embargo on foreign cultural products of all kind: music, films, foreign literary translations, and the staging of theater performances, opera, and operetta.

One social group particularly affected by the adoption of these measures was the urban youth. Most of these youngsters were high school boys and, in some cases, male students of different social backgrounds and nationalities (Romanian, Hungarian, or German). They lived mainly in Bucharest and other urban centers in Romania, some of which also contained universities. During the 1970s, improved living standards made audio players (especially radios) available at affordable prices. However, traveling abroad to buy foreign records, cassettes, and magazines, or attend music concerts was an activity reserved only for individuals whose families were financially secure, or who had relatives living in other East bloc countries (such as Hungary), or in the West (like France, the United States, and especially West Germany). Despite all these differences, youngsters' appetites for anything that came from outside the Iron Curtain—mostly music, film, and fashion—had been stirred at the beginning of Nicolae Ceaușescu's rule, which had been characterized by political relaxation and cultural liberalization. As such, their reactions to these measures were among the most diverse and intense. In this chapter, I analyze how Romanian youth responded to the suppression of cultural products from the West after 1971. More precisely, I show how, in spite of the ban, young people identified alternative ways to access foreign music and how, based on precarious sources of information, they began to emulate the styles of countercultures such as punk, new wave, and rock trends. At the same time, I identify what appears to be a somewhat paradoxical evolution, but one that gained a distinct significance in Romania in the 1970s and 1980s. Specifically, I show that, by imitating the behavioral norms and fashion styles introduced by Western musical countercultures, young people in Romania sought to create and express an alternative and seemingly more authentic subjectivity that rejected the impositions of the communist regime and created space for personal experimentation and freedom. For the regime, the idea that the new generation could define itself in this way constituted a cause for concern. Through its secret police, the "Securitate," the regime constantly tried to eliminate all potential sources of contamination containing Western values.

The debate over the definition of what it meant to be young in Romania during the 1970s and 1980s was played out in the context of the Cold War. Each side put forward its own version of personal authenticity and, in different ways, the adoption and contestation of Western cultural values played a major role in both. For the Romanian youth, the West symbolized authenticity because it was seen to oppose the official values of the communist regime and the Securitate. Romanian youths therefore contested the ideal subjectivity that the regime imagined to be worthy of its younger generation. From this perspective, the competition for the minds of Romanian youth was, in fact, a struggle for supremacy between two sets of distinct social and cultural values that were constructed on the long cleavage of the Cold War. As a result, the youths' appropriation of a countercultural model over a socialist one marked not only the failure of Romanian educational policies, but also its loss of initiative in the face of its Western political and ideological adversary.

The theoretical perspective of the "field," as formulated by Pierre Bourdieu,[2] helps us to explain the nature of young people's relationship with the Securitate with regard to the appearance and consumption of Western countercultural products. The Romanian communist regime represented a political power that set the general limits of the social sphere, within which the Securitate occupied a distinct position. The regime and Romanian youth competed to gain control over the circulation of Western cultural products, a development that helped them to redefine the positions attained inside the social field. The identification of certain channels, which enabled alternative access to foreign cultural goods and their circulation, allowed young people to challenge the general rules of the social arena. From the Securitate's perspective, conserving the social field by limiting the circulation of cultural products imported from the West consolidated its position as a guardian charged not only with protecting the regime, but also its future citizens.

Young people's growing appetite for Western countercultural products in Romania stemmed from their cultural fixation with Western music and everything associated with it. Thomas Cushman explains that "cultural fixation" appears when cultural products "of an important but limited range" are "seized upon early and become the central objects," therefore forming the basis of subsequent cultural practices.[3] The exaggeration of their cultural value was due to an idealization process through which they received new aesthetic cognitive significations. As a consequence, these cultural goods became mandatory benchmarks upon which Romanian youth created "a local cultural and imaginary construct that was based on the forms of knowledge and aesthetics associated with the 'West,' but not necessarily referring to any 'real' West," namely the "Imaginary West."[4] Importantly, here was a delay in the time that it took foreign music trends to reach Romania in comparison to the West. According to the Securitate, when punk (including the genre's ethnicized Hungarian version, known as the csöves) became highly fashionable among urban Romanian youth at the end of the 1970s and 1980s, it had already lost most of its appeal in the Western world.[5]

I chose the term "counterculture" to ascribe a label to the emergence of new punk, rock, and new wave trends among Romanian youth, because it best explains the nature of their development in the Romanian context from 1970 to 1980. In line with Thomas Cushman, I define counterculture as "practical knowledge which is the result of engagement in alternative forms of communication among actors engaged in the collective pursuit of alternative ways of life," which "runs counter to the dominant stock of knowledge in a society."[6] To express their authentic subjectivity through the imitation of countercultural styles, young people primarily sought to "exercise conscious control over their personal appearance." To this end, they used artifacts like clothes, accessories, and haircuts, but also bricolage.[7] In this way, the young fans ascribed new meanings to familiar and mundane objects, integrating them as essential parts of their countercultural lifestyle.[8] Herein lies another difference between the experiences of Romanian and Western fans. While the latter had a variety of products at their disposal that they could turn into artifacts, the Romanian urban youth imitated the same style employing whatever was available, using, for instance, safety pins instead of earrings and piercings, and ornaments made of razor blades instead of metal necklaces.

In this chapter, after examining the political context that led to the imposition of the official embargo on the import of cultural products from the West, I address two distinct issues. First, I show how young people found alternative channels to listen to punk, new wave, and rock music, examining how they used artifacts and bricolage to imitate the behaviors and dress code of their idols, and to create and express what they believed represented a true self. Second, I analyze how the Securitate understood and reacted to the dissemination of musical countercultures among Romanian youth and their attempts to create an authentic subjectivity based on a set of norms that diverged from those provided through official channels.

Containing the Western Influence: The July Theses of 1971

At the beginning of July 1971, Romanian communist leader Nicolae Ceaușescu announced a series of proposals that were designed to improve the "political, ideological, and Marxist education of Party members and of all members of the working class." Unanimously adopted by the decision-making bodies of the party and the state, "The July Theses 1971" marked the beginning of "Romania's mini-cultural revolution."

Unlike the Chinese version, the Romanian "cultural revolution" was largely aimed at implementing measures that would contribute to the making of the "new man." In order to successfully fulfill his role as the "builder of socialism," the "new man" needed to gain a high level of consciousness. Arts, culture, education, and propaganda were considered essential to this effect. Aside from the fact that the above-mentioned domains would be subordinated to the political sphere and its ideological tenets, all cultural and educational forms accessible to the population needed to be inspired by contemporary Romanian realities. As a consequence, in his interventions of July 1971, Nicolae Ceaușescu denounced a perceived moral capitulation to Western culture, suggesting that its ideological, bourgeois message undermined the healthy foundations of socialist consciousness. In order to counter this damaging influence, Ceaușescu proposed that bodies within the Party assume more rigorous control of the channels that made the encroachment of Western culture—and its hostile message—possible. To this end, and in an attempt to enhance the educational role of cultural products, the measures put forward in July 1971 required that all artistic productions included in the repertoire of cultural institutions, the shows broadcast on national radio and television, and printed works, to be Romanian, to have "an educational purpose," and "a military, revolutionary character." These cultural products were supposed to replace the imports that cultivated "ideas and principles alien to our philosophy and socialist morals" and "promoted the spirit of violence, a bourgeois way of life, and toxic mentalities for the education of youth."[9] The July Theses of 1971 advocated increased agitation and propaganda. These techniques were not simply limited to promoting officially sanctioned ideological and educational messages; the regime also aimed to arm the masses—especially the youth—with the skill to distinguish and understand the significance of the harmful messages that came disguised as the content of highly attractive Western cultural formulas.[10]

Therefore, the subordination of cultural productions and propaganda to the purpose of constructing the "new socialist man," the invalidation of Western cultural superiority through the exposure of its hostile ideological message, and the assertion of Romanian culture's primacy within global cultural heritage, all justified the measures taken in July 1971.[11] As a consequence of these measures, all imported artistic productions, notably films and music, were removed from radio, television, and cinema listings. Translations that did not comply with the new cultural line were excluded from editorial plans, and all shows that were perceived to praise a bourgeois way of life were eliminated from the repertoires of theateres, opera, and operetta. They were replaced by Romanian productions that glorified either the country's past or the achievements of its socialist present.[12]

The focus of the 1971 July Theses on the superiority of national culture mirrored the nationalist policy readily embraced by the Romanian Communist Party (RCP) from the early 1960s onward. It not only aimed to bolster its right to adopt a strategy for building a socialism appropriate to the specific needs of the country, but also underlined the exceptionalism of the Romanian historical experience.[13] From this perspective, Nicolae Ceaușescu did not simply reject any cultural borrowings due to their ideological unreliability. These foreign influences were also deemed ineffectual because Romanian cultural achievements had preceded and successfully surpassed them in both the distant past and socialist present.[14] Even if the measures adopted in July 1971 targeted Romanian society as a whole, young people, and especially those living in urban areas, were the most affected by the strengthening of the Communist Party's control over cultural life and, consequently, their leisure time. The restriction of free access to cultural imports, as well as various educational activities outside of school and the workplace, was meant to protect young people from the supposedly negative influences of the West. These actions were based on two main considerations. On the one hand, young people were perceived to represent the prototype of the new man. They had a pure human essence that remained uncontaminated by the values of the old society, and they were responsible for constructing socialism to ensure the future of communism. On the other hand, due to their inexperience and insufficient political-ideological education, it was feared that young people could easily fall prey to bourgeois influences, which would hamper their formation of a socialist consciousness and divert them from fulfilling their fundamental role as builders of socialism.

The July Theses formalized the framework that the Romanian regime used to prevent young people from being contaminated by Western cultural influences. Despite this control over distribution and, implicitly, cultural consumption, it was unable to stop either the diffusion of Western influences, or Romanian youth's contact with them. In fact, the restrictive measures of July 1971 actually contributed to the strengthening of young people's cultural fixation with everything Western. By listening to foreign music and adopting a type of behavior and style inspired by Western magazines, young people represented their free choice, defining and redefining the self in opposition to the regime's obtuse and abusive attempts to establish norms and define culture in 1970s and 1980s Romania. In this way, the emergence of youth counterculture and the regime's attempt to stop its dissemination, represented pieces of the same symbolic conflict. In it, both sides viewed the consumption of music and its associated practices as contributing to the creation of an alternative subjectivity: one that the youth wanted to achieve, and one that the regime wished to see gone.

Gazing to the West

Western radio stations such as Radio Free Europe, Voice of America, and Deutsche Welle were the main channels through which Romanian youth kept up to date with the latest musical releases. Reports compiled by the Securitate in the 1970s and 1980s show an increase in the number of young people listening to musical programs on radio stations west of the Iron Curtain, especially Radio Free Europe.[15] Polls conducted by the Audience and Public Opinion Research Department of Radio Free Europe showed that 40 percent of listeners aged between eighteen and twenty regularly listened to musical shows during the 1980s.[16] In Romania, unlike in other Eastern European countries, the frequencies of foreign radio stations were not jammed. Young people could therefore listen to their broadcasts without difficulty, though not without a certain degree of personal risk.[17] As a consequence, their favorite place for such activity was almost always at their own residence, family home, or at boarding school. Foreign radio stations were also commonly listened to at school parties.[18]

Listening to radio programs was done either individually or in groups. Securitate reports noted with great concern that young people formed groups to listen to Radio Free Europe and other Western stations' music shows. Within these groups, young people encouraged one other to listen to certain genres of music, to adopt particular behaviors, and to wear certain clothing specific to particular Western countercultures. Worst of all, it was infectious: Securitate officers noted that groups of young people that exhibited such styles in public spaces like coffee shops, bars, discotheques, or clubs were quickly imitated by others equally attracted to the novelty and uniqueness of their appearance.[19]

Romanian fans were not satisfied with only being able to listen to music being chosen by foreign radio stations. They also wrote letters to the producers of Western radio programs requesting they air their favorite songs. Because letters posted through the Romanian postal circuit were generally confiscated by the Securitate, young people frequently chose to send their letters via unassuming tourists, foreign students, truck drivers, friends, or relatives who traveled abroad.[20] In addition, Romanian fans created their own channels in order to listen to foreign music. The most passionate of them made recordings of songs broadcast during radio shows on magnetic tapes and, later, on cassettes, which they would then play at festive occasions or lend to other people—friends and colleagues who then also familiarized themselves with Western artists and their music.[21]

Trips abroad were yet another opportunity for some young people to not only listen to Western music, but also observe the styles of clothing and behaviors that were specific to certain musical countercultures. Traveling abroad was obviously not possible for all youth because it was very expensive. Interestingly, the Securitate reports noted that the young people who acted as group leaders, or whose countercultural behavior became particularly contagious among their friends and colleagues, came from a secure financial background and lived in one of Romania's main cities (such as Bucharest, Iași, Craiova, Timișoara, Oradea, Cluj Napoca, Târgu Mureș, all of which were also university centers). Along with other members of the family, they traveled abroad or visited relatives who lived in other East bloc countries (especially Hungary), or in the West (particularly West Germany, but also France and the United States). During these journeys, they bought vinyl discs, cassettes, and magazines, such as West Germany's *Bravo* and *Youths Magazine* or *Youth of the World* from Hungary, attended concerts, or simply met up and became acquainted with punk, new wave, rock or csöves friends. Once back home, young people changed their appearance and behavior in order to express their allegiance to a counterculture.[22] Their peers not only envied the clothes that they wore but also the music magazines, vinyl discs, or cassettes that they had managed to smuggle back home.

Attendance at the concerts of rock bands from Hungary (Omega, Piramis, Edda, Illes, Lokomotiv), Poland (Skaldowie), Serbia (Generacija 5), Czechoslovakia (M-Effekt) provided young people with another opportunity to get a glimpse of what global music was like. These concerts, however, were not accessible to all since they were mainly organized in Bucharest and other urban centers in Romania. The regime and local authorities allowed these performances. They were aware of young people's quest for rock music and therefore tried to satisfy this need in a controlled environment. Moreover, from their perspective, rock music from the East was more ideologically reliable than that which came from the West.[23]

Interestingly, in their efforts to find out as much as they could about various musical countercultures, young people used official media products that were specifically designed to counter such tendencies. Shows on national television that painted an extremely unflattering picture of punk only increased its attractiveness among the young generation.[24] In a similar vein, Securitate officers noted that young people of Hungarian ethnicity who read Hungarian magazines such as *Youth Magazine* and *Youth of the World* "took only the negative aspects" of musical counterculture, and therefore its activities degenerated into "an improper and toxic behavior of the 'csöves' type."[25]

Counterculture, Imitation, Authenticity

Despite strict control from the authorities, young people in Romania identified alternative channels that ensured their access to Western music and information concerning the emergence and the expression of countercultures in the West. As a consequence, under the country's restrictive conditions, Romanian youth began imitating and publicly expressing their choice for countercultural styles. Furthermore, young people believed that imitating the behavior and styles of Western countercultures afforded them the opportunity to form and express a distinct subjectivity that provided them with a particular place in Romanian society. Therefore, their expression of authenticity came, paradoxically, from the consumption of mass cultural products from abroad and even the repackaging and remodeling of some local ones.

This "cultural fixation" on the West explains why Romanian youth saw, through the imitation of Western cultural products, a desirable way to express and showcase themselves in the most genuine manner. The cultural embargo imposed after July 1971 resulted in the social individualization of those who had access to newly prohibited cultural products. By identifying with the West, youngsters had a means of expressing their uniqueness within the mass of a homogenized youth who were all consumers of the same material goods. Importantly, imitation did not mean a faithful recreation of Western countercultural styles, but rather a re-establishment, in which the youth's ability to substitute some products that were not available on the Romanian market, such as safety pins instead of earrings, played a major role and provided a unique and authentic character to the consumption of foreign cultural products.[26]

For young people in Romania, "the imaginary West" also won the battle of authenticity in a different way. The West was seen as the repository of a multiplicity of values, emotions, and feelings that allowed for a variety of lifestyles and which, in the eyes of Romanian youngsters, were freely shared and unanimously accepted by political authorities and society as a whole. In contrast, the Romanian regime strove to impose on its youth only one set of communist values, and a single communist perspective. Under such circumstances, the adoption of a countercultural style signified not only the possibility of a free choice that expressed the young person's sense of self, but also the opportunity for indirect experimentation with the Western way of life. In fact, young people's main motivation to become members of a particular group based on their common preference for a specific musical style, was the idea, as one youngster stated, of "having a free and independent view of life, one that could provide an escape from social norms."[27] At the same time, young fans formed what the Securitate identified as "youth entourages" (informal gatherings for hanging out or listening to foreign music) whose purpose, according to the Romanian secret police, was to "act against Marxist-Leninist education measures," which would lead to "the limitation of youth liberties."[28]

Elements of "the imaginary West" appeared in the language of its fans and signaled individual and collective identification. For example, young people mostly chose English names for themselves and their bands: The Club of Free Kings, The Kid Klan, and Punk.[29] In the latter example, the nicknames were used not only during the group's interactions but also to sign letters to Radio Free Europe so that their authors would not be identified by the Securitate. Young people drew on extremely diverse sources of inspiration when formulating their nicknames, with some replicating the main protagonists of the international musical scene, such as Michael Jackson, Rod Stewart, Freddie Mercury, and Dire Straits.[30]

Young people not only chose English nicknames, but also used bricolage and artifacts to create a unique appearance that would substantiate their subjectivity. Unlike Western fans, who had a variety of products at their disposal that they could turn into artifacts, Romanian fans imitated the same style using whatever was available. Punk fans opted for "eccentric outfit, clothes in strident colors" that they adorned with "large safety pins, fibulae, beads, badges, lacing, animal teeth" or wore "T-shirts with bizarre animal figures and skulls, with chains and wires on which they had strung nuts and washers, etc. and wore them around their neck, with metallic clips and safety pins of unusual size" in order to create "a behavior and an appearance out of the ordinary."[31] As members of different groups, young people respected a series of rules that strengthened the authenticity of their appearances and manifestations. Rules included: giving an oath, making insignia and badges featuring the name of the group and its members, the adoption of a common piece of clothing, and the establishment of a meeting place, such as a discotheque, pastry shop, bar, or park.[32]

Willing to "distinguish themselves from the rest of the common and ordinary people," as one of the Securitate report noted in April 1983, young new wave fans dressed in "green shirts and wide-legged trousers, some of them wearing white trousers and black underwear." In regard to their hairstyles, the same document mentioned that "some are shaved above the ears, with a Mohawk in the middle of the head, others combed with many partings or with hair falling over their eyes to the chin." [33]

The csöves clothing followed on from the hippie style of the 1960s. Influenced by articles in Hungarian and West German magazines, the Romanian csöves "went so far as to paint their face and hands." Their outfits included "tight pants, long and large shirts, overabundant hair, shoes with sharp edges." They accessorized their outfits with "metal chains, ornaments made of razor blades, scallops, crosses, knives introduced in the clothes' loops."[34] As reported by the Securitate of Brașov County in December 1983, other csöves wore "red ties with white dots, some rubber bracelets, blue jeans, T-shirts with different initials, etc."[35] They also paid special attention to adornments on their bodies, choosing to "introduce safety pins under their skin in the visible parts of their bodies: on hands, throat and face."[36] The greetings among csöves were addressed in Hungarian—"servus csü" (hello pipers!) or "elgen csü" (long live the pipers!)—and were accompanied by specific gestures such as raising the arm and forming a "V" shape with two fingers.[37] While not necessarily an overt provocation to the authorities, the csöves use of Hungarian asserted their belonging to a minority group that had been subjected to an intense policy of denationalization by the Romanian regime. In Romania, the fact that young people with Hungarian nationality imitated a version of Western counterculture that was disseminated via their kin state, not only indicated their strong national identity, but also demonstrated the important role that ethnicity played in the creation of authentic subjectivities in a countercultural context.

The way in which music consumption influenced behavior and appearance further affirmed the development of an authentic "youth" subjectivity in Romania. Romanian punk, rock, and new wave fans used bricolage and nicknames to create unique appearances that matched their newly acquired subjectivity. Since they originated in the West, countercultures contained the promise of personal freedom and the opportunity to express and redesign oneself without constraints. This was an ideal situation to which young Romanians, living under a restrictive communist regime, aspired. Moreover, young people were inclined to consider Romanian values, norms, and even cultural goods as inferior to those that came from the West, as they were imbued with a political message that failed to inspire them. As demonstrated in the next section, their attempts to forge a distinct subjectivity brought young people into conflict with the regime and its secret police.

The Securitate and Youth Counterculture

Throughout the 1970s and 1980s, the Romanian secret police tried to limit and subsequently eliminate young people's countercultural manifestations. As discussed above, the Securitate sought to police these activities because it saw itself as a gatekeeper, and believed that the emergence of countercultures, as inspired by the West, undermined the fundamental health foundations of the younger generation's consciousness.

The elimination of musical countercultures and their influence was primarily justified on ideological grounds, with the Securitate claiming it to be hostile Western propaganda. The Western enemy was said to consist of "the espionage services, the reactionary circles and organizations from abroad,"[38] to which Nicolae Ceaușescu added "some elements of the former exploiting classes and reactionary circles [who had] fled abroad."[39]

According to the Securitate, these "external hostile circles" directed their attention "in all directions and in a diversified range of preoccupations toward youth," taking advantage of their "lack of experience, insufficiently shaped judgment, increased receptivity and non-conformist tendencies" that made them "more vulnerable to influences." Secret police agents stated that the aim of such "ideological diversion" was "to create within the groups a mass of people that could be easily manipulated for antisocial purposes, and subsequently pose serious problems for the state's internal order and security."[40] In the Securitate's eyes, these "reactionary circles make use of all available means" to cause "diversion among the youth." "Western written and oral propaganda" was ascribed an important role in producing "hostile materials and shows dedicated to young people, aiming to misinform, create distrust in the policy promoted by our party and state, inflate, and determine their involvement in hostile actions."[41] The Securitate's documents also emphasized the fact that foreign radio stations, especially Radio Free Europe, exploited young people's desire to listen to music by inculcating them with "reactionary ideas and views," therefore creating "confusion ... and mainly distrust in the party and the state's policy."[42] Moreover, in a 1984 report regarding the problem "of negative influencing of the youth" by "reactionary circles from abroad," authorities noted (correctly) that Radio Free Europe hoped to appeal to young Romanian listeners by increasing and diversifying its broadcasting time with this specific audience in mind:

> The diverse problems discussed in broadcasts are meant to attract a wide range of listeners: school children, students, young workers, who are subject to an intense and subtle hostile propaganda, with a view to indoctrinating them, to [encourage them to] adopt an attitude of insubordination and rejection of communist education, to create an ideological diversity.[43]

As previously shown, the strategy of Western radio stations to attract young listeners through their music programs was not without results. During the 1970s and 1980s, an ever growing number of young people listened to the music shows individually or in groups, and tried to contact the collaborators and producers of radio stations "in order to broadcast their musical preferences."[44]

The Securitate's hostile reaction to musical countercultures was also related to its officials' lack of proper knowledge about Western music. The Securitate justified their interventions on the false belief that Romanian punk, heavy metal, and new wave fans were driven by the same rebellious stance toward authority and the status-quo as their Western counterparts.[45] Securitate documents highlighted the dissenting voice of punk music, which was especially popular among young Romanians, in different contexts. In June 1984, the Iași branch of the Securitate reported that "the punk fashion ... is imitated by young people between the ages of 15 and 22 as a form of 'anarchic discontentment,' having as sources of influence the punk groups from the capitalist states. The behavior of these young people is characterized by a specific non-conformist outfit and haircut, plus a certain attitude of rebelliousness."[46] Another Securitate report, dated May 1984, adopted an even more alarmist tone: "The punk fans argue that society and everything around them should be despised and destroyed; they support disobedience of laws, school and family, they advocate for violence and moral self-destruction, they run away from home, neglect or abandon school, drink alcohol, commit immoral acts."⁴⁷ Moreover, these reports, mostly written during the 1980s, insisted on using various negative meanings of the word "punk, invariably translating it as "loiterer, hooligan, and libertine."⁴⁸

The Securitate's lack of knowledge about Western musical culture became apparent through the way that it defined youth countercultures. A report from May 1984 noted that the Romanian youth imitated "the members of the British band of light music called PUNK (loiterer, hooligan, and libertine) founded in 1978 which was on several occasions the object of some programs broadcast by the Romanian Television."⁴⁹ As well as the fact that officials described punk music as "light," a description far removed from its rock sensibilities, and regarded punk as a British band rather than a culture in itself, it also appears that the Securitate had "found" the answer to ongoing debates about whether the genre was British or American in origin.⁵⁰

The Securitate's officials also misunderstood the connection between punk and new wave. They believed that "the followers of the PUNK culture" concealed themselves "under the more respectable designation of New Wave,"⁵¹ and that punk culture provided the foundations for "a new form of manifestation called *new wave,* which is distinguished only through the clothing of its followers, the behavior being identical."⁵² At the end of the 1970s, new wave followers were indeed considered to be imitators of punk, but soon afterwards they began to individualize themselves by developing a music style closer to pop rather than rock music.⁵³ Even after several years, it appears that Securitate officials had failed to overcome their initial confusion between punk and new wave.

As for the csöves, in April 1983 the Securitate incorrectly associated them with hippie culture but also noticed several similarities with punk, particularly regarding their "anti-social" behavior:

> The young *csöves* and *punk* adopt a parasitic lifestyle, refuse to carry out socially useful activities, promote a strong maverick spirit, of parasitic type, wishing to live at the edge of the so-called complete liberty; they enter into a moral conflict with their society and families; they indulge in antisocial actions; [are] violence prone, having a profound aversion toward everything that renders order and discipline in the society, some of them leave their homes, surviving on expedients, thefts, and begging; they wear cloths of *pipe type,* live under the bridges and in sewerage pipes (hence the name csöves—pipers).⁵⁴

Securitate officials incorrectly labeled young people as csöves if they wore a particular style of clothing that resembled the outfits worn by Western hippies. However, as Timothy W. Ryback has argued, these young people often identified themselves with British punk rock.[55]

Heavy metal fans also came under the scrutiny of the Securitate, largely due to the names of the foreign bands who played this type of music. In a report produced in September 1989, one of the Securitate's county branches meticulously recorded, sometimes using "original" translations, the names of bands that were popular among "the followers of the Heavy Metal culture": "Killer's Vampir, Maniac, DAF (a band from the anticommunist German Federal Republic), AC/DC (*Anticiștii contra comuniștilor*—Those Who Were against Communism)." The same document mentioned how these bands popularized "anti-communist, neo-Nazi, and anti-state ideas" through their "musical texts and forms of manifestation."[56]

Having construed a negative perspective about Western music and its influence, Securitate documents produced in the 1980s expressed particular concern that the involvement of young people in "a series of actions with an anti-social character"—including the creation of groups and entourages, "malicious and critical comments" about the country's internal situation, and "the manifestation of excessive liberalism"—were precisely the result of "reactionary propaganda" produced by foreign radio stations.[57] The Securitate's July 1988 report highlighted the fact that existing "deficiencies" in young people's education encouraged their "subduing to hostile influences" from outside.[58] The report concluded that "in order to have a vigorous youth, with healthy conceptions about the world and life, fully devoted to motherland and socialism," all institutions that involved young people must dutifully fulfill their tasks, "because one cannot allow and must not allow any failure regarding the youth, the harm done in this domain being very difficult to undo or [it may] even [be] irreparable."[59]

Securitate authorities became involved in active surveillance in order to prevent the contamination of young fans with "ideas and conceptions ... foreign to the character of the ruling system we are building, and contrary to our healthy traditions of our people."[60] Together with the Communist Militia,[61] its officials raided culture houses, youth clubs, or discotheques; places where young people congregated and where it was likely that they would be listening and dancing to Western music.[62] At the same time, Securitate county authorities tried to identify, monitor, and break up groups that had developed with the sole purpose of listening to Western music.[63]

Most frequently, the Securitate used warnings and positive influencing measures against young people who listened to Western music. Initially, the young person was invited to the local Securitate headquarters for a meeting with an officer. During this meeting, he was cautioned about the gravity of his actions. The meeting ended when the person "fully admitted and apologized for his deeds, and made a written commitment not to engage in similar types of behavior in the future." Sometimes the person bolstered their commitment "that he or she will restrain from similar acts" with the promise that he or she "will contribute to the identification of other similar elements" and inform the Securitate authorities about their existence.[64]

By adopting positive influencing tactics, Securitate authorities attempted to use a network of informants, family members, and educational agents to protect young people from the negative influences that might lead to them taking part in "anti-social and potentially harmful actions."[65] Securitate officials usually requested the help of "teachers and local factors" from educational institutions to carry out "measures to positively influence those in question" after their intervention.[66] On occasion, Securitate agents "entrusted young people to the care of educational figures and parents in order to guarantee their surveillance and positive influencing."[67]

The Securitate also used public debates to remodel the behavior of young people who loved Western music. This measure reflected their belief that public disavowal was a useful tool of social control for all types of unorthodox behavior.[68] As a result, the young person found guilty of being "an admirer of Punk" or a hardcore fan of Western radio shows was brought in front of his class, in the presence of teachers, students, and a representative of the Union of Communist Youth.[69] Lastly, in order to correct and impose on young people certain norms and attitudes, the Securitate organized "actions of counterintelligence work ... with the aim of raising the combative spirit for defending the revolutionary achievements in our country, and vigilance against the external harmful influence."[70]

The political purpose behind the Securitate's attempts to eradicate these countercultural manifestations can be seen most clearly when considering the concept of the "new man," an ideal that the Romanian regime sought to strengthen through the July Theses of 1971. From the perspective of the Romanian secret police, this plan was jeopardized by the ease with which younger generations could be influenced by hostile Western propaganda. Moreover, assuming that Romanian fans were not only copying the attire and behaviors of Western countercultures, but also their rebellious pose toward authority and political order, the Securitate underlined the specific ways in which new youth subjectivities undermined young people's transformation into strong builders of socialism and communism.

Conclusion

Through their consumption of Western popular culture, Romanian youngsters created a subjectivity that brought them into conflict with the regime over an essential issue: what it meant to be young in Romania during the last decades of communist rule. Both young people and the regime put forward a particular vision of authentic subjectivity and ascribed a different role to the West in order to support their case. For young people, the West and its music allowed them to express themselves freely and differently, providing new ways of understanding reality and their place within it. The embargo on Western cultural products, enacted in July 1971, forced Romanian fans to look for alternative ways to access music outside the Iron Curtain. Consequently, they began to increasingly listen to foreign radio stations, avidly read all that they could find about their favorite bands and artists, energetically shared music and information with their peers, chose English nicknames for themselves and their friends, and imitated the countercultural styles of punk, new wave, and rock by using the limited means they had at their disposal. Young people therefore devised a variety of initiatives in order to sidestep interdictions. Furthermore, they challenged the regime by listening to foreign music in boarding schools and at school parties, and by dressing as punk, new wave, and rock fans in public spaces like coffee shops, bars, discotheques, or clubs.

The Romanian regime reacted to young people's consumption of Western cultural goods by enlisting its secret police. This episode describes a lesser known aspect of the Securitate's work during the 1970s and 1980s: its officials monitored and took measures not only against political dissidents or hostile foreigners, but also against young punk, new wave, and rock fans. The Securitate tried to contain the spread of Western cultures among young people because it was assumed that Romanian fans were not only imitating their countercultural dress style, but also their rebellious stance toward authority and official order. Moreover, the Securitate and the regime saw the youth's familiarization with a set of ideas that deviated from its official values as a danger to its plan of forging a "correct" and thus socialist subjectivity for the future builders of socialist Romania. By engaging with punk, rock, or new wave countercultures, youngsters denied the regime the right to define what it meant to be young, creating an alternative subjectivity for themselves instead. These contrasting attitudes and responses shed new light on relations between the regime and significant aspects of Romanian society.

These conflicts led to different imaginings of "authentic" subjectivity. The regime argued that youth should build their subjectivity on socialist values that were neither ideologically subversive nor borrowed from the West. Above all, these values were seen to help young people understand the great importance of their assigned task, that of building socialism in Romania. For young people, the consumption of Western cultural goods was, paradoxically, their central means of forging what they identified to be an authentic subjectivity. Their adoption of countercultural styles was seen to signify the possibility of free choice, and the opportunity to work on one's self independently, rather than in accordance with terms that were officially prescribed. Their attire, behavior, and English nicknames were outward signs of young people's newly acquired subjectivity, providing them with a particular place in Romanian society that drew them closer to their imaginary West, the land of unlimited personal and political freedom.

The regime understood the dissemination of Western countercultures as a real threat to its political survival, because punk, rock, or new wave countercultures purportedly encouraged a disobedient and rebellious stance toward its authority. These countercultures were seen to empower young people to refuse and resist their officially assigned role: that of the "new man" and future builder of socialism in Romania. The involvement of the Romanian secret police, and the array of preventive measures that it took to limit the spread of countercultures among youth, speaks tellingly of the regime's growing concern about the issue. The extent to which Romanian youth actually attributed political significance to its consumption of foreign music varied from case to case. Ultimately, whether they were simply imitating what they saw and read about Western countercultures, or were consciously making political statements with their style of dress or choice of music, young people learned that every aspect of their lives, no matter how ordinary it was, could trigger the unwanted attention of the regime.

Manuela Marin, Ph.D., is a postdoctoral researcher at Babeș-Bolyai University, Cluj-Napoca, Romania. She received her Ph.D. in Romanian contemporary history in 2008. Her main research interest is related to Nicolae Ceaușescu's regime and his cult of personality, on which she published two books, *Nicolae Ceaușescu: Omul și Cultul* [Nicolae Ceaușescu: The man and his cult] (Editura Cetatea de Scaun, 2016) and *Între trecut și prezent: cultul personalității lui Nicolae Ceaușescu și opinia publică românească* [Between past and present: Nicolae Ceaușescu's cult of personality and Romanian public opinion] (Editura Mega, 2014). Other areas of interest include the history of communism in Romania, everyday life during communism, national minorities, and Muslim religion during communism.

Notes

1. Archive of the National Council for the Study of the Securitate Archives (hereafter abbreviated as ACNSAS), Informative Fund, file 3032 vol. 1, folio 21f. All translations are mine unless otherwise stated.
2. Patricia Thomson, "Field," in *Pierre Bourdieu: Key Concepts*, ed. Michael Grenfell (Durham, NC, 2008), 69–74.
3. Thomas Cushman, *Notes from the Underground: Rock Music Counterculture in Russia* (New York, 1995), 43.
4. Alexei Yurchak, *Everything Was Forever, Until It Was No More: The Last Soviet Generation* (Princeton, NJ, 2006), 34–35.
5. Hugh Fielder and Mike Gent, *PUNK: The Brutal Truth* (London, 2012).
6. Cushman, *Notes*, 7–8.
7. D. G. Leathers, *Successful Nonverbal Communication: Principles and Applications* (New York, 1992), 157, cited in Eric Batson, "Youth Culture, Clothing, and Communicative Messages," MA thesis (Las Vegas, 2005), 8.
8. Dick Hebdige, *Subculture: The Meaning of Style* (London, 2002), 102–106; Andy Bennet, *Cultures of Popular Music* (Buckingham, UK, 2001), 63.
9. "Propuneri de măsuri pentru îmbunătățirea activității politico-ideologice, de educare marxist-leninistă a membrilor de partid, a tututor oamenilor muncii. 6 Iulie 1971" in Ana-Maria Cătănuș, ed., *Sfârșitul perioadei liberale a regimului Ceaușescu: Minirevoluția culturală din 1971* (București, 2005), 121–130.
10. Cătănuș, *Minirevoluția culturală din 1971*, 25–26, 33–37, 127; Mary Ellen Fischer, *Nicolae Ceausescu: A Study in Political Leadership* (Boulder, CO, 1989), 180.
11. For further details, see Katherine Verdery, *National Ideology under Socialism: Identity and Cultural Politics in Ceausescu's Romania* (Berkeley, CA, 1991).
12. Cătănuș, *Minirevoluția culturală din 1971*, 33–37, 127; Fischer, *Nicolae Ceausescu*, 180, 186–197.
13. Robert R. King, *A History of the Romanian Communist Party* (Stanford, CA, 1980), 120–134; Verdery, *National Ideology*.
14. Anneli Ute Gabanyi, *The Ceausescu Cult* (Bucharest, 2000), 155–168; Manuela Marin, "The Nationalistic Discourse in Communist Romania: A General Perspective," *Studia Universitatis Babeș-Bolyai, Historia* 56, no. 2 (2011): 80–104.
15. Manuela Marin, "Ascultând Radio *Europa Liberă* în România lui Nicolae Ceaușescu," in *Între transformare și adaptare: Aspecte ale cotidianului în regimul comunist din România*, ed. Luciana M. Jinga and Ștefan Bosomitu (Iași, 2013), 218–224; ACNSAS, fond Documentar, dosar 8833 vol. 45, f. 75f, 116; dosar 8833 vol. 41, f. 35 verso.
16. Marin, "Ascultând Radio," 218–219.
17. RFE/RL. RFE Listening Patterns in Romania, February 1980, OSA Archivum, HU OSA 300-6-2 Box 4, East Europe Area and Opinion Research, September 1971–December 1980; RFE/RL. Reasons for not listening to RFE in Romania, October 1986, HU OSA 300-6-2 Box 7, East Europe Area and Opinion Research, March 1986–November 1988.
18. ACNSAS, Documentary Fund, file 8833 vol. 47, folio 342; vol. 36, folio107; Informative Fund, file 3032 vol.1, folios 115, 173.

19. ACNSAS, Documentary Fund, file 8833 vol. 15, folio 217 f-v; vol. 10, folio 227 f-v; file 18306 vol. 11, folios 250–251; Network Fund, file 423391 vol. 1, folio 8.
20. ACNSAS, Documentary Fund, file 8833 vol. 15, folios 211 f-v, 217 f-v, 415–419; vol. 10, folio 262 f-v; vol. 11, folio 118 f-v; vol. 36, folios 107–109.
21. ACNSAS, Documentary Fund, file 8833, vol. 43, folios 146–147; file 12550 vol. 1, folio 15v; file 8697 vol. 2, folio 66 f; Informative Fund, file 3032 vol. 1, folios 12 v, 114 f, 115; file 906390, folio 6; file 759981, folio 65 bis.
22. ACNSAS, Documentary Fund, file 8833 vol. 10, folio 441; vol. 25, folio 395; file 18306 vol. 7, folio 184 v; Informative Fund, file 906390, folio 86 v.
23. ACNSAS, Documentary Fund, file 8833 vol. 45, folio 439 v; Nelu Stratone and Florin Silviu Ursulescu, *Stratonelu (un rocket atipic): Nelu Stratone în dialog cu Florin Silviu Ursulescu* (București, 2016), 34, 55–57.
24. ACNSAS, Documentary Fund, file 8833 vol. 18, folio 318 f.
25. ACNSAS, Documentary Fund, file 8833 vol. 11, folio 23 f; Network Fund, file 423391 vol. 1, folio 7. Csöves, or the pipers, were part of punk subculture that originated in Hungary at the end of 1970; the Csöves part of punk subculture was adopted by ethnic Hungarians living in Romania as well. For more details see Timothy W. Ryback, *Rock around the Bloc: A History of Rock Music in Eastern Europe and the Soviet Union* (Oxford, 1990), 171.
26. ACNSAS, Documentary Fund, file 8833 vol. 41, folio. 68 f-v.
27. ACNSAS, Informative Fund, file 906390, folio 38. Also see Informative Fund, file 855732 vol. 1, folio 18.
28. ACNSAS, Documentary Fund, file 13365 vol. 1, folio 39.
29. ANCAS, Informative Fund, file 906390; file 3032 vol.1; file 855732 vol. 1.
30. ACNSAS, Documentary Fund, file 8833 vol. 15, folio. 211 f; file 8687 vol. 2, folios 62, 67, 153.
31. ACNSAS, Documentary Fund, file 8833 vol. 41, folio 68 f-v; Informative Fund, file 855732 vol. 1, folio 17.
32. ACNSAS, Documentary Fund, file 13365 vol.1, folio 38; Informative Fund, 3032 vol.1, folio 30; file 855732 vol. 1, folios 4 f, 18, 27 f.
33. ACNSAS, Documentary Fund, file 8833 vol. 18, folio 4 f.
34. ACNSAS, Documentary Fund, file 8833 vol. 14, folio 322 f.
35. ACNSAS, Documentary Fund, file 8833 vol. 11, folio 23 f-v.
36. ACNSAS, Documentary Fund, file 8833 vol. 14, folio 322 f.
37. ACNSAS, Documentary Fund, file 8833 vol. 10, folio 343 f.
38. ACNSAS, Documentary Fund, file 8833 vol. 45, folio 113.
39. ACNSAS, Documentary Fund, file 8833 vol. 45, folio 74 v.
40. ACNSAS, Documentary Fund, file 8833 vol. 45, folio 113.
41. Ibid.
42. ACNSAS, Documentary Fund, file 8833 vol. 45, folio 74 v.
43. ACNSAS, Documentary Fund, file 8833 vol. 41, folio 35 f.
44. ACNSAS, Documentary Fund, file 8833 vol. 45, folio 75 f.
45. See Mark Paytress, *The History of Rock: The Definitive Guide to Rock, Punk, Metal and Beyond* (Bath, UK, 2011), 186; Cari E. Byres, "The Sex Pistols: Punk Rock as Protest Rhetoric," MA thesis (Las Vegas, 2002), 3–25; Fielder and Gent, *PUNK*; Penelope Spheeris, foreword to *The Encyclopaedia of Punk* by Brian Cogan, (New

York, 2008), vii; Adrian Boot and Chris Salewicz, *Punk: The Illustrated History of a Music Revolution* (New York, 1997), 9.
46. ACNSAS, Documentary Fund, file 8833 vol. 45, folio 427 v.
47. ACNSAS, Documentary Fund, file 8833 vol. 18, folio 318 v.
48. ACNSAS, Documentary Fund, file 8833 vol. 41, folio 68 f; file 8833 vol. 18, folio 318 f.
49. ACNSAS, Documentary Fund, file 8833 vol. 18, folio 318 f.
50. For more details see Cogan, *The Encyclopedia of Punk*, viii–x; Boot and Salewicz, *Punk*, 9.
51. ACNSAS, Documentary Fund, file 8833 vol. 18, folio 1 f.
52. ACNSAS, Documentary Fund, file 8833 vol. 45, folio 427 v.
53. Paytress, *The History of Rock*, 190–191, 317.
54. ACNSAS, fond Documentar, dosar 8833 vol. 14, folios 322 v-323. The last part of the description of young csöves does not identify very clearly the two elements that determined their labeling as *pipers*. Therefore, the word csöves is used in reference to the wandering way of life of these young people, and at the way they wore their trousers, which resembled drain pipes. For more details, see Anna Szemere, *Up from the Underground: The Culture of Rock Music in Postsocialist Hungary* (University Park, PA, 2001), 39.
55. Ryback, *Rock around the Bloc*, 171.
56. ACNSAS, Documentary Fund, file 8833 vol. 25, folio 381 f.
57. ACNSAS, Documentary Fund, file 8833 vol. 45, folio 75 f-v.
58. ACNSAS, Documentary Fund, file 8833 vol. 45, folio 74 v.
59. ACNSAS, Documentary Fund, file 8833 vol. 45, folios 112–113.
60. ACNSAS, Documentary Fund, file 8833 vol. 45, folio 114.
61. The Romanian police force was known as *Miliție* during Ceaușescu's regime.
62. ACNSAS, Documentary Fund, file 8833 vol. 45, folio 439 v; vol. 43, folio 142.
63. ACNSAS, Documentary Fund, file 8833 vol. 10, folios 335–337; file 12550 vol. 1, folio 9 f-v; file 13365 vol. 1, folios 38–39, etc.
64. ACNSAS, Documentary Fund, file 8833 vol. 43, folio 143; vol. 45, folio 427v.
65. ACNSAS, Documentary Fund, file 123 vol. 41, folios 24–26 cited in Liviu Burlacu, "Preventive Measures Used by the Securitate," in *Learning History through Past Experiences: Ordinary Citizens under the Surveillance of Securitate during the 1970–1980s*, ed. Virgiliu Țârău (Bucharest, 2009), 64.
66. ACNSAS, Documentary Fund, file 8833 vol. 11, folio 23.
67. ACNSAS, Documentary Fund, file 8833 vol. 10, folio 336.
68. See Dumitru I. Mazilu, *Opinia publică în socialism* (București, 1971).
69. ACNSAS, Documentary Fund, file 8833 vol. 43, folios 146–147.
70. ACNSAS, Documentary Fund, file 8833 vol. 25, folios 381 v, 384 v.

Bibliography

Batson, Eric. "Youth Culture, Clothing, and Communicative Messages." MA thesis. Las Vegas: University of Nevada, 2005.
Bennet, Andy. *Cultures of Popular Music*. Buckingham, UK: Open University Press, 2001.

Boot, Adrian, and Chris Salewicz. *Punk: The Illustrated History of a Music Revolution*. New York: Penguin Studio, 1997.
Burlacu, Liviu. "Preventive Measures Used by the Securitate." In *Learning History through Past Experiences: Ordinary Citizens under the Surveillance of Securitate during the 1970–1980s*, edited by Virgiliu Țârău, 64–66. Bucharest: Editura CNSAS, 2009.
Byres, Cari E. "The Sex Pistols: Punk Rock as Protest Rhetoric." MA thesis. Las Vegas: University of Nevada, 2002.
Cătănuș, Ana-Maria, ed. *Sfârșitul perioadei liberale a regimului Ceaușescu: Minirevoluția culturală din 1971*. București: Institutul Național pentru Studiul Totalitarismului, 2005.
Cogan, Brian. *The Encyclopaedia of Punk*. New York: Sterling, 2008.
Cushman, Thomas. *Notes from the Underground: Rock Music Counterculture in Russia*. New York: State University of New York Press, 1995.
Fielder, Hugh, and Mike Gent. *PUNK: The Brutal Truth*. London: Flame Tree Publishing, 2012.
Fischer, Mary Ellen. *Nicolae Ceausescu: A Study in Political Leadership*. Boulder, CO: L. Rienner, 1989.
Gabanyi, Anneli Ute. *The Ceausescu Cult*. Bucharest: The Romanian Cultural Foundation Publishing House, 2000.
Hebdige, Dick. *Subculture: The Meaning of Style*. London: Routledge, 2002.
King, Robert R. *A History of the Romanian Communist Party* (Stanford, CA:Hoover Institution Press, 1980)
Marin, Manuela. "Ascultând Radio *Europa Liberă* în România lui Nicolae Ceaușescu." In *Între transformare și adaptare: Aspecte ale cotidianului în regimul comunist din România*, edited by Luciana M. Jinga and Ștefan Bosomitu, 209–230. Iași: Polirom, 2013.
———. "The Nationalistic Discourse in Communist Romania: A General Perspective." *Studia Universitatis Babeș-Bolyai, Historia* 56, no. 2 (2011): 80–104.
Mazilu, Dumitru I. *Opinia publică în socialism*. Bucharest: Editura Politică, 1971.
Paytress, Mark. *The History of Rock: The Definitive Guide to Rock, Punk, Metal and Beyond*. Bath, UK: Parragon Books, 2011.
Ryback, Timothy W. *Rock around the Bloc: A History of Rock Music in Eastern Europe and the Soviet Union*. Oxford: Oxford University Press, 1990.
Spheeris, Penelope. Foreword to *The Encyclopaedia of Punk* by Brian Cogan. New York: Sterling, 2008, VII.
Stratone, Nelu, and Florin Silviu Ursulescu. *Stratonelu (un rocker atipic): Nelu Stratone în dialog cu Florin Silviu Ursulescu*. Bucharest: Casa de Pariuri Literare, 2016.
Szemere, Anna. *Up from the Underground: The Culture of Rock Music in Postsocialist Hungary*. University Park: The Pennsylvania State University Press, 2001.
Thomson, Patricia. "Field." In *Pierre Bourdieu: Key Concepts*, edited by Michael Grenfell, 67–84. Durham, NC: Acuman, 2008.
Verdery, Katherine. *National Ideology under Socialism: Identity and Cultural Politics in Ceausescu's Romania*. Berkeley: University of California Press, 1991.
Yurchak, Alexei. *Everything Was Forever, Until It Was No More: The Last Soviet Generation*. Princeton, NJ: Princeton University Press, 2005.

Chapter 10

Punk Authenticity

Difference across the Iron Curtain

Jeff Hayton

> Living means more than simply existing: Are you living?
>
> —*Hamburger Mottenpost* no. 2

In its second issue, the Hamburg punk fanzine *Hamburger Mottenpost* touched on important issues governing the subculture in Germany: how to live and not merely exist? What did living imply? Which actions constituted living and not simply existing? Such a binary implies that certain ideas and practices were considered more authentic than others in the pursuit of living and suggest that debates over authenticity were critical to the pursuit of meaningful life for alternative groups like punk. Thus, exploring what authenticity meant for punks can shed light on the evolution of the subculture across the Iron Curtain. Emerging in East and West Germany in the late 1970s, punk as both a musical genre and a subcultural lifestyle, provided youths with alternative identities and unconventional communities in contrast to what they felt to be the dulling grays of everyday life in real-existing socialism or the shallow materialism of the Federal Republic. At the heart of their rejection was the pursuit of individuality and difference, which they postulated would enable them to live more authentic lives: as the slogan above suggests, living meant more than existing and for German punks, subculture was a means of pursuing authentic living.

Scheiß Norm: Articulating an Inauthentic World

> Norm, norm, norm
> You're born to fulfill norms
>
> —Schleim-Keim, "Scheiß Norm"

The lyrics to "Scheiß Norm" (Fuck Norms) by the Erfurt punk band Schleim-Keim presents a society that is rigid and unforgiving.[1] From its first line reminding listeners that they are born to fulfill norms dictated to them from on high to its contention that failure will lead to ruin, the song marks out how school, work, and even trips to heaven have forced East Germans to forfeit all individuality in the interests of the party-state.[2] While Schleim-Keim's examples were specific to the German Democratic Republic (GDR), nonetheless, the belief that conformity and oppression were robbing individuals of a more authentic living experience was a hallmark of German punk on either side of the Berlin Wall: in both East and West, claims that social pressures were denying individual self-expression were common currency within the subculture. While such understandings of contemporary society were dramatically shaped by the particularities of national historical contexts, nonetheless, a shared sense of oppression speaks to the cross-Bloc nature of the subculture. By examining how punks understood the mechanics of an inauthentic world, we can see how and why they sought to redefine authenticity.

Frustration and disappointment with the status quo evident in punk songs and statements can be tracked on both sides of the Iron Curtain, a similarity suggesting that regardless of democratic capitalism or state socialism, punk complaints about an inauthenticity hinged not in the specifics of the politico-socio-economic order, but rather in a condemnation of the structures of modern life itself. A Düsseldorf punk fanzine illustrated such complaints well when its author tabulated the pluses and minuses of modern human existence: "Bureaucracy + Arbitrariness + Drunkenness + Job + State Control + Contamination − Individuality − Living Space − Happy Experience − Health = Life."[3] Here we see the hallmarks of punk critiques of the modern world: the creeping bureaucratization of society that can only lead to individual corruption; the arbitrariness of authoritative power and state control; and an (over-)emphasis on work that drove many to numb themselves with alcohol. Even worse were the consequences: loss of individuality, happiness, and health. What these binaries indicate is how the very structures of the modern state (bureaucracy, state power) were, according to punks, degrading individual self-realization.

Furthermore, such a schematic lays out a binary between control and loss of individuality that is essential for understanding how German punks understood the world in which they lived. Above all, punk complaints about an inauthentic world recorded fears that individuality and distinctiveness—and as such, the individual self—were being trampled by conformist attitudes and behavior. Such concerns were numerous. On the one hand, many punks rejected mainstream youth culture, which they condemned as unadventurous and lacking in distinctiveness. As an East Berlin punk explained, "I came to punk because all the others, the people, made me sick. It's always the same wherever you go."[4] Another youth, in justifying his decision to become a punk, told his Stasi interrogator that, "everyone in our society is the same as the next one," uniformity that pushed him toward nonconformity.[5] If outward behavior reflected inner genuineness then those attracted to punk viewed conventionality as an attack on their personal authenticity with its rejection being an expression of legitimacy. On the other hand, some youths also feared being caught up in social structures that threatened to trap them and oppress them with falsehoods as "Scheiß Norm" suggested. Here, bourgeois society before all else was viewed with skepticism and disgust: speaking to the West Berlin newspaper *TAZ* in 1982 about why he turned to punk, Schleim-Keim's singer "Otze" responded, "The petit-bourgeoisie, for example, makes me sick. … This whole affectation bothers me, this mask that is there that no one takes off. That no one does what they want, is spontaneous; that rules are always laid down."[6] Even the family was considered a form of structural oppression. When asked about marriage, one punk explained that, "that isn't really a thing with us. Anyway, I think that to get married and all that is bullshit; and also bringing children into the world."[7]

Since punks in both East and West felt their societies to be marked overwhelmingly by conformity and boredom—feelings which they believed divorced individuals from meaningful lives—the pursuits that prior generations had found fulfilling were considered nothing more than deceptions. Such sentiments account for the famous punk slogan "no future," which rejected any sort of progressive narrative about upcoming possibilities as a delusion.[8] But if many early punks cried "no future" because they lacked prospects, not all were looking that far in advance. For some in the West, with the future irrelevant, "no fun" became "more fun," an invitation to present-day debauchery. Youths in the East, by contrast, complained of "too much future" because life was seemingly set in stone: shuttled from school to work until retirement after decades of service to the state, youths in the GDR had their lives mapped out in advance by the SED (Socialist Unity Party of Germany).[9] GDR education policy was designed to transform youths into "socialist personalities" who could then contribute to the historic victory of communism.[10] Outside school, youths were expected to participate in state-sponsored youth culture such as in the Young Pioneers and the Free German Youth (FDJ).[11] The education system and mass youth organizations were meant to foster obedience and conformity not creativity, which meant that socialist youth culture was dull and regimented. For youths attracted to punk, the conformity that marked school and youth culture was despised: as "Mike" spat to *Der Spiegel* in 1982, "This whole upbringing to become a machine … the whole state-run youth scene makes me sick. There was nothing there. So boring. When I think about our discotheques, I think: Vomit!"[12]

State socialism, of course, retained no monopoly on boredom in the minds of young punks as life in West Germany was similarly derided as overly monotonous. And what especially came in for criticism was a perceived loss of agency. As a West German female punk put it, modern life had been reduced to waiting: "In practice, life consists solely of waiting. To wait for next Friday; to wait for somebody; to wait to become an adult; to wait for the end of school; oh, what do I know. We are so busy waiting, that we don't see at all what we are waiting for."[13] To wait meant to accept passivity and become a subject in history. Easterners too lamented that modern life meant waiting for possibilities to present themselves rather than acting and seizing them, which were all the more dangerous in a society where opportunities seemed to never appear. As one punk put it, "For the things that you somehow really want to achieve you have no future, that is a fact, as you won't achieve them as a matter of course."[14] Or, as another East Berlin punk lamented sadly, "I had so much to experience but I wasn't going to be able to do anything at all," a sentiment speaking to the frustrations of wasting one's youth on tasks which appear anathema to the authentic construction of the self.[15] The punk subculture was therefore conceived as an antidote to tediousness; if contemporary life was reduced to waiting, then punk could speed up time and make daily life meaningful.

For punks, the levers of conformity that were most immediate to them were, in the first instance, musical. Punk is a musical subculture and as such, aural considerations played a critical role in shaping youth visions of the world. Punks in both East and West despised contemporary pop music as not only banal and insipid, but also dangerous in its ability to perpetuate oppression and circumscribe authenticity. In the GDR, to tame the disruptiveness of rock and roll, the music industry was completely co-opted by the SED.[16] Over the 1960s and 1970s, the East German state instituted a system in which bands were subject to state licenses and controls. In such a system, musical opportunities were rewards for political loyalty rather than artistic merit, which resulted in conservatism when it came to sonic production. Moreover, because the Eastern rock industry was funded and organized by the state, successful bands supported the system and were instrumental in maintaining the dominant position of acceptable mainstream music until the end of the regime. Likewise, in the West, the capitalist music industry promoted a variety of pop music in the 1970s and 1980s (mainstream rock, disco, *Neue Deutsche Welle*) in its pursuit of profits that punks condemned as artificial and commercial.[17] To punks, the popularity and corresponding conventionality of these genres were barometers of inauthenticity, especially as fashion trends exploited their consumer potential. Thus, in each case, capitalism or socialism, those attracted to punk saw the music industry as working to restrict, subdue, and repackage any manifestations of alternativeness, oppression that threatened individual authenticity. The consequence for punks was popular music devoid of individuality and distinctiveness whose politics and sounds were anodyne and bereft of substance: as one East Berlin punk lamented, "Other music is all so plain because, after all, there is no message there anymore."[18]

If apprehensions about a lack of originality and mass conformity in society and music represented one pole on the spectrum of punk concerns about an inauthentic world, then at the other end was a furious rejection of the student movement and the politics of the Alternative Left. Such hatred was part and parcel of punk provocations. While most observers of the subculture document punk's shock value extensively, some misidentify the target of such provocations as mainstream society. Except it was not primarily the establishment that was the focus of punk incitements, but rather '68ers and hippies; it was they who dominated the field of protest politics and alternative identities in the late 1970s. Following the collapse of the student movement in the late 1960s, its remnants entered a period of leftist dogmatism that was seen to some as inhibiting rather than liberating.[19] Punks came overwhelmingly from an age cohort too young to have participated the 1960s, but who had grown up in a society reeling from its aftermath. However, the Manichean world view put forward by students that equated their generational revolt with progressivism and any deviation with fascism fueled a negative response by punks.[20] Likewise in the East, by the late 1970s, students, hippies and other nonconformists populated what existed as social alternativeness and punks found their lifestyles, practices, and moralizing grating. While the latter's hatred of the former did not reach the same levels of their counterparts in the West, nonetheless, the belief that the 1960s generation was fundamentally erroneous in their narrow-mindedness was transposed eastwards, as yet another example of transnational cultural transfer.

Hatred for hippies and the Alternative Left ran deep among German punks on both sides of the Berlin Wall. And what late-1970s youth hated most about them was their monopoly of difference, which precluded any alternative oppositional positions that might become platforms for individual authenticity. What punks wanted was liberty, and the moral righteousness of the '68ers who decided what was good and what was bad was an unwanted restriction on this drive; as Düsseldorf punk artist padeluun has noted, at this time, hippies "occupied everything called protest."[21] Much of the concerns and political positions that dominated leftist circles then—Marxism, environmentalism, or pacifism, to take a few prominent examples—were considered the only acceptable subjects and politics. Punks believed that such hegemony of thought and action was alienating and threatened their personal authenticity. Moritz Rrrr, a musician in the influential Düsseldorf band Der Plan, has perceptively argued that punk was an important corrective to the dogmatism of the Alternative Left. "Everything was so unfree then. And I wanted to feel free again. I wanted to be as free as possible," Rrrr remembered. "If you talked with hippies, guaranteed that after five minutes you were talking about nuclear power, and after ten minutes you had such a gloomy image of the world that you wanted to kill yourself. And for this reason, punk was necessary."[22]

The belief by punks that the Alternative Left had failed to imagine multiple pathways of protest is evident in the subculture's criticisms of hippie appearances. According to Peter Hein, aka Janie Jones, the singer for Mittagspause and later Fehlfarben, to be different back then meant above all, to wear "overly long hair and baggy clothes," a narrow aesthetic position that could not account for diversity or individuality.[23] Punks chafed at the insistence by the Alternative Left that only such an appearance could constitute protest. Coroners guitarist Gode, for example, explained that the rigidity of the Left was just as bad as the conservatism of the Right: "I quickly noticed that all these '68er hippie-teachers with their long hair were basically as fascist as any priest. Already among the hippies were many who reacted in an extreme manner over my short hair. For them, there only existed short-haired philistine 'squares' and long-haired cool dudes. I didn't make any sense in this dialectal ideology."[24] Having long hair was the means by which one "protested" in the 1970s, and youths drawn to punk rejected such a limitation: Nor was this sentiment confined to Westerners: as a young woman in East Berlin told *Der Spiegel* in 1982, "GDR hippies make me puke, these softies with their tattered parkas and sneakers. I also had hair down to my ass but I just had to cut it off."[25]

The vitriol punks poured on the hippies attests to the angry generational conflict lurking beneath the surface of the subculture. As Frank Bielmeier alerts us, known as Mary Lou Monroe and founding member of Charley's Girls and Mittagspause, punks embraced the modern world, a stance reflecting the genre's realism, which put them at odds with the Alternative Left's utopianism: "the hippies always claimed that the world was good and everything was possible. We were overjoyed that the world was terrible and bad. From this perspective, there was also considerable potential."[26] Nowhere is this celebration better exemplified than in the song "Die Welt ist Schlecht, das Leben ist schön" (The world is terrible, life is beautiful) by Der Plan that insisted that, while the world was perhaps not ideal, nonetheless, life was grand. For punks, the industrial cityscapes of the Federal Republic were sites ripe with potential, not spaces to avoid or reform as ecologists desired, and indeed, for some Easterners, it was the ruins of cities that attracted them.[27] One anthem of West German punk, S.Y.P.H.'s "Zurück zum Beton" (Back to Concrete), reveled in the landscapes of the industrial Ruhr and the materials of modern society:

> Nausea, Nausea, Nature, Nature
> I want concrete pure
> Blue sky, blue sea
> Long live the Concrete Fairy!
> No birds, fish, or plants
> I'd rather dance on concrete.[28]

Youths were enamored with industry—"Industriegelände als Abenteuerspielplatz" (Industrial sites as adventure playground*)* as one song by Der Plan put it—in a way that the '68ers found horrifying.[29] To punks, everyday life needed to be depicted realistically, and fashion, music and aesthetics, all marked punk off from the idealism of the 1960s.[30] And by embracing such modernity, punks sought emancipation from the 1960s as Moritz Rrrr again astutely observed: "There was this feeling that there were many themes that one could not talk about. If in 1977, you said 'I like high-rise apartment buildings,' then you were a real reactionary. Concrete, plastics. All was forbidden."[31]

Thus, punk visions of an inauthentic world rested on two beliefs understood to be stifling authenticity. On the one hand was the certainty that contemporary society was conformist and boring and needed to be overcome for more meaningful life to ensue. On the other hand, there was a belief that current efforts at challenging such oppression (hippies and the Alternative Left) were lacking in their limited vision of what protest and difference might look like. What was needed was a renewed drive for authenticity that rejected conformity. For these reasons, youths who were attracted to punk saw within the subculture strategies for staking out alternative outposts of genuineness that could act as platforms for more meaningful living. In so doing, punk functioned as a positive movement for recuperating individual and communal authenticity in a world that threatened to abolish it.

Anderssein: Punk Authenticity and the Politics of Instability

> In an inexplicable manner and way, these people and their music spoke to that which had for so long been desired unconsciously. One could also be different differently! (*Man konnte auch anders anders sein!*)
> —Peter Hein, *Zurück zum Beton*

At the heart of German punk was a desire for difference.[32] *Anderssein*—to be different or the condition of being different—is the most important ideological referent for understanding punk visions of authenticity in Germany. Underwritten by notions of independence, individuality, and an intense desire for originality, *Anderssein* was an attempt to escape mainstream conformity and leftist dogmatism, both of which—according to punks—stifled meaningful life. In this manner, *Anderssein* functioned as an expression of autonomy and a drive for freedom whereby difference was posited as the authentic future of Germany. Despite claims by the Alternative Left to support nonconformity, punks found their articulations of difference to be as doctrinaire as those to whom they opposed. In response, punks embraced *Anderssein* and its stress on individualism and antagonism as an avenue of pursuing authentic living. Such expressions of provocation and hostility meant there was considerable instability in punk authenticity as it was often dependent upon specific contexts. *Anderssein* was therefore at times contradictory because the demands of subculture often clashed with the pursuit of authenticity, an inconsistency leading to numerous irreconcilable paradoxes that punks were never able to wholly resolve. Nevertheless, early on, *Anderssein* was understood as a credible alternative to both the mainstream and to the Alternative Left as Peter Hein has suggested when he realized that being different from those who claimed to be different was possible through punk (*Man konnte auch anders anders sein!*). Being different meant reworking one's identity in an uncompromising manner and taking pleasure in one's own conception of what it meant to be free, regardless of the friction that such pursuits might generate. To do so, punks pursued *Anderssein* through numerous strategies—music, aesthetics, behaviors—whereby the very structures and practices of subculture became the launching points in their re-evaluation of authenticity.

Ideologically, punk authenticity trafficked above all in a celebration of individuality. In this endeavor, originality, creativity, experimentation, difference, all coalesced in a subculture that would reverse the crushing uniformity and conformity that we have seen define punk visions of the inauthentic world. *Anderssein* meant more than just a rejection of conformity; it was an absolute commitment toward rebelliousness, as one fanzine writer modified Descartes, "I rebel, therefore I am."[33] In this, insurgency became an end not a means. Or, as the East German punk slogan put it somewhat differently, "Better dead than uniform" (*Lieber sterben als genormt sein*).[34] Rather than directed towards a tangible goal, individuality itself became the objective wherever it might be found. As we will see below, making music and aesthetic style were several concrete embodiments of these endeavors. But the impulse towards originality was meant to be all-encompassing in contradistinction to the destruction of individuality that youths believed was a consequence of mass-market consumer culture—the successes of the *Wirtschaftswunder* and the hard work of the postwar generation in the West—and by the socialist party-state in the East. As youths sought freedom in punk to pursue identities and behaviors that ran counter to the mainstream, the genre authorized radical communities and positions with which Germans could experiment. The slogan "no future" was thus both a condemnation of past traditions and present accomplishments, but more importantly, a belief that the future was a blank slate full of possibilities. Suddenly, the boredom and disappointment that had previously characterized contemporary life for youth was replaced by moments pregnant with anticipation.

Faced with the omnipresence of conformity in East and West, punk pointed its adherents towards the possibilities of individuality that promised to enable a more authentic embodiment of their selves. For example, with the regimentation and uniformity of growing up in the GDR pressing heavily on East German youths, punk music became appealing to those who thought or wanted to listen differently. As Jörg Löffler, a member of the Dresden-based band Paranoia, later explained, hearing punk on the radio was an immediate release from the crush of the collective: "For me and a few of my schoolmates, the English program on RTL [Radio Luxembourg] ... was *the discovery.* At last, music that was acceptable. No pop, no Schlager, no disco; we didn't want to do the same as the other 90 percent of our class."[35] With musical choices circumscribed by the dictates of the SED, punk music coming from the West became an illicit form of pleasure that opened up new vistas about the possibilities of cultural production.[36] The music not only offered different sounds, but it also enabled like-minded individuals to connect around their shared love for sonic alternatives, thus becoming a central building block of subculture. In cities across East and West Germany, youths quickly established local scenes so that by the late 1970s, a thriving German punk scene existed on both sides of the Iron Curtain.

These comments about the discovery of punk music being a springboard for subcultural practice illustrates how efforts at making music were essential in driving the movement. Already by 1976, youths began forming bands and making music. Cities developed distinctive sounds—Düsseldorf was more experimental while Hamburg was more hard rock—as punks sought to reignite the rebelliousness of popular music, which they claimed had been defanged by the music industry. When it came to making punk music, German youths wanted to break with the rules governing rock and roll and especially with the conventions of 1970s popular music. Songs were reduced to their bare minimum, both instrumentally and compositionally, in contrast to the extravagant opuses that marked 1970s rock. Danceable rhythms were sped up and variable in contrast to the steady pounding of disco. Simplicity reigned supreme as elaborate arrangements were ditched in favor of fast, hard, and loud music. Punk musicians were marked overwhelmingly by dilettantism as their studied unprofessionalism became a badge of integrity because it closed them off from any commercial appeal. Singing and lyrics were marked with contempt and sarcasm rather than virtuosity and allusions. Instruments and non-instruments—violins, saxophones, vacuums, drills—which rarely populated rock and roll, offered new sonic avenues for punks to explore.[37]

These examples indicate how musical experimentation became a key hallmark of punk aural authenticity with bands endeavoring to make music that would provide a soundtrack of difference. The mood among punk musicians was thus directed at stretching the boundaries of conventional music and their criticisms of contemporary music ("no fun") were reverse-engineered towards the new. If innovation was a source of punk authenticity, then in many ways, experimentation became its ends not its means. Bernward Malaka, bassist for Male, the first West German punk band, suggested that at its heart, punk was about musically testing the limits of the possible: "How far can you go, until the others can't follow? Until they say: 'Enough! This is too hard!'"[38] Ralf Dörper, a member of S.Y.P.H., an early Düsseldorf band, put it perhaps even more succinctly: "We played with what was possible."[39] These comments point to a fundamental truth about punk music: rather than an effort at composing commercial rhythms or even pleasant sounds, punk music—and the authenticity that flowed from it—stemmed from a push to redefine the sonic in new and exciting ways. Sometimes this meant trying to capture the "sound" of West Berlin in the early 1980s as Einstürzende Neubauten attempted.[40] Or when they tried to write songs reflecting a specifically feminine understanding of contemporary society, which bands like Malaria! and Kleenex tried to do.⁴¹ But regardless, the contrast between established audio conventions and what punk music sought to accomplish is no clearer than in the excitement that gripped youths when they were introduced to punk music: as Harty Sachse, singer from Müllstation in the GDR remembered, after listening to punk on the radio, "About the lyrics, I had no clue; it could have been right-wing music … At that moment, it didn't matter. For the first time, only the music and this snotty singing was what counted."⁴²

The rudeness that punks accentuated in their music was an important innovation. And insolence was not only musical but also political, a challenge to the hegemony of both the music industry and the Alternative Left. Part of the punk critique of the world was its condemnation of profit and professionals who, in their minds, had ruined popular music through professionalism and calculation. Instead, punks wanted to construct a parallel independent music industry to produce musical alternatives to the mainstream, an endeavor they believed would restore autonomy to their actions and leave them in control of their cultural productions. Musical dilettantism was important here as was the Do-It-Yourself ethos that authorized individual initiative and ignored the conventions of commercial enterprise; DIY concerned the pleasure of doing things yourself regardless of profit.⁴³ Whether making clothes or music, setting up record shops or distribution networks, or even organizing concerts and tours, punks engaged in a wide variety of activities that offered alternative creative productions to the mainstream. By the late 1970s, a plethora of independent music labels had been created to distribute records that bands had produced themselves. Bars and concert halls were set up to host live events and national tours were organized by amateurs.⁴⁴ Even in the East, several independent cassette labels were created to distribute music while semi-legal music venues were opened for punk bands throughout the 1980s.⁴⁵ These activities point to the busyness of punks who, with complete disregard for expertise or experience, set out to create an alternative music industry in the belief that such initiatives would restore authenticity to their actions and achievements. Thus, perhaps even more attitudinal than musical, punk was the unshakable belief that, according to Klaus Maeck, owner of the seminal record store Rip-Off in Hamburg, "we couldn't do it but we simply did it anyway."⁴⁶

Such endeavors meant that punk offered an alternative to contemporary society. Whether through fashion or music, punks undertook actions that marked them off from the mainstream. Such alternativeness represented efforts at dramatizing their dissatisfaction with both capitalist democracy and state socialism. But even more important for punks was their opposition to the Alternative Left. As we have seen, punks saw the conformity of the Alternative Left as dreadful, perhaps even more insidious than the mainstream since "hippies" claimed to be oppositional. *Anderssein*, with its rejection of all conformity, mobilized youths against the hippies. To do so, punks antagonized their enemies through provocations that attacked their political ideals. For example, the many *bêtes noires* of the political Left were mocked by punks who wore buttons like "Nuclear Power, Yes!," "Hippies? No Thank You!," and "Vietnam War is Fantastic!," not because they believed in such positions, but because they knew they would upset the Left.[47] Use of the swastika and right-wing language by punks were other instances of needling hippies, not expressions of Nazism, despite the outraged claims of the mainstream media.[48] Such efforts were done to expose the Left as equally fascist; these provocations were about the present not the past. At the same time, punks also sought to reorient music and difference away from the Alternative Left's definition of genuineness. Bielmeier, in an important statement highlighting how punks believed their musical revolution was as much an attack on the dominance of leftist conceptions of authenticity, suggested that punk music was "all about originality, but in a clear and defined direction. This direction was oriented, above all, against any form of depth. Against [depth] in music for instance. Against enigmatic remarks. Because back then everything was so full of cryptic remarks."[49] By shifting legitimacy to the superficial level, punks sought to generate new instances of import that could lead youths to more meaningful lives.

The importance of shallowness as a site for authenticity cuts to the heart of the punk reorientation of alternativeness. Instead of the inner self as the object of cultivation—an assumption of the Alternative Left—it was surfaces and the consequences of external interactions and provocations that punks identified as the location of legitimacy. Aesthetically, we can see how such concerns were expressed above all in youth's experimentation with fashion.[50] In both East and West, fashion functioned as a marker of identity to bind the subculture together. At the same time, fashion provided youths with an outlet for individual expression. While a Mohawk haircut and leather jacket is the central image of punk, this conformist fashion only became dominant with the triumph of Hardcore in the early 1980s.[51] Punk fashion in the first years, by contrast, was unrestricted, indicating the importance of heterogeneity with key features being spontaneity, elasticity, and an ability to change course quickly depending on context.

In the late 1970s, punk fashion encompassed a variety of styles that sought to mark youths off from the mainstream. Some youths dressed in a patchwork of different materials and designs, crisscrossed with texts and slogans, while others deliberately mismatched them to produce cognitive dissonance. Clothing was ripped and torn with patches, safety pins, or chains holding together the fabrics.[52] In the West, youths often took their cues from the Anglo-American world that they read about in the press or even visited in person, while in the East, youths above all gravitated to any clothes that distanced them from mainstream GDR society: the clean-cut look of FDJ youth, the denim world of workers, and the long hair of the hippies.[53] In both Germanys, hair was cut short and rough to mark punks off from long-haired alternatives, and then cola, glue, or cream was used to spike it and dye it a variety of colors.[54] Accessories like badges and pins were self-made, sometimes baked in the oven or glued onto beer bottle caps; one youth, some remember, fastened cheese slices to his jacket.[55] Trash was also acceptable as punk couture meant the detritus of the past was the fashion of the future. Youths flocked to second-hand stores to discover hidden gems to be customized along individual tastes since at the outset youths could not buy punk fashions.[56]

Such inaccessibility drove the creativity marking early punk style. Until the late 1970s, the scarcity of punk meant that many German youths did not know what punks wore abroad and dressed accordingly. As a result, Thomas Schwebel from S.Y.P.H. and Fehlfarben has remembered that, "we were in these absurdist fantasy-costumes because we had no idea how punks were supposed to look at all."[57] Ignorance led to exciting experiments on both sides of the Berlin Wall. While in the West, youths colored their faces in elaborate makeup, in the East, artist Conny Schleime recollected how she donned four hats at once because that was punk.[58] For some, instability and unpredictability made punk attractive: Jürgen Muschalek, guitarist for the early Düsseldorf band Charley's Girls, loved that you could wear a leather jacket "and put your own symbols on it ... and next week, discard it all. [There was] flexibility in the message."[59] For others, originality was a breath of fresh air: as 16-year old "Carmen" told *Bravo* in 1977, "During the summer holidays I was in London. There, I had already seen punk bands in the Roxy. I found the fashion funny. At last, there's something original and not boring or unimaginative."[60] Indeed, style changed so quickly that it took substantial awareness to stay on top of recent developments though punk fanzines helpfully directed youths: *The Anschlag* assured its readers in 1979 that safety pins were out and parkas were now in.[61]

Creativity was intended as an antidote to the perceived loss of individuality that punks claimed accompanied mass society. Bielmeier has suggested that punk fashion was an explicit attack on packaged consumer culture and a means of showcasing one's inner originality through personal style.[62] But equally important, punk fashion was deliberately designed to provoke and indeed, the reactions that punks produced were a critical part of the equation for many youths: as Inga Humpe from the Neonbabies put it, "I really wanted to be unconditionally set off and difficult."[63] The point of dressing confrontationally was to shock, part and parcel of the punk's invasion of public space. As Dick Hebdige argued classically, the appearance of everyday items in outrageous positions—a safety pin in a cheek—produced cognitive dissonance because the brain associated these objects elsewhere.[64] The movement of household items and more intimate, often sexual commodities—toilet chains, handcuffs, dildos—into public space was a means of upsetting the public/private dichotomy. As Hein has suggested, youths used fashion to explore themselves, but also quite deliberately to experiment with the reactions their fashion produced: "with these clothes we experimented a lot with the effects that our fashion produced."[65] These reactions were important because, in many ways, punk pleasure came as much from responses as they did from dressing up. But provocation in the pursuit of reaction meant equally that instability was built into the punk aesthetic, which jeopardized any stable authentic core.

At the same time, how fashion was used by youths and the very content of punk fashion became a running commentary on mainstream society and the subculture itself. Punk outfits were intended to highlight the hypocrisy and contradictions of German society. Clothes meant to be tight were ill-fitting, while those meant to be loose were too small or too short. Such experiments created an anti-fashion. The use of common or base materials like PVC or faux leopard print fur suggested the cheapness of society, the disposable nature of consumerism, and the ugliness of contemporary society. Garish colors were used to brighten the dull and boring everyday while chains and leather pointed to sexual fantasy and violence that punks felt society kept repressed behind closed doors. At the same time, fashion was also a marker of subcultural devotion with considerable criticism heaped upon youths who were only "part-time punks": as one East Berlin punk criticized, "there are also many who even dress like that when their parents are not there, and when they come back, they immediately run to the basement, hide their clothes, and dress differently. That makes me sick. If they participate then they should also show it."[66] Thus while punk fashions offered the possibility of salvation, such remarks hint at the disciplining nature of the subculture in which marginality and commitment were necessary sacrifices for belonging in an authentic community.

Conclusion

Slowly, the paradox of trying to create a community based on extreme individuality caught up with punk. To hold the subculture together, invariably rules came to govern the pursuit of punk authenticity as the comment by the East Berliner above suggests. By the early 1980s, uniformity had come to dominate punk whether from the standpoint of fashion and music or behavior and mentality. Leather-clad punks listening to fast and hard music replaced the experiments of the late 1970s. Instead of being a platform for alternativeness, punk degenerated into a sullen body whereby provocation was undertaken not to challenge society to think differently about itself but as a nuisance. By the mid-1980s at the latest, punk had ceased to offer exciting opportunities for difference and instead settled into existence as an unimaginative thorn in the side of mainstream society. Certainly punks have continued to produce music and the subculture has continued to grow. But afterwards, punk too succumbed to the conformity and uniformity that only a few years prior to its adherents had condemned. Such a defeat speaks not necessarily to an intrinsic failure of punk specifically, but perhaps rather to the seeming impossibility of constructing a subculture (which demands collectivity) centered around absolute originality (which elevates individuality).

If punk as a subculture ultimately failed in its promise of offering individuals an alternative version of authenticity to pursue, for a brief period, the genre was nonetheless an exciting attempt at reworking contemporary understandings of genuineness. Disappointed with both mainstream and alternative constructions of society, punks in East and West Germany in the late 1970s and early 1980s tried to circumvent the boredom and convention, which they believed characterized their world, by positing difference and originality as a means to a more meaningful life. With clear mental conceptions and a multitude of practices, punks pursued activities that they believed would lead them to living, not merely existing, whether through provocative fashions or rejecting the politics of their elders. Punk intrusion into both the mainstream and the Alternative Left were disconcerting; but it was precisely this disquiet that was evidence to them that they were indeed living. Perhaps what was most disturbing about the subculture was that punk indicated that authenticity was in fact not a stable entity to be found, cultivated, or nurtured, rather it could be fundamentally unstable. While instability meant punk had difficulty reconciling itself coherently as a subculture, as an individual identity and as a means of pursuing individual genuineness, the genre's redefinition of authenticity remains as challenging today as it did back in the 1970s.

Jeff Hayton is Assistant Professor of Modern European History at Wichita State University. He received his Ph.D. from the University of Illinois at

Urbana-Champaign in 2013. He is currently completing a manuscript, *Culture from the Slums: Punk Rock, Authenticity and Alternative Culture in East and West Germany*, and he has published numerous articles on popular culture, rock 'n' roll, and German history. His next project investigates the cultural integration of Europe in the postwar era.

Notes

1. Schleim-Keim, "Scheiß Norm," *DDR von Unten* (West Berlin: Aggressive Rockproduktionen, 1983). All translations are mine, unless otherwise stated.
2. On Schleim-Keim, see Anne Hahn and Frank Willmann, *Satan, kannst du mir noch mal verzeihen: Otze Ehrlich, Schleimkeim und der ganze Rest* (Mainz, 2008).
3. *Deutschland Ruhmeshalle*, no. 3 (1980), 7.
4. BStU, MfS, HA XXII, no. 17742, Erinnerung an eine Jugendbewegung: P U N K, n.d., 3.
5. BStU, MfS, BV Erfurt, AOP 614/86, Bd. V/1, OV "Herbege," Bericht über durchgeführte Aussprache, 28 March 1983, 80.
6. "Sobald ich auf die Straße gehe, fange ich an, mich zu bekotzen," *Tageszeitung*, 31 August 1982, 9.
7. BStU, MfS, HA XXII, no. 17742, Erinnerung an eine Jugendbewegung: P U N K, n.d., 20.
8. On punk temporality, see Greil Marcus, *Lipstick Traces: A Secret History of the Twentieth Century*, 2nd ed. (Cambridge, MA, 2009); Neil Nehring, *Flowers in the Dustbin: Culture, Anarchy and Postwar England* (Ann Arbor, MI, 1993).
9. Michael Boehlke and Henryk Gericke, eds. *Too Much Future: Punk in der DDR* (Berlin, 2007), 13. For a discussion of specifically East German futures, see Seth Howes, "Pessimism and the Politics of the Future in East German Punk," *Journal of Popular Culture* 49, no. 1 (2016): 77–96.
10. On the development of socialist education, see Benita Blessing, *The Antifascist Classroom: Denazification in Soviet-occupied Germany, 1945–1949* (New York, 2006); John Rodden, *Repainting the Little Red Schoolhouse: A History of Eastern German Education, 1945–1995* (Oxford, 2002).
11. On youth politics in the GDR, see Alan McDougall, *Youth Politics in East Germany: The Free German Youth Movement 1946–1968* (Oxford, 2004).
12. "Auf die Sahne," *Der Spiegel*, no. 24 (14 June 1982), 59.
13. Günter Franzen and Boris Penth, *Last Exit. Punk: Leben im toten Herz der Städte* (Reinbek bei Hamburg, 1982), 197.
14. BStU, MfS, HA XXII, no. 17742, Erinnerung an eine Jugendbewegung: P U N K, n.d., 13.
15. BStU, MfS, HA XXII, no. 17742, Erinnerung an eine Jugendbewegung: P U N K, n.d., 14.
16. On postwar East German popular music, see Mark Fenemore, *Sex, Thugs and Rock 'n' Roll: Teenage Rebels in Cold-War East Germany* (New York, 2009); Bernd Lindner, *DDR: Rock & Pop* (Cologne, 2008); Olaf Leitner, *Rockszene DDR: Aspekte einer Massenkultur im Sozialismus* (Reinbek bei Hamburg, 1983).

17. On postwar West German popular music, see Christoph Wagner, *Der Klang der Revolte: Die magischen Jahre des westdeutschen Musik-Underground* (Mainz, 2013); Detlef Siegfried, *Time Is On My Side: Konsum und Politik in der westdeutschen Jugendkultur der 60er Jahre* (Göttingen, 2006); Hermann Haring, *Rock aus Deutschland West: Von den Rattles bis Nena: Zwei Jahrzehnte Heimatklang* (Reinbek bei Hamburg, 1984).
18. BStU, MfS, HA XXII, no. 17742, Erinnerung an eine Jugendbewegung: P U N K, n.d., 18.
19. For a succinct overview, see Nick Thomas, *Protest Movements in 1960s West Germany: A Social History of Dissent and Democracy* (Oxford, 2003).
20. See, for example, Hans Kundnani, *Utopia or Auschwitz: Germany's 1968 Generation and the Holocaust* (New York, 2009).
21. Jürgen Teipel, *Verschwende Deine Jugend: Ein Doku-Roman über den deutschen Punk und New Wave* (Frankfurt a. M., 2001), 73.
22. Ibid., 83.
23. Peter Hein, "Alles ganz einfach," in *Zurück zum Beton: Die Anfänge von Punk und New Wave in Deutschland 1977–'82*, ed. Ulrike Groos et al. (Cologne, 2002), 131–132.
24. Teipel, *Verschwende*, 60.
25. *Spiegel*, no. 24, 1982, 60
26. Teipel, *Verschwende*, 38–39.
27. Sven Marquardt, *Die Nacht ist Leben: Autobiographie*, with Judka Strittmatter (Berlin, 2014), 14–17.
28. See Teipel, *Verschwende*, 89.
29. Ibid. Peter Hein has claimed that punk originality lay with their acceptance and joy in reality. See Hein, "Alles ganz einfach," 133.
30. Diedrich Diederichsen, "Intensität—Negation—Klartext: Simultanes und Inkommensurables zwischen Theorie, Bildender Kunst und Musik im deutschen Punk," in *Zurück zum Beton: Die Anfänge von Punk und New Wave in Deutschland 1977–'82*, eds., Ulrike Groos et al. (Cologne, 2002), 142. In *Utopia Limited*, Marianne DeKoven argues that utopian thinking died between the 1960s and the 1990s, although she links its death to postmodernism. Both authors agree, however, that the 1960s were the last moment of utopian thinking. See Marianne DeKoven, *Utopia Limited: The Sixties and the Emergence of the Postmodern* (Durham, NC, 2004).
31. Teipel, *Verschwende*, 83.
32. Hein, "Alles ganz einfach," 132.
33. *Ffurs*, no. 0 (West Berlin, 1978), cited in Hollow Skai, *Punk: Versuch der künstlerischen Realisierung einer neuen Lebenshaltung* (Berlin, 2008), 61.
34. BStU, MfS, HA XXII, no. 17742, Erinnerung an eine Jugendbewegung: P U N K, n.d., 11.
35. Harald Heusner, "Jörg Löffler: ein Punk-pionier aus der DDR," *Trust 77* (Bremen: 1999), n.p. Punctuation as in original.
36. See Jeff Hayton, "Crosstown Traffic: Punk Rock, Space and the Porosity of the Berlin Wall in the 1980s," *Contemporary European History* 26, no. 2 (May 2017): 353–377.

37. See Jeff Hayton, "Culture from the Slums: Punk Rock, Authenticity, and Alternative Culture in East and West Germany," Ph.D. dissertation (Urbana-Champaign: University of Illinois at Urbana-Champaign, 2013), chapters 2–5.
38. Teipel, *Verschwende*, 35.
39. Teipel, *Verschwende*, 42.
40. On Einstürzende Neubauten, see Jennifer Shryane, *Blixa Bargeld and Einstürzende Neubauten: German Experimental Music: 'Evading do-re-mi'* (Surrey, 2011).
41. The history of German punk women remains to be written. But see Teipel, *Verschwende*, 72, 195–198, and 233–234.
42. Mark M. Westhusen, *Zonenpunkprovinz: Punk in Halle (Saale) in den 80er Jahren* (Halle, 2005), 15.
43. On DIY, see George McKay, *Senseless Acts of Beauty: Cultures of Resistance since the Sixties* (London, 1996),
44. On DIY in German punk, see Jeff Hayton, "'The Revolution is Over—and We Have Won!': Alfred Hilsberg, West German Punk and the Sixties," in *The Global Sixties in Sound and Vision: Media, Counterculture, Revolt*, ed. Timothy S. Brown and Andrew Lison (Palgrave, 2014), 135–150.
45. On cassette labels in the GDR, see Susanne Binas, "Die 'anderen Bands' und ihre Kassettenproduktionen: Zwischen organisiertem Kulturbetrieb und selbstorganisierten Kulturformen," in *Rockmusik und Politik: Analysen, Interviews und Dokumente*, ed. Peter Wicke and Lothar Müller (Berlin, 1996), 52–54.
46. Cited in Hollow Skai, *Alles nur geträumt: Fluch und Segen der Neuen Deutschen Welle* (Innsbruck, 2009), 191.
47. See Teipel, *Verschwende*, 22, 52; Franzen and Penth, *Last Exit*, 11; and *Der Aktuelle Mülleimer* no. 2 (1980): 24.
48. See Albrecht Koch, *Angriff auf's Schlaraffenland: 20 Jahre deutschsprachige Popmusik* (Frankfurt a.M., 1987), 168–169.
49. Teipel, *Verschwende*, 34.
50. For an introduction to punk's fashion interventions, see Andrew Bolton et al., *Punk: Chaos to Couture* (New York, 2013).
51. See Frank Cartledge, "Distress to Impress?: Local Punk Fashion and Commodity Exchange," in *Punk Rock: So What? The Cultural Legacy of Punk*, ed. Roger Sabin (London, 1999), 143–153.
52. See Teipel, *Verschwende*, 29, 32, 101–102, and 153.
53. See Kate Gerrard, "From London to the GDR: Symbols and Clothing in East German Punk," "Rhythms of Rebellion, Part I," special issue, *United Academics Journal of Social Sciences*, no. 11 (June 2012): 56–70.
54. Teipel, *Verschwende*, 32, 35, 51, and 212.
55. Teipel, *Verschwende*, 86.
56. Hein, "Alles ganz einfach," 132.
57. Teipel, *Verschwende*, 46.
58. Konstantin Hanke, "Ostpunk auf Schallplatte," in *Ox-Fanzine* no. 73 (August/September 2007): 120.
59. Teipel, *Verschwende*, 55.
60. "Punk-Pleite Made in Germany," *Bravo* no. 49 (24 November 1977): 67.
61. *The Anschlag* no. 1 (1979): 4.

62. Teipel, *Verschwende*, 37. See Alfred Hilsberg, "Die Revolution ist vorbei—wir haben gesiegt!" *Sounds* no. 2 (February 1978): 36.
63. Teipel, *Verschwende*, 70.
64. Dick Hebdige, *Subculture: The Meaning of Style*, revised ed. (New York, 1979).
65. Teipel, *Verschwende*, 37.
66. BStU, MfS, HA XXII, no. 17742, Erinnerung an eine Jugendbewegung: P U N K, n.d., 9.

Bibliography

Binas, Susanne. "Die 'anderen Bands' und ihre Kassettenproduktionen: Zwischen organisiertem Kulturbetrieb und selbstorganisierten Kulturformen." In *Rockmusik und Politik: Analysen, Interviews und Dokumente*, edited by Peter Wicke and Lothar Müller, 48–60. Berlin: Ch. Links Verlag, 1996.

Blessing, Benita. *The Antifascist Classroom: Denazification in Soviet-occupied Germany, 1945–1949*. New York: Palgrave Macmillan, 2006.

Boehlke, Michael, and Henryk Gericke, eds. *Too Much Future: Punk in der DDR*. Berlin: Verbrecher, 2007.

Bolton, Andrew, Richard Hell, John Lydon, and Jon Savage, eds. *Punk: Chaos to Couture*. New York: The Metropolitan Museum of Art, 2013.

Cartledge, Frank. "Distress to Impress?: Local Punk Fashion and Commodity Exchange." In *Punk Rock: So What? The Cultural Legacy of Punk*, edited by Roger Sabin. London: Routledge, 1999, 143–153.

DeKoven, Marianne. *Utopia Limited: The Sixties and the Emergence of the Postmodern*. Durham, NC: Duke University Press, 2004.

Diederichsen, Diedrich. "Intensität—Negation—Klartext: Simultanes und Inkommensurables zwischen Theorie, Bildender Kunst und Musik im deutschen Punk." In *Zurück zum Beton: Die Anfänge von Punk und New Wave in Deutschland 1977–'82*, edited by Ulrike Groos, Peter Gorschlüter, and Jürgen Teipel, 137–146. Cologne: Verlag der Buchhandlung Walther König, 2002.

Fenemore, Mark. *Sex, Thugs and Rock 'n' Roll: Teenage Rebels in Cold-War East Germany*. New York: Berghahn Books, 2009.

Franzen, Günter, and Boris Penth. *Last Exit. Punk: Leben im toten Herz der Städte*. Reinbek bei Hamburg: Rowohlt, 1982.

Gerrard, Kate. "From London to the GDR: Symbols and Clothing in East German Punk." In "Rhythms of Rebellion, Part I," special issue, *United Academics Journal of Social Sciences* no. 11 (June 2012): 56–70.

Hahn, Anne, and Frank Willmann, *Satan, kannst du mir noch mal verzeihen: Otze Ehrlich, Schleimkeim und der ganze Rest*. Mainz: Ventil Verlag, 2008.

Haring, Hermann. *Rock aus Deutschland West: Von den Rattles bis Nena: Zwei Jahrzehnte Heimatklang*. Reinbek bei Hamburg: Rowohlt, 1984.

Hayton, Jeff. "Crosstown Traffic: Punk Rock, Space and the Porosity of the Berlin Wall in the 1980s." *Contemporary European History* 26, no. 2 (May 2017): 353–377.

———. "'The Revolution is Over—And We Have Won!': Alfred Hilsberg, West German Punk and the Sixties." In *The Global Sixties in Sound and Vision: Media,*

Counterculture, Revolt, edited by Timothy S. Brown and Andrew Lison, 135–150. New York: Palgrave, 2014.

———. "Culture from the Slums: Punk Rock, Authenticity, and Alternative Culture in East and West Germany." Ph.D. dissertation. Urbana-Champaign: University of Illinois at Urbana-Champaign, 2013.

Hebdige, Dick. *Subculture: The Meaning of Style,* revised ed. New York: Routledge, 1979.

Hein, Peter. "Alles ganz einfach." In *Zurück zum Beton: Die Anfänge von Punk und New Wave in Deutschland 1977–'82,* edited by Ulrike Groos, Peter Gorschlüter, and Jürgen Teipel, 131–134. Cologne: Verlag der Buchhandlung Walther König, 2002.

Heylin, Clinton. *Babylon's Burning: From Punk to Grunge.* London: Viking, 2007.

Howes, Seth. "Pessimism and the Politics of the Future in East German Punk." *Journal of Popular Culture* 49, no. 1 (2016): 77–96.

Koch, Albrecht. *Angriff auf's Schlaraffenland: 20 Jahre deutschsprachige Popmusik.* Frankfurt a. M.: Ullstein, 1987.

Kundnani, Hans. *Utopia or Auschwitz: Germany's 1968 Generation and the Holocaust.* New York: Columbia University Press, 2009.

Leitner, Olaf. *Rockszene DDR: Aspekte einer Massenkultur im Sozialismus.* Reinbek bei Hamburg: Rowohlt, 1983.

Lindner, Bernd. *DDR: Rock & Pop.* Cologne: Komet, 2008.

Marcus, Greil. *Lipstick Traces: A Secret History of the Twentieth Century.* 2nd ed. Cambridge, MA: Belknap, 2009.

Marquardt, Sven. *Die Nacht ist Leben: Autobiographie.* With Judka Strittmatter. Berlin: Ullstein Extra, 2014.

McDougall, Alan. *Youth Politics in East Germany: The Free German Youth Movement 1946–1968.* Oxford: Clarendon Press, 2004.

McKay, George. *Senseless Acts of Beauty: Cultures of Resistance since the Sixties.* London: Verso, 1996.

McNeil, Legs and Gillian McCain. *Please Kill Me: The Uncensored Oral History of Punk,* reprint ed. New York: Grove Press, 2006.

Nehring, Neil. *Flowers in the Dustbin: Culture, Anarchy and Postwar England.* Ann Arbor: University of Michigan Press, 1993.

Reichardt, Sven. *Authentizität und Gemeinschaft: Linksalternatives Leven in den siebziger und frühen achtziger Jahren.* Berlin: Suhrkamp Verlag, 2014.

———. "Authentizität und Gemeinschaftsbindung: Politik und Lebensstil im linksalternativen Milieu vom Ende der 1960er bis zum Anfang der 1980er Jahre." *Forschungsjournal Neue Soziale Bewegungen* 3 (2008): 118–130.

Rodden, John. *Repainting the Little Red Schoolhouse: A History of Eastern German Education, 1945–1995.* Oxford: Oxford University Press, 2002.

Saupe, Achim. "Authenticity." *Docupedia-Zeitgeschichte.* 12 April 2016. Retrieved 16 June 2017 from http://docupedia.de/zg/saupe_authentizitaet_v3_en_2016.

Savage, Jon. *England's Dreaming: Anarchy, Sex Pistols, Punk Rock, and Beyond,* revised ed. New York: St. Martin's Griffin, 2002.

Shryane, Jennifer. *Blixa Bargeld and Einstürzende Neubauten: German Experimental Music: 'Evading do-re-mi.'* Surrey, UK: Ashgate, 2011.

Siegfried, Detlef. "Superkultur: Authentizität und politische Moral in linken Subkulturen der frühen siebziger Jahre." In *Bürgersinn mit Weltgefühl: Politische Moral und soidarischer Protest in den sechziger und siebziger Jahren*, edited by Habbo Knoch, 251–270. Göttingen: Wallstein, 2007.

———. *Time Is On My Side: Konsum und Politik in der westdeutschen Jugendkultur der 60er Jahre*. Göttingen: Wallstein, 2006.

———. "White Negroes: The Fascination of the Authentic in the West German Counterculture of the 1960s." In *Changing the World, Changing Oneself: Political Protest and Collective Identities in West Germany and the U.S. in the 1960s and 1970s*, edited by Belinda Davis, Wilfried Mausbach, Martin Klimke, and Carla MacDougall, 191–215. New York: Berghahn Books, 2010.

Skai, Hollow. *Alles nur geträumt: Fluch und Segen der Neuen Deutschen Welle*. Innsbruck: Hannibal, 2009.

———. *Punk: Versuch der künstlerischen Realisierung einer neuen Lebenshaltung*. Berlin: Archiv der Jugendkulturen, 2008.

Teipel, Jürgen. *Verschwende Deine Jugend: Ein Doku-Roman über den deutschen Punk und New Wave*. Frankfurt a. M.: Suhrkamp Verlag, 2001.

Thomas, Nick. *Protest Movements in 1960s West Germany: A Social History of Dissent and Democracy*. Oxford: Berg, 2003.

Wagner, Christoph. *Der Klang der Revolte: Die magischen Jahre des westdeutschen Musik-Underground*. Mainz: Schott, 2013.

Westhusen, Mark M. *Zonenpunkprovinz: Punk in Halle (Saale) in den 80er Jahren*. Halle: Zeit-Geschichte(n) e. V., 2005.

Chapter 11

Humanitarianism on Stage
Live Aid and the Origins of Humanitarian Pop Music

Benjamin Möckel

On 13 July 1985, three major crowds gathered to attend what the organizers had repeatedly heralded in advance as "the greatest show on earth." In London, seventy-two thousand people flocked to Wembley Stadium to see artists such as David Bowie, Dire Straits, and Queen perform live. At the same time, a hundred thousand people gathered at the John F. Kennedy Stadium in Philadelphia to see Bob Dylan, Paul McCartney, Madonna, and other US and international artists. And in front of TV screens all over the world, an estimated crowd of 1.5 billion people watched both shows through an all-day live broadcast. Irish pop singer Bob Geldof was the main organizer of Live Aid, and the concerts were the climax of his fundraising endeavors in aid of those affected by a major famine crisis in Ethiopia. Contemporary critics were not sure what was more symptomatic about the event: the fact that pop music was able to generate such an immense response to a humanitarian plea (Live Aid resulted in an estimated £150 million in donations), or the fact that a humanitarian catastrophe and the charitable response to it could so seamlessly be transformed into a modern consumer and lifestyle event.

A chapter on Live Aid might appear slightly out of place in a volume on protest cultures of the 1970s and 1980s. When thinking about political and cultural protests and the "authentic subjectivities" connected to them, we are inclined to focus on oppositional groups, generational conflicts, and deviant subcultures that put into question the political dogmas of their time—and more often than not, it is protest movements from the Left that have caught the attention of contemporary historians.[1] Similarly, attempts to construct an "authentic subjectivity" have largely been understood through protest movements that articulated their dissent through idiosyncratic practices, aesthetics, and lifestyles that did not conform to mainstream culture.

All this is certainly not what Live Aid was about. The concert was far away from constituting a countercultural event. It was openly directed toward a mainstream audience; it depended on close cooperation with mainstream media outlets; and, in order to secure this cooperation, the organizers were very conscious to refrain from any explicit political agenda. Even more importantly, the audience was not expected to participate in any political or countercultural activities. To support the event, it was only necessary to attend the concert or watch it on television, to buy a record or some of the other specially produced merchandise, and to give some money to the humanitarian cause that the event was supporting. At first glance, one might be tempted to point to the concept of "culture industry" as a reasonable starting point for analyzing the event, rather than to look for "authentic subjectivities" that might have played out in this context.[2]

Nonetheless, Live Aid and the three other events discussed in this chapter—the production of the *Sun City* album by the collaborative project Artists United Against Apartheid in 1985, the Human Rights Now! tour organized by Amnesty International in 1988, and the Nelson Mandela 70th Birthday Tribute Concert held at Wembley Stadium in the same year—raise interesting questions concerning the role of protests in 1980s political culture. Since at least the 1960s, protest movements and subcultures had become inseparably intertwined with consumer society, the entertainment industry, and pop culture.[3] Obviously, this had consequences for the ways in which alternative lifestyles and subjectivities could emerge and for the way these lifestyles were continually absorbed by mainstream consumer cultures. We should not, therefore, too readily accept a dichotomy between consumerist lifestyles on the one hand and authentic subjectivities on the other. Instead, it seems more interesting to ask how political protests were framed in the context of mass consumer societies and how "authenticity" was produced in highly mediatized events like Live Aid and other pop concerts. Hence, my aim in this chapter is not to ask for the "authenticity" of the pop albums and concerts themselves, but for the strategies that organizers like Bob Geldof and institutions like Amnesty International employed to create events that were perceived to be and experienced as "authentic" by their audiences.

This chapter thus presents a different kind of inquiry into authentic subjectivity. Instead of asking how and why pop music lost its authenticity as a means of political protest during the 1980s, the chapter examines why the question of "authenticity" became so important in precisely this period. As many scholars have argued, authenticity is not a given attribute of objects or persons, but a quest and a demand formulated toward people, objects, activities, and—not least—toward oneself. Talking about authenticity therefore primarily means to analyze the different ways in which individuals and institutions try to fabricate and verify authenticity.[4] This argument is particularly relevant for the time period of the 1980s. As Sven Reichardt has argued, "being authentic" became one of the key demands that members of the so-called alternative milieu were confronted with. In this context, "being authentic" attained a performative dimension: it no longer referred to objects or products but instead to the idea of "being true to oneself."[5] Looking at the issue from a different perspective, scholars of consumption have argued that the quest for authenticity has become particularly important in the context of modern consumer societies. In a rather apodictic manner, James Gilmore and Joseph Pine, for example, have claimed that authenticity became a key term of modern consumerism precisely because false and inauthentic objects have come to dominate the social sphere of modern capitalism; or in their own words, because of the "toxic levels of inauthenticity we're forced to breathe" in contemporary society.[6] Pop music is, of course, a good example for this ambivalence: while the music industry has to continually adapt to consumer demands and expectations, it is at the same time paramount to emphasize the authentic quality of the music and the authentic lifestyles of the musicians themselves. Richard Peterson has shown, for example, how the fabrication of "authentic" music and artistic personalities in modern country music is an indispensable part of the very process of making the music saleable on the consumer market, an argument that can easily be applied to other music genres like folk, punk, or rap music.[7]

In this argumentative framework, the question is not whether a certain event was an authentic manifestation of protest, subculture, or humanitarian empathy. Instead, one needs to examine how the organizers of events such as Live Aid tried to create an "authentic" experience.[8] In this context, Live Aid is indeed a significant example for the issues involved in searching for authenticity because it highlights the blurring distinctions between "authentic" manifestations of political protest and its commodification and eventization through charity concerts, charity singles, and celebrity activism. Thus, by explicitly referring to the context of mass consumerism as the general framework for all protest movements of the 1970s and 1980s, in this chapter I highlight the way political and humanitarian pop music became caught between countercultural attitudes and the perils of being commodified and absorbed into conformist consumer practices.

Live Aid: The Invention of a Humanitarian Pop Concert

The history of Live Aid is closely connected to the humanitarian endeavors that Bob Geldof began in the summer of 1984 in response to a famine crisis in Ethiopia.⁹ The first project was the recording of a song, "Do They Know It's Christmas," for which Geldof was able to secure an all-star line-up of British musicians.¹⁰ It was released as a single on 28 November 1984 and became a number-one hit in all major European countries. In the following months, several national offshoots were recorded, most notably the song "We Are the World" by a group of US artists, which even surpassed the sales figures of the original single. But the climax of media attention was only reached in the summer of 1985, when the project was transformed into a live spectacle, with concerts held simultaneously at John F. Kennedy Stadium in Philadelphia and Wembley Stadium in London. Aside from the sold-out concert venues, the live broadcasting of the event allowed it to reach an estimated audience of 1.5 billion viewers globally.

For Lilie Chouliaraki, Live Aid is one of the prime examples of what she terms "ceremonial humanitarianism."¹¹ As she highlights, Live Aid was characterized by a highly mediatized "theatricality" that put the question of "authenticity" at its center and made it necessary to look for "strategies of authentication." According to Chouliaraki, the mediatization of human suffering and charitable actions makes it necessary for all humanitarian protagonists to explicitly stage "authentic" feelings like empathy or solidarity. The question of "authentic subjectivities" is therefore highly relevant for the analysis of Live Aid. How Geldof himself described his motivation for organizing these events is noteworthy in this regard. In his autobiography, published in 1986, he described in close detail how the famine in Ethiopia had captured his attention and how this had been the decisive moment that transformed the pop star's faltering career and led to him becoming a global humanitarian icon. The key moment, he claimed, was seeing a BBC news report in the summer of 1984.¹² The piece he referred to was a report by Mohamed Amin and Michael Buerk from a refugee camp in Korem in the Northern part of Ethiopia.¹³ It is no coincidence that it was this particular report that triggered Geldof's attention: the report was a hugely influential piece of humanitarian news coverage that, within a day, put the Ethiopian famine on the global political agenda and in the news bulletins of the mainstream media.¹⁴ It was shown by more than four hundred TV stations around the globe and found an audience of approximately 470 million people.¹⁵ According to Geldof's account, he had just come home from disappointing office work for his band when he switched on the TV and, by coincidence, saw the report by Amin and Buerk:

> From the first seconds it was clear that this was a horror on a monumental scale. The pictures were of people who were so shrunken by starvation that they looked like beings from another planet. Their arms

and legs were as thin as sticks, their bodies spindly. Swollen veins and huge, blankly staring eyes protruded from their shriveled heads. The camera wandered amidst them like a mesmerized observer, occasionally dwelling on one person so that he looked directly at me, sitting in my comfortable living room surrounded by the fripperies of modern living which we were pleased to regard as necessities. Their eyes looked into mine. ... All around was the murmur of death, like a hoarse whisper, or the buzzing of flies.[16]

In his memoirs, Geldof used this account to emphasize the radical conversion he experienced that evening. Even though there is no reason to doubt his sincere shock and dismay, which he would later repeatedly refer to as the main motivation for his humanitarian commitment, it is nonetheless significant to ask why exactly he was framing his experience in this way. On the one hand, the paragraph is part of the broader narrative of the book, which brings together his childhood, his musical career, and his humanitarian activities to produce a coherent life-story that gives enough substance to an autobiography of a 35-year-old man. But more importantly, the passage was an attempt to claim an "authentic" experience: it was the immediate shock (albeit triggered by the indirect account of a TV report) that Geldof claimed as the initial motivation for his humanitarian activity. And this authentic experience was a decisively apolitical one. Geldof has often been criticized for not taking into account the political circumstances of the famine in Ethiopia. While this is certainly true, this apolitical interpretation of the situation was key for the kind of "authentic" experience he claimed for himself—namely a personal and emotionalized humanitarian reaction toward a suffering that had to be stopped without asking for any political reasons or circumstances.[17]

Taking this apolitical setting of the event as a starting point, it is possible to analyze how Live Aid tried to merge commercial pop music with charitable and humanitarian efforts. In doing so, one can examine how the organizers of Live Aid reflected on the humanitarian catastrophe they were dealing with and what kind of pictures and narratives they used to describe the situation in Ethiopia.

The connection between pop music and global charity—soon afterward described with the term "charity rock"—became of predominant importance for 1980s pop culture. Live Aid has often figured as the key reference for this development, both affirmatively as an event that was able to generate unprecedented media attention for a global humanitarian crisis, but also negatively as an event that oversimplified and depoliticized its message and thereby reaffirmed existing stereotypes about Africa, its people, and its political development.

The concept of using pop music as a means for humanitarian relief was not new in 1984/85. In 1971, George Harrison and Ravi Shankar had organized the Concert for Bangladesh at Madison Square Garden, which can be interpreted as the first charity concert that reached a global audience through a live performance and the subsequent release of an album. Oxfam is another example of a charity organization that cooperated with actors, musicians, and other celebrities. Amnesty International began to use music and comedy events in the 1970s and even UNICEF began to organize rock/pop music events around this time.

Live Aid's main innovation must rather be seen in its explicitly consumerist approach and its media dimension.[18] Most importantly, it was the adoption of the concept of the "mega-event" that was unique to Live Aid as a charity event.[19] In this context, Live Aid was not so much a successor to Woodstock or the Concert for Bangladesh, but to events such as the Football World Cup and, in particular, the Los Angeles Olympics that had taken place only one year before.[20] In keeping with these events, Live Aid primarily followed a TV-choreography with which the live event had to comply.[21] Equally important was the consumerist dimension of the event. Geldof himself stated quite bluntly at multiple occasions that he was not interested in the musical quality of the event as long as it generated as much money as possible. Evidently, this approach embodied quite perfectly the essence of standard capitalist thinking about consumer products; however, here it could be stated much more openly because the goal of making profit had morphed into a humanitarian endeavor. One obvious example of the commodification of the event was the immense amount of merchandise that appeared in the context of the festival; apart from the concert itself, the event created revenues through the issuing of LPs and videotapes, books, t-shirts and other products as well as the TV rights. This kind of all-embracing marketing chain was extremely influential for similar events in the future.

The decision to organize Live Aid as a charitable consumer event required several decisions concerning its musical and political content. Because the concerts had to appeal to a mass audience, artists and performances were explicitly meant to be nonsubversive and noncontroversial—in other words, apolitical. It also followed that even though Live Aid was meant to be a global event, its performers were almost exclusively top-40 artists from Western Europe and the United States, while other musical styles—particularly African music or Caribbean music styles like reggae or ska—did not feature in the program. As a consequence, there was no real correlation between the cause of the event and its musical content.

More importantly, this also holds true for the educational aspect of the concert. On the one hand, the organizers claimed that they did not only want to raise money, but also raise awareness about the Ethiopian famine and similar humanitarian crises. On the other hand, just as African musicians were not considered to have sufficient appeal to a global audience, neither, ultimately, was the topic of the Ethiopian famine itself. The whole event was defined by a tension that was almost impossible to dissolve: while the intention of the organizers was to provide help for a "Third-World" country in a humanitarian crisis, the event itself remained a symbol of Western consumerism and hedonism.

The accompanying "star-book" to the concerts, which was published only six weeks after the event, demonstrates this tension. Although the author did refer to the Ethiopian famine as the sole purpose of the event, he carefully avoided all references to the political situation in Africa, global problems of hunger and poverty, or any other topics of global politics. Throughout the book, Ethiopia was clearly not the center of attention. The only exception was a nine-page chapter under the heading "They Are the Children," which was illustrated with pictures of starving children and a photo from an Ethiopian refugee camp. The text acknowledged:

> Live Aid may have been a triumph. But it was a triumph born out of a tragedy; the tragedy of famine, the tragedy of starvation. This was what the concert was all about: not about the pulsing, energetic music of rock and roll played by the world's greatest musicians, not about the wonders of technology that spanned the globe and united the continents—but about hunger. About hunger, about drought, about famine. About despair.[22]

In all other chapters of the book, however, the reader gets the opposite impression. Contrary to the author's claim in the paragraph above, most of the book was actually devoted to the European and US rock stars that had participated in the event and to the "wonders of technology" that had been necessary to organize it. The implicit dichotomy of the cited paragraph is nevertheless telling. While the "Western" world was described as active and dynamic, the situation in Ethiopia was pictured as exclusively defined by hunger, passivity, and despair. This was particularly problematic because there was no attempt to differentiate between the specific situation in Ethiopia in 1984 and the much more diverse developments in other African countries or even the "Third World" in general. This highly problematic confrontation between "the West and the rest" was further emphasized by the two pictures that were juxtaposed on the inner side of the book jacket, the first showing a crowd of people at an Ethiopian refugee camp, while the second one directly below picturing the cheering crowd at the Live Aid concert.

Live Aid is therefore an intriguing case study for the concept of the "politics of authentic subjectivity." Geldof was very successful in framing the event as an alternative to traditional politics; he and the other organizers claimed time and again that the concerts were apolitical. Instead of political protest, they mobilized through emotional categories like compassion, solidarity, and empathy. While politics was interpreted as a realm of contest and controversy, these emotional categories seemed to be universally shared and in this way more suitable for a global media event.[23] In this way, Live Aid owed much of its success to its ability to create an imagined community of moral and emotional concern that everybody could join simply by watching TV and donating a certain amount of money.

Live Aid's Ambivalent Legacy: Sun City (1985), Human Rights Now! (1988), and the Concert for Nelson Mandela (1988)

In the late 1980s, Live Aid inspired a number of other projects that made use of pop music as a means to raise awareness for political or humanitarian causes. Apart from the numerous offshoots that explicitly built on the original Band Aid-concept (such as Farm Aid, Self Aid, or Sport Aid), there were two main features of the Band Aid/Live Aid-concept that profoundly influenced future projects in the realm of humanitarian pop music. First, the "charity single," which evolved as a genre of its own in the aftermath of "Do They Know It's Christmas" and "We Are the World"; and second, the concept of pop concerts as highly mediatized "mega-events" that tried to raise money and awareness for social and political causes.[24]

The tension between the self-proclaimed humanitarian intentions and the intrinsically hedonistic character of modern pop music remained a main feature of these subsequent events, as did the tension between "raising money" and "raising awareness" as two separate goals that were not always easy to reconcile. While Live Aid clearly focused principally on generating charitable donations, the three case studies under scrutiny in this section shared a much more ambiguous attitude to such an approach. Looking at them in comparison will therefore further illuminate the tensions between the political, awareness-raising dimensions, and the charitable, fundraising dimensions of such events. Nevertheless, Live Aid served as an important point of reference in all three cases: both as a role model for how to attract large audiences and to generate global media attention, but also as a negative example of a politically inconsiderate or even naïve event.

The song "Sun City" was written by Steven Van Zandt and recorded by the collaborative project Artists United against Apartheid.[25] The title referred to the Las Vegas-style luxury resort 160 km north of Johannesburg that had opened its doors in 1979.[26] The place became notorious because of its location in Bophuthatswana, one of the infamous "homelands" that were nominally declared independent by the South African state (though never recognized by any other state). Because of this official status, Sun City was partly able to avoid the cultural boycott sanctioned by the United Nations against the South African state. Several Western pop musicians used this loophole to play concerts at Sun City, including Frank Sinatra, The Beach Boys, Elton John, and Queen. The song addressed this issue and with its main chorus line ("I ain't gonna play Sun City") called on all artists to comply with the cultural boycott.[27]

The song was released in October 1985, only three months after Live Aid. It is therefore no surprise that the different approaches of both projects have often been compared and contrasted with each other. For some interpreters, Van Zandt attained an almost saintly status as a counterexample to Live Aid and a role model for how to attach political meaning to contemporary pop music while avoiding the pitfalls of traditional charity and philanthropy.[28] One should of course be careful with such normative evaluations, especially because both projects pursued very different targets from the outset. While Live Aid was a charity project that along the way tried to raise awareness for a humanitarian crisis, Sun City was a decidedly political song that along the way raised money by giving its royalties to the New York-based charity The Africa Fund.[29] It is nevertheless useful to highlight both the differences and the similarities between both approaches.

The first difference is obvious: while the organizers of Live Aid tried their best to depoliticize the event, Sun City was an explicitly political record. These opposite approaches had several consequences. For Live Aid it meant, for example, that the lyrics of the charity songs left out all political statements and were restricted to supposedly "universal truths" that no one could reasonably contest ("feed the world," "the world must come together as one"). Consequently, Live Aid presented the Ethiopian famine solely as a natural catastrophe without reflecting upon the much more complicated political and military context. Finally, the event also refrained from drawing any connections to Western politics or calling for a change of one's individual lifestyle.

Sun City followed a completely different script. The lyrics were explicit in condemning the South African regime and referred to specific topics like the forced relocation policies and the denial of voting-rights for black people. The song denounced Western governments for not being able to agree on a full economic and political boycott of South Africa. It even referred explicitly to Ronald Reagan and his politics of "constructive engagement" and "quiet diplomacy." Finally, by calling on all artists to boycott South Africa and Sun City, the record pointed to an individual act of support for the political fight against apartheid. The strategies for generating political protest therefore differed substantially from the ones used at Live Aid. And while the book that accompanied the record also used a personalizing rhetoric and strong visualizations in order to generate empathy and a personal emotional reaction, the intended reaction was not a purely humanitarian one. The goal was to encourage reflection on the political situation in South Africa, on the connections to political decisions in the United States and Europe, and especially on the personal decisions one could make to hinder the South African regime. People were not primarily asked to donate money, but rather to gather information on South African politics, to support protest or boycott movements, and to consider joining an anti-Apartheid group.

The second major difference lay in the musical content of the song. Here, too, Sun City was much more ambitious than Live Aid. While Live Aid had been criticized for not having included any African musicians or avant-garde musical styles, Sun City was much more sensitive about trying to mirror the political statement of the project in the musical content of the song. African-American musicians played an important role in the project and artists from different ethnic backgrounds shared lines of the song as if to practically thwart South African policies of segregation. More importantly, the song was a mixture of very different musical styles. It featured jazz artists such as Herbie Hancock and Miles Davis and was also influenced by rap and hip hop, which had not yet become part of mainstream musical culture. Finally, the music videos also reflected these different approaches. While "Do They Know It's Christmas" and "We Are the World" featured the cliché footage of celebrities singing the song in the studio, the video for Sun City was mainly shot on the streets of New York and juxtaposed with footage of political protest and police violence in South Africa.

Clearly, the differences between Live Aid and Sun City are significant; however, one should not be too fast to interpret Live Aid and Sun City along a dichotomy of authenticity and inauthenticity. The video that accompanied the Band Aid single showed the participating pop stars in their everyday dresses, uncombed hair and ostensibly without make-up. This was, of course, a carefully staged expression of authenticity. In the same spirit, the images of multi-ethnic urbanism created in the New York City street scenes of the Sun City video were not "more authentic" in this manner, but rather constituted a different strategy of authentication. The main difference lies in the alternative cultural sensitivities shown in both approaches—one decidedly Western-centered, the other trying to build iconographic bridges between the Western artists and the people struggling for freedom in South Africa—and the cultural heterogeneities taken or not taken into account. In this matter, Sun City was much more sensitive and followed a much more radical approach.

But this came at a price. It is no coincidence that the song did not even come close to repeating the success of the Band Aid charity singles. Because of its rather demanding musical style it was not able to reach a comparable audience. More importantly, many US radio stations refused to play the song because they deemed it too political to be played on a public radio station.[30] This, of course, further diminished public attention and commercial success. Sun City can therefore be interpreted as a counterexample to Live Aid, but it can also be seen as a reinforcement of the validity of Bob Geldof's approach. In order to create a global mega-event, it seemed necessary to radically depoliticize and universalize the topic that was being dealt with. It was exactly this idea that re-occurred in the preparation of two other events that clearly stood in the tradition of Live Aid.

In 1988, two other pop music events with a human rights inspired agenda took place and reached a global audience. In June, the British Anti-Apartheid Movement (AAM) organized a concert in London to celebrate Nelson Mandela's seventieth birthday and to call for his liberation from prison. In September, the US wing of Amnesty International launched its Human Rights Now! world tour to mark the fortieth anniversary of the Universal Declaration of Human Rights. Both cases call for a much more detailed examination than can be provided here.[31] For this analysis, I concentrate on how the organizers of these events tried to profit from the example of Live Aid, asking which lessons they drew from the successes and shortcomings of the Live Aid concerts.

In the case of the Concert for Nelson Mandela, the most obvious parallel to Live Aid was the choice of venue: by holding the event at Wembley Stadium, the organizers stood inevitably in the tradition of Bob Geldof's charity concert three years earlier. There were also several other ways in which the concert learned from its precursor, for example in organizational matters, in the way the media were integrated, and in its iconography and choice of the musical line-up. Even more importantly, the success of Live Aid made it much easier for the organizers to secure initial media attention, to persuade musicians to participate, and to sell the event to domestic and international TV stations.

As discussed above, the commercial success of Live Aid was intricately linked to a process of depoliticization. The Concert for Nelson Mandela is another example for this interrelation. The concert was organized by Tony

Hollingsworth, who had the difficult task of navigating between the AAM activists, who insisted on a decidedly political approach, and the expectations of TV stations, sponsors, and other institutions that were needed to support and finance the concert. It was Hollingsworth who insisted on focusing on a solely humanitarian message about Nelson Mandela and his sixteen years of imprisonment. By personalizing the message, Hollingsworth argued, it would be much easier to create an emotional relationship to the topic, as well as helping to secure the support of the BBC and other international TV stations.[32]

The internal debates of the AAM show that this approach was met with a distinctly mixed response.[33] Looking back at the event at the end of the year, the AAM was on the one hand enthused by the immense support they had gained through the concert:

> The past year in the Anti-Apartheid Movement has been dominated by one event, the 70th birthday of Nelson Mandela, which took place on 18 July. It is literally true that virtually the whole world knew of this event as a result of the great pop concert at Wembley in June which was the preparation for it. A billion people saw on their television screens some of the greatest stars in the world who gave their services free for this event. In spite of considerable pressure from our opponents, the BBC transmitted the whole event live for over 10 hours.[34]

On the other hand, the AAM emphasized that the concert was only one event in a larger campaign that aimed not only at the release of Mandela, but of all political prisoners and ultimately at the dismantling of the Apartheid system:

> The most important task, however, now facing the campaign is to ensure that should Mandela's release be secured, it in fact achieves the wider objective of the release of all political prisoners and the unbanning of his organization, the ANC and other banned organizations, so that Mandela's freedom becomes the key to the freedom of all the people of South Africa.[35]

In this way, the AAM navigated quite successfully between its own political agenda and the intrinsic requirements of modern pop culture and entertainment industry. For Robin Denselow, the concert was therefore "a more political version of Live Aid," aimed at "raising consciousness" and not at "just raising money."[36] At first sight this argument seems convincing. But under closer scrutiny one might come to ask whether the degree of politicization was really the key difference between the two events. A more detailed analysis shows that the tension between politicization and mass media appeal produced very similar dynamics. The main factor that set the Concert for Nelson Mandela apart from Live Aid was the fact that the AAM had a tradition of three decades of political protest against the Apartheid regime and was thus able to generate a political context in which the concert could be framed.

This kind of political contextualization was also important for the Human Rights Now! concert tour. The tour was organized by the US strand of Amnesty International, which, like the Anti-Apartheid Movement, had a long institutional history dating back to the mid-1960s.[37] After a first concert tour through the United States in 1986, this second tour—organized in celebration of the fortieth anniversary of the Universal Declaration of Human Rights – adopted a global perspective. Bringing together Bruce Springsteen, Peter Gabriel, Sting, Tracy Chapman, Youssou N'Dour, and additional local artists, the tour visited nineteen cities in Europe, Asia, Africa, and North and South America.

Like Live Aid, Human Rights Now! targeted a mass audience, but its approach differed significantly from its predecessor. While Live Aid was held in two Western cities, the Human Rights Now! tour covered Eastern Europe and the Global South, and was even able to play close to the borders of both Chile and South Africa, two of the most infamous human rights violators at the time. Second, its lineup was not exclusively shaped by the public appeal and commercial success of the artists. All participants were, at the time, in some way considered politically and socially conscious artists. Peter Gabriel and Sting were particularly natural choices, as they had both written songs on topics directly related to Amnesty International's key areas of activity.[38] In addition to the musical performances, the tour also featured a supporting program of press conferences and other activities that aimed to raise awareness of human rights issues. For this reason, the touring group also contained human rights activists from the United States, Cambodia, South Africa, and Chile.[39] These activists were the main protagonists of the press conferences, but the musicians were also expected to participate at these events and talk about their motivation to engage in human rights activism. At the concerts, brochures of the Universal Declaration of Human Rights were handed out to every concert-goer and the stage-talk of the musicians also regularly referred to human rights issues.

With the help of these strategies, the organizers tried to combine the goals of raising money and raising awareness that Live Aid had largely separated. Different from Geldof and his co-organizers, they were sensitive about attaching political meaning to the concerts and not letting them appear as mere fundraising events. At the same time, Human Rights Now! owed a lot to Live Aid: it copied the all-star-mechanism that Live Aid had applied so successfully and used similar marketing techniques. When funds were running low, Amnesty even accepted a multi-million-dollar sponsorship deal from Reebok, the athletic shoe manufacturer.[40] It might therefore not come as a surprise that many Amnesty members—particularly from the European sections—remained quite skeptical about the whole idea of the concert tour.[41]

As these three case studies have shown, Live Aid was an important—albeit ambivalent—point of reference. On the one hand, activists hoped to repeat the immense success of Live Aid and to generate comparable media attention. On the other hand, the completely apolitical character of Live Aid was often seen very critically, and activists tried to link their concerts in some way to a political message. Nevertheless, rather than drawing a clear line between Live Aid and its successors, the section has shown that the tension between the political agendas of the campaigns and the expectations of mass media, sponsors and consumers were structurally very similar in all cases. The fierce rejection of Live Aid by many contemporary critics in the 1980s can therefore only be explained by the symbolic meaning the event acquired as a symbol for a presumed decline of pop music as a means of political protest.

Protest, Consumption, and Authenticity: Contemporary Criticism of Live Aid

One of the most perplexing aspects of Live Aid was how fiercely the event was criticized by journalists, pop critics, and other protagonists during the 1980s. The numerous relaunches of the project in following years triggered similar criticisms.[42] There were, of course, plenty of reasons to disapprove of the event, for example the monolithic picture of Africa as a "dark continent" that was present in the whole event, the absence of African or other non-Western artists, or Bob Geldof's uncompromising and often highly narcissistic behavior (and this is before one even begins to think about the musical and aesthetic qualities of the event). Nevertheless, the vigor of contemporary criticism is from today's perspective surprising, and shows that for many interpreters Live Aid was not only an entertainment event with doubtful musical quality, but posed a much deeper challenge to the idea of pop music as a form of political protest and countercultural habitus. In this reading, Live Aid appeared as a symbolic event that was emblematic for the development of pop music in the 1980s. While the 1960s were seen as a decade in which pop music had become a means of articulating political and cultural dissent, the 1980s now appeared as the endpoint of a process of commodification in which pop music had lost its countercultural significance.

Rather ironically, this interpretation in a sense paralleled the way the organizers of Live Aid themselves tried to stage the event as the defining moment of 1980s pop culture. Live Aid was a phenomenon of self-historicizing *in actu*, in which participants were continually reminded that they were part of a historical event. One key example for this kind of self-historicizing was the appearance of folk icon Joan Baez at the festival. Like the critics of the event, Baez referred to the 1960s in order to put Live Aid in a historical perspective. When she made her entrance onto stage in Philadelphia on 13 July 1985, she welcomed the audience with an exclamation that was repeatedly cited by journalists in the following days. After having been introduced to the audience by Jack Nicholson—another icon of the 1960s—she exclaimed: "Good Morning, Children of the 80s.… This is your Woodstock and it's long overdue."[43] The audience responded with cheers and applause and Baez sang two songs: "Amazing Grace" and "We Are the World," the charity single by USA for Africa released earlier in the same year.

Woodstock was a predictable association. At the same time, it was not clear what this comparison really meant. Baez tried to put Live Aid in the tradition of a renewed social and political commitment of pop music and pop musicians. For her, the festival showed that the members of the "young generation" were still able to commit themselves to a common cause at a time in which individualism, hedonism, and greed appeared to dominate public discourse. For many critics, a different interpretation seemed much more compelling. For them, Live Aid was not the antithesis to the individualistic mentality of its time, but just another symbol for the depoliticized culture of the 1980s. They had the uncomfortable feeling that Joan Baez was indeed right and that Live Aid showed what had happened to the political dimension of pop music in the preceding fifteen years. In this interpretation, the comparison between Woodstock and Live Aid seemed to reflect quite adequately the perceived dichotomy of pop music and politics and its reconfigurations in the 1980s.

These interpretations followed a narrative of steady decline in which pop music had deteriorated from "authentic protest" into "commodified dissent."[44] While this dichotomy between the political and the commercial dimension of pop music was immensely influential for contemporary critics, analytically, it is not particularly convincing. On the one hand, it is obvious that pop music had already become a mass consumer market in the 1950s and 1960s. More importantly, the rebellious attitudes of pop musicians and the commercialization of their music were by no means antagonistic, but inseparably intertwined. Thomas Frank's argument concerning the alliance of counterculture and consumer culture in the 1960s is therefore particularly important in the case of modern pop music: instead of interpreting the 1980s as a time in which 1960s counterculture became commodified as a consumer product, it might be much more useful to look for similarities and continuities.[45] Pop music could then be characterized by an entanglement between changing styles of rebellion and their commodification as mass consumer products. Of course it remains possible to question the "authenticity" of such gestures of subversion; but this distinction seems only of minor relevance for the analysis of pop music as a consumer product.[46] For the case studies considered here, this means that it is not fruitful to differentiate between genuinely "authentic" and "inauthentic" forms of political protests or humanitarian activities. Instead we should concentrate on analyzing the different strategies with which the organizers of these events tried to construct subjectively authentic experiences within a framework of a consumer and media society. In this context, all four case studies faced closely related challenges. While Bob Geldof emphasized the sincerity of his humanitarian commitment by referring to his personal shock from the Amin/Buerk report from the refugee camp in Ethiopia, organizations such as Amnesty International and the Anti-Apartheid Movement had to make clear that they were not sacrificing their own political agenda when they cooperated with TV stations and sponsors in order to organize their concerts.

Conclusion

In conclusion, two broader contexts seem significant for the cases analyzed in this chapter. First, from the perspective of pop music and politics, all four examples point to a reinterpretation of pop music as a means of generating moral concern and empathy instead of political protest and rebellion. Not only Live Aid, but also Amnesty International and the Anti-Apartheid Movement tried to communicate their political agenda in an apolitical language in order to reach as many people as possible. Only "Sun City" could be analyzed along the lines of a traditional political protest song. This strategy of depoliticization was often effective, but as the case study of the Concert for Nelson Mandela has shown, it was also very contentious for activists within these organizations and movements.

Second, the phenomena I described must be considered in connection to a more general development of consumer patterns during the 1970s and 1980s. The use of pop music as a means of political communication is only one facet of a development in which NGOs like Oxfam, Amnesty International, or the Anti-Apartheid Movement began to use consumer products to communicate their political objectives.[47] To use the example of the Anti-Apartheid Movement: in the same time period in which the AAM began to organize music events like the Concert for Nelson Mandela, it also began to produce and sell consumer products and everyday items like coffee mugs, t-shirts, and jewelry in order to raise funds for their political work and to win new supporters and members for the movement. Other developments like the Fair Trade movement and the market for green consumerism also show that ethical values began to have an impact on consumer markets. These developments can therefore be put into a wider context of the post-1968 period. Not only did pop music become linked to humanitarian efforts, but consumerism in general was partly reinvented as an ethically significant practice of the everyday life.

Taking these developments into account, this chapter has analyzed the way pop music engaged with political and social causes during the 1980s. One important aspect was the moralization of pop music—the attempt to add an ethical dimension to specific songs, LPs, or concerts. Instead of political rebellion and cultural nonconformity, artists were now asked to represent compassion and empathy and to participate in charity events and other acts of philanthropy and benevolence. If political pop music was a key phenomenon of the 1960s, this emergence of humanitarian pop music might be interpreted as an equally important development of the 1980s.

Benjamin Möckel is Assistant Professor at the University of Cologne. After finishing his dissertation on the youth generations of the postwar era in East and West Germany, he is currently working on a history of "ethical consumerism" in the United Kingdom and West Germany since the 1960s. He is currently a research fellow at Oxford University and the Oxford Centre for European History.

Notes

1. As a case study that shows how productive it can be to divert from this research agenda, see Anna von der Goltz, "A Polarized Generation? Conservative Students and West Germany's '1968,'" in *"Talkin' 'Bout My Generation": Conflicts of Generation Building and Europe's "1968,"* ed. Anna von der Goltz (Göttingen, 2001).
2. Theodor W. Adorno and Max Horkheimer, "The Culture Industry: Enlightenment as Mass Deception," in *Dialectic of Enlightenment: Philosophical Fragments* (Stanford, CA, 2002).
3. Thomas Frank, *The Conquest of Cool: Business Culture, Counterculture, and the Rise of Hip Consumerism* (Chicago, 1997); Detlef Siegfried, *Time Is on My Side: Konsum und Politik in der westdeutschen Jugendkultur der 60er Jahre* (Göttingen, 2006).

4. For the vast literature on authenticity, see Lionel Trilling, *Sincerity and Authenticity* (Cambridge, MA, 1972), Charles Taylor, *The Ethics of Authenticity* (Cambridge, MA, 1992), Charles Lindholm, *Culture and Authenticity* (Malden, MA, 2008), Phillip Vannini and J. Patrick Williams, ed., *Authenticity in Culture, Self, and Society* (Surrey, UK, 2009).
5. Sven Reichardt, *Authentizität und Gemeinschaft: Linksalternatives Leben in den Siebziger und frühen Achtziger Jahren* (Berlin, 2014). For a similar argument concerning the 1970s and 1980s as the decades in which the "quest for authenticity" became of predominant importance, see Achim Saupe, "Authenticity," in *Docupedia-Zeitgeschichte*. On the performative aspect of authenticity see Erika Fischer-Lichte and Isabel Pflug, eds., *Inszenierung von Authentizität* (Tübingen, 2000).
6. James H. Gilmore and B. Joseph Pine, *Authenticity: What Consumers Really Want* (Boston, MA, 2007). A kindred interpretation, but more open for ambivalences is Jörn Lamla, "Consuming Authenticity: A Paradoxical Dynamic in Contemporary Capitalism," in *Authenticity in Culture, Self, and Society*, ed. Phillip Vannini and J. Patrick Williams (Surrey, UK, 2009).
7. Richard A. Peterson, *Creating Country Music: Fabricating Authenticity* (Chicago, 1997). See also for other genres Joseph A. Kotarba, "Pop Music as a Resource for Assembling an Authentic Self: A Phenomenological-Existential Perspective," in *Authenticity in Culture, Self, and Society*, ed. Phillip Vannini and J. Patrick Williams (Surrey, 2009).
8. For a similar argument, see Lilie Chouliaraki, *The Ironic Spectator: Solidarity in the Age of Post-Humanitarianism* (Cambridge, 2013), 108–114.
9. On the history of Live Aid, see T. V. Reed, "Famine, Apartheid and the Politics of 'Agit-Pop': Music as (Anti)colonial Discourse," *Cercles* 3 (2001): 96–113; Stan Rijven and Will Straw, "Rock for Ethiopia (1985)," in *World Music, Politics and Social Change*, ed. Simon Frith (Manchester, 1989); Neal Ullestad, "Rock and Rebellion: Subversive Effects of Live Aid and 'Sun City,'" *Popular Music* 6, no. 1 (1987): 67–76.
10. Band Aid, *Do They Know It's Christmas*, Phonogram, UK 1984, Vinyl 7".
11. Chouliaraki, *Ironic Spectator*, 106–137.
12. Bob Geldof, *Is That It?*, with Paul Vallely (London, 1986), 215–216.
13. For the video see https://www.youtube.com/watch?v=XYOj_6OYuJc, retrieved 27 January 2018.
14. As Susan Moeller has shown, several newspapers had reported on the famine in the preceding months without triggering any significant attention. It was only the TV report that was able to generate a significant public reaction, see Susan D. Moeller, *Compassion Fatigue: How the Media Sell Disease, Famine, War, and Death* (New York, 1999), 111–125. See also Greg Philo, "From Buerk to Band Aid: The Media and the 1984 Ethiopian Famine," in *Getting the Message: News, Truth and Power*, ed. John Eldridge (London, 1993), 104–125.
15. For the numbers, see Philo, "From Buerk to Live Aid," 121.
16. Geldof, *Is That It?*, 215–216.
17. On this claim of "humanitarianism" as being nonpolitical, see Michael N. Barnett, *Empire of Humanity: A History of Humanitarianism* (Ithaca, NY, 2011).

18. Daniel Dayan and Elihu Katz, *Media Events: The Live Broadcasting of History* (Cambridge, MA, 1992).
19. For an overview on the concept of "mega-events" and its significance for global cultures of modernity, see Maurice Roche, *Mega-Events and Modernity: Olympics and Expos in the Growth of Global Culture* (London, 2000). Focusing on the connection between "mega-events" and political and moral protest is Christian Lahusen, *The Rhetoric of Moral Protest: Public Campaigns, Celebrity Endorsement and Political Mobilization* (Berlin, 1996); Christian Lahusen, "Mobilizing for International Solidarity: Mega-Events and Moral Crusades," in *Political Altruism: The Solidarity Movement in International Perspective*, ed. Marco Giugni and Florence Passy (Lanham, 2001): 177–195. On Live Aid as a "mega event," see H. Louise Davis, "Concerts for a Cause (Or, 'Cause We Can?)," in *The Routledge History of Social Protest in Popular Music*, ed. J. C. Friedman (London, 2013), 211–226, Reebee Garofalo, "Understanding Mega-Events: If We Are the World, Then How Do We Change It?," in *Rockin' the Boat: Mass Music and Mass Movements*, ed. Reebee Garofalo (Boston, 1992).
20. The Olympics in Los Angeles have been interpreted as the first event of this kind that fully embraced the potential of sport performances as a global media event. See among others: Roche, *Mega-Events*.
21. Contemporary critics noticed this difference and emphasized that while Woodstock, for example, had ended in total chaos, Live Aid finished its program only three minutes late. See Samuel G. Freedman, "Live Aid and the Woodstock Nation," *New York Times*, 18 July 1985.
22. Peter Hilmore, *Live Aid* (London, 1985), 40.
23. On the pitfalls of this approach of framing global humanitarian crises in a narrative of individual empathy, see Paul Bloom, *Against Empathy: The Case for Rational Compassion* (New York, 2016).
24. For the renaissance of the "charity single" in the 1980s, see Lucy Robinson, "Putting the Charity Back into Charity Singles: Charity Singles in Britain 1984–1995," *Contemporary British History* 26, no. 3 (2012): 405–425.
25. Artists United Against Apartheid, *Sun City* (Vinyl/LP), Manhattan Records/EMI UK, 1985.
26. For Sun City as an entertainment venue and the concerts held during Apartheid, see Torsten Thomas Sannar, *Playing Sun City: The Politics of Entertainment at a South African Mega-Resort* (Proquest Umi Dissertation, 2012).
27. For a more elaborated analysis of "Sun City" and the context of the cultural boycott, see Benjamin Möckel, "'Free Nelson Mandela': Popmusik und zivilgesellschaftlicher Protest in der britischen Anti-Apartheid-Bewegung," *Jahrbuch des Zentrums für populäre Kultur und Musik*, 60/61(2016): 199–217. For the internal debates and ambivalent effects of the cultural boycott, see Detlef Siegfried, "Aporien des Kulturboykotts: Anti-Apartheid-Bewegung, ANC und der Konflikt um Paul Simons Album 'Graceland' (1985–1988)," *Zeithistorische Forschungen/Studies in Contemporary History* 13, no. 2 (2016): 254–279.
28. Reed, for example, compares Live Aid and Sun City along this dichotomy, see Reed, *Famine*, 96–113.
29. See the back sleeve of the record where "The Africa Fund" is presented as "a charitable trust based in New York City and registered with the United Nations." The text

further states: "The income will benefit political prisoners and their families in South Africa, educational and cultural needs of South African exiles, and educational work of anti-apartheid groups in the United States."
30. Reed, *Famine*, 108.
31. For a more detailed analysis, see the existing literature on both events. For the "Concerts for Nelson Mandela," see Lahusen, *Rhetoric*, 100–106, Christian Lahusen, "Nelson Mandela als Pop-Ikone: Mega-Events und politische Mobilisierung im globalen Dorf," in *Events: Soziologie des Außergewöhnlichen*, ed. Winfried Gebhardt et al. (Opladen, 2000): 284–304; Reebee Garofalo, "Nelson Mandela, the Concerts: Mass Culture as Contested Terrain," in *Rockin' the Boat: Mass Music and Mass Movements*, ed. Reebee Garofalo (Boston, MA, 1992). Literature on "Human Rights Now!" is scarce. The official tour book is helpful but is itself part of the iconography of the event, see James Henke and Human Rights Foundation, Inc., *Human Rights Now! The Official Book of the Concerts for Human Rights Foundation World Tour* (Topsfield, MA, 1988). Helpful, but also written from a contemporary perspective is Deena Winstein, "The Amnesty International Tour: Transnationalism as Cultural Commodity," *Public Culture* 1, no. 2 (1989): 60–65. Stephen Hopgood mentions the event only briefly, but rightly points to the controversies the tour caused within Amnesty International, see Stephen Hopgood, *Keepers of the Flame: Understanding Amnesty International* (Ithaca, NY, 2006), 108–113.
32. Ex post, Tony Hollingsworth has regularly referred to this strategy of personalization and depoliticization as a means to secure maximum media support and attention. See, for example, his statements in an interview with the South African TV program "Carte Blanche": https://www.youtube.com/watch?v=0FQTYIiqp5s, retrieved 27 January 2018.
33. For the internal debates and correspondences, see Archive of the Anti-Apartheid Movement, Bodleian Library (Oxford), MSS AAM 2361–2375.
34. Archive of the Anti-Apartheid Movement, Bodleian Library (Oxford), MSS AAM 13, Annual Report 1987/88, 2.
35. Ibid, 17.
36. Robin Denselow, *When the Music's Over: The Story of Political Pop* (London, 1990), 276.
37. The national sections of Amnesty International act rather independently. Amnesty International was founded in 1961, the US section (AI USA) was founded in 1966.
38. Peter Gabriel's song "Biko" was about South African anti-Apartheid activist Steve Biko who had been killed in custody in 1977. Sting's song "They Dance Alone" referred to the women of the "Disappeared" in Pinochet-Chile.
39. See Henke, *Human Rights Now!*, 33–37.
40. Cyndee Miller, "Reebok Pays Cost of Human Rights Concert Tour," *Marketing News* 22, no. 19 (1988): 6–7.
41. See, for example, Hopgood, *Keepers of the Flame*, 106–107.
42. See as only one of many examples in the context of the media coverage of "Band Aid 30" in 2014, Bim Adewunmi, "Band Aid 30: Clumsy, Patronizing and Wrong in So Many Ways," *The Guardian*, 11 November 2014.
43. For the video footage of the scene, including the introduction by Jack Nicholson, see https://www.youtube.com/watch?v=qD9kcvIc48M, retrieved 28 January 2018.

44. Thomas Frank and Matt Weiland, *Commodify Your Dissent: Salvos from the Baffler* (New York, 1997).
45. For the interconnectedness between 1960s counterculture and consumer cultures, see Frank, *Conquest of Cool*. For the German case, see Siegfried, *Time*.
46. The self-staging as rebellious and nonconformist is of course not solely a phenomenon of pop music; generating attention in the "literary field" or the "artistic field" can contain similar gestures of rebellion and nonconformity. See Pierre Bourdieu, *The Field of Cultural Production: Essays in Art and Literature* (New York, 1993).
47. For the connections between consumption, political protest and campaigns of protest movements, and NGOs, see Jörn Lamla and Sighard Neckel, *Politisierter Konsum: konsumierte Politik* (Wiesbaden, 2006).

Bibliography

Adewunmi, Bim. "Band Aid 30: Clumsy, Patronizing and Wrong in So Many Ways." *The Guardian*, 11 November 2014.

Adorno, Theodor W., and Max Horkheimer. *Dialectic of Enlightenment: Philosophical Fragments*. Stanford, CA: Stanford University Press, 2002.

Barnett, Michael N. *Empire of Humanity: A History of Humanitarianism*. Ithaca, NY: Cornell University Press, 2011.

Bloom, Paul. *Against Empathy: The Case for Rational Compassion*. New York: Harper Collins, 2016.

Bourdieu, Pierre. *The Field of Cultural Production: Essays in Art and Literature*. New York: Columbia University Press, 1993.

Chouliaraki, Lilie. *The Ironic Spectator: Solidarity in the Age of Post-Humanitarianism*. Cambridge: Polity Press, 2013.

Davis, H. Louise. "Concerts for a Cause (Or, 'Cause We Can?)." In *The Routledge History of Social Protest in Popular Music*, edited by J. C. Friedman, 211–226. London: Routledge, 2013.

Dayan, Daniel, and Elihu Katz. *Media Events: The Live Broadcasting of History*. Cambridge, MA: Harvard University Press, 1992.

Denselow, Robin. *When the Music's Over: The Story of Political Pop*. London: Faber and Faber, 1990.

Fischer-Lichte, Erika, and Isabel Pflug, eds. *Inszenierung von Authentizität*. Tübingen: Francke, 2000.

Frank, Thomas. *The Conquest of Cool: Business Culture, Counterculture, and the Rise of Hip Consumerism*. Chicago: University of Chicago Press, 1997.

Frank, Thomas, and Matt Weiland. *Commodify Your Dissent: Salvos from the Baffler*. New York: Norton & Company, 1997.

Garofalo, Reebee. "Nelson Mandela, the Concerts: Mass Culture as Contested Terrain." In *Rockin' the Boat: Mass Music and Mass Movements*, edited by Reebee Garofalo, 55–65. Boston, MA: South End Press, 1992.

———. "Understanding Mega-Events: If We Are the World, Then How Do We Change It?" In *Rockin' the Boat: Mass Music and Mass Movements*, edited by Reebee Garofalo, 15–35. Boston, MA: South End Press, 1992.

Geldof, Bob. *Is That It?* With Paul Vallely. London: Sidgewick & Jackson, 1986.
Gilmore, James H., and B. Joseph Pine. *Authenticity: What Consumers Really Want.* Boston, MA: Harvard Business School Press, 2007.
Goltz, Anna von der. "A Polarized Generation? Conservative Students and West Germany's '1968.'" In *"Talkin' 'Bout My Generation": Conflicts of Generation Building and Europe's "1968,"* edited by Anna von der Goltz, 195–215. Göttingen: Wallstein, 2001.
Henke, James, and Human Rights Foundation, Inc. *Human Rights Now! The Official Book of the Concerts for Human Rights Foundation World Tour.* Topsfield, MA: Salem House, 1988.
Hilmore, Peter. *Live Aid.* London: Sidgewick & Jackson, 1985.
Hopgood, Stephen. *Keepers of the Flame: Understanding Amnesty International.* Ithaca, NY: Cornell University Press, 2006.
Kotarba, Joseph A. "Pop Music as a Resource for Assembling an Authentic Self: A Phenomenological-Existential Perspective." In *Authenticity in Culture, Self, and Society,* edited by Phillip Vannini and J. Patrick Williams, 153–168. Surrey, UK: Ashgate Publishing, 2009.
Lahusen, Christian. "Mobilizing for International Solidarity: Mega-Events and Moral Crusades." In *Political Altruism: The Solidarity Movement in International Perspective,* edited by Marco Giugni and Florence Passy, 177–195. Lanham, MD: Rowman & Littlefield, 2001.
———. "Nelson Mandela als Pop-Ikone: Mega-Events und politische Mobilisierung im globalen Dorf." In *Events: Soziologie des Außergewöhnlichen,* edited by Winfried Gebhardt, Ronald Hitzler, and Michaela Pfadenhauer, 284–304. Opladen: Leske + Budrich, 2000.
———. *The Rhetoric of Moral Protest: Public Campaigns, Celebrity Endorsement and Political Mobilization.* Berlin: De Gruyter, 1996.
Lamla, Jörn. "Consuming Authenticity: A Paradoxical Dynamic in Contemporary Capitalism." In *Authenticity in Culture, Self, and Society,* edited by Phillip Vannini and J. Patrick Williams, 171–185. Surrey, UK: Ashgate Publishing, 2009.
Lamla, Jörn, and Sighard Neckel. *Politisierter Konsum: konsumierte Politik.* Wiesbaden: Verlag für Sozialwissenschaften, 2006.Lindholm, Charles. *Culture and Authenticity.* Malden, MA: Blackwell Publishing, 2008.
Miller, Cyndee. "Reebok Pays Cost of Human Rights Concert Tour." *Marketing News* 22, no. 19 (1988): 6–7.
Möckel, Benjamin. "'Free Nelson Mandela': Popmusik und zivilgesellschaftlicher Protest in der britischen Anti-Apartheid-Bewegung." *Jahrbuch des Zentrums für populäre Kultur und Musik* 60/61 (2016): 199–217.
Moeller, Susan D. *Compassion Fatigue: How the Media Sell Disease, Famine, War, and Death.* New York: Routledge, 1999.
Peterson, Richard A. *Creating Country Music: Fabricating Authenticity.* Chicago: University of Chicago Press, 1997.
Philo, Greg. "From Buerk to Band Aid: The Media and the 1984 Ethiopian Famine." In *Getting the Message: News, Truth and Power,* edited by John Eldridge, 104–125. London: Routledge, 1993.

Reed, T. V. "Famine, Apartheid and the Politics of 'Agit-Pop': Music as (Anti)colonial Discourse." *Cercles* 3 (2001): 96–113.
Reichardt, Sven. *Authentizität und Gemeinschaft: Linksalternatives Leben in den Siebziger und frühen Achtziger Jahren*. Berlin: Suhrkamp Verlag, 2014.
Rijven, Stan, and Will Straw. "Rock for Ethiopia (1985)." In *World Music, Politics and Social Change*, edited by Simon Frith, 198–209. Manchester: Manchester University Press, 1989.
Robinson, Lucy. "Putting the Charity Back into Charity Singles: Charity Singles in Britain 1984–1995." *Contemporary British History* 26, no. 3 (2012): 405–425.
Roche, Maurice: *Mega-Events and Modernity: Olympics and Expos in the Growth of Global Culture*. London: Routledge, 2000.
Sannar, Torsten Thomas. *Playing Sun City: The Politics of Entertainment at a South African Mega-Resort*. Proquest Umi Dissertation, 2012.
Saupe, Achim. "Authenticity." In *Docupedia-Zeitgeschichte*. Retrieved 27 January 2018 from http://docupedia.de/zg/saupe_authentizitaet_v3_en_2016.
Siegfried, Detlef. "Aporien des Kulturboykotts: Anti-Apartheid-Bewegung, ANC und der Konflikt um Paul Simons Album 'Graceland' (1985–1988)." *Zeithistorische Forschungen/Studies in Contemporary History* 13, no. 2 (2016): 254–279.
———. *Time Is on My Side: Konsum und Politik in der westdeutschen Jugendkultur der 60er Jahre*. Göttingen: Wallstein, 2006.
Taylor, Charles. *The Ethics of Authenticity*. Cambridge, MA: Harvard University Press, 1992.
Trilling, Lionel. *Sincerity and Authenticity*. Cambridge, MA: Harvard University Press, 1972.
Ullestad, Neal. "Rock and Rebellion: Subversive Effects of Live Aid and 'Sun City.'" *Popular Music* 6, no. 1 (1987): 67–76.
Vannini, Phillip, and J. Patrick Williams, ed. *Authenticity in Culture, Self, and Society*. Surrey, UK: Ashgate Publishing, 2009.
Winstein, Deena. "The Amnesty International Tour: Transnationalism as Cultural Commodity." *Public Culture* 1, no. 2 (1989): 60–65.

Chapter 12

Embedded Abstractions
Authenticity, Aura, and Abject Domesticity in Hamburg's Hafenstraße

Jake P. Smith

Authenticity as a Structure of Meaning

In November 1984, an article in the conservative West German newspaper, *Die Welt*, jubilantly proclaimed that the squatting movement in West Berlin was "nothing but a memory."[1] Striking a similar note, Heinrich Lummer, West Berlin's Interior Secretary (*Innensenator*), triumphantly declared that law-abiding West Berliners could once again be proud of their city now that the last squats had been cleared and the protesting youth defeated.[2] The situation was similar in cities across Northern and Central Europe: the utopian dreams of the 1980–1981 youth movements were fading fast; the "hot summer" that had been so joyfully celebrated by youth activists in places like Zurich, Freiburg, and West Berlin was steadily dissolving into a long, cold winter.[3] There were, however, exceptions to this downward trajectory. In the wealthy West German city of Hamburg, for example, a group of squatters living in a dilapidated building on the Elbe River managed to weather the storms of reaction and conservative retrenchment and, in so doing, slowly ascended to a dominant position within the symbolic landscape of the radical left.[4] As the historian George Katsiaficas has argued, even as "the squatters' movement elsewhere suffered a series of defeats, the Hafenstraße's capability to remain intact made it a symbol of almost mythic proportions."[5] Indeed, the colorful "House of Horrors," which was covered with striking murals that implored residents and visitors to show "Solidarity with the RAF" and which served as a meeting point for various countercultural and radical leftist groups, provocatively countered the claims that the youth movements were finished.[6]

Especially when compared to the raucous squatting movements taking place concurrently in places like Amsterdam, Freiburg, and West Berlin, the

Hafenstraße in Hamburg-Altona began rather inauspiciously in 1980 when the Siedlungs-Aktiengesellschaft Altona (SAGA), one of the city agencies responsible for housing issues, allowed students, recovering drug addicts, and other at-risk social groups to occupy a number of empty apartments in the seedy, riverfront neighborhood of St. Pauli for a nominal fee.[7] While ostensibly meant to assist at-risk populations find affordable housing, such short-term rental agreements were also explicitly designed to facilitate future urban renewal projects since they not only enabled the city to protect otherwise empty properties from being squatted and from legal challenges stemming from a "misuse of living space" but also made it easy, when the time came, to terminate the leases and evict the residents prior to the building's demolition.[8] In the case of the Hafenstraße, though, nothing went according to plan. Indeed, between 1983 and 1987, the Hafenstraße steadily developed into one of the city's premiere countercultural meeting points. Thomas Osterkorn, a journalist for the *Hamburger Abendblatt*, described the cast of characters who populated the Hafenstraße in this period as "punks and youth from broken homes, orphanages, and prisons, as well as militant left-extremists such as Spontis and anarchists"—in short, not the sort of people the city wanted living without social supervision in what was deemed to be prime real estate along the Elbe River.[9] Repeated efforts to evict the residents only managed to further exacerbate an already tense situation, which, in late 1987, seemed likely to erupt in violence. Although Hamburg Mayor Klaus Dohnanyi's November 1987 compromise proposal to extend the residents' leases initially succeeded in preventing a violent showdown between police and the thousands of activists who had gathered in the city, the conflict continued to simmer for another decade as lease agreements were continually renegotiated and as conservative politicians and pundits incessantly railed against the dangers of such "lawless zones" in the centers of West German cities.[10]

The extraordinary duration of the conflict over the Hafenstraße coupled with the extreme emotions that it generated opens up a number of potential avenues for academic research. One could, for example, explore the experimental architectural forms developed in the squat; the shifting alliances within Hamburg city politics; the role of the mainstream press in exacerbating social tensions; or the effects of leftist activism on urban development policies—all of which would be beneficial for understanding the complex interrelationship between politics, activism, and urban transformation in late twentieth-century West Germany.[11] This chapter, though, takes a different tack and uses the conflict as a lens through which to examine the shifting and contested meaning of authenticity—in particular surrounding domestic spaces—in the West German Left-alternative milieu during the turbulent 1980s.[12]

Authenticity is by no means an understudied concept in scholarship on the West German left. Indeed, recent years have witnessed a spate of publications on the relationship between leftist practices and broader transformations in the meaning of authenticity. As historians such as Pascal Eitler and Sven Reichardt have convincingly argued, for example, leftist activists in the years following the student movements of the late 1960s were obsessed with the desire to develop authentic subjectivities, authentic social relationships, and authentic modes of expression.[13] Drawing from theories developed by the French philosopher Michel Foucault on the technologies of self-fashioning, Reichardt and others have illustrated how the concept of authenticity provided leftist youth with a powerful corpus of linguistic and behavioral tools that they could use both to demarcate themselves from mainstream West German society and to solidify their membership in an oppositional community. The actual meaning of authenticity was immaterial. What mattered was how and to what ends it was employed. Authenticity, in this line of analysis, served as a technique for disciplining the self, a seemingly liberatory set of discourses and practices through which ever more people in modern societies voluntarily submitted to regimes of governmentality and power.[14]

These arguments have, without question, radically improved our understanding of left-alternative practices and their role in transforming large-scale systems of social and cultural values in the last three decades of the twentieth century. However, by focusing primarily on the sociological dimensions of authenticity—its functional role as a tool of self-fashioning—scholars have largely elided its more "structural" aspects. Authenticity was not, I contend, merely an empty category that leftists employed to distinguish themselves from mainstream society; it was part of a broader urban "habitus," an underlying structure of meaning that helped to determine the lived experience of urban "lifeworlds" throughout the postwar period.[15] Authenticity, in short, structured behavior. It was a concept with agency, an idea with its own volition. This is not to suggest that authenticity had a fixed definition in these years; on the contrary, it encompassed at least two oppositional sets of meaning.[16] On the one hand, urban authenticity was understood as a mode of transcending social and cultural contexts, of liberating one's true self from the anchors of everyday existence, from what might be called the unbearable heaviness of being. Indeed, whether it was modernist architects rethinking the nature of postfascist urbanism or Reichian-inspired activists experimenting with psychoanalytic techniques of self-discovery, a number of West Germans believed that authentic expressions of individuality could only emerge when people were freed from their existential contexts.[17] On the other hand, though, authenticity was premised on the belief that one could and indeed should embrace embedded—or what, drawing from Walter Benjamin, we might call "auratic"—lifeworlds, those which exhibited a more "natural," more unmediated connection between sociocultural context and subjectivity.[18] Some, on the left and in society more broadly, sought to discover these auratic enclaves within the traditional spaces and populations of the nation such as rural villages and agricultural communities; others insisted that truly authentic environments could only be found well beyond the borders of Europe. Native Americans, anticolonial resistance fighters, African American musicians, East Asian religious communities, and the international working classes, among many others, were seen as more authentic due to their seemingly unmediated connection to their surroundings and to their exclusion from Western modernity.[19]

While not discounting arguments that stress the sociological importance of authenticity for constructing oppositional identities, this chapter thus suggests that authenticity was more than an empty signifier passively waiting to be employed as a tool of disciplinary power. Rather, it comprised a deeply meaningful set of practices and assumptions that structured how leftists (and society more broadly) thought about and behaved in urban space. This is not to argue that West Germans robotically acted out the dictates of underlying structural codes. Indeed, given the deep tensions between what I will be calling *transcendent* and *auratic* forms of urban authenticity, social actors were able to express their own agency by modifying, channeling, and controlling the relationship between these two oppositional sets of meaning as well as their actualization in the world.[20] Such attempts at controlling the meanings and expressions of authenticity were particularly evident in the discourses surrounding postwar domesticity. As I argue in the fourth section of this essay, the postwar home in West Germany served as a disciplinary space that utilized the practices and ideologies of domesticity to channel the underlying structures of urban authenticity as tools of governmentality and social control. The postwar home's role as a channeling device for structures of meaning was both a highly effective technique of governmentality and a potential weak point. Indeed, the squatters and supporters of the Hafenstraße used the unique structural position of the postwar home to recombine some of the central elements of transcendent and auratic forms of urban authenticity into an overarching framework of "abject domesticity," an interrelated set of discourses and practices that fundamentally challenged dominant forms of postwar dwelling. The Hafenstraße thus served as a framing device with which leftists could think through and creatively rearrange the underlying structures of urban authenticity. It was, to paraphrase the prolific structural anthropologist, Claude Levi-Strauss: "good to think with."[21]

Transcendent Authenticity

In the years following the global student movements of 1968, many leftists evinced an obsessive desire to transcend what they understood to be the oppressive social and cultural contexts of the postwar era. Declarations of existential liberation from the surrounding world were a central theme, for example, in the manifold coming of age narratives produced in the period. In Leonie Ossowski's 1982 novel *Wilhelm Meister's Abschied*, the novel's young working-class protagonist, Wilhelm, makes the fateful decision to leave the comfortable domestic environment of his family home in Lichterfelde for a squat in Kreuzberg. In an imagined speech to his father—which he theatrically reenacts with the assistance of his new family in the squat—Wilhelm proclaims his freedom: "I am not your monument. I have a right to my own life about which I will decide. My experiences are my own. Can you not understand that yours do not interest me? The world that you made remains your world and does not concern me."[22] Like Wilhelm, many left-alternative youth viewed life in postwar Germany as thoroughly contaminated by the oppressive, alienating forces of capitalist modernity.[23] From the cold functionalism of the built environment to the monotonous routines of work and leisure, urban life, they argued, had become a nightmarish iron cage of bourgeois morality, capitalist ethics, and state violence, a disciplinary arena that constrained their behavior and thus prevented authentic forms of community and self-expression.

Whereas some chose to confront the injustices of the postwar order through street protests or even through acts of terrorism, others looked to create autonomous spaces within which they could immediately begin to cultivate more authentic subjectivities.[24] They sought, in other words, to build utopian islands in the midst of an alienating and deeply hostile everyday environment. Communes, shared living spaces (*Wohngemeinschaften*), and autonomous youth centers, for example, were widely believed to offer spaces in which youth could discover and freely develop their true, authentic selves.[25] According to members of the Kommune 2 project in West Berlin, communal living spaces combined a widespread rejection of prevailing work and education systems with "disgust over capitalist consumption, the feeling of unspeakable isolation [and] the hope for psychological liberation."[26] Although they were certainly easier to create in rural areas, leftist communal living projects also proliferated in urban centers throughout Europe. In the late 1970s and early 1980s, for example, groups of squatters occupied empty spaces in cities across West Germany and Western Europe in the hopes of simultaneously combating capitalist property relations and creating alternative, utopian communities. For many squatters, the empty factories, dilapidated buildings, and decaying neighborhoods of Europe's crumbling inner cities were seen as largely independent from the otherwise ubiquitous power of capitalism and the state, and, as such, provided the perfect setting in which to cultivate autonomous (and thus authentic) subjectivities.

Drawing from the rhetoric and practices developed by earlier generations of leftist activists, the occupants of the Hafenstraße sought to create conditions within which authentic social relationships could flourish. One way of accomplishing this goal was to forcibly remove all vestiges of bourgeois mores and capitalist ethics from the squatted landscape. Many of the squatters relished this atmosphere of freedom that was created inside the squat. One resident, for example, described the experience of eating in the *Volksküche* (the Hafenstraße's communal kitchen) as the diametrical opposite of the bourgeois dining experience: "Sometimes you cooked, sometimes others cooked, and some days there was no dinner at all because everyone felt like being alone."[27] In his pop ethnography of the squat, Carl-Heinz Mallet also depicted the moral laxity and social freedom that characterized life at the Hafenstraße in glowing terms, writing:

> I could speak or stay silent, daydream, forget myself in the music, or look out the window. I could stretch out my legs as far as I wanted, sit or stand on the podium, loll about with Josef or take a nap, like Olaf once did. I could dress however I liked, have a beard or a shaved head. I could get up and leave without any explanation and without saying goodbye, and no one would ask where I was going. No matter what I might do, no one would stare at me. Where else in the entire world can one conduct oneself with so little compulsion?[28]

As a space that was understood to be devoid of social obligations, the Hafenstraße, theoretically at least, offered an environment where people were free to be themselves.

This focus on radically autonomous individualism in the Hafenstraße was not, however, antithetical to community and social warmth. Indeed, liberating the individual from oppressive, alienating social conditions was seen as the necessary precondition for building authentic relationships. In addition to sharing the responsibilities for cooking, cleaning, and childcare, the squatters also tried to increase communication and conviviality among the residents by abolishing what they viewed as bourgeois practices of privacy by leaving their doors open and sharing their possessions. One resident directly contrasted the communal organization of everyday life in the Hafenstraße with the private property relations that reigned in other residential buildings in the area, noting: "We do not even shut the doors here. Here everything is much opener. I wanted to borrow a filter full of coffee from a stupid rental building next door. The woman just looked at me. Coffee? We don't have any. And bang, she shut the door. They don't let anything leave their own four walls."[29] The Hafenstraße was a space where, as one squatter put it, "there is room for people to actualize themselves, where communication can be supported through space."[30] By extricating themselves from what they viewed as the oppressive social and economic forms that structured mainstream society, the squatters sought to create more authentic, more natural modes of sociability that were based not on one's social position or functional value within the economic system but on inherent human worth. The Hafenstraße thus came to be thought of as a unique, communal space in which residents knew "almost everyone by their first name, but almost never by their last name."[31]

Residents not only conceived of the identity being forged inside the Hafenstraße in positive terms, but also in relation to the dangerous terrain outside of the complex. Indeed, the ideal life of existential freedom and authentic community that was to be forged inside the heavily defended walls of the Hafenstraße was constantly compared to the violence, injustice, and loneliness of life on the outside. One resident discussed his feelings toward the West German state at length, noting:

> I want to be finished with this pig system. Do you know where they have tried to stick me? In psychiatric wards, in prison, in special schools, in a home for those with behavioral problems. And do you know why? Because I am too strong. ... I no longer want to be a German. I don't want the judges to pass sentences in my name which make me want to puke. In the name of the people! Without me.[32]

Mobilizing phrases such as "No Pasaran!" and "We won't let our lives be prescribed. Period," the residents of the Hafenstraße exerted considerable energy to demarcate life inside the squat from the outside world.[33] In so doing, they hoped to "remove all forms of alienation" from their community, and thus create a space where everyday life could again be filled with joy and hope, where social relationships could flourish, and where people could engage in acts of self-discovery.[34]

At the height of the conflict from late 1986 to the signing of the extended leases in 1987, activists from cities across West Germany as well as from Amsterdam, Copenhagen, London, and Zürich expressed support for the liberated zone surrounding the Hafenstraße. They traveled to Hamburg to man the barricades, penned letters of support in local newspapers, and organized protests in their own cities—all of which deeply worried Hamburg city officials and conservative pundits throughout West Germany who warned that the Hafenstraße was becoming an "unconquerable fortress," a leftist enclave that threatened the very legitimacy of the state.[35] It was abundantly clear for both the right and the left that the Hafenstraße was not only a place to live—it was a tool for transcending and subverting the established order, a "Free Space" (*Freiraum*) where one could take refuge from the alienation, violence, and exhaustive temporalities that were believed to structure everyday life in the late twentieth century. As I argue in the following section, though, this attempt at transcending local contexts to cultivate one's authentic, inner self was often paired with a longing for a more grounded identity, one in which people interacted symbiotically with their surrounding environment. Transcendent authenticity was, in other words, paired with its opposite: with a search for aura.

Auratic Authenticity

As the leftist youth withdrew behind the protected walls of the Hafenstraße, they increasingly sought to forge connections with groups that they believed had been marginalized or criminalized by capitalism, nationalism, and the West. Countless flyers, for example, made the connection between the squatters' battles against the senate and international liberation movements ranging from Latin American revolutionaries to the IRA (Irish Republican Army). On the occasion of Prince Charles's 1987 visit to Hamburg, the squatters hung signs that read: "Smash the H-Block! Victory to the IRA!" Explaining these actions, Radio Hafenstraße reported: "What binds us with the colleagues in Northern Ireland is that we are both resisting the anti-human system that built such torture chambers. This is international solidarity."[36] Another claimed that the Hafenstraße belonged "to those in the world that struggle against the Deutsche Bank, whether it's because they support the racist system in South Africa and earn billions on the hunger and blood of those forced into perpetual underdevelopment, or because [in Hamburg, they] press the Senate to remove us."[37] As was the case with numerous leftist groups in the decades following 1968, the squatters also looked to Native American groups for inspiration. One of the wall murals, for example, depicted native peoples dancing amid corn, flowers, and wild animals and a Mayan saying: "they rip off our fruit, they cut our branches, and they burn our trunk, but they cannot kill our roots."[38] The residents of the Hafenstraße did not restrict themselves to forging international connections but found comrades in history as well. Some authors, for example, allied themselves with Klaus Störtebeker, Hamburg's own Robin Hood who was executed for piracy in the early fifteenth century. Störtebeker's popularity among the squatters was unrivaled: not only did they name an antifascist information and communication center after him, but one pamphlet even proclaimed him to be mayor of the Hafenstraße.³⁹ Even the press took notice of the Hafenstraße's catchall approach to revolution, noting that Radio Hafenstraße played "a confused mixture of Palestinian freedom songs, hardcore punk, [and] communist fighting songs."⁴⁰

As these examples indicate, many of the residents of the Hafenstraße—like numerous leftist activists and theorists before them—imagined themselves to be part of an international network of abjection: an army of the excluded, whose revolutionary authenticity was premised not on uncovering and fostering some truer version of the self that lay buried beneath layers of alienation and social control, but on embodying negation.⁴¹ In a system where everything was corrupt, they reasoned, only those who had been entirely excluded exhibited a modicum of revolutionary authenticity. The relationship between the European left and romanticized visions of the "other"—evident, for example, in the late 1960s deification of Mao, the Socialist Patient Collective's valorization of the mentally ill, and the Red Army Faction's incessant invocation of the will of "the people"—is far too complex to explore in any detail in this chapter. Suffice it to say that these actions represented an alternative vision of authenticity, one which was based not on the principle of transcending all forms of locality and sociocultural context in order to liberate a more authentic version of the self but on re-embedding oneself in a fundamentally different lifeworld, a romantic space of alterity and opposition.⁴² This vision of authenticity, in other words, embraced auratic identities, but only if they were entirely uncontaminated by capitalism and Western modernity.

If dissolving one's identity into an amorphous network of outsiders reflected the common slogan that the squatters of the Hafenstraße were "everywhere" (*überall*), a somewhat different vision of embedded authenticity was reflected in the equally ubiquitous phrase "Hafenstraße remains" (*Hafen bleibt*), which appeared on the walls of the squat, on pamphlets, and in graffiti scrawled throughout the city. Although one could certainly interpret this slogan merely as a defiant statement against eviction, I would also suggest that it points to something much broader, to a notion that the Hafenstraße was not an empty space of transcendence, but an embedded locality, a symbolically loaded landscape with deep historical roots. One of the most striking expressions of this valorization of the Hafenstraße's emplaced qualities came from a squatter who vehemently rejected the notion that residents could end the conflict by putting down their weapons and moving into the country to form a commune, noting: "Old houses are full. Full of work, full of history, their history, the history that they embody; of the people that have lived there and how they have lived. our life, our ten years of a hundred, in which the walls with their cracks leave traces. our walls, our traces. *hafen bleibt.*"⁴³ Rather than an abstract, empty space, the Hafenstraße was heavily laden with its own contextual significance. It had a unique history. It had memories etched into its walls. The Hafenstraße, in other words, was no mere *space* but a *place*. It was an auratic location rich with memories, with unique references, with its own embedded temporalities. It was, to quote the cultural theorist Robert Pogue Harrison, a "memory of itself—a place where time reflects back upon itself."⁴⁴

In a number of respects, this valorization of the emplaced, auratic qualities of the local was very much in tune with the times. Especially in the wake of the economic "boom years" of the 1950s and 1960s, paeans to the vanishing qualities of authentic places proliferated across the Western world.⁴⁵ From the careful reconstruction of historic buildings to the memory boom that manifested itself in tourism, media, and interior design aesthetics, the long 1970s was indeed an era characterized by a nostalgia for place. At the same time, though, such praise for the unique qualities of local place-worlds was not particularly common for the activists and theorists of the West German left.⁴⁶ Indeed, given the close association between German landscapes and Nazi "blood and soil" ideology, many on the left preferred to avoid evocations of localized contexts in favor of either romanticized visions of alterity or a transcendent dismissal of local lifeworlds altogether. As will become clear in the following section, however, the Hafenstraße's emplaced qualities—its imbrication in the dense materiality of the German place-world—proved to be vital for formulating an alternative approach to urban authenticity, one that was both embedded and transcendent.

Abject Domesticity

As a number of scholars have convincingly argued, domestic spaces in West Germany played an inordinately large role in forging meaningful identities after the collapse of the Third Reich.⁴⁷ According to historian Paul Betts, "the postwar focus of aesthetics had moved from the public and spectacular … to the mundane and private …, from the glorification of the united Volk to the cultivation of consumer difference and individual lifestyle."⁴⁸ In the immediate postwar era, many West Germans took refuge in a romanticized version of the *Heimat*, which "came to embody the political and social community that could be salvaged from the Nazi ruins."⁴⁹ Whether through bucolic films from the 1950s, through a renewed focus on the nuclear family, or through the numerous housing exhibits that proliferated in the postwar period, many West Germans came to believe that the auratic landscapes of the home and the neighborhood could serve as ideal locations in which to forge a meaningful postfascist life, one that was both oriented toward the future and grounded in the nostalgic comforts of the romantic past. *Heimat*, in this reading, had two interrelated functions, both of which facilitated the exercise and reification of postwar state power. On the one hand, it served as a necessary counterweight to the exhausting tempo and disorienting futurity of postwar capitalism by providing West Germans with a sense of stability in what, by all accounts, was a deeply unsettled historical moment. On the other hand, the auratic landscapes of the German *Heimat* also served as disciplinary spaces where a diverse array of bodies and objects that had been devastated by more than three decades of social, cultural, and political upheaval could be reconfigured into legible constellations of meaning; into what, drawing from arguments developed in a different context by the gender theorist Judith Butler, we might call "bodies that matter."[50]

Building on Butler's theories of gender normativity, I suggest that we can think of the postwar West German home as a disciplinary space that instrumentalized both auratic and transcendent forms of authenticity as tools of governmentality and social control. As a deeply auratic locale, the home enabled the disconnected fragments of the national body to be re-embedded into the romanticized landscape of the German *Heimat*, thus providing citizens with a seemingly authentic connection to the national past and to their compatriots. It transformed them, in other words, into a collectivity who could dwell authentically in the national landscape. At the same time, though, the home also constrained and channeled the population's desires for transcendence by allowing normalized national subjects to momentarily escape their immediate sociocultural contexts and bask in a controlled utopia of democracy and consumption. One could, in other words, cautiously reach toward the shining, capitalist future while remaining safely ensconced in the fundamentally nationalist landscape of the German *Heimat*.[51] The home, as the primary locus of *Heimat*, was thus a disciplinary space where German subjects could reaffirm their connections to the aura of the nation while, at the same time, safely stretching these contextual dependencies in pursuit of progress. It was a tool of postwar governmentality that mobilized and channeled the underlying structures of urban authenticity to produce and discipline bodies, to create intelligible, postfascist identities.

By occupying the symbolic landscapes of the postwar home and by "abjectly citing" its concomitant rituals, however, the residents of the

Hafenstraße managed to develop a novel and fundamentally subversive form of urban dwelling: an "abject domesticity" which, theoretically at least, recombined auratic and transcendent forms of authenticity in three interrelated ways.[52] First, by welcoming excluded populations into the subject-generating space of the German home, the squatters grafted "otherness" onto the auratic landscapes of the nation, and, in so doing, folded together the different iterations of auratic authenticity. Rather than being forced to choose between a potentially reactionary form of valorizing locality and a deeply romantic fascination with the embedded authenticity of the other, the squatters of the Hafenstraße used the integrative power of the home to merge locality and alterity. The abject home, in this vision, became a cosmopolitan landscape of communication, a space where one could simultaneously engage with the local and the global, where one could be here, there, and everywhere all at once. Second, by transforming the banal iterations of everyday domesticity into acts of subversion, the practices of abject domesticity enabled the residents of the Hafenstraße to embody oppositional subjectivities without being forced into romantic appropriations of the innately revolutionary other. They could transcend the dictates of national belonging while simultaneously reaffirming a sense of embedded place. Being at home, in other words, became itself an antinationalist act that facilitated closer connections with oppositional groups around the world. Finally, and most abstractly, by abjectly citing the practices of domesticity, squatters appropriated the postwar home's monopoly on controlled transcendence. As I argued above, the postwar home allowed residents to transcend their immediate sociocultural contexts but only in a heavily proscribed fashion—for example, by incorporating cutting-edge appliances like television sets into domestic environments. The abject home, by contrast, gave its occupants license to radically transcend contextualized identities while remaining grounded in an embedded lifeworld. Residents of the Hafenstraße who wished to engage in acts of subjective transcendence were not restricted to the cut-and-paste futures offered by postwar capitalism, but could instead experiment with a wide array of possible futures, all while remaining firmly embedded in an auratic environment.

Over the course of the decade-long battle over the Hafenstraße, these interrelated elements of abject domesticity manifested themselves in a number of different ways. One of the most common was the visual juxtaposition of traditional and seemingly benign evocations of nostalgic, domestic scenes with depictions of defiant abjection, which appeared in much of the imagery surrounding the squat. One image, for example, showed a group of women in ski masks happily engaging in domestic chores like vacuuming. Another particularly clever illustration transformed the RAF symbol—which consisted of a star with a machine gun—by replacing the machine gun with a power drill, thus suggesting that everyday domestic acts could themselves be revolutionary.[53] The murals that decorated the house also illustrated the novel connections between oppositional social forms and auratic lifeworlds. Indeed, the walls of the Hafenstraße were covered with symbolic representations of resistance including an image of a black cat that represented the workers' struggle in the United States, a Palestinian woman engaged in acts of resistance with the words "shit state, let's fight for our rights," Disney characters with guns, images of skyscrapers and wrecking balls, and a highly comical phrase reading "if you evict us, we're calling in the Russians."[54] In the Hafenstraße, representations of abjection and resistance were defiantly and provocatively included in the auratic space of the home thus indicating that dwelling itself could be a subversive act.

Much of the literature depicting life in the Hafenstraße also focused on themes of abject domesticity. The authors of a 1984 "Open Letter," for example, explicitly argued that the Hafenstraße provided a home for those who had been cast out by society.[55] One squatter reminisced about the crazy dogs, the noisy kids, and the open windows. It was a place with "more sense for justice than for law," a "tranquil" spot in which "the foreign (*Fremde*) found a home (*Heimat*)." "Like weeds in dog shit," the houses grew out of tainted society to provide a place where one could "live together without strangeness (*Fremdheit*)."[56] Another described how the beauty of everyday life in the Hafenstraße convinced her to militantly defend the houses from the police. When drinking coffee and making flyers, she always felt as if she were in her "own village."[57] Another clearly stated: "It doesn't matter how you feel about yourself, here you are at home, here you can be human."[58] In a set of letters reproduced in *St. Pauli Einschnitt*, two men from the former GDR expressed gratitude that the Hafenstraße offered them a place where they could finally feel at home again. In the first letter, Hans-Jürgen Neumann began abruptly with "I know who I am again! Since I visited you, I know who I am again. One from below, just like it was in the DDR." He went on to note: "I am no longer homeless, and I know that we can only live in this *Heimat* collectively."[59] As Neumann's comments—"I know who I am again!"—indicate, the downtrodden collectively became "bodies that mattered" in the crucible of the abject home. They were not relegated to a zone outside of the realm of intelligible subjectivity but included in the very center of meaningful communal life.

Throughout the conflict over the Hafenstraße, the squatters and their supporters produced a number of films, many of which clearly illustrate the practices of abject domesticity that were being developed in the squat. Indeed, the films are filled with images of everyday acts of domestic resistance:

people of various ethnic backgrounds relaxing outside of the houses, punks washing clothes, children playing in front of the barricades.[60] In the film *Terrible Houses in Danger*, for example, banal domestic practices like cooking dinner and repairing the buildings are paired with official voices declaring the squatters terrorists as well as with the sound of war drums and Native American chanting. At one point in the film, we see an image of a sign hanging from a window that reads: "the great white man has made many promises but he has only held true to one of them; namely to try and destroy us."[61] On the one hand, this sign is indicative of the West German left's romantic attachment to groups that had been excluded from modernity. On the other hand, though, it reflects the concept of abject domesticity by suggesting an analogical identity. The sign, like the practices and discourses of abject domesticity more broadly, posits a relationship of unity in difference, a creative recombination of auratic and transcendent authenticity into a technique of resistance.

Conclusion

As the preceding discussion indicates, the squatters of the Hafenstraße utilized the unique structural position of the postwar home—its role as a mediating, channeling device for the underlying structures of urban/domestic authenticity—to develop a novel set of practices and discourses that can best be understood as a form of abject domesticity. Combining auratic and transcendent forms of authenticity, they created a vision of urban space that was liberating, autonomous, and transcendent even as it remained embedded and auratic. Through processes of occupation and critical citation, the residents of the Hafenstraße both embraced the contextual specificity, the innate aura, of the German place-world *and* transcended their spatiotemporal contexts by connecting to oppositional populations around the world and by freely experimenting with new modes of transgressive behavior. Authenticity, in this reading, was thus far from the empty category that scholars such Reichardt have made it out to be. It was a structure of meaning, a mediating device that determined the ways in which people engaged with their environments. The seemingly interminable battle over the Hafenstraße was not, then, merely a conflict over living space. Nor was it simply an iteration of some larger discursive struggle over how to strategically employ the language of authenticity for the purposes of power. It was a hard-fought battle over meaning, a battle to determine the nature of urban existence and oppositional identity in the late twentieth century.

Jake P. Smith teaches Modern European History at Colorado College. He is currently working on a book manuscript based on his Ph.D. dissertation, "Strangers in a Dead Land: Redemption and Regeneration in the European Counterculture," which focuses on the experimental practices developed by European countercultures after the student movements of 1968 and argues that these groups played an important role in shifting patterns of spatial and temporal perception in the late twentieth and early twenty-first centuries.

Notes

1. "Hausbesetzungen sind nur noch Erinnerung," *Die Welt*, 13 November 1984.
2. Heinrich Lummer, "Hausbesetzungen – Probleme und Lösungen," 8 November 1984, Landesarchiv Berlin, BRep 002, 17125.
3. The youth movements of these years consisted of a wide array of (largely uncoordinated) forms of activism ranging from protests against nuclear power plants to campaigns for autonomous youth centers to the widespread squatting of empty buildings. Although most pronounced in Northern and Central Europe, similar protests also occurred in France, Italy, and Great Britain. For a good overview of these movements, see Knud Andresen and Bart van der Steen, eds., *A European Youth Revolt: European Perspectives on Youth Protest and Social Movements in the 1980s* (New York, 2016).
4. On the squatting movement in Europe, see, among others, Amantine, *Gender und Häuserkampf* (Münster, 2011); Harald Bodenschatz, *Schluss mit der Zerstörung: Stadterneuerung und städtische Opposition in West-Berlin, Amsterdam und London* (Giessen, 1983); Claudio Cattaneo and Miguel Martinez, eds., *The Squatters' Movement in Europe: Commons and Autonomy as Alternatives to Capitalism* (London, 2014); Eric Duivenvoorden, *Een voet tussen de deur: Geschiedenis van de kraakbeweging (1964–1999)* (Amsterdam, 2000); Armin Kuhn, *Vom Häuserkampf zur neoliberalen Stadt: Besetzungsbewegungen und Stadterneuerung in Berlin und Barcelona* (Münster, 2014); Alan Moore, *Occupation Culture: Art and Squatting in the City from Below* (New York, 2015); Lynn Owens, *Cracking under Pressure: Narrating the Decline of the Amsterdam Squatters' Movement* (University Park, PA, 2009); Squatting Europe Kollective, *Squatting in Europe: Radical Spaces, Urban Struggles* (New York, 2013); Bart van der Steen and Ask Katzeff, eds., *The City is Ours: Squatting and Autonomous Movements in Europe from the 1970s to the Present* (Oakland, CA, 2014); Andreas Suttner, *"Beton brennt": Hausbesetzer und Selbstverwaltung im Berlin, Wien und Zürich der 80er Jahre* (Vienna, 2011); Alexander Vasudevan, *Metropolitan Preoccupations: The Spatial Politics of Squatting in Berlin* (Malden, MA, 2015).
5. George Katsiaficas, *The Subversion of Politics: European Autonomous Social Movements and the Decolonization of Everyday Life* (Atlantic Highlands, NJ, 1997), 128.
6. "Dr. Terror's House of Horrors," *Bild*, 15 November 1987, reproduced in *10 Meter Ohne Kopf*, 44, [Rote Flora, Box 09.400, HH Hafenstraße I]. RAF refers to the West German terrorist group the Red Army Faction.

7. Carl-Heinz Mallet, *Die Leute von der Hafenstraße: Über eine andere Art zu leben* (Hamburg, 2000), 176. See also Bürgerschaft Drucksache 10/56 (13.7.82), Abgeordneten Klimke (CDU), Staatsarchiv Hamburg, 136-1, 4927.
8. See, for example, Heiko Artkämpfer, *Hausbesetzer, Hausbesitzer, Hausfriedensbruch* (Berlin, 1995).
9. Thomas Osterkorn, "Hafenstraße: Senat legt die Glacehandschuhe ab," *Hamburger Abendblatt*, 10 August 1985.
10. "Wunder oder Illusion: Hamburg, Hafenstraße, Hafenstraßenbild," *Spiegel*, 23 November 1987.
11. Some of these themes have been covered in the existing literature on the Hafenstraße. See, for example, Joist Groll, "Der Hamburger Hafenstraßenkonflikt und der Geisterkrieg um die Vergangenheit," *Zeitschrift des Vereins für Hamburgische Geschichte* 91 (2005): 133–158; Michael Herrmann, ed., *Hafenstrasse: Chronik und Analysen eines Konfliktes* (Hamburg, 1987); Werner Lehne, Die *Konflikt um die Hafenstrasse: Kriminalitätsdiskurse im Kontext symbolischer Politik* (Pfaffenweiler, 1994).
12. Throughout this essay, I will be focusing on discourses and practices of authenticity connected to domestic spaces. My use of domesticity is somewhat heterodox. Rather than restricting the concept to gendered practices of housework such as childcare, cleaning, and cooking, I use domesticity to refer to a broader feeling of being-at-home. This expands the traditional meaning of the term both spatially and in terms of practice. Housework, according to my reading, is certainly part of domesticity but so are intimate conversations between friends and other forms of non-familial conviviality. Furthermore, given the expansive notions of being-at-home practiced by the West German squatting milieu, these domestic activities took place well beyond the traditional walls of the home. This blurring of the boundaries between private and public was, after all, one of the signature elements of radical leftist practices during these years.
13. See, among others, Pascal Eitler, *Das beratene Selbst: zur Genealogie der Therapeutisierung in den "langen" Siebzigern* (Bielefeld, 2011); Sven Reichardt, *Authentizität und Gemeinschaft: Linksalternatives Leben in den siebziger und frühen achtziger Jahren* (Berlin, 2014); Sven Reichardt and Detlef Siegfried, eds., *Das Alternative Milieu: Antibürgerlicher Lebensstil und linke Politik in der Bundesrepublik Deutschland und Europa, 1968–1983* (Göttingen, 2010).
14. Reichardt, *Authentizität und Gemeinschaft*, 57–71.
15. On "habitus," see Pierre Bourdieu, *Outline of a Theory of Practice* (Cambridge, 1977). On authenticity as an empty category, see Reichardt, *Authentizität und Gemeinschaft*, 67. On the idea of "lifeworlds," see Michael Jackson, *Lifeworlds: Essays in Existential Anthropology* (Chicago, 2012).
16. For a classic statement on the tendency of structural categories to encompass multiple meanings, see Claude Levi-Strauss, "The Structural Study of Myth," *The Journal of American Folklore* 68, no. 270 (1955): 428–444.
17. On Wilhelm Reich and the German Left, see Joachim Häberlen, "Feeling like a Child: Dreams and Practices of Sexuality in the West-German Alternative Left During the Long 1970s," *The Journal for the History of Sexuality* 25, no. 2 (2016): 219–245; Dagmar Herzog, *Sex after Fascism: Memory and Morality in Twentieth-Century*

Germany (Princeton, NJ, 2005). On postwar urban planning as a technique for creating postfascist identities, see Sandra Wagner-Conzelmann, *Die Interbau 1957 in Berlin: Stadt von heute—Stadt von morgen: Städtebau und Gesellschaftskritik der 50er Jahre* (Petersberg, 2007).

18. On the concept of aura, see Walter Benjamin, "The Work of Art in the Age of Mechanical Reproduction," in *Illuminations*, ed. Hannah Arendt (New York, 1968); Miriam Hansen, "Benjamin's Aura," *Critical Inquiry* 34, no. 2 (2008): 336–375.
19. On the Left's fascination with the authentic other, see Detlef Siegfried, *Time Is on my Side: Konsum und Politik in der westdeutschen Jugendkultur der 60er Jahre* (Göttingen, 2006); Quinn Slobodian, *Foreign Front: Third World Politics in Sixties West Germany* (Durham, NC, 2012).
20. On the relationship between structural categories and their actualization in the world, see Marshall Sahlins, *Islands of History* (Chicago, 1985).
21. See Claude Levi-Strauss, *The Savage Mind* (Chicago, 1966).
22. Leonie Ossowski, *Wilhelm Meisters Abschied* (Weinheim, 1982), 123. All translations are mine unless otherwise noted.
23. For a discussion of the ways in which radical leftists in West Germany sought to demarcate themselves from capitalist values, see Joachim Häberlen and Jake P. Smith, "Struggling for Feelings: The Politics of Emotions in the Radical New Left in West Germany, c. 1968–84," *Contemporary European History* 23, no. 4 (2014): 615–637.
24. On the turn toward militancy, see, among many others: Martin Klimke, Jacco Pekelder, and Joachim Scharloth, eds., *Between Prague Spring and French May: Opposition and Revolt in Europe, 1960–1980* (New York, 2011); Wolfgang Kraushaar, *Die Bombe im Jüdischen Gemeindehaus* (Hamburg, 2005); Jeremy Varon, *Bringing the War Home: The Weather Underground, the Red Army Faction, and the Revolutionary Violence in the Sixties and Seventies* (Berkeley, CA, 2004).
25. See, for example, Johannes Feil, *Wohngruppe, Kommune, Grossfamilie: Gegenmodelle zur Kleinfamilie* (Reinbek bei Hamburg, 1972); Reichardt, *Authentizität und Gemeinschaft*; David Templin, *Freizeit ohne Kontrollen: Die Jugendzentrumsbewegung in der Bundesrepublik der 1970er Jahre* (Göttingen, 2015).
26. Quoted in Reichardt, *Authentizität und Gemeinschaft*, 383.
27. Annette, "Was halt mich hier bloß?" *St. Pauli Einschnitt* (Hamburg, 2000), 13.
28. Mallet, *Die Leute von der Hafenstraße: Über eine andere Art zu leben*, 172–173.
29. "Rote Ernte," *Wiener*, 1 February 1987.
30. "Bauen," *St. Pauli Einschnitt*, 22.
31. Dorit van Aken, Monika Bischoff-Gombert, Martin Schirmacher, Simone Borgstede, Claus Petersen, Mathias Böge, Martin Junk, and Annette, "Annäherung," *St. Pauli Einschnitt*, 17.
32. "Rote Ernte," *Wiener*, 1 February 1987.
33. *10 Meter Ohne Kopf*, 14.
34. Alfred Stümper, "Antifastische Arbeit—Teil autonomer Politik," (November 1986). Reproduced in *Gewalt Gegen Frauen*.
35. Thomas Ruhmöller, "Hafenstraße: Peinliche Polizei-Panne" *Hamburger Abendblatt*, 13 October 1986.

36. Radio broadcast from 11 June 1987, *Hier Spricht Radio Hafenstraße*, 19.
37. "Deutsche Bank und deutsches Geld morden mit in aller Welt," November 1989. Reproduced in *StaatsTerrorismus Hat Kontinuität: Lever Dot as Slav* (1990) 15, [Rote Flora, Box 09.400 HH Hafenstraße I].
38. Monika Sigmund and Marily Stroux, *Zu bunt: Wandbilder in der Hafenstraße* (Hamburg, 1996), 86.
39. "Unser Bürgermeister heisst Klaus Störtebeker," [Rote Flora, Hafenstrasse Flugblätter 88–89].
40. "Hönkel, Grummel, Hönkel, Grummel: Der illegal Sender 'Radio Hafenstraße,'" *Spiegel*, 23 November 1987.
41. For an early formulation of this idea, see Herbert Marcuse, "Political Preface 1966," *Eros and Civilization: A Philosophical Inquiry into Freud* (Boston, MA, 1974). For Marcuse, the traditional locus of authentic revolutionary action was represented by the working classes. In conditions of late capitalism, however, the working class had been entirely incorporated into consumer culture and thus could no longer be counted on to serve as the primary carriers of revolutionary consciousness. As an alternative, Marcuse suggested that the European Left look to build alliances with third world liberation movements and with the civil rights movement in the United States.
42. On the concept of "re-embedding," see Anthony Giddens, *The Consequences of Modernity* (Stanford, CA, 1990).
43. *10 Meter Ohne Kopf*, 14. Capitalization as in original.
44. Robert Pogue Harrison "Hic Jacet," in *Landscape and Power*, ed. W. J. T. Mitchell (Chicago, 2002), 353.
45. On the concept of the boom years and the structural effects engendered by their conclusion, see Anselm Doering-Manteuffel and Lutz Raphael, *Nach dem Boom: Perspektiven auf die Zeitgeschichte seit 1970* (Göttingen, 2008); Anselm Doering-Manteuffel, Lutz Raphael, and Thomas Schlemmer, eds., *Vorgeschichte der Gegenwart: Dimensionen des Strukturbruchs nach dem Boom* (Göttingen, 2016). On nostalgia and the memory boom in this period, see among many others: Aleida Assmann, "Transformations of the Modern Time Regime," in *Breaking Up Time: Negotiating the Borders between Present, Past, and Future*, ed. Chris Lorenz and Berger Bevernage (Göttingen 2013); Svetlana Boym, *The Future of Nostalgia* (New York, 2001); Hans Ulrich Gumbrecht, *Our Broad Present: Time and Contemporary Culture* (New York, 2014); Andreas Huyssen, *Present Pasts: Urban Palimpsests and the Politics of Memory* (Stanford, CA, 2003); Rudy Koshar, *Germany's Transient Pasts: Historical Preservation and National Memory in Twentieth Century Germany* (Chapel Hill, NC, 1998).
46. For a general discussion of the place-world and the differences between space and place, see Edward Casey, *Getting Back into Place: Toward a Renewed Understanding of the Place-World* (Bloomington, IN, 2009).
47. See, for example, Greg Castillo, *Cold War on the Home Front: The Soft Power of Midcentury Design* (Minneapolis, MN, 2010); Johannes von Moltke, *No Place Like Home: Locations of Heimat in German Cinema* (Berkeley, CA, 2005); and the essays in the April 2005 special issue of *The Journal of Contemporary History*, "Domestic Dreamworlds: Notions of Home in Post 1945 Europe."

48. Paul Betts, *The Authority of Everyday Objects: A Cultural History of West German Industrial Design* (Berkeley, CA, 2007), 16.
49. Celia Applegate, *A Nation of Provincials: The German Idea of Heimat* (Berkeley, CA, 1990), 242. Although difficult to translate, *Heimat* refers to a German vision of the domestic place-world. For a classic statement on the relationship between locality and conceptions of national identity, see Alon Confino, *The Nation as a Local Metaphor: Württemberg, Imperial Germany, and National Memory, 1871–1918* (Chapel Hill, NC, 1997).
50. In her book *Bodies that Matter*, Butler argues that intelligible selves, or bodies that matter, are produced and reproduced through banal, everyday performances of normal identity such as those that take place in domestic settings. Dominant power structures are thus naturalized through the repetitive, humdrum actions undertaken by people in their everyday lives. In the process of producing these putatively normal categories of being, though, other bodies and objects are relegated to the unintelligible realm of the abject. "The abject designates here precisely those 'unlivable' and 'uninhabitable' zones of social life which are nevertheless densely populated by those who do not enjoy the status of the subject" (Butler, *Bodies that Matter: On the Discursive Limits of "Sex,"* [New York, 1993], 3). Thus, people assume intelligible identities both by embodying and performing discourses sanctioned by power and by disavowing their connections to the abject.
51. For an excellent discussion of the ways in which domestic spaces in postwar West Germany facilitated a controlled engagement with capitalist modernity, see Erica Carter, *How German Is She? Postwar West German Reconstruction and the Consuming Woman* (Ann Arbor, MI, 1997).
52. According to Butler, it is possible to disrupt the regimes of normalization by abjectly "citing" them. Citation, she argues, should be understood "*as an insubordination that appears to take place within the very terms of the original, and which calls into the question the power of origination,*" (Butler, *Bodies that Matter*, 45; italics in original).
53. *Hafenstrasse Chronologie Eines Konflikts*, 5.
54. For images and information on the art of the Hafenstraße, see Sigmund and Stroux, *Zu Bunt: Wandbilder in der Hafenstraße*.
55. "Offener Brief." Reproduced in *Gewalt Gegen Frauen*.
56. Simone Borgstede, "Liebeserklärung," *St. Pauli Einschnitt*, 5.
57. Annette, "Was halt mich hier bloß?" *St. Pauli Einschnitt*, 12–13.
58. Simone Borgestede, "Volksküche," *St. Pauli Einschnitt*, 19.
59. "Zwei Briefe aus Saalfeld (ehemals DDR)," *St. Pauli Einchnitt*, 37.
60. See, for example, *Die Augen schließen um besser zu sehen* (Hamburg, 1986) and the compilation *St. Pauli Hafenstraße Nr. 7* (Hamburg, 1995).
61. *Terrible Houses in Danger* (Hamburg, 1985).

Bibliography

Amantine. *Gender und Häuserkampf.* Münster: Unrast Verlag, 2011.
Andresen, Knud, and Bart van der Steen, eds. *A European Youth Revolt: European Perspectives on Youth Protest and Social Movements in the 1980s.* New York: Palgrave, 2016.

Applegate, Celia. *A Nation of Provincials: The German Idea of Heimat*. Berkeley: University of California Press, 1990.
Artkämpfer, Heiko. *Hausbesetzer, Hausbesitzer, Hausfriedensbruch*. Berlin: Springer Verlag, 1995.
Assmann, Aleida. "Transformations of the Modern Time Regime." In *Breaking Up Time: Negotiating the Borders between Present, Past, and Future*, edited by Chris Lorenz and Berger Bevernage. Göttingen: Vandenhoeck & Ruprecht, 2013.
Benjamin, Walter. "The Work of Art in the Age of Mechanical Reproduction." In *Illuminations*, edited by Hannah Arendt. New York: Schocken Books, 1968.
Betts, Paul. *The Authority of Everyday Objects: A Cultural History of West German Industrial Design*. Berkeley: University of California Press, 2007.
Bodenschatz, Harald. *Schluss mit der Zerstörung: Stadterneuerung und städtische Opposition in West-Berlin, Amsterdam und London*. Giessen: Anabas, 1983.
Bourdieu, Pierre. *Outline of a Theory of Practice*. Cambridge: Cambridge University Press, 1977.
Boym, Svetlana. *The Future of Nostalgia*. New York: Basic Books, 2001.
Butler, Judith. *Bodies that Matter: On the Discursive Limits of "Sex."* New York: Routledge, 1993.
Carter, Erica. *How German Is She? Postwar West German Reconstruction and the Consuming Woman*. Ann Arbor: University of Michigan Press, 1997.
Casey, Edward. *Getting Back into Place: Toward a Renewed Understanding of the Place-World*. Bloomington: Indiana University Press, 2009.
Castillo, Greg. *Cold War on the Home Front: The Soft Power of Midcentury Design*. Minneapolis: University of Minnesota Press, 2010.
Cattaneo, Claudio, and Miguel Martinez, eds. *The Squatters' Movement in Europe: Commons and Autonomy as Alternatives to Capitalism*. London: Pluto, 2014.
Confino, Alon. *The Nation as a Local Metaphor: Württemberg, Imperial Germany, and National Memory, 1871–1918*. Chapel Hill: University of North Carolina Press, 1997.
Die Augen schließen um besser zu sehen. Hamburg: Medien Pädagogik Archiv, 1986.
Doering-Manteuffel, Anselm, and Lutz Raphael. *Nach dem Boom: Perspektiven auf die Zeitgeschichte seit 1970*. Göttingen: Vandenhoeck & Ruprecht, 2008.
Doering-Manteuffel, Anselm, Lutz Raphael, and Thomas Schlemmer, eds. *Vorgeschichte der Gegenwart: Dimensionen des Strukturbruchs nach dem Boom*. Göttingen: Vandenhoeck & Ruprecht, 2016.
Duivenvoorden, Eric. *Een voet tussen de deur: Geschiedenis van de kraakbeweging (1964–1999)*. Amsterdam: De Arbeiderspers, 2000.
Eitler, Pascal. *Das beratene Selbst: zur Genealogie der Therapeutisierung in den "langen" Siebzigern*. Bielefeld: transcript, 2011.
Feil, Johannes. *Wohngruppe, Kommune, Grossfamilie: Gegenmodelle zur Kleinfamilie*. Reinbek bei Hamburg: Rowohlt, 1972.
Giddens, Anthony. *The Consequences of Modernity*. Stanford, CA: Stanford University Press, 1990.
Groll, Joist. "Der Hamburger Hafenstraßenkonflikt und der Geisterkrieg um die Vergangenheit." *Zeitschrift des Vereins für Hamburgische Geschichte* 91 (2005): 133–158.

Gumbrecht, Hans Ulrich. *Our Broad Present: Time and Contemporary Culture*. New York: Columbia University Press, 2014.
Häberlen, Joachim. "Feeling Like a Child: Dreams and Practices of Sexuality in the West-German Alternative Left During the Long 1970s." *The Journal for the History of Sexuality* 25, no. 2 (2016): 219–245.
Häberlen, Joachim, and Jake P. Smith. "Struggling for Feelings: The Politics of Emotions in the Radical New Left in West Germany, c. 1968–84." In "Emotions in Protest Movements in Europe since 1917," edited by Joachim Häberlen and Russell A. Spinney, special issue. *Contemporary European History* 23, no. 4 (2014): 615–637.
Hansen, Miriam. "Benjamin's Aura." *Critical Inquiry* 34, no. 2 (2008): 336–375.
Harrison, Robert Pogue. "Hic Jacet." In *Landscape and Power*, edited by W. J. T. Mitchell, 349–364. Chicago: University of Chicago Press, 2002
Herrmann, Michael, ed. *Hafenstrasse: Chronik und Analysen eines Konfliktes*. Hamburg: Verlag am Galgenburg, 1987.
Herzog, Dagmar. *Sex after Fascism: Memory and Morality in Twentieth-Century Germany*. Princeton, NJ: Princeton University Press, 2005.
Huyssen, Andreas. *Present Pasts: Urban Palimpsests and the Politics of Memory*. Stanford, CA: Stanford University Press, 2003.
Jackson, Michael. *Lifeworlds: Essays in Existential Anthropology*. Chicago: University of Chicago Press, 2012.
Katsiaficas, George. *The Subversion of Politics: European Autonomous Social Movements and the Decolonization of Everyday Life*. Atlantic Highlands, NJ: Humanities Press, 1997.
Klimke, Martin, Jacco Pekelder, and Joachim Scharloth, eds. *Between Prague Spring and French May: Opposition and Revolt in Europe, 1960–1980*. New York: Berghahn Books, 2011.
Koshar, Rudy. *Germany's Transient Pasts: Historical Preservation and National Memory in Twentieth Century Germany*. Chapel Hill: University of North Carolina Press, 1998.
Kraushaar, Wolfgang. *Die Bombe im Jüdischen Gemeindehaus*. Hamburg: Hamburger Edition, 2005.
Kuhn, Armin. *Vom Häuserkampf zur neoliberalen Stadt: Besetzungsbewegungen und Stadterneuerung in Berlin und Barcelona*. Münster: Westfälisches Dampfboot, 2014.
Lehne, Werner. *Die Konflikt um die Hafenstrasse: Kriminalitätsdiskurse im Kontext symbolischer Politik*. Pfaffenweiler: Centaurus, 1994.
Levi-Strauss, Claude. *The Savage Mind*. Chicago: University of Chicago Press, 1966.
———. "The Structural Study of Myth." *The Journal of American Folklore* 68, no. 270 (1955): 428–444.
Mallet, Carl-Heinz. *Die Leute von der Hafenstraße: Über eine andere Art zu leben*. Hamburg: Lutz Schulenburg, 2000.
Marcuse, Herbert. *Eros and Civilization: A Philosophical Inquiry into Freud*. Boston, MA: Beacon Press, 1974.
von Moltke, Johannes. *No Place like Home: Locations of Heimat in German Cinema*. Berkeley: University of California Press, 2005.
Moore, Alan. *Occupation Culture: Art and Squatting in the City from Below*. New York: Minor Compositions, 2015.
Ossowski, Leonie. *Wilhelm Meister's Abschied*. Weinheim: Beltz Verlag, 1982.

Owens, Lynn. *Cracking under Pressure: Narrating the Decline of the Amsterdam Squatters' Movement*. University Park: Pennsylvania State University Press, 2009.
Reichardt, Sven. *Authentizität und Gemeinschaft: Linksalternatives Leben in den siebziger und frühen achtziger Jahren*. Berlin: Surkamp Verlag, 2014.
Reichardt, Sven, and Detlef Siegfried, eds. *Das Alternative Milieu: Antibürgerlicher Lebensstil und linke Politik in der Bundesrepublik Deutschland und Europa, 1968–1983*. Göttingen: Wallstein, 2010.
Sahlins, Marshall. *Islands of History*. Chicago: University of Chicago Press, 1985.
Siegfried, Detlef. *Time Is on My Side: Konsum und Politik in der westdeutschen Jugendkultur der 60er Jahre*. Göttingen: Wallstein, 2006.
Sigmund, Monika, and Marily Stroux. *Zu bunt: Wandbilder in der Hafenstraße*. Hamburg: St. Pauli Archiv, 1996.
Slobodian, Quinn. *Foreign Front: Third World Politics in Sixties West Germany*. Durham, NC: Duke University Press, 2012.
Squatting Europe Kollective. *Squatting in Europe: Radical Spaces, Urban Struggles*. New York: Minor Compositions, 2013.
van der Steen, Bart, and Ask Katzeff, eds. *The City is Ours: Squatting and Autonomous Movements in Europe from the 1970s to the Present*. Oakland, CA: PM Press, 2014.
St. Pauli Einschnitt. Hamburg: Hafenrand verein für selbstbestimmtes Leben und Wohnen in St. Pauli e.V., 2000.
St. Pauli Hafenstraße Nr. 7. Hamburg: Medien Pädagokik Archiv, 1995.
Suttner, Andreas. *"Beton brennt": Hausbesetzer und Selbstverwaltung im Berlin, Wien und Zürich der 80er Jahre*. Vienna: Lit, 2011.
Templin, David. *Freizeit ohne Kontrollen: Die Jugendzentrumsbewegung in der Bundesrepublik der 1970er Jahre*. Göttingen: Wallstein Verlag, 2015.
Terrible Houses in Danger. Hamburg: Medien Pädagokik Archiv, 1985.
Varon, Jeremy. *Bringing the War Home: The Weather Underground, the Red Army Faction, and the Revolutionary Violence in the Sixties and Seventies*. Berkeley: University of California Press, 2004.
Vasudevan, Alexander. *Metropolitan Preoccupations: The Spatial Politics of Squatting in Berlin*. Malden, MA: Wiley-Blackwell, 2015.
Wagner-Conzelmann, Sandra. *Die Interbau 1957 in Berlin: Stadt von heute—Stadt von morgen: Städtebau und Gesellschaftskritik der 50er Jahre*. Petersberg: Michael Imhof Verlag, 2007.

Afterword

Concluding Thoughts
Authenticity's Visual Turn

Sara Blaylock

Politics as Image

Undoubtedly the most prominent icon of the Cold War's dramatic (and by all accounts unpredicted) end remains the dismantling of the Berlin Wall on 9 November 1989.[1] When visual culture scholar Sunil Manghani calls the fall of the wall one of the first "image-events" of the contemporary era, he points not just to the significance of the global circulation of the documentation of this event, but also to its importance in asserting the power of the visual to define political rupture.[2] The jubilant bodies of people celebrating atop one of modern Europe's most entrenched defensive icons clearly contested state power. These East and West Germans also laid claim to a new kind of subjectivity—postcommunist, postideological, postdivision. The fall of the wall came to represent the union of East and West. Its documentation, that is to say its image, dramatically reformulated the East bloc's political power. The visual markers of that loss of power, which circulated globally, made it appear unequivocal.

The fall of the Berlin Wall remade the optics of the Cold War. While certainly the events of 9 November 1989 resulted from years of political assertion, in fact it only took a matter of hours for the visual impact of this event to solidify the global change that had been long since demanded.

The capacity of the visual to embody and represent a new subjectivity accelerates the political claim of defiant or change-seeking subjects. Quite simply, visual cues make manifest the difference between the "us" and the "them," whether these schematics define the revolutionary and the oppressor, the punk and the square, or some mark along a social continuum. The point is that the politics of subjectivity are enacted with great consequence in visual form. Similarly, authenticity—the ideal of autonomous subjectification—produces a unique visual language that counters or contests hegemonic discourse. Living a full and meaningful life necessitates a feeling of authenticity, which is typically visually marked. These visual signs, from hairstyle to dress to public affect to the ways that one inhabits space, become cues for both the subject and the interpellator. How we look can help us to conform to, resist, or redefine the expectations of our onlookers.

If optics count not just in defining the one-on-one encounter, but also in the definition of the politics of that encounter, then how might the larger implications of the visual cultures of the twelve case studies examined in this volume be defined? How did the externalization of political subjectivity contribute to people's claims to authenticity and difference? Whereas I will not examine the particulars of any of this volume's examples, these two framing questions insinuate the role that the visual played in each. My visual turn implicitly supports the arguments each author makes with regard to the formation of and claim to a new political subjectivity, even as it suggests an alternative direction of analysis.[3]

Interpellation and the Right to Look

As Louis Althusser demonstrated, simply the act of hailing an individual turns that person into a subject.[4] This encounter is the rudiment of interpellation. In other words, a person becomes a subject (i.e., a type or class of person) when another subject recognizes her as such. Althusser defined the ability to name a subject as central to the power of ideology. In this account, the very act of naming a person as a specific subject compels that person to internalize and thus conform to that subjectification. To this theory of subject formation, I wish to emphasize the implication of the visual in that encounter—this is to say, the inclusion, even the necessity, of the visual in the formation of a subject. The assessment inherent to interpellation is for most a principally visual encounter insofar as it begins with seeing, recognizing, and identifying a person's place within the seer's limited set of expectations (as well as preferences) for personhood, gender, race, ethnicity, age, ability, beauty, fashion, and so on. Even for the non-sighted, the primacy of sight in the modern world has produced a textual and verbal language of description that prioritizes external appearance as a primary qualification for categorization.[5] Thus, the moment when a person who is traditionally hailed as one thing resists or retools that interpellation, she engages in a confrontation against hegemony—or, at the very least against the conventions of hegemonic culture. A homosexual woman is typically hailed as heterosexual in East Germany, and begins to bear her sexual identification as a lesbian publicly. When another recognizes her difference—even if that difference is ultimately deemed unacceptable—the woman represents a radical break, and becomes a new kind of subject. A feminist in the United Kingdom or West Germany presents a new mode of identifying herself within the movement. When others take the fact of her subjectivity (if not its politics) seriously, they initiate an expanded definition of womanhood, femininity, and political power. The same logic may be applied to objects and space. On 9 November 1989, the Berlin Wall was no longer an "anti-fascist protection rampart," but a stage and a canvas. Likewise, activists redefine the shape of public life by inhabiting it anew—from politicizing domestic spaces to claiming public ones for mass assembly.

Althusser defines encountering difference as a "swerve"—a description, which accounts for both the mental shift and the imbalance that such confrontations often produce.[6] Combined, Althusser's theories of interpellation and the generative impact of the swerve help to explain the continued and unanticipated ("aleatory") effects of difference on an adapting society.[7] Of course, difference describes a fundamental aspect of authenticity explored in this volume. When Althusser writes that "every accomplished fact, even an election, like all the necessity and reason we can derive from it, is only a provisional encounter," he opens up the possibility for a limitless and self-perpetuating world of new subjectification wrought in the encounter of difference, as well as in an evolving and contextual definition of authenticity.[8] Indeed, because ideology encourages people to categorize, classify, and make sense of the people, places, and things they encounter, the yearning to identify difference within a familiar frame of reference can initiate the undoing of oppressive social power.

The visual culture scholar Nicholas Mirzoeff's recent and significant claim to defining a politics of visuality through counterdiscourses (what he terms countervisuality) offers a methodology for describing the union of a swerving Althusserian interpellation with the power of the visual in the creation of a politics of authenticity.[9] Mirzoeff's metaphorical call for "the right to look" defines the act of a person looking where one is not meant to look as a kind of political action: "The right to look claims autonomy, not individualism or voyeurism, but the claim to a political subjectivity and collectivity."[10] Here, "looking" describes not just seeing, but redefining the rules of culture, space, and sovereignty: a gay man in France in the 1970s claims the right to look by participating in a political movement. At the same time, Mirzoeff's framework invites the political agency of subjects to claim the right to be looked at on their own terms: a gay man in France in the 1970s claims the right to look by being seen as a participant in a political movement. At best, the right to look is a "right to the real"—an action of reciprocation, exchange, equality, and humanity.[11] The real, like authenticity, is political subjectification or a way of living that is produced autonomously. It depends upon the "swerve" insofar as it invites the unanticipated. In other words, a political encounter does not necessarily know how to, or even aspire to, control its outcomes. It is the unknowability inherent to one subject meeting another that perhaps makes the most impactful political or social shifts.

The impact of a political or social change is often most immediately visibly marked. I call these markers "image vocabularies." West German squatters made their subject positions known by inhabiting and making strange the urban space of Hamburg. Autonomists in Italy dressed as Native Americans to reference a common cultural vocabulary in a unique and unexpected context. In both cases, visual intervention contested the definitions of normalcy. Even more explicitly discursive groups, such as the consciousness-raising organizations of women in the United Kingdom and West Germany, or the lesbians in East Germany and gay rights activists in France, advanced their political claim through visible contestation. Of course discourse is not simply talk, but the performance of talk with all its attendant optics, including the circulation of speech in autonomously produced publications, posters, and films or in mass protests that take to the streets. Similarly, the visual artifacts of the post-1968 humor in Czechoslovakia, such as cartoons and television programs, most certainly helped to disseminate, expand, and ultimately normalize this new brand of humor.[12] The visual, too, accompanies music—arguably turning a sound into a scene. One wonders, then, how much more immediately worrisome the look of West German punks or Romanian metal heads and hippies were to their respective governments than were their lyrics or the quality of their music. The visual is the aggressor for or against uniformity, and is thus the site of greatest contestation and the origin of political advancement.

Whereas policing normalcy is generally described as the work of governance, several of the examples in this volume likewise demonstrate how group dynamics might likewise lend themselves to interpersonal observation.[13] For example, the British and the German cases explored by Kate Mahoney and Jane Freeland clearly articulate how well-intentioned activists themselves policed definitions of feminism. Antoine Idier describes the challenges the gay rights movement of a 1970s France faced in terms of its celebration of individuation, a controversy within classical Marxist thought. Similarly, Angelo Ventrone delineates conflicts within the dynamic scope of radical politics and their relation to a history of activism in a 1960s and 1970s Italy.

Perhaps Benjamin Möckel's descriptions of the trappings of the commercialization of political movements illustrate most succinctly the worry that group members in a variety of subcultures face vis-à-vis the risk of diluting a movement, and ultimately "selling out" down the road. The metrics of authenticity are thus paradoxical: both improvisational and unpredictable, but nevertheless also in need of legibility—a characteristic that makes them vulnerable to institutionalization, especially in capitalist systems.

An Optic Union

Taken as a whole, the contributions to this volume contest the Cold War's geopolitically inscribed divisions. Specifically, one pertinent contribution of a volume of this nature resides in the way its authors demonstrate that citizens on either side of the Cold War divide asserted and maintained a political agency with a variety of real material traces. In other words, the image vocabularies of punks, metal heads, and hippies, feminists, squatters, and other activists for social justice, influenced, and even sometimes redefined, the language of hegemonic culture. That argument may be made even plainer in analysis of the impact and import of visual culture, including historical and cultural transfer or comparison. In fact, it is interesting that the politics of authenticity often looked alike across the Iron Curtain. Nevertheless, to raise one example, West German versus East German punks produced image vocabularies with highly differing and contextually specific registers. Dwelling on a parallel trajectory thus risks a significant dilution through the production of aggregate claims based on surface, which tend to prioritize the Western perspective over others.[14] Indeed, to this point dominant narratives of the culture of the East bloc tend not to account for the kinds of citizen-led, and often state-critical, impacts on official culture that, for example, Zsófia Lóránd describes in terms of women's groups in Yugoslavia or Barış Yörümez offers in terms of humor in the former Czechoslovakia. These examples help to dismantle the binaries of official versus unofficial culture or dissident versus conformist behavior that still define the Cold War-era in the common vernacular. They likewise contest the traditional refrain that communism either fell under the weight of its own inadequacy or was defeated by the triumph of the free market.[15]

In contrast, the impact of subcultures or political movements on normative culture forms an important part of the story of the Cold War's "free West." To wit, Möckel's text on aid concerts and protest music demonstrates the unintended, if cynical, impacts of the countercultures of the 1960s on a burgeoning neoliberal, global identity. In other words, the absorption of politics of authenticity—and especially their image vocabularies—into everyday culture is now understood as a predictable, if unavoidable, outcome of capitalism.[16] From the conversion of punk into a fashion style to the cultural cache of protest movements being used to define a brand, nonnormative and critical culture in the West ran (and continues to run) the risk of commercial appropriation. Of course, on the other hand, the absorption of different political subjectivities and the invitation of a diversity of self-presentation into the Western cultural vernacular remains a paramount achievement of Western democracy.[17] Similarly discussion of the role that mass media played in the formation and dissemination of protest movements in the West—certainly sometimes to their detriment—would help to clarify fundamental differences between the development of alternative subjects in Western versus East bloc contexts.[18]

What remains to be interrogated further are the ways in which subcultures and political movements impacted the hegemonic cultures of the East bloc. Certainly state socialist governments also assimilated counter and critical culture into the mainstream.[19] Tracing the material effects—the ambiguities in national culture that reveal the influence of experimental culture—across film, design, and art, as well as their impacts on national discourse, would contribute a great deal to understanding how governments on this side of the Iron Curtain accommodated or prohibited a greater inclusivity in mass culture. Indeed, it is quite important to consider how those accommodations represent a spectrum of compromise and control.

It is then within the realms of subculture, and their incorporation into everyday life, that the "passing of mass utopia in East and West" that Susan Buck-Morss has theorized in her path-breaking research on the rise and fall of the Cold War era's two grand powers are best materialized.[20] The research in this volume furthers Buck-Morss's brilliant claim that the Cold War represented a final test and ultimate failure of predictable, mass forms of culture, itself a utopian ideal of modernity.[21] The desire for something different—to be authentic—was a shared desire, and in hindsight an inevitable outcome, for citizens on both sides of the Cold War divide who no longer wished to be hailed as anticipated, classifiable, and predictable subjects. That union remains optically inscribed on historical memory in the image of a crumbling Berlin Wall—an ideological dissolution made material, a repair through rupture.

Sara Blaylock is Assistant Professor of Art History at the University of Minnesota at Duluth. To date, the bulk of Blaylock's research has concerned the experimental art, film, and visual culture of the German Democratic

Republic during the 1980s. Broader interests include the culture of the Cold War East and West, fiction and documentary film from the East bloc, and global histories of modernism and postmodernism. She received her Ph.D. in Visual Studies from the University of California at Santa Cruz in 2017. Recent publications include "Bringing the War Home to the United States and East Germany: *In the Year of the Pig* and *Pilots in Pajamas*," *Cinema Journal* 56, no. 4 (2017); "Being the Woman They Wanted Her to Be: Cornelia Schleime Performs her Stasi File," *Gradhiva* 24 (2016); and "A Material Revolt: Body Portraits in the Prenzlauer Berg of the 1980s," which appeared in the exhibition catalogue for *Gegenstimmen: Kunst in der DDR 1976–1989* (2016).

Notes

1. On the unexpected, but nevertheless unsurprising collapse of the Soviet Union, see, for example, Alexei Yurchak, *Everything Was Forever Until It Was No More: The Last Soviet Generation* (Princeton, NJ, 2005).
2. Sunil Manghani, *Image Critique and the Fall of the Berlin Wall* (Bristol, UK, 2008), 30. The field of Visual Culture Studies also asks the question of image presence, that is to say, the power of images to impart messages beyond the intention of their makers, and often unconsciously absorbed by their recipients. This power of an image is described by Keith Moxey as "what comes to meet us, rather than what we bring to the encounter." See Keith Moxey, "Visual Studies and the Iconic Turn," *Journal of Visual Culture* 7, no. 2 (2008): 133. Understanding the fall of the Berlin Wall as an image-event likewise allows for the spontaneity of this event to persist and evolve as an outcome of its circulated images.
3. Scholars use the phrase "visual turn" to describe a significant change in scholarship in the 1990s toward interrogation of the role of the visual as not simply a reflection, but a driver and a representation of social and political change. See, for example, Martin Jay, "The Visual Turn: The Advent of Visual Culture," *Journal of Visual Culture* 1, no. 1 (2002): 87–93. See, also, Svetlana Alpers, "The Visual Culture Questionnaire," *October* 77 (1996): 25–70.
4. Louis Althusser, "Ideology and Ideological State Apparatuses," in *Lenin and Philosophy and Other Essays* (New York, 2001), 85–126.
5. On the relationship between the standardization of visual imagery and the creation of the modern subject in the late nineteenth century, Jonathan Crary writes, "Crucial to the developments of … new disciplinary techniques of the subject was the fixing of quantitative and statistical *norms* of behavior. The assessment of 'normality' in medicine, psychology, and other fields became an essential part of the shaping of the individual to the requirements of institutional power in the nineteenth century, and it was through these disciplines that the subject in a sense became *visible*." See Jonathan Crary, *Techniques of the Observer: On Vision and Modernity in the Nineteenth Century* (Cambridge, MA, 1990), 15–16. Emphasis in original.

6. Louis Althusser, "The Underground Current of the Materialism of the Encounter," in *Philosophy of the Encounter, Later Writings, 1978–87*, ed. François Matherton and Oliver Corpet (London, 2006), 169.
7. Ibid., 167.
8. Ibid., 174.
9. Nicholas Mirzoeff, *The Right to Look: A Counterhistory of Visuality* (Durham, NC, 2011).
10. Ibid., 1.
11. Ibid.
12. Of course, Alexei Yurchak has described the production of a kind of critical consumerist humor in this way in his chapter "Imaginary West: The Elsewhere of Late Socialism" in Yurchak, *Everything Was Forever*, 158–206.
13. See, for example, Michel Foucault, *Discipline and Punish: The Birth of the Prison* (New York, 1977).
14. Reactions against this East/West comparison have been particularly strong in studies of experimental art from the Cold War East. On performance art in the East bloc in relation to the West, see, for example Bojana Cvejić, "A Parallel Slalom from BADco: In Search of a Poetics of Problems," *Representations* 136, no. 1 (2016): 21–35.
15. Recent scholarship on the postsocialist era contests this binary. See, for example, Jodi Dean, "The Communist Horizon," in *Former West: Art and the Contemporary after 1989*, ed. Maria Hlavajova and Simon Sheikh (Cambridge, MA, 2016), 168.
16. Of course, Max Horkheimer and Theodor Adorno laid important groundwork for this critique of mass culture in anticipation of the Cold War West's consumerist turn. See Max Horkheimer and Theodor W. Adorno, *Dialectic of Enlightenment* (Stanford, CA, 2002), esp. "The Culture Industry."
17. Although this diversity is under serious threat at this time.
18. It is significant, for example, that in their edited volume *Media and Revolt: Strategies and Performances from the 1960s to the Present* (New York, 2014), which investigates the interrelationship between the mass media and protest movements, Kathrin Fahlenbrach, Erling Siversten, and Rolf Werenskjold carefully situate their discussion within Western contexts only.
19. See, for example, the absorption of punk music into East Germany's official culture, as evident in the state documentary *flüstern & SCHREIEN: Ein Rockreport* (*whisper and SHOUT: A Rock Report*), directed by Dieter Schumann (1988), or the status of performance art and other avant-garde practices across the East bloc, as explored by Klara Kemp-Welch, *Antipolitics in Central European Art: Reticence as Dissidence under Post-Totalitarian Rule, 1956–1989* (London, 2014), as well as in the volume edited by Aleš Erjavec, *Postmodernism and the Postsocialist Condition: Politicized Art under Late Socialism* (Berkeley, CA, 2003).
20. Susan Buck-Morss, *Dreamworld and Catastrophe: The Passing of Mass Utopia in East and West* (Cambridge, MA, 2000).
21. The legacies of that loss continue to reverberate in our postsocialist contemporary. See, for example, the work of the Former West research initiative (2008–2016), including Susan Buck-Morss's contribution to their recent edited volume. "Theorizing Today: The Post-Soviet Condition," in Hlavajova and Sheikh, *Former West*.

Bibliography

Alpers, Svetlana. "The Visual Culture Questionnaire." *October* 77 (1996): 25–70.
Althusser, Louis. "Ideology and Ideological State Apparatuses." In *Lenin and Philosophy and Other Essays*, 85–126, New York: Monthly Review Press, 2001.
———. "The Underground Current of the Materialism of the Encounter." In *Philosophy of the Encounter, Later Writings, 1978–87*, edited by François Matherton and Oliver Corpet, 163–207. London: Verso, 2006.
Buck-Morss, Susan. *Dreamworld and Catastrophe: The Passing of Mass Utopia in East and West*. Cambridge, MA: MIT Press, 2000.
———. "Theorizing Today: The Post-Soviet Condition." In *Former West: Art and the Contemporary after 1989*, edited by Maria Hlavajova and Simon Sheikh, 157–165. Cambridge, MA: MIT Press, 2016.
Crary, Jonathan. *Techniques of the Observer: On Vision and Modernity in the Nineteenth Century*. Cambridge, MA: MIT Press, 1990.
Cvejić, Bojana. "A Parallel Slalom from BADco: In Search of a Poetics of Problems." *Representations* 136, no. 1 (2016): 21–35.
Dean, Jodi. "The Communist Horizon." In *Former West: Art and the Contemporary after 1989*, edited by Maria Hlavajova and Simon Sheikh, 167–178. Cambridge, MA: MIT Press, 2016.
Erjavec, Aleš, ed. *Postmodernism and the Postsocialist Condition: Politicized Art under Late Socialism*. Berkeley: University of California Press, 2003.
Fahlenbrach, Kathrin, Erling Siversten, and Rolf Werenskjold, eds. *Media and Revolt: Strategies and Performances from the 1960s to the Present*. New York: Berghahn Books, 2014.
Foucault, Michel. *Discipline and Punish: The Birth of the Prison*. New York: Pantheon Books, 1977.
Horkheimer, Max, and Theodor W. Adorno. *Dialectic of Enlightenment: Philosophical Fragments*. Stanford, CA: Stanford University Press, 2002.
Jay, Martin. "The Visual Turn: The Advent of Visual Culture." *Journal of Visual Culture* 1, no. 1 (2002): 87–93.
Kemp-Welch, Klara. *Antipolitics in Central European Art: Reticence as Dissidence under Post-Totalitarian Rule, 1956–1989*. London: I. B. Tauris, 2014.
Manghani, Sunil. *Image Critique and the Fall of the Berlin Wall*. Bristol, UK: Intellect Books, 2008.
Mirzoeff, Nicholas. *The Right to Look: A Counterhistory of Visuality*. Durham, NC: Duke University Press, 2011.
Moxey, Keith. "Visual Studies and the Iconic Turn." *Journal of Visual Culture* 7, no. 2 (2008): 131–146.
Schumann, Dieter, dir. *flüstern & SCHREIEN: Ein Rockreport*, produced by Deutsche Film-Aktiengesellschaft, East Berlin, 1988, 35mm film, 100 mins.
Yurchak, Alexei. *Everything Was Forever Until It Was No More: The Last Soviet Generation*. Princeton, NJ: Princeton University Press, 2005.

Index

1968, 4, 5, 6, 27, 46, 48, 49, 50, 52, 53, 56, 58, 68, 90, 92, 93, 94, 95, 97, 98, 99, 104, 106n11, 131, 132, 135, 182, 183, 185, 260, 263, 270
'68ers, 216, 217, 218
May, 90, 91, 95, 104, 105
Movement of, 185
post-, 45, 46, 54, 59, 89, 90, 92, 94, 95, 100, 103, 249, 281

abjection, 264, 267, 268
abortion, 67, 103, 113, 119, 121, 132, 134, 135, 137, 143, 147n30, 160, 164
AC/DC, 204
Action Council for the Liberation of Women, 132
Afia, Rukshana, 75
Africa Fund, The, 241, 251n29
Agnelli, Gianni, 178
AIDS, 121, 151
Althusser, Louis, 95, 279, 280
Amin, Mohamed, 236
Amnesty International, 234, 238, 243, 245, 246, 248, 252n31, 252n37
Amsterdam, 183, 256, 262
Anschlag, The, 224
Anti-Apartheid Movement (AAM), 243, 244, 245, 248, 249, 252n33
Antonioni, Michelangelo, 28
Arbeitskreis (AK) Homosexualität, 154, 155, 157
Dresden, 156, 157, 163
Leipzig, 156
Arcadie, 101
Argan, Giulio Carlo, 178
Arnaud, Claude, 93
Artists United Against Apartheid, 234, 241

Ash, Timothy Garton, 59
Asor Rosa, Alberto, 31, 41n18
A/traverso, 1, 37, 175, 176, 177, 178
autonomism, 13, 174–77, 183, 185
Autonomia Operaia, 26, 33, 37, 174
See also operaismo
Avanguardia nazionale, 26, 27
avant-garde art movement, 174, 175, 177, 180, 181, 182, 186, 193, 285n19

Baez, Joan, 247
Bailey, Cathryn, 66, 67
Bangladesh, 238
Bascher, Anne de, 100
Beat generation, 32, 37
Beatniks, 32, 34
Beck, Julian, 33
Beckett, Samuel, 28
Belgrade, 112, 113, 117, 121, 122
Belsize Lane Women's Liberation Group, 70
Benjamin, Walter, 259, 272n18
Berardi, Franco "Bifo", 178, 186
Berlin, 136, 143, 144, 177, 183, 216
East, 2, 6, 154–58, 214, 215, 216, 217, 225, 226
West, 1, 3, 4, 132, 134, 135, 136, 144, 158, 214, 221, 256, 260
Berlin Wall, 58–59, 213, 216, 224
fall of the, 58, 59, 151, 167, 278, 280, 283, 284n2
Bielmeier, Frank (Mary Lou Monroe), 217, 223, 224
Birmingham, 69, 75
Birmingham Women's Liberation, 69, 75
Birmingham Women's Liberation Newsletter, 69
Black Mask, 183

Index

body, 1, 2, 3, 10, 13, 18n51, 26, 28, 30, 32, 33, 36, 38, 39, 92, 116, 118, 121, 123, 133, 134, 135, 136, 137, 138, 140, 141, 144, 145, 160, 164, 181, 182, 200, 226, 237, 266, 268, 274n50
    female, 119, 120, 121, 136, 137, 141, 142, 145, 160
    national, 266
    social, 104
Bologna, 27, 38, 175, 177, 179, 186
Bolsheviks, 185
Boltanski, Luc, 11
Bolton, Jonathan, 7, 61n18, 61n19
Bonnet, Marie-Jo, 101
boredom, 14, 33, 214, 215, 220, 226
Bophuthatswana, 241
Bourdieu, Pierre, 19n51, 89, 90, 101, 192, 253n46, 271n15
Bowie, David, 233
Bradford, 76
Brașov, 200
Bratislava, 45, 46, 48, 55, 59n1, 61n15.
Braun, Sarah, 71, 72
Bravo, 197, 224
Bren, Paulina, 47, 60n6, 61n30
Brezhnev, Leonid, 49
bricolage, 193, 194, 199, 201
Brigate Rosse (Red Brigades), 26, 29, 34, 36, 37, 39, 41n16, 186
Bristol, 71, 73, 74
Britain, 66, 68, 73, 81n1, 82n12, 122, 183, 270n3
Bröckling, Ulrich, 11
Brooke, Dinah, 78
Browne, Sarah, 72
Bucharest, 191, 197, 198
Buck-Morss, Susan, 283, 285n21
Budapest, 6
Buerk, Michael, 236, 248
Bulgaria, 2, 49
Butler, Judith, 266, 274n50, 274n52

Calvesi, Maurizio, 183, 189n29
Calvino, Italo, 32
Cambodia, 245

Cambridge (UK), 68
Camden, 68. *See also* London
Carnation Revolution, 6
Carter, Sally, 73, 76
Castro, Roland, 98
Castrovillari, 177
Ceaușescu, Nicolae, 191, 194–95, 201
Centre d'études, de recherches et de formations institutionnelles (CERFI), 104, 108n57
Chapman, Tracy, 245
Charley's Girls (band), 217, 224
Chiapello, Eve, 11
Chile, 245, 252n38
Chinese Cultural Revolution, 98, 185
Chouliaraki, Lilie, 236, 250n8
Christian Democrats, 174, 178
church, 8, 104,
    Protestant, 151–52, 155, 157–58, 162
class, 30, 33, 48, 56, 76, 92, 98, 101, 115, 122, 145, 146, 174, 176, 182, 201
    capitalist, 102
    intellectual, 176
    middle, 76, 134
    urban, 56
    working, 36, 96, 97, 136, 175, 176, 183, 185, 194, 259, 260, 273n41, 279
Club of Free Kings, The (band), 199
Cluj Napoca, 197
Cold War, 3, 192, 278, 282, 283
comics, 174, 177, 179, 180
coming out, 153, 156, 161–2, 166
Communards, 185
Communist Party, 90, 102
    of Czechoslovakia, 54–56
    of Great Britain, 73
    French, 106
    Italian, 27, 174, 178, 182, 183, 183, 185
    Romanian, 195
commune, 33, 98, 260, 265
consciousness-raising, 1, 3, 10, 12, 33, 65–81, 117, 118, 134, 153, 162-7

negative experiences, 65, 70, 71, 73, 74, 77–80
personal transformation, 66, 71–74, 81
consumerism, 14, 225, 235, 239, 249,
consumption, 6, 30, 31, 33, 47, 192, 196, 198–199, 201, 206–7, 235, 246, 253n47, 260, 266,
Coroners (band), 217
Cosenza, 177
Cossiga, Francesco, 178
Costruiamo l'azione, 26
Counterculture, 3, 4, 5, 6, 9, 11, 12, 33, 53, 54, 90, 98, 100, 112, 119, 191–94, 196–203, 205–7, 234, 235, 246, 247, 248, 256, 270, 282
Courage, 133, 141, 142, 143
Craiova, 197
Cressole, Michel, 93
csöves, 193, 197, 198, 200, 203, 209n25, 210n54
Cuninghame, Patrick, 183, 187
Curcio, Renato, 39
Cushman, Thomas, 193
Czechoslovakia, 2, 5, 6, 7, 12, 45–59, 166, 198, 281, 282

Dadaism, 174–75, 178, 183. *See also* Mao-Dadism
D'Amico, Tano, 182
Danube, the, 6
Dauenheimer, Karin, 163
Davis, Miles, 242
Deleuze, Gilles, 10, 19n52, 101, 105
Delphy, Christine, 100
Denselow, Robin, 244
desire, 7, 9, 10, 13, 14, 19n52, 33, 56, 91, 92, 103, 105, 119, 132, 139, 141, 151, 153, 154, 157, 159, 160, 161, 163, 167, 174, 175, 177, 179, 181, 182, 183, 186, 187, 219, 283
Deutsche Welle, 196
détournement, 175, 177, 178, 181, 183, 188n25
Deudon, Catherine, 100
Disgruntled Hazel, 76
Dire Straits (band), 199, 233

disguise, 175, 182–86
dissidence, 46, 50, 53, 110, 112, 151
dissidents, 2, 5, 7, 46, 47, 48, 50, 52, 53, 54, 59, 61n18, 110, 112, 206, 282
Dixon, Thomas, 75
Dohnanyi, Klaus, 257
Do-It-Yourself (DIY), 12, 222, 229n43, 229n44.
domesticity, 259, 271n12
abject, 256, 259, 265–69
everyday, 267
Dörper, Ralf, 221
Dresden, 156–7, 163, 220
Dubček, Alexander, 5, 48
Düsseldorf, 213, 217, 221, 224
Dylan, Bob, 233
Dziggel, Bettina, 155–6

East bloc, 2, 3, 5, 15, 46, 48, 49, 51, 166, 191, 196, 197–98, 278, 282, 283, 284, 285n14, 285n19
East Berlin. *See* Berlin
East Germany. *See* German Democratic Republic
Eastern European Information Pool, 166
Eaubonne, Françoise d', 101
Echaurren, Pablo, 185
écriture feminine, 114, 115, 123
Eco, Umberto, 182
Edda (band), 198
Einstürzende Neubauten (band), 221
EMMA, 133, 134
emotion work 153, 156, 162–67
emotions, 2, 10, 25, 26, 29, 38, 39, 46, 47, 51, 56, 65, 67, 68, 70, 72, 77, 75, 78, 79, 80, 81, 90, 91, 92, 94, 99, 100, 110, 111, 131, 140, 143, 152, 153, 156, 157, 159, 162, 166, 167, 199, 237, 240, 242, 244, 257
emotional distress, 78, 79, 81
emotional habitus, 152, 162, 167
emotional politics, 100, 152, 166
emotional regime, 152, 167
emotional style, 159
emotional subject, 80
emotional support, 74–77, 81

England, 1, 10, 12, 65–81, 118
Enzensberger, Hans Magnus, 180
Erfurt, 156, 213
Erfurter Lesben, 156
Ethiopia, 233, 236, 237, 239, 241, 248
everyday life, 47, 52, 80, 114, 143, 175, 176, 177, 179, 207, 212, 218, 249, 261, 262, 263, 268, 283. *See also* domesticity

Fair Trade, 249
falsity, 9, 13, 175, 178, 182, 183
Fanon, Frantz, 68
Fascism, 25, 26, 27, 28, 29, 35, 37, 40n10, 216, 217, 223, 264, 280
post-, 5, 258, 266, 271n19,
fashion, 6, 191, 192, 202, 216, 218, 222, 223, 224, 225, 226, 229n50, 279, 283,
Fauret, Anne-Marie, 101
Fawkes, Guy, 187
Federal Republic of Germany, 5, 124, 131–50, 153–55, 158, 160–61, 164–65, 183, 191, 197, 212, 215, 220, 226, 257, 259, 260, 262, 263, 265, 272n23, 274n51, 280, 281
Fehlfarben, 217, 224
feminism, 19n55, 65, 66, 67, 73, 90, 100–3, 110, 112, 115, 116, 117, 118, 123, 124, 126n17, 154, 281
Black, 67, 82n12
intergenerational debates within, 66, 67
socialist, 75, 113
in West Germany, 124, 131–46, 280
in the United Kingdom, 280
in the United States, 66, 68, 69, 70, 71, 83n24, 113, 124, 126n18, 132, 133, 134, 135, 147n30, 142, 166
New Yugoslav, 13, 110–124
radical, 77–78, 126n18, 133, 134
third-wave, 66, 67
second-wave, 66
See also women's liberation movement
feminist, 2, 13, 67, 75, 77, 93, 100–3, 110–24, 125n9, 126n18, 132, 133, 138, 139, 140, 141, 142, 143, 145, 146, 154, 155, 156, 157, 158, 159, 160, 161, 166, 167, 282
authenticity, 65, 66–67, 68, 70, 71, 72, 73, 74, 75, 77, 80, 81, 133,
periodicals, 65
politics, 67, 81, 110–30
subject, 67
subjectivity, 131, 133, 134,
See also women's liberation movement
Feministička grupa žena i društvo (FGŽD), 121, 127n27
Feminist Women's Health Center (FFGZ), 137, 140, 144,
Fenzi, Enrico, 34, 35, 37
Filip, Jaroslav, 45–46, 55, 59n1, 59n2
Fioravanti, Giusva, 36
Flins-sur-Seine (France), 93
Foa, Vittorio, 31
Foucault, Michel, 8, 9, 18n48, 96, 104, 167, 258, 285n13
Fouque, Antoinette, 100
France, 1, 3, 6, 7, 9, 11, 13, 89–105, 114, 188n25, 191, 197, 270n3, 280, 281
Frank, Thomas, 247–48
Fraser, Sally, 70
frau anders, 157, 164
Frauen für den Frieden, 158
Frankfurt Institute for Social Research, 28
Free German Youth (FDJ), 157, 215, 224
Freiburg, 256
Freie Deutsche Jugend (FDJ). *See* Free German Youth (FDJ)
Front homosexuel d'action révolutionnaire (FHAR), 89–94, 96, 98–103, 104, 105, 107n52
Futurism, 174, 175

Gabriel, Peter, 245, 252n38
Gauche prolétarienne, 94, 96, 97
gauchism, 90, 92, 93, 101, 103–4
cultural, 103–5
gauchiste, 92, 94, 99, 103, 104
gay rights movement, 4, 6, 94, 281
Geldof, Bob, 233, 234, 235, 236, 237, 238, 240, 243, 245, 246, 248

gender, 12, 13, 33, 65, 115, 121, 122, 123, 124, 134, 137, 138, 139, 140, 142, 143, 145, 146, 157–58, 160–61, 167, 187n1, 266, 271n12, 279
  equality, 65, 111, 113, 160
Generacija 5, 198
general intellect, 174
Gerard, J., 69
Gerassi, Jean-Michel, 93
German Democratic Republic, 2, 9, 10, 13, 151–67, 212, 213, 220, 226, 280, 281, 285n19
Germany, 5, 14, 144, 183, 212, 219, 224, 260. *See also* Federal Republic of Germany, German Democratic Republic
Gilmore, James, 235
Glucksmann, André, 95
Godard, Jean-Luc, 28
Gorlier, Claudio, 37
Gouines rouges (Red Dykes), 103
Gould, Deborah, 152–53
Graziani, Clemente, 28, 29, 40n11
Groupe d'information sur les prisons (GIP), 104
Gruber, Klemens, 175
Guattari, Félix, 10, 19n52, 95, 101, 104

Hafenstraße (Hamburg), 9, 10, 14, 256–69
Hagen, Nina, 2
Hamburg, 9, 10, 14, 212, 221, 222, 256–69, 281
Halle, 156
Hancock, Herbie, 242
Hanstorf, 157
happening, 182, 183, 184. *See also* National Happening of the Youthful Proletariat
hardcore, 223, 264
Harrison, George, 238
Havel, Václav, 2, 5, 9, 50–52, 59, 61n24, 125n4
heavy metal, 202, 204
Hebdige, Dick, 225

Heimat, 265, 266, 268, 273n47, 274n49
Hein, Peter (Janie Jones), 217, 219, 225, 228n29
heteronormativity, 151, 155, 167
heterosexuality, 138, 160, 161
hidden transcripts (of resistance), 46, 47, 52, 58, 49
hippies, 4, 10, 14, 33, 41n30, 200, 203, 204, 216, 218, 223, 224, 281, 282
Hocquenghem, Guy, 1, 13, 89–105
Hoffman, Abbie, 98
Hollingsworth, Tony, 244, 252n32
homosexuality, 6, 77, 78, 89–105, 151–167
Homosexuelle Initiative Wien, 158
human rights, 46, 243, 245
Human Rights Now!, 234, 240–46, 252n31
Humpe, Inga, 224
Hungary, 6, 13, 31, 49, 50, 59, 166, 191, 193, 197, 198, 200, 209n25
Husák, Gustav, 54

Iași, 197, 202
identity, 97, 112, 140, 145, 154, 157, 160, 161, 185, 219, 223, 226, 262, 263, 269, 274n50, 282
  collective, 8, 66, 76, 77
  European, 6
  feminist, 67, 81
  gender, 145, 146
  lesbian, 166
  national, 3, 200, 274n49
  sexual, 118, 160
  women's, 123, 142
Illes (band), 198
Illuminati, Augusto, 185
inauthenticity, 124, 213, 216, 235, 242
individuality, 30, 66, 67, 212, 213, 214, 216, 217, 219, 220, 224, 225, 226, 258
Irish Republican Army (IRA), 263
Iron Curtain, 1, 3, 4, 5, 6, 111, 191, 196, 206, 212, 213, 221, 282, 283
Italian General Confederation of Labor, 179, 183

Italian Movement of 1977, 9, 175, 176, 178, 182, 183, 185
Italy, 1, 3, 9, 10, 11, 12, 13, 25–44, 174–87

Jackson, Michael, 199
Jacobins, 185
Jena, 154, 156, 157, 164
Jeunesse communiste révolutionnaire (JCR), 92, 93, 95, 106n11
Jones, Janie. *See* Hein, Peter (Janie Jones)

Katsiaficas, George, 256
Kenney, Padraic, 8, 17n33
Kid Klan, The (band), 199
King Mob, 183
Klässner, Bärbel, 154, 158, 164
Kleenex (band), 222
Klein, Carola, 78
Koedt, Anna, 138–142
Kolesárová, Ľudmila, 57, 58
Kommune 1, 183
Korem, 236
Körzendörfer, Marinka, 158–59, 164
Krapfl, James, 58
Kreuzberg, 136, 260
Krug, Marina, 155
Kryl, Karel, 56–58
Kubišová, Marta, 56–58,
Kuroń, Jacek, 5

Lama, Luciano, 179, 183–85
Larzac, 6
Leeds, 75
lesbian(s), 9, 12, 13, 77, 78, 101, 103, 107, 142, 151–67, 280. *See also* homosexuality
Lesben in der Kirche (LiK), 152–56, 158–63, 166, 167
Leterrier, Anne-Sophie, 29
Liberatore, Gaetano, 179
lifeworld, 258, 259, 264, 265, 267, 268, 271n15
Ligue Communiste, 95, 106n11
Lila Pause, 156
Linhart, Robert, 97

Linhart, Virginie, 97
Live Aid, 11, 14, 233–49
Living Theater. *See* Beck, Julian
Ljubljana, 112, 113, 117, 118
Löffler, Jörg, 220
Lokomotiv (band), 198
London, 66, 68, 70, 72, 76, 77, 78, 79, 81, 224, 233, 236, 243, 262,
London Women's Liberation Workshop, 66, 68, 76, 78, 79
  Psychology Group, 66, 77–80, 81
Lorde, Audre, 158
Lorez, Gudula, 142
Lorusso, Francesco, 179, 186
Lotta Continua, 26, 38
Lyotard, Jean-François, 104, 105

Madonna, 233
Maeck, Klaus, 222
Majakovskij, Vladimir, 176, 178
Malaka, Bernward, 221
Malaria! (band), 222
Malý, Václav, 49
Mandela, Nelson, 234, 240, 243, 244, 245, 248, 249, 251n27
  Concert for, 240–46, 252n31
Mao-Dadaism, 175–76
Maoism, 68, 93, 94, 96, 97, 98, 99, 101
Mao Zedong, 68
Marx, Karl, 116, 175–76, 179, 185
Marxism, 29, 30, 48, 89, 92, 95, 96–101, 104, 105, 106n11, 113, 116, 124, 125n9, 126n18, 174–177, 183, 194, 217, 281
Marxism-Leninism, 29, 96, 97, 167, 199
Mattioli, Massimo, 179
McCartney, Paul, 233
M-Effekt (band), 198
mental health, 78, 122, 139
Mercury, Freddie, 199
Metropolitan Indians, 175, 177, 182, 183, 185, 186, 187
Milan, 175, 177, 182, 183
Miłosz, Czesław, 2
Mirzoeff, Nicholas, 280
Mittagspause (band), 217, 218

Modzelewski, Karol, 5
Monday Consciousness-Raising Group, 69. *See also* Birmingham Women's Liberation
Monroe, Mary Lou. *See* Bielmeier, Frank (Mary Lou Monroe)
Morgan, Robin, 68, 83n24
Moroni, Primo, 177
Moseley Group, 70, 75. *See also* Birmingham Women's Liberation
Mouvement de libération des femmes (MLF), 91, 98, 100–102
Movimento sociale italiano, 27
Müllstation (band), 222
Muschalek, Jürgen, 224
music, 3, 4, 6, 55, 56, 57, 58, 98, 125n4, 181, 191, 192, 193, 195, 196, 197, 198, 199, 201, 202, 203, 204, 206, 207, 216, 218, 219, 220, 221, 226, 235, 236, 238, 239, 242, 2443, 245, 246, 247, 249, 259, 261, 281, 282. *See also* hardcore, heavy metal, pop, punk, new wave

Naples, 177
National Happening of the Youthful Proletariat, 184
Native American(s), 177, 259, 263, 269, 281
Nava, Mica, 72
Nazism, 153, 156, 204, 223, 265
N'Dour, Youssou, 245
Negri, Antonio (Toni), 30, 33, 36, 41n19, 174
neo-fascism, 26, 27, 28, 29, 35, 37, 40n10
Neonbabies (band), 224
Netherlands, the, 158, 161
Neue Deutsche Welle, 216
New Left, 112, 132, 133, 135
  in Britain, 68
  in Italy, 26, 30
  in West Germany, 124, 132, 133, 135
new man, 30, 31, 112, 123, 194–95, 205, 207

new wave, 192, 193, 194, 197, 200, 201, 202, 203, 206, 207
New York, 69, 98, 183, 241, 242, 251n29
Nicholson, Jack, 247, 252n43
normalization, 2, 49, 50, 153, 158, 274n52
nostalgia, 54, 75, 265, 273n45
Notting Hill, 78. *See also* London
Nuclei Armati Rivoluzionari (NAR), 36

Omega, 198
Oradea, 197
operaismo, 30, 31, 41n18, 96, 174–75, 186
Ordine Nuovo, 26, 27, 28, 40n11
Orwell, George, 31
Oxfam, 238, 248

Packard, Vance, 31
padeluun, 217
Palandri, Enrico, 178
Palestine, 264, 268
Panunzio, Sergio, 25
Panzieri, Raniero, 30
Paranoia (band), 220
Paris, 3, 4, 89, 98, 100, 105, 144, 182
Pazienza, Andrea, 179, 180
Parco Lambro, 182
Peci, Patrizio, 34
performance, 138, 142, 145, 164, 181, 183, 185, 191, 198, 238, 245, 251n20, 274n50, 281, 285n14, 285n19
Pershore Road Group, 75. *See also* Birmingham Women's Liberation
personal, 1, 4, 5, 34, 48, 49, 53, 54, 65, 66, 70, 80, 97, 110, 111, 112, 114, 115, 122, 123, 124, 131, 133, 155, 156, 157, 158, 160, 161, 162, 163, 164, 167, 192, 193, 196, 201, 207, 224
  authenticity, 11, 214, 217, 237, 242, 244, 248, 252n32
  is political, 67, 68, 75, 99, 111, 112, 114, 116, 123, 179

personal *(cont.)*
  subjectivity, 96
  transformation, 1, 71–74, 81, 95, 152
Peterson, Richard, 235
Philadelphia, 233, 236, 247
Pine, Joseph, 235
Piramis (band), 198
Pithart, Petr, 52
Plan, Der (band), 217, 218
Plzeň, 2
Poland, 5, 6, 59, 166, 198
politics of the first person, 99, 00
Pollock, Friedrich, 28
pop, 175, 191, 203, 215, 216, 220, 233, 234, 235, 236, 237, 240, 241, 242, 243, 244, 246, 247, 248, 249, 253n46
Pope Paul VI, 178
Portugal, 6
poststructuralism, 174–75, 186
Potere Operaio, 26, 38
Prague, 3, 4, 6, 7, 46, 47, 48, 54, 56, 57, 58
Prague Spring, 7, 46, 47, 48, 49,56
Prima Linea, 26, 32
private, 47, 52, 116–19, 132, 152, 155, 158, 265
  life, 93, 100, 101, 116
  -public, 36, 114–16, 123, 163, 225, 271n12
  sphere, 47, 132, 151,
Provos, 183
psychoanalysis, 79, 113, 117
psychotherapy, 10, 66, 77, 79, 104, 127n29
punk, 3, 4, 12, 14, 19n55, 192–94, 197–98, 200, 201, 202–7, 209n25, 212–26, 227n8, 228n29, 229n41, 229n50, 235, 264, 278, 283, 285n19
punks, 2, 4, 12, 14, 212–26, 257, 269, 281, 282
Punti Rossi Cooperative, 177
PVC, 225

Queen (band), 233, 241

Radio Alice, 13, 175, 178–81, 183, 186
Radio Free Europe, 57, 191, 196–97, 199, 202
Ramones (band), 3, 4
Rancière, Jacques, 95
rape, 132, 143, 144
Ravensbrück, 156
Reagan, Ronald, 54, 242
Red Army, 49, 50
Red Army Faction (RAF), 256, 264, 267, 270n6
Red Brigades. *See* Brigate Rosse (Red Brigades)
Red Dykes. *See* Gouines rouges (Red Dykes)
Red Rag, 75
refusal of labor, 174, 176, 187
Reichardt, Sven, 7, 8, 124, 235, 258, 269
revolution, 12, 25, 32, 34, 37, 47, 58, 69, 89, 90, 93, 94, 95, 97, 99, 102, 103, 120, 223, 264
  communist, 34
  countercultural, 100
  cultural, 96, 98, 100, 194,
  proletarian, 185
  sexual, 119, 120, 135,
  socialist, 99, 132
  symbolic, 89, 95
  See also Carnation Revolution; Chinese Cultural Revolution; Velvet Revolution
Ricci, Paolo, 178
Richman, Geoff, 68
Rip-Off (store), 222
rock, 3, 45, 192–94, 197, 198, 201, 203–4, 206–7, 215, 216, 221, 237, 238, 239
Rogers, Anna E., 70, 75, 76–77
Rolin, Jean, 93
Rolin, Olivier, 94
Romania, 11, 13, 191–94, 196–201, 206–7
Rome, 175, 177, 178, 183
RosaLinde, 157
Ross, Kristin, 7, 16n15, 17n26, 91, 104–5
Rosser, Jilly, 74–75

Rothenburg, Marcia, 102
Roussopoulos, Carole, 93, 100
Rrr, Moritz, 217, 218
Rubin, Jerry, 33, 98
Ruhr, 218
Ryan, Joanna, 68

Sachse, Harty, 222
Salaris, Claudia, 183
Salvaresi, Elisabeth, 100
Sander, Helke, 131, 132
San Giovanni in Monte, 186
San Precario, 187
Sappho Collective, 69
satire, 54–56
Sartre, Jean-Paul, 96
Schleime, Conny, 224
Schleim-Keim (band), 213, 214
Schwarzer, Alice, 132, 134, 135, 136, 139, 140, 145
Schwebel, Thomas, 224
Scotland, 81n1
Scott, James C., 46, 52, 58
Scozzari, Filippo, 179
Scuro, Enrico, 182
Securitate, 13, 191–94, 196–206
self-help, 134–38, 144
  therapy, 78, 79
self-representation, 175–77, 185
Sensibili alle foglie, 39
Serbia, 198
sexuality, 3, 6, 12, 33, 90, 92, 93, 99, 103, 104, 115, 118, 119, 120, 133, 134, 135, 137, 138, 139, 140, 141, 142, 143, 144, 145, 146, 153, 154, 155, 157, 158, 159, 160, 161, 162, 163, 164, 166, 167, 181, 182
Shaktini, Namaskar, 101, 102
Shankar, Ravi, 238
Siedlungs-Aktiengesellschaft Altona (SAGA), 257
Šimečka, Milan 50, 52
Situationism, 174
Skaldowie, 198
socialism, 5, 9, 13, 14, 47, 48, 49, 50, 54, 57, 75, 99, 111, 119, 121, 122, 124, 132, 133, 135, 151, 152, 157, 167, 181, 192, 194, 195, 196, 204, 205, 206, 207, 212, 216, 220, 227n10, 285n15, 285n21
  Eastern, 14, 46
  state, 1, 5, 110, 111, 112, 121, 213, 215, 222, 283
socialist internationalism, 2
socialist personality, 167
Socialist Patient Collective (SPK), 264
Socialist Unity Party of Germany (SED), 151, 214, 215
Socialist Worker's Party (UK), 73
Sonntags-Club
  Berlin, 157
  Cottbus, 157
Spare Rib, 70, 72, 79
Spiegel, Der, 215, 217
Springsteen, Bruce, 245
squatting, 270n3, 271n12
  movement, 136, 256, 270n4
  urban, 4
squatters, 9, 10, 14, 256, 259, 260, 261, 262, 263, 264, 267, 268, 269, 281, 282
St. Albans, 73
Stasi (Ministerium für Staatssicherheit) 151, 158, 159, 167, 214
Stewart, Rod, 199
Sting, 245
St. Pauli., 257, 268
student movement, 216, 258, 260, 270
subjectivity, 1, 7, 9, 11, 19n54, 94, 98, 99, 110, 111, 116, 125n9, 174, 175, 181, 186, 198, 199, 201, 206, 259, 268, 278, 280
  alternative, 13, 196, 206
  authentic, 3, 4, 8, 11, 134, 136, 143, 161, 192–194, 201, 206–7, 233, 234, 240
  feminist, 133, 134, 140, 145, 1–50
  individual, 90
  lesbian, 13, 152, 154, 161, 162, 164
  politics of, 10, 13, 89, 90, 91, 94, 95, 96, 100, 105, 279, 280
  socialist, 206

subjectivity *(cont.)*
  women's, 110, 111, 114, 116, 123, 124, 136, 145,
Sunshine, A., 69
Surrealism, 174, 182, 183
S.Y.P.H. (band), 218
Szilard, Leo, 31

Tamburini, Stefano, 179
Târgu Mureș, 197
Taylor, Barbara, 75
TAZ, 214
terrorism, 4, 29, 92, 93, 94, 260,
Terza Posizione, 26, 29
therapy. *See* psychotherapy
Third International, 185
Third Reich, 265
Third World, 34, 239, 273n41
Thompson, Paul, 47
Timișoara, 197
Tout!, 98–99
transgression, 12, 45, 46, 48, 51–56, 58, 59
Tronti, Mario, 30, 41n19
Trotskyism, 92, 93, 95, 106n10, 106n11, 185,
  Trotskyists, 93, 101
Truffaut, François, 28
Tufnell Park Women's Liberation Group, 68
Turin, 183

Unabhängige Frauengruppe Brandenburg, 156
Unabhängige Frauengruppe Magdeburg, 156
UNICEF, 238
uniformity, 25, 214, 220, 226, 281
Union des étudiants communistes (UEC), 92, 106n11
Union des jeunesses communiste marxistes-léninistes (UJC(ml)), 97
Union nationale des étudiants de France (UNEF), 92
Union of Communist Youth, 205
United Kingdom, 61n22, 153, 280, 281

United States, 9, 31, 32, 33, 68, 69, 70, 71, 89, 98, 101, 110, 111, 113, 114, 116, 124, 126n18, 132, 133, 134, 138, 142, 143, 153, 161, 164, 191, 196, 197, 203, 238, 242, 245, 251n29, 259, 268, 273n41,

Vaculík, Ludvik, 52
Van Zandt, Steven, 241
Velvet Revolution, 54, 58, 59, 62n36
violence, 12, 14, 27, 29, 32, 34, 35, 36, 37, 38, 93, 118, 119, 195, 202, 203, 225, 257, 262, 263
  against women, 113, 116, 121, 122–23, 133, 134, 142–5, 148n62
  domestic, 113
  gender-based, 113, 121
  police, 242
  sexual, 164
  state, 260
Vive La Révolution (VLR), 98
Voice of America, 196

Wales, 81n1
Walker, Alice, 66
Walker, Rebecca, 66
Walpurgis Night, 144
Warsaw, 3
Warsaw Pact, 46, 48, 49, 50, 56, 57, 58, 59n3
Weber, Henri, 93
Werner, Pascale, 93
West, 2, 4, 5, 11, 14, 30, 50, 61n22, 111, 158, 166, 191–99, 201, 206–7, 213, 214, 215, 216, 220, 223, 224, 239, 278, 282, 283
West Berlin. *See* Berlin
West Berlin Women's Center, 134, 135, 136, 144
West Germany. *See* Federal Republic of Germany
Wirtschaftswunder, 220
Wittig, Gille, 102
Wittig, Monique, 100, 101, 102
women's health, 78, 117, 118, 120, 121, 122, 133, 134–38, 145

women's liberation movement, 1, 3, 4, 10, 12, 13, 68–81, 101, 102
  American, 66, 68, 69, 70, 71, 83n24
  conferences, 67
  groups, 68, 69, 70, 75
  politics, 66, 67, 71, 72, 73, 74, 79, 80
women's movement, 12, 13, 19n55, 66–67, 81, 131, 132, 133, 139, 140, 142
  in West Germany, 145
women's question, 111
Women's Revolutionary Council, 132, 135
women's shelter, 113, 133, 144
women's writing. *See* écriture féminine
Woodstock, 238, 247, 251n21
workerism. *See* operaismo

Yorkshire, 70, 72
Young Pioneers, 215
Young Proletarians, 9, 174–77, 180–84
Youth Magazine, 197–98
Youth of the World, 197–98
Youthful Proletariat, 174–76, 183–84. *See also* National Happening of the Youthful Proletariat
Yugoslavia, 5, 13, 50, 60n13, 68, 110, 111, 114, 117, 119, 120, 121, 124, 282

Zagreb, 112, 113, 117, 118
Žena i društvo (Woman and society), 110, 112, 117, 118, 121
žensko pismo, 114, 115
Zhivkova, Lyudmila, 2
Zurich, 256, 262

Protest, Culture, and Society

General editors:
Kathrin Fahlenbrach, Institute for Media and Communication, University of Hamburg
Martin Klimke, New York University, Abu Dhabi
Joachim Scharloth, Waseda University, Japan

Protest movements have been recognized as significant contributors to processes of political participation and transformations of culture and value systems, as well as to the development of both a national and transnational civil society.

This series brings together the various innovative approaches to phenomena of social change, protest, and dissent which have emerged in recent years, from an interdisciplinary perspective. It contextualizes social protest and cultures of dissent in larger political processes and socio-cultural transformations by examining the influence of historical trajectories and the response of various segments of society, political, and legal institutions on a national and international level. In doing so, the series offers a more comprehensive and multi-dimensional view of historical and cultural change in the twentieth and twenty-first century.

Volume 1
Voices of the Valley, Voices of the Straits: How Protest Creates Communities
Donatella della Porta and Gianni Piazza

Volume 2
Transformations and Crises: The Left and the Nation in Denmark and Sweden, 1956–1980
Thomas Ekman Jørgensen

Volume 3
Changing the World, Changing Oneself: Political Protest and Collective Identities in West Germany and the US in the 1960s and 1970s
Edited by Belinda Davis, Wilfried Mausbach, Martin Klimke, and Carla MacDougall

Volume 4
The Transnational Condition: Protest Dynamics in an Entangled Europe
Edited by Simon Teune

Volume 5
Protest beyond Borders: Contentious Politics in Europe since 1945
Edited by Hara Kouki and Eduardo Romanos

Volume 6
Between the Avant-Garde and the Everyday: Subversive Politics in Europe from 1957 to the Present
Edited by Timothy Brown and Lorena Anton

Volume 7
Between Prague Spring and French May: Opposition and Revolt in Europe, 1960–1980
Edited by Martin Klimke, Jacco Pekelder, and Joachim Scharloth

Volume 8
The Third World in the Global 1960s
Edited by Samantha Christiansen and Zachary A. Scarlett

Volume 9
The German Student Movement and the Literary Imagination: Transnational Memories of Protest and Dissent
Susanne Rinner

Volume 10
Children of the Dictatorship: Student Resistance, Cultural Politics, and the "Long 1960s" in Greece
Kostis Kornetis

Volume 11
Media and Revolt: Strategies and Performances from the 1960s to the Present
Edited by Kathrin Fahlenbrach, Erling Sivertsen, and Rolf Werenskjold

Volume 12
Europeanizing Contention: The Protest against "Fortress Europe" in France and Germany
Pierre Monforte

Volume 13
Militant around the Clock? Left-Wing Youth Politics, Leisure, and Sexuality in Post-Dictatorship Greece, 1974–1981
Nikolaos Papadogiannis

Volume 14
Protest in Hitler's "National Community": Popular Unrest and the Nazi Response
Edited by Nathan Stoltzfus and Birgit Maier-Katkin

Volume 15
Comrades of Color: East Germany in the Cold War World
Edited by Quinn Slobodian

Volume 16
Social Movement Studies in Europe: The State of the Art
Edited by Guya Accornero and Olivier Fillieule

Volume 17
Protest Cultures: A Companion
Edited by Kathrin Fahlenbrach, Martin Klimke, and Joachim Scharloth

Volume 18
The Revolution before the Revolution: Late Authoritarianism and Student Protest in Portugal
By Guya Accornero

Volume 19
The Nuclear Crisis: The Arms Race, Cold War Anxiety, and the German Peace Movement of the 1980s
Edited by Christoph Becker-Schaum, Philipp Gassert, Martin Klimke, Wilfried Mausbach, and Marianne Zepp

Volume 20
A Fragmented Landscape: Abortion Governance and Protest Logics in Europe
Edited by Silvia De Zordo, Joanna Mishtal, and Lorena Anton

Volume 21
Hairy Hippies and Bloody Butchers: The Greenpeace Whaling Campaign in Norway
Juliane Riese

Volume 22
The Women's Liberation Movement: Impacts and Outcomes
Edited by Kristina Schulz

Volume 23
The Virago Story: Assessing the Impact of a Feminist Publishing Phenomenon
Catherine E. Riley

Volume 24
Taking on Technocracy: Nuclear Power in Germany, 1945 to the Present
Dolores L. Augustine

Volume 25
The Politics of Authenticity: Countercultures and Radical Movements across the Iron Curtain, 1968–1989
Edited by Joachim C. Häberlen, Mark Keck-Szajbel, and Kate Mahoney

www.ingramcontent.com/pod-product-compliance
Lightning Source LLC
Chambersburg PA
CBHW072145100526
44589CB00015B/2100